Juvenile Offenders for a Thousand Years

JUVENILE OFFENDERS

FOR A THOUSAND YEARS

Selected Readings
from Anglo-Saxon Times to 1900

Edited by WILEY B. SANDERS

The University of North Carolina Press
Chapel Hill

To my wife
DOLLY COOPER SANDERS

Acknowledgments

During the years while this collection of readings was being assembled a number of people connected with the University of North Carolina contributed to the study in one way or another. A few figures, however, stand out clearly. Dr. Howard W. Odum, Kenan Professor of Sociology, who always stressed research by his staff, made it possible for the author to visit London and study in such libraries as the British Museum, the Guildhall Library, the Goldsmiths' Library, and the library of the Howard League for Penal Reform. Dr. Katharine Jocher, Research Professor of Sociology and closely associated with Dr. Odum, gave constant encouragement to this historical project. The Institute for Research in Social Science gave invaluable aid in typing the early copies of the selections. Reference librarians were most helpful in locating scarce documents. This was particularly true of Miss Georgia Faison, Chief Reference Librarian of the Louis Round Wilson Library of The University of North Carolina at Chapel Hill.

A final acknowledgment should be made of the skilled services of "old book dealers" in London and New York, who on numerous occasions located books and pamphlets on delinquency which were long out of print.

Contents

xiii

Introduction

So many books, pamphlets and articles on juvenile delinquency are pouring from the presses that the reading public is becoming skeptical as to whether anything new can be written about the subject. The author of another book on juvenile delinquency therefore is morally bound to show that his work is not simply a restatement of well known and generally accepted facts about delinquency. He must show that he has discovered new facts based upon his own research, or that he has approached the subject from a fresh new angle. This volume is new in the sense that it includes material so old it has been long forgotten and is practically unknown to the present generation of social scientists, or old material of a local nature which though important never had wide circulation, and is now to be found rarely in scattered libraries throughout the world.

This book is the outgrowth of more than a quarter century of study, teaching and research in the field of juvenile delinquency. The idea of the desirability of a source book on the historical background of juvenile delinquency began to take shape in 1929 when the author ran across in the Crerar Library in Chicago Walter Buchanan's privately printed pamphlet describing "the state of juvenile crime in the metropolis" of London in 1846. Extensive browsing in libraries has failed to locate another copy of this classic work. A rare pamphlet of such value and interest should not be buried in library stacks gathering dust but should be made readily available to the reading public today. Subsequent exploration in other libraries has revealed many other interesting pamphlets and documents on delinquency which should see the light of day. A major purpose of this volume therefore is to render more accessible rare and valuable books, pamphlets and other data on juvenile delinquency. Incidentally, it may be pointed out that the danger of destruction by bombing attacks of the great libraries housing these rare documents on delinquency is a very real threat as shown by repeated bombings of the British Museum and other English libraries during World War II. To preserve copies of these valuable pamphlets and reports would tend to minimize the loss of the originals.

The extracts finally selected have been drawn from many places. The chief American sources were the Library of Congress, Crerar Library, the libraries of the University of Chicago, Columbia University, Yale, Harvard Law School, Duke University, The University of North Carolina at Chapel Hill, Boston Public Library, New York Public Library, and the North Carolina Department of Archives and History. The British Museum, the Goldsmiths' Library of the University of London, and the Library of the Howard League for Penal Reform were the principal English sources. In addition to these the editor over a period of years through old book dealers has been able to locate and add to his own library a number of rare and in some cases unique documents and pamphlets dealing with juvenile delinquency. These too have been drawn upon.[1] Numbered notes have been supplied by the editor; asterisk notes appeared in the original.

For historical perspective the extracts have been arranged in chronological order from Anglo-Saxon times down to 1900. Material since 1900 has not been included since it is usually quite accessible and generally known.

Although satisfied that the great majority of the extracts included here will appear as new to the reading public, the editor has presented for the sake of completeness some material relating to the early houses of refuge in America, the development of probation in Boston, and the early days of the Chicago Juvenile Court, which has already appeared in other works.

The group to which this volume will offer the strongest appeal will be teachers of college courses dealing with crime, delinquency, and social problems. It should provide valuable background material for judges, social workers, social historians, and educators. Perhaps parents and citizens may find some of the selections of more than passing interest.

In the minds of many intelligent and educated people juvenile delinquency is a twentieth century problem, receiving its first public recognition from the passage of the first juvenile court act in Illinois in 1899. Such people assume that before the beginning of this century child lawbreakers were tried and punished in exactly the same way, and with the same severity, as adult offenders. There are of course records of children who were hanged for picking pockets, and for committing other offenses. These selections, however, make it abundantly clear that as far back as written records go children who have broken the law have been treated on the whole more leniently than have adult offenders. This is the central theme of this book of readings.

1. For the convenience of the reader, in checking or verifying the material, the name of the library is given in addition to the source of the extract for those documents which are particularly rare.

A Good Historian by running back to ages past, and by standing still and viewing the present times, and comparing the one with the other, may then run forward, and give a Verdict of the State almost Prophetick.

—Edward Chamberlayne's
Angliae Notitia, 1669.

PART I

England, Scotland, and Australia, 688-1898

Delinquent Children
under Anglo-Saxon Laws

Benj. Thorpe (ed.), *Ancient Laws and Institutes of England*
(London, 1840), pp. 47, 85, 103 (Brit. Mus.)

I. THE LAWS OF KING INE [688 A.D.–725 A.D.]
Of Stealing

7. If any one steal, so that his wife and his children know it not,
let him pay LX. shillings as 'wite.' [punishment]. But if he steal
with the knowledge of all his household, let them all go into slavery.
A boy of X. years may be privy to a theft. . . .

II. THE LAWS OF KING AETHELSTAN [924 A.D.]

(A) Council of Greatanlea.
Of Thieves

1. First: that no thief be spared who may be taken 'handhaeb-
bende,' [i.e. with the goods in his hand] above XII. years, and above
eight pence. And if any one so do, let him pay for the thief according to his 'wēr,' [*pretium nativitatis*] and let it not be the more
settled for the thief, or that he clear himself thereby. But if he will
defend himself, or flees away, then let him not be spared. If a thief
be brought into prison: that he be XL. days in prison, and then let
him be released thereout with CXX. shillings, and let the kindred
enter into 'borh' [security] for him that he evermore desist. And if
after that he steal, let them pay for him according to his 'wēr,' or
bring him again therein: and if any one stand up for him, let him
pay for him according to his 'wēr,' as well to the king as to him to
whom it lawfully belongs: and let every man of those who there
stand by him pay to the king CXX. shillings as 'wite.' . . .

(B) Judicia Civitatis Lundoniae.
Twelfth:
1. That the king now again has ordained to his 'witan' [as-
sembly] at* 'Witlanburh,' and has commanded it to be made known
to the archbishop by bishop† Theodred, that it seemed to him too
cruel that so young a man should be killed, and besides for so little,

*Whittlebury, Northamptonshire?
†Bishop of London A.D. 900 until about 921.

3

as he has learned has somewhere been done. He then said, that it seemed to him, and to those who counselled with him, that no younger person should be slain than XV. years, except he should make resistance or flee, and would not surrender himself; that then he should be slain, as well for more as for less, whichever it might be. But if he be willing to surrender himself, let him be put into prison, as it was ordained at 'Greatanlea,' and by the same let him be redeemed.

2. Or, if he come not into prison, and they have none, that they take him in 'borh' by his full 'wēr,' that he will evermore desist from every kind of evil. If the kindred will not take him out, nor enter into 'borh' for him, then let him swear as the bishop may instruct him, that he will desist from every kind of evil, and stand in servitude by his 'wēr.' But if he after that again steal, let him be slain or hanged, as was before done to the older ones.

3. And the king has also ordained, that no one should be slain for less property than XII. penceworth, unless he will flee or defend himself. . . .

The City of London Chamberlain's Court, or the City Custom of Apprenticeship, 1299—

[A] A. H. Thomas (ed.), *Calendar of Plea and Memoranda Rolls, Preserved among the Archives of the Corporation of the City of London at the Guild-hall, A.D. 1364-1381* (Cambridge: At the University Press, 1929), pp. 16, xl, xlvi.

. . . The City Chamberlain's Court for dealing with offences of masters and apprentices was in existence in 1299. *Cal. of Early Mayor's Court Rolls*, pp. 46-8. Next year the procedure was regulated, two Aldermen being associated with the Chamberlain for the purpose of ensuring that all indentures were registered at Guildhall, and for taking fines from apprentices. More serious cases were brought before the Mayor's Court by bill or petition. See *Cal. of Letter Book C*, p. 78, and *Cal. of Early Mayor's Court Rolls*, pp. 82-3. . . .

CITY CUSTOM OF APPRENTICESHIP

It has been noted above that already in 1299-1300 there was a considerable body of City law and custom regulating apprenticeship. This was enlarged and defined by civic ordinances, by case and statute law, and by such ordinances of the misteries as were sanctioned by the Courts of Aldermen and Common Council and therefore were enforceable in the courts.

A primary qualification for apprenticeship was that a boy or girl should be of free condition and not a villein. . . .

In the 15th century it was usual to insist that all apprentices should be English born. . . .

A further limitation was temporarily introduced by the Statute 7 Henry IV c. 17 which, after confirming the Statute of Labourers and 12 Ric. II. c.3, recites how children from the country were put as apprentices at the age of twelve years in towns*. . . .

The apprentice for his part, was expected to be obedient, industrious and orderly, and he must not waste his master's goods. If it were a serious matter he could be sued in the Mayor's Court; for small breaches of discipline he was brought before the Chamberlain —committals by the Chamberlain to Newgate or Bridewell continued within living memory. . . .

[B] Evans Austin, *The Law Relating to Apprentices, including those Bound According to the Custom of the City of London* (London, 1890), pp. 110-11.

Ch. V. London (City) Apprentices

The jurisdiction of the Chamberlain over apprentices is founded on custom, and only extends to those bound to freemen of the city, and according to the "custom of London." His Court is an intermediate Court below the Mayor's Court, and if he cannot settle a dispute in his Court he remits the matter to the Mayor's Court, and there an action is brought on the covenants of the indenture. In any matter arising in the Chamberlain's Court, carried or remitted to the Mayor's Court, the parties concerned may, if they desire it, have the matter submitted to a jury. The Chamberlain sits as a magistrate in his Court, and hears the cases that are brought before him on a summons previously taken out by the complainant, and, after hearing the evidence, adjudicates. The Chamberlain's Court is, in fact, a Court of arbitration between masters and their apprentices, for the Chamberlain generally gives advice, and endeavours to settle the disputes, rather than exercise the powers of punishment which are vested in him; and it is only after repeated cautions and admonitions that he really does so. He usually admonishes the parties, and lets

*This was taken in the City to fix the age under which no child could be apprenticed. I, fo. 258 b, "and that the apprentices shall be of full age according to the statute of apprentices lately made at Cambridge.

the case stand over for a fortnight or so, and, as a rule, the parties in the meantime come to a better understanding, and nothing more is heard of the case. This jurisdiction extends to all kinds of disputes between masters and apprentices. . . .

[C] Sir William Maitland, History of London (1739), p. 433.

[PRISONS FOR APPRENTICES]

On each side of the steps ascending to the Mayor's Court are situate the Hall-Keepers Offices. . . .

Underneath these offices are two prisons, denominated Little-Ease, which appellation was given to them for the lowness of their ceilings, whereby the prisoners are oblig'd to sit on the floor during their confinement. The persons for whom these prisons were erected are the City apprentices, who in cases of obstinacy are thither committed by the Chamberlain of London, till they submit themselves to their injur'd Masters, by begging pardon for their past offences.

[D] P. E. Jones, The Corporation of London. Origin, Constitution, Powers and Duties (Oxford University Press, 1950), pp. 90-91.

CHAMBERLAIN'S COURT

For many centuries the Chamberlain has exercised a jurisdiction in respect of apprentices bound by the London indenture, the terms of which are peculiar to the City.

. . . Decisions of the Chamberlain's Court have been questioned by mandamus and upheld in the superior Courts and their jurisdiction has been preserved by modern statutes, 30 & 31 Vict., c. 141, s. 24 and 38 & 39 Vict., c. 90, s. 131. A kindly master much preferred to proceed here than to invoke the stigma of a police court prosecution.

Generally the Chamberlain sought to smooth out difficulties rather than pronounce judgements. He preferred to arbitrate or admonish and only when these measures proved unavailing did he commit to prison, and even then was ever ready to release the penitent. In the middle of last century the Clerk of the Chamber stated that he, personally, was able to "arrange" five cases out of six without troubling the Chamberlain. Commitals to Bridewell in 1830 were 40, by 1850 the number had decreased to 20, and the last apprentice was detained there in 1916. True apprenticeship in the City is now rare and cases are few. Recent disputes brought before the Chamberlain have related to the refusal of an apprentice

6

to work overtime, bad time-keeping, irregular attendance, unlawful use of an apprentice as a menial or to run errands, and lack of instruction.

At one time apprentices sent to Bridewell were permitted to mingle with vagrants and other prisoners confined there. Segregation of apprentices in sound-proofed cells was arranged in 1800. When Bridewell prison was closed and the Hospital reconstituted as King Edward's School, the Corporation insisted that some provision should be made for the reception of recalcitrant apprentices. The scheme approved by the Charity Commissioners in 1860 required the Governors to reserve three rooms at Blackfriars for apprentices committed from the Chamberlain's Court. A subsequent scheme of 1931 reduced the number of rooms to two, each of which was furnished with a bedstead, iron washbasin, desk, and chair. It was customary for a copy of Bunyan's *Pilgrim's Progress* to be placed upon the desk.[1]

Delinquent Children in the Sixteenth Century: Illustrative Cases

Charles Wriothesley (Windsor Herald), *A Chronicle of England During the Reigns of the Tudors, from A.D. 1485 to 1559*, edited by William Douglas Hamilton (Printed for the Camden Society), Vol. I, M.S. 11 (1875), pp. 73, 134-35; Vol. II, p. 129.

This yeare, the 29 of Januarie [1537/8] was arreigned at Westminster in the afternoone a boye of Mr. Culpepers, Gentleman of the Kings Privie Chamber, which had stolne his maisters purse and £11 of money, with a jewell of the Kinges which was in the same purse, and there condemned to death; but the morrowe after when he was brought to the place of execution, which was at the ende of the tylt yeard afore the Kinges Pallace at Westminster, and that the hangman was takinge the ladder from the gallowes, the Kinge sent his pardon for the sayde boye, and so he was saved from death, to the great comforte of all the people there present, &c. . . .

1. The writer in talking with Mr. Jones in the Corporation Records Office, 55 Moorgate Street, London, in November 1950, suggested that the Chamberlain's Court might be regarded as a forerunner of the present day juvenile court. In his opinion, however, the jurisdiction of the Chamberlain extended only to controversies between apprentices and masters, while ordinary offences committed by apprentices were handled by other courts.

Note, too, that parish or pauper apprentices, who were frequently mistreated, and in some instances were beaten to death, were not subject to the jurisdiction of the Chamberlain, and for all practical purposes they were unable to appeal to magistrate's courts for protection.

This yeare, the 17th of March [1542], was boyled in Smithfeild one Margret Davie, a mayden, which had poysoned 3 househouldes that she dwelled in, one being her Mrs, which dyed of the same, and one Darington and his wyfe, which also she dwelled with in Coleman Streat, which dyed of the same; and also one Tinleys wyfe, which dyed allso of the same. . . .

Mundaye the first of Julie [1555] John Bradford and a boye were brent [burnt] in Smythfielde for heresie.[1]

John Calvin's Catechism Describes the Punishment for Disobedient Children, 1556

> John Calvin, *The Catechisme or Manner to teache children the Christian religion, wherin the Minister demandeth the question, and the childe maketh answere*. Made by the excellent Doctor and Pastor in Christes Churche, John Calvin ([Pub.] By John Crespin, 1556), p. 74 (Brit. Mus.)

THE MINISTER

And what is to be sayd of them that be disobedient unto father and mother?

THE CHILDE

God will not onely punish them with everlasting payne in the day of judgement, but he will execute also punishmente on theyr bodyes here in thys worlde; eyther by shortnynge their life, eyther by procuring them a shameful death, either at the least a life most miserable.

London City Council Bars Delinquent Children from Inheriting from Their Parents, 1580

> *Orders Taken and Enacted, for Orphans and their Portions* (Imprinted at London for Gabriel Cawood, Anno MDLXXX). [Black Letter—not paged] (Brit. Mus.)

1. A blind boy was burned for heresy at Gloucester about May 5, 1556, and a twelve-year-old boy of Worcester, imprisoned in chains for several months for alleged heresy, narrowly escaped a similar fate by the death of Henry VIII. *Narratives of the Days of the Reformation, Chiefly from the Manuscripts of John Foxe the Martyrologist*, edited by John Gough Nichols (Printed for the Camden Society [1859]), Vol. 77, pp. 18-20; 60-68.

Forasmuch as the Citie of London, is of late yeres sore decayed, and dayly is lyke to decaye, more and more: A great cause and occasion whereoff among other, hath ben, for that free mens children, (Orphanes of the sayd Citie) sometimes in the lyves of their Parents, and sometimes after their deceases, being lefte wealthy and rich, doe bestow themselves in ungodly Marriages, for the most part in their young age, at their owne wills and pleasures, without the consent and against the mindes of their friends, saying and affirming, that the Law and custome of the said Citie giveth unto them their portions, whether they mary by the assent of their friends or not (and so do daily cast away and undoe themselves, in trust to have their saide portions, whether their parents or friends will or will not. And thereby doe they bestow themselves upon simple and light persons, having neither cunning, knowledge, substance, ne good or honest conditions. By reason where-off, such Orphanes, inordinately, and insolently, do spende and consume their patrimony and portions in short time, not only to the undoing of themselves, and to the great ignomie and shame of their friends, but also to the great slaunder of the Lord Mayor and Aldermen of this citie (who bene reputed and taken as Fathers and Protectors of the same Orphanes) and to the great losse and hinderaunce of the sayd Citie.

And forasmuch as the sayd Lord Mayor and Citizens; have by theyr lawes and customes, power and authoritie to make lawes and ordinances, by their common counsaile, for redresse of the same. It is therefore now (to the intent to reduce the same to a more godly, more profitable and decent order and conformitie) by the said Lord Mayor, and Communaltie, and Citizens, in this present common counsayle assembled ,and by authoritye of the same common Counsaile, enacted, ordeined, authorized, and established for a Law perpetually to be observed and kept within the said Citie. That if any Orphane, or childe of anye free man or free woman, of the sayd Citie doe offend in any the things heereafter expressed, and be thereoff lawfully convicted, afore the Lorde Mayor and the Aldermen or els where, that then they and every of them, shall to al entents purposes, constructions and meanings, be unabled and barred to demaund and claime their portion or portions, and also shal lose and forgoe and be barred forever, of all and every his, hir, or their part or parts, and portions to him or them belonging, by and after the death of his or their said father or mother, of ye goods and cattalles, of every such father and mother, by reason of any Law, custome, ordinance, usage, fraunches, priviledge, act of Commune Counsale, or other thing, heretofore had or used, within ye sayd Citie. . . . That is to wit, First, if any manchild, or womanchild, shal malitiously go about or attempt to do, or cause to be done, any bodily harm, death, or destruction to his or their Father or Mother: of if any manchild do heerafter mary or contract mariage in the life of his father or mother (by whom he will clayme any portion) under the age of xxi yeres, without ye consent of his sayd Father, or Mother, by whom hee will claime any portion: [same for girl under xviii years] . . . or, if any manchilde bee a Thiefe, or a Fellon, or a common player at unlawfull games notoriously known: Or if any womanchilde shal heerafter commit any whoredome, or be a common Picker, that then every of ye persons so offending, shalbe barred and excluded to have, or demaund any portion.

[It is provided, however, that the parent can bequeath in legacy any or all of the portion of the orphan in writing, etc.]

A School of Crime in London as Described by William Fleetwood, Recorder of London, 1585

Charles M. Clode, *The Early History of the Guild of Merchant Taylors of . . . London* (1888), Part II, p. 294 (UNC Lib.)

Amongst our travells this one matter tumbled out by the waye, that one Wotton, a gentilman borne, and sometime a merchantmane of good crydit, who falling by time with decay kepte an alehouse at Smart's Key, near Billingsgate, and for some misdemeanour put downe. He reared up a new trade in lyfe and in the same house he procured all the cut-purses about this city to repair to the same house. There was a school house set up to learn young boys to cut purses. There were hung up two devyses, the one was a pocket and the other was a purse. The pocket had in it certain counters and was hung about, with hawks bells, and over the top did hang a little sacring bell,* and he that could take out the counters without any noyse was allowed to be a public foyster, and he that could take a piece of sylver out of the purse without the noyse of any of the bells he was adjudged a judicial nypper.

Legal Status of the Child Offender during the Seventeenth Century

[A] Michael Dalton, *The Countrey Justice, Conteyning the Practise of the Justices of the Peace out of their Sessions . . .* (1st

* A bell used to be rung in churches at the elevation of the Host.

Ed.; London, 1618), pp. 204-6, 215, 226, 229, 237-38 (Brit. Mus.) Many later editions.

PETIE TREASON

Petie Treason is when wilfull Murder is committed (in the estate Oecomenicall) upon any subject, by one that is in subjection, and oweth faith, duetie, and obedience, to the partie murdred; as in these cases following. . . .

A servant of the age of thirteene yeares, killed her Mistresse, it was adjudged in her Petie Treason. . . .

The childe maliciously killeth the father, or mother; this is Pettie treason (although the father or mother at the same time give neither meate, drinke, nor wages to such child:) But it is Treason in the child, in respect of the duetie of nature violated. . . .

The punishment for pettie treason is this, The man so offending, shalbe drawen and hanged: the woman shall be burned alive, in case as well of pettie Treason, as of high Treason. But in the case of felonies, the judgement both of the man and woman is to be hanged. . . .

WHAT PERSONS ARE CHARGEABLE WITH HOMICIDE?

An infant of eight yeares of age, or above, may commit homicide, and shall be hanged for it, *viz.* If it may appeare (by hyding of the person slaine, by excusing it, or by any other act) that he had knowledge of good and evill, and of the perill and danger of that offence. See *3.H.7. 1 & 12. Stamf. 27. Fitz. Coron. 118. 129 & Br. Coron. 133.*

But an infant of such tender yeares, as that he hath no discretion or intelligence, if he kill a man, this is no felonie in him. 3.H.7.1.b. . . .

BURGLARY

Note also by *Britton,* fol. 17. it is not Burglary in an Infant of fourteene years of age; nor in poore persons that upon hunger shall enter a house for victuall under the value of twelve pence; nor in naturall fooles, or other persons that bee *non compos mentis.* . . .

ROBBERIE

If one shall cut my purse, or take, or picke my purse out of my pocket secretly, or privily and fraudulently, it is felonie of death without benefit to Clergie, if it be above the value of xij. d. [12 pence]. . . .

11

Grand Larceny, is when the goods stollen be above the value of xij. d. and this is felonie of death, Sc. wherin judgement of death shall be given upon the offendor (except be he saved by his book.)

And yet if the goods stollen be to the value of x. s. if the Jurie that passeth upon his arraignement, shall find that the goods did not exceed the value of xij. d. then that offence shall be taken but for petie Larcenie.

Petie Larcenie, is when the goods stollen, doe not exceed the value of xij. d. & for this the offendor shalbe imprisoned for some certaine time, and after shall be whipped, or otherwise punished by the discretion of the Justices before whom he is arraigned; but it is not felony of death. . . .

An Ideot, Lunatike, dumbe and deafe person, and an Enfant, are chargeable in Larceny, after the same sort, as they are chargeable in Homicide; which see here before in Manslaughter. And yet if an Enfant shall commit Larcenie, and shall be found guiltie thereof before the Justices of P. it shall not be amisse for them to respite the judgement, & so hath it often bin done by the Judges; see Stamf. 27 et H.7. fol. 1.b. et 12.b.

[In the 1626 edition of Dalton's *Countrey Justice* (p. 267) the following citations are given of respite of judgement for infants found guilty of larceny:]

At Cambridge Assizes in Lent, 1619, before Sir Henry Montague, and Sir John Doddridge Judge of Assize there, they sitting together upon the prisoners, an Infant, about 14 yeares of age, was arraigned before them of Larceny, and was found guilty, and upon demand of his Clergy had the same allowed him, and was burned in the hand.

The like was done there at Lent Assizes, 1624 before Sir Randall Crew, Lord Chiefe Justice.

[In Dalton's *Countrey Justice*, 1630 (pp. 199-200, 244, 335):]

FORCIBLE ENTRIE, &C.

An infant of the age of eighteen years, by his own act may commit a forcible entry or deteiner: & so he may though he be under eighteen, if so be that he be of the age of discretion; (sc. of the age of 14 yeares.) See *Perk.f.10.b.* and it seemeth the Justice may fine him therefore. But yet it shall be good discretion in the Just. of peace to forbeare the imprisonment of such infants. See B. imp. 43.45.75.101. . . .

For an Infant shall suffer no imprisonment or corporall paine for any offence committed against any statute, wherein an Infant is not expressly named. . . .

[HOMICIDE]

An Infant of eight yeares of age, or above, may commit Homicide, and shall be hanged for it. . . .

And yet Sir *Edw. Coke* upon *Littleton fol.* 147, saith, that it is of an Infant, untill he be of the age of 14 yeares (which in law is accounted the age of discretion) as it is with a man *Non compos mentis;* and that in criminal causes (as felony &c.) his act and wrong shall not be imputed to him, for that *Actus non facit reum, nisi mens sit rea,* &c.

ARREST, AND IMPRISONMENT

An Infant (though of yeeres of discretion, yet he shall suffer no imprisonment, nor other corporall paine, for any offence committed or done by him against any statute, except that an infant be expressed by name, in the statute. *Br. Impris.* 101. *Covert.* 68. *Plo.* 364. *Doct & Stu.* 147.148.

> [B] J[ohn] B[rydall], Esq.; *A Compendious Collection of the Laws of England, Touching Matters Criminal. Faithfully collected and Methodically digested, not only for the use of Sheriffs, Justices of the Peace, Coroners, Clerks of the Peace, and others within that Verge; but of all the People in general* (London, 1675), pp. 13-14, 55-56, 58, 114 (Brit. Mus.)

OF MURDER IN RESPECT OF ANOTHER

. . . Whether an Infant within the age of Nine Years can be guilty of Murder?

Un Infant deins age ix ans occist un Enfant de ix ans & Confesse le Felony, & auxi fuit trove que quant il luy avoit tue, il luy occult & auxi le Sanke que fuit sur luy effundes, si il ceo excuse; And the Judges held, that he ought to be hanged. But *Fairefax* said, that the words of Fortescue were, viz. That the Reason why a person is executed for Murder, is for example, that others may fear to offend; But such punishment can be no example to such an Infant or to a person that hath not discretion.

Le Recorder de Londes monstre coment un enfant entra le age de x. ans & xii. ans fuit endite de mort, & il fuit appose de ceo, & il dit, que il gard barbettes ove cestuy que est mort & ils happen a variance per que il luy ferist en le gule, puis en le Teste & issent en divers

Lieux del corps tanque qu'il fuit mort, & donques il trahist le corps en le corne, & les Justices pur son rendr', & pur ceo que il narroit le matter playnem ent respite le Judgment, & plusours Justic' disont, que il fuit deigne mort &c. And the Reason is, quia malitia supplet etatem: With this our Rule do concur the Roman Laws. . . .

OF LARCENY

Larceny, by the Common Law, is the felonious and fraudulent taking, and carrying away by any man or woman, of the meer personal goods of another, neither from the person, nor by night in the house of the owner: This Larceny is twofold, the one so called Simply, and the other Petit, or Little Larceny.

The first is where the thing stollen exceeds the value of 12 pence, and that is felony.

The other (which is called little, or petit Larceny) is where the thing stollen doth not exceed the value of 12 pence, and that is not felony.

From the Description and Division of Larceny, I proceed to propose these following Queries, with Resolutions on them. . . .

Whether an Infant, that is under the age of discretion, can commit Larceny?

An Infant, until he be of the age of 14, which in Law is accounted the age of discretion cannot commit Larceny, or other felony; for the principal end of punishment is, that others by his example may fear to offend: But such punishment can be no example to Infants, that are not of the age of Discretion.

But it appears by Lambard f.2 nu. 7. that the Law was heretofore thus: Infans decem annorum furti reus censeatur. . . .

The principal end of punishment in our Law is, that others by example may fear to offend. *Ut poena unius sit metus multorum;* and therefore a man that is *non compos mentis*, or an Infant that is within the age of discretion, is not (un home) within the statute of 25.E.3.c.2 *de proditionibus;* for the end of punishment is that others may be deterred from the perpetration of similar offences. But such punishment can be no example to mad Men, or Infants, that are not of the age of discretion.

[C] [Anon.], *The Infant's Lawyer: or, The Law, Ancient and Modern Relating to Infants, etc.* (2nd Ed.; London, 1712), pp. A2, 18, 21-23, 32, 34, 40, 45, 50, 346 (Brit. Mus.)

[This is a scholarly legal treatise by an unknown hand, setting forth the privileges of infants, "their several Ages for divers Purposes; Guardians and *Prochein amy,* as to Suits and Defences by them; Actions brought by and against them . . . likewise, of Devises by and to Infants, Apprentices, Custom of *London* and Pleadings, Orphans, Tryals of Infancy, Portions and Legacies, and Resolutions and Decrees at Common Law and *Chancery* concerning the same." The first edition of this work appeared in 1697 and a third edition in 1726.]

To the Reader

It is a frequent Saying in our Law-Books, *De minimis non curat Lex,* which is true if it be understood of petty Things and minute Circumstances, but if we apply it to Persons, it is not so; for it is most certain, that our Law hath a very great and tender Consideration for Persons naturally disabled, and especially for *Minors.* The Law protects their Persons, preserves their Rights and Estates, excuseth their Laches, and assists them in their Pleadings. And as it is ingenuously observed in *Holford* and *Platt's* Case, 2 *Roll.* Rep. 18. *The Judges are their Counsellors, the Jury are their Servants,* (for they ought to find the Title at large in an Assize) *and the Law is their Guardian.* And let me add, They are under the special Aid and Protection of his Equity, who is no less than Keeper of the King's Conscience.

It hath been computed by some (whose Genius lies that Way), That Infants make up a Third Part of the Nation; which if so, (as the Guess seems not very improbable) then I suppose a Treatise of this Kind (and never before attempted) may be acceptable.

It is but Small, and therefore more analogous to the Subject of it; and yet the Matter is full of Weight and Variety.

The Method which I have used is, I conceive, as proper and apt as a Treatise of this Sort is capable of. And indeed it is the Nature of the Subject, which ought to direct the Method.

But be that as it will, it appears without either a *Parent* or a *Patron;* and therefore, as an *Orphan,* claims *Pity,* and hopes for a *favourable* Construction. . . .

Our Common Law looks upon Infancy as an Age of Impotence, Weakness and Disability, not capable of managing their Concerns with Discretion, and for their better Profit and Advantage; and therefore is very favourable to them in preserving their Rights and Estates, inabling them in their Suits, assisting them in their Pleadings, excusing their Laches, and in protecting their Persons. . . .

Infant of 10 Years outlaw'd, he was not awarded to Prison for the Tenderness of his Age. 38 Ed. 3. 5. b. . . .

Infant named a Disseisor, voucheth a Record and fails, he shall not be imprison'd on the Statute W. 2. *cap.* 25. *Com.* 364. *a.*

So if Infant be Bail, &c. and on Account he is found in Arrear, the Auditors may not commit him to the next Gaol, upon the Statute of W. 2. c. 11. . . .

He is not guilty of Felony till the Age of Discretion, 3 Inst. 4, 5. . . .

It's said generally, Statutes which give Corporal Punishment shall not extend to Infants. But 30 Ass. 18. Infant brought an Attaint, and the first Verdict was affirmed, and the Infant was awarded to Prison. . . .

But though an Infant is generally favoured in the Law, (as hath been represented to you) yet this Favour doth not extend to all Cases; the Consideration whereof shall be the Subject of the next Section. . . .

2. In case of Criminal Actions, and Wrongs and Injuries done to the Person or Estate of another, an Infant shall not be priviledg'd for in such Cases *Malitia Supplet Aetatem;* but then he must be of the Age of Discretion. . . .

Statutes which give Corporal Punishment, shall not extend to Infants, contrary of other Statutes, 36 Ed. 3. If Infant be Keeper of a Prison, and suffer an Escape, he shall be subject to the Escape. . . .

One and twenty is accounted the full Age in our Law, and Twenty five by the Civil Law, for then the *Romans* accounted the Man to have *plenam Maturitatem;* and the *Lombards* counted the Age of Eighteen to be Full Age, 1 *Inst.* 78. b.

At Fourteen Years in our Law is accounted the Age of Discretion, and in several Cases at that Age an Infant, shall be priviledged, punished or chargeable, as you will find in this Treatise. . . .

Infant under the Age of Seven Years shall not be said to be a Wanderer within the Statute of 39 *Eliz. cap.* 4. for the *Punishment of Rogues,* 2 *Bulstr.* 352. . . .

Of Punishment of Infants for Criminal Matters

If Infant be indicted of Felony, and arraigned, and pleads Not guilty, and found Not guilty, yet the Justices may dismiss him by their Discretion, if it appear to them to be of such an Age that he had not Discretion, 35 H. 6. 11. b. And the Reason is, that in Felony he had no other Remedy but to plead Not guilty, for Felony may not be justified.

Per Doctor and *Student* 149. a. If Infant commit Felony at such an Age that he had Discretion to know the Law, he shall have

Punishment of the Law. One of 12 Years or over kills another, this is Felony; if he were but of 9 Years, if by any Signs it may be intended that he had Conisance of Good and Evil; as by his Excuses, or any other Act that he did after the killing, to wit, in hiding the Dead in any secret Place; for in such a Case *Malitia Supplebit Aetatem, ut patet*, 3 H. 7. 12. b.

Per Doctor and *Student* 149 a. If Infant does a Trespass at such an Age that he had Discretion to know the Law, he shall have Punishment of the Law.

Com. 19. a. Infant of tender Years kills one, it is not Felony, because he had not Discretion to understand.

Cok. 3 Inst. 47. Murder is when one of Age of Discretion kills one: So of Homicide.

Children of Winchester Punished for Playing on Sunday, 1656

Charles Bailey,[1] *Transcripts from the Municipal Archives of Winchester, and Other Documents, Elucidating the Government, Manners, and Customs of the Same City, from the Thirteenth Century to the Present Period* (Winchester, 1856), pp. 72-73 (Brit. Mus.)

[IDLE CHILDREN PLAYING IN THE GREAT CHURCH YARD] 1656

Forasmuch as the Lord's day is very much pphaned [profaned] by a disorderly sort of idle children in unlawfull Exercises and pastimes in the greate church yarde, and the streets, and divers other places within this citty, It is therefore ordained and established by the Assemble, that the Parents of such children doe for the tyme to come take care that their sayd children doe not offend herin, upon paine of Two Shillings for evry tyme that they shall neglect the same; and for ye better discovrry of such unlawfull exercises and pastimes, It is ordained and established that the constables and Beedle of the sayd citty doe apprhend all such idle children who shall offend herein, and that they cause them to go before ye Maior, or some other Justice W^th in the sayd citty, there to be dealt withall according to the Law.

1. Town clerk.

Thomas Firmin, London Philanthropist, Establishes a Spinning School to Keep Children out of Mischief, 1677

Thomas Firmin, *Some Proposals for the Imployment of the Poor* (2nd. Ed.; London, 1681), pp. 1-4, 37 (editor's lib.)

It is now above four years since I erected my Work-House in *Little Britain* for the Imployment of the Poor in the Linnen Manufacture, which hath proved so great a Help, and afforded such Relief to many Hundreds of poor Families, that I never did, nor I fear ever shall do an Action more to my own satisfaction, nor to the good and benefit of the Poor. . . .

To the end therefore that Poverty, together with that wicked Trade of Begging (which so many thousands of late years have taken up, to the dishonour of Almighty God, and the great scandal of the Government of this Nation) may be prevented, I shall humbly propose a few things, which being put in practice, may with Gods Blessing, prove effectual to the ends designed.

And the first is this, That every Parish that abounds with Poor People, would set up a School in the nature of a Workhouse, to teach their poor Children to work in, who for want thereof, now wander up and down the Parish and parts adjacent, and between Begging and Stealing, get a sorry liveing; but never bring any thing to their poor Parents, nor earn one Farthing towards their own maintenance, or good of the Nation.

This, in a short time, would be found very advantagious, not only to the poor Children themselves, who by this means, whilst young should be inured to labour, and taught to get their own Livings, but also to their Parents, who should hereby both be freed from the Charge of keeping them, and in time, be helpt by their Labours, as it is in other places; and moreover the Parish should be freed from much Charge which many times they are at, to keep such poor Children, or at least which they are necessitated to allow their Parents towards it.

Nothing being accounted a better Argument for a large Pension, than that a Man or Woman hath six or seven small Children, whereas unless they were all born at a time, or came faster into the World than ordinarily so many Children do, it is very hard if some of them are not able to work for themselves. I my self have at this time many poor Children, not above five or six years old, that can earn two pence a day, and others but a little older, three pence or four pence, by spinning Flax which will go very far towards the maintenance of any poor Child. Not that I would have these

Schools confined only to Spinning, but left at liberty to take in any other work that the Children shall be capable of, as knitting of Stockings, winding of Silk, making of Lace or plain Work, or the like: For it matters not so much what you employ these poor Children in, as that you do employ them in some thing, to prevent an idle, lazy kind of Life, which if once they get the habit of, they will hardly leave; but on the contrary, if you train up a Child in the way that he should go, when he is old, he will not depart from it.

And this is the way (as I am informed) that is practiced in *Holland* and other places, with so great advantage, that there is very few Children who have attained to seven or eight years of age, that are any charge to their Parents, or burthensome to the Parish. And Mr. *Chamberlain* in his Book, Intituled, *The Present State of England,* hath observed, that in the City of *Norwich,* it hath been computed of late years, and found, that yearly, Children from six to ten years old, have gained twelve thousand pounds a year more than they have spent, chiefly by knitting fine Jersey Stockings.

This School would be of no great Charge, but many ways advantagious to the Parish. At this time I have a person who for five shillings a week, doth constantly teach between twenty and thirty poor Children to spin; Some that are little, upon the single Wheel, and others that are bigger, upon the double, or two handed Wheel (like that which you have at the beginning of these Papers, which I esteem the best way for spinning, and full as proper for Wooll as Flax) which when they are expert in, I give the Children leave to carry away with them to their several places of abode, that so there may be room for others; and of these, there are divers that can earn six pence a day, and some more, allowing them two hours in a day to learn to read in, instead of that time which is allotted to the poorest of our Children to play in; a custom that I verily believe hath been the ruin of many thousand poor Children, and hath nothing in the World to justifie it but an old Proverb, which yet we have not fully observed: For instead of giving them all work and no play, the generality of our poor Children have all play and no work, which is a thousand times more mischievous than the other. Not that I would have all manner of Recreation and Divertisement prohibited to Children, nor will it be hard to find some others besides playing at push-pin, or hide-Farthing, neither of which, nor twenty others now in use, are any ways conducing to the health of their Bodies, or to the improvement of their minds; but are only fit to teach them lying and wrangling, with twenty cheating Tricks, which many times they retain as long as they live.

I believe there are very few persons who have had occasion to take one of these poor Children for a Foot-boy, or other-wise, but can tell you the sad Effects of such an idle Life as they have been brought up in; the Lad having from his Cradle, if he had any, been permitted to play, has made it so natural to him, that send him in what haste you will, upon any Errand, if he meets with a Play-fellow, will have a touch of his old Sport, and many times for want of such a one, will be exercising his hand alone, rather than forbear his old Trade.

Let any man that hath occasion either to walk or ride through the Out-parts of this City, (where mostly our poor people inhabit) tell but what he hath seen of the Rudeness of young Children, who for want of better Education and Employment, shall sometimes be found by whole Companies at play, where they shall wrangle and cheat one another, and upon the least Provocation, swear and fight for a Farthing, or else they shall be found whipping of Horses, by reason of which, they sometimes cast their Riders, to the hazard or loss of their Lives or Limbs; or else they shall be throwing of Dirt or Stones into Coaches, or at the Glasses, insomuch that I have been a hundred times greatly troubled, to see the Rudeness and Mis-behaviour of the poorer sort of Children, (especially of late years) they having been generally so much neglected, that they have neither been taught their Duties either towards God or Man. . . .

But further, to encourage the setting up of Schools in every great Parish, for the Instruction of young Children, and bringing them to labour; and also for providing Work for such as are of Age, which they may carry to their own Habitations: I have a few things more to say.

First, By means hereof, you will prevent much of that mischief that happens to young Children, by suffering them to wander up and down without any Care or Government, by reason of which, they do not only get a lazy, idle Habit, which yet is no small Evil, but learn all manner of Wickedness that they are capable of, as Lying, Swearing, Thieving, and such like, which by sad experience, we find many times they retain as long as they live, being bred in the Bone, will hardly be got out of the Flesh, it being almost as possible to wash the *Blackamore* white, as it is to teach them to do well, that have been long accustomed to do evil: Whereas, if due Care were taken to instruct young Children, and to put them into a good Course of Life, before Evil had taken hold of them, both Labour and Vertue would be much more pleasing to them, than Idleness, Sloth and Vice.

20

Children's Cases Tried in Old Bailey, London, 1681-1836

Cases of Children Charged with Crime and Handled by the
Quarter Sessions of Gaol Delivery Held in the Old Bailey[1] in
London, 1681-1836 (Brit. Mus.)

[The published accounts of trials of criminals in the court sessions in the Old Bailey in London are widely scattered in the British Museum, are not always arranged chronologically in the collections, and there are many gaps in the series. Unfortunately some whole volumes of court reports were destroyed in the bombing of London during World War II. It is impossible to locate a full set of court reports for the Old Bailey sessions for any extended period. It is believed, however, that the following extracts of children's cases taken from available reports are representative. In the reports examined all children's cases have been reported as found, except for a very small number where the child was acquitted for lack of evidence, or where the prosecutor failed to appear against the child.

Anyone familiar with court records knows that for a variety of reasons the sentence imposed by the court is not always put into effect. Frequently his Majesty upon recommendation of the judge passing the sentence has been pleased to pardon the offender or to respite the sentence. Usually there were no published accounts of the pardons and commutations of sentences with which to supplement the court records of trials. This fact should be kept in mind when noting in the following extracts several sentences of death passed upon young children. It is possible, in fact, highly probable, that most of these death sentences for children were never carried out due to executive clemency. Many writers after 1800, particularly the Ordinary of Newgate, give strong evidence supporting this view.

In this connection it may be noted that the proportion of children's cases compared with those of adults in the Old Bailey sessions is extremely small. In many sessions of the court no children appeared. In one collection of proceedings covering seventeen Old Bailey court sessions during the period February 1683/4-January 1702, only four boys, and no girls, were reported among the six hundred and fifty-four criminals on whom sentences were passed. The sentences imposed on these criminals were as follows: burnt in the hand, 262; death, 172; whipped, 110; burnt on cheek,

1. The popular name for the central criminal court in London. A bailey is an open space enclosed by a fortification. The Old Bailey derives its name from its situation in one of the baileys that was a part of the old city fortifications.

33; fined (sometimes with pillory sentence added), 32; transported, 28; his Majesties service, 10; prison, 5; sent to sea, 1; sent to Bedlam, 1.]

1681
July 6, 7, 8, 9.

[William Buckley, a Youth, charged with murdering a Bailiff's follower who tried to arrest his master, was found guilty and was condemned to death.]

Oct. 17, 18, 19.

Mary Marshall was tryed for stealing a Curral, with a Silver chain, valued at twenty Shillings; which being proved against her, she was Convicted of the Felony; but not being above twelve years of age, though an old Offender, having been in Newgate before, for the like Robberies, she received Sentence with the rest; but notwithstanding, was reprieved after Judgment, for Transportation. [At this session seven criminals were sentenced to be burnt in the hand, six were condemned to die, four sentenced to be whipped, and one transported (Marshall).]

Dec. 7, 8.

Lydia Arlington, a Girl of about ten years of Age, was Indicted with three more supposed to be her Accomplices, for picking two several Pockets, and Stealing Money to the value of six pounds, but the former taking it upon her Self, having (past doubt) received her Instructions in *Newgate* she was only found Guilty, and the rest acquitted. [This child's name was not listed among the six condemned to death, nor does it occur elsewhere in the sentences.]

1683/4
Feb. 27, 28.

Charles Atlee, a little Boy, Indicted for stealing out of the Shop of Obadiah Bennet, in the Parish of Stepney, 28 s. and 11 d. on the 26th of *January* last: a Maid proved, she saw him run into the Shop, and that it was taken out of the Money-Box, but upon a quick pursuit, he was apprehended, and the Money taken out of his Pocket: He was found Guilty of the said Felony. [Sentenced to be transported.]

1684
Jan. 17, 18.

John Atkins, a little Boy, (but said to be an old Pickpocket) was, however, now Indicted for stealing a Silver Tankard, valued at Ten Pound, being the Goods of *Henry Smith* and taken upon him: he was therefore found Guilty. [Sentenced to be transported.]

May 15, 16.

Jane Owen, Indicted for Stealing a Silver Mustard-Pot, and three Silver Spoons, of the Goods of William Hannuay: It appeared, that the said Jane Owen having lately gone in Mans Cloaths as a Youth to wait upon a Gentleman, she was as such entertained into the Service of Mr. William Hanuay, waiting upon him as his Boy until she had gotten a new Suit of Cloaths, and then with the said Plate run away from him. She was found Guilty to the Value of nine Shillings. [Sentenced to be burnt in the hand.]

1686
May 20, 21, 22.

Nathaniel Johnson, a boy about Ten Years of Age, was Indicted for stealing £30 in money from Charles Hare—[evidence given which the boy did not deny] he was found Guilty of the Felony. [No disposition is listed.]

John Colwell, a Boy about Ten Years of Age, of the Parish of St. Butolph without Bishop's-gate, was Indicted for stealing Thirty Yards of Lemon-Colour'd Satin Ribbon, on the 21st of April last, from Ann Lee of the same Parish. The Evidence against the Prisoner was, that he coming to the House of the Prosecutor about Ten of the Clock at Night, and that he pretended to buy a Hatband, upon which the Maid let him in and called down her Mistress, and the Prisoner under pretence of desiring to see a piece of Ribbon, ran away with the said Ribbon; but he coming by the next day, the Maid saw him, whereupon, her Mistress caused him to be Apprehended. The Prisoners Defence was, that he was going to Rumford for a Horse for his Master (as he pretended, and that he knew nothing of the Ribbon; but he having none to appear in his behalf, and it being look'd upon as a frivilous Excuse, and the Prosecutor Swearing possitively, that he was the person; he was found Guilty to the value of 10 d. [Ordered to be whipped.]

1689
Dec. 11, 12, 13, 14.

Daniel Groves, a Boy about 16, of St. Alhallows-Lumbard street, was Indicted for Firing the House of *John Foster*, on the 27th of *October* last. The Evidence was Mr. *Foster*, with whom the Prisoner was an Apprentice, who said, That he Chopt a piece of Link, and clapt it between the Boards in a partition in the Cellar, where it took Fire, but was soon quench'd. The Prisoner confest it before the Justice, and said, that he was Instigated to Commit the Fact by the Temptations of the Devil, and one *Baker;* yet he deny'd it upon his Tryal. So he was found Guilty. [He was sentenced to be transported.]

Martin Seward and William Harwood, two little Youths, were both Tryed for Robbing one Richard Hall on the 14th of Novemb. last. Seward confest before the Justice, that he being Servant in the next House, got into Halls, and let in Harwood, and that Harwood took away 12 pair of Silver Clasps value 30 s. 20 Gold Rings value £5. One Silver Belt value 5 s. 40 Ounces of silver value £10 with some Silver Buttons value 20 s. It was Credibly Evidenced, that the Proscutor's Cellar was broke, and that Seward let the other Boy into the House, and put him into the Dust-hole for 6d. and about 4 or 5 a Clock in the Morning Committed the Robbery: but *Harwood* had good Evidence to prove his Honesty, so he was Acquitted; and Seward found Guilty of the Felony and Burglary. [He was sentenced to be transported.]

Jane Peel, a Girle was Indicted the first time for Stealing 9s. from Mary Peekworth a second time for Stealing, 5 Gold Rings value £5. 5 more value 40s. . . . found Guilty . . . to the value of 10d. [Sentenced to be whipped.]

1690
Jan. 15, 16, 17, 19.

Nicholas Carter, and Giles Webb, two Pick-pocket Boys, were Tryed for taking a Beaver Hat off the Head of one Mr. William Cummins, value £3 2s. on the 2d of December last, as he was passing along Brumley street, near Shorts Gardens, which was fully sworn against Carter, besides he did confess it when taken, and they were both together when the Robbery was done. They both denyed it stiffly, and were known in Court. Carter was found Guilty to the value of 10d. but Webb was acquitted. [Carter received sentence of death.]

Jan. 26.[2]

Nicholas Carter, about fourteen Years of Age, condemned for Robbery. He said, That his Father imployed him in sewing and making of Gloves: But he being Idle, and regardless of his Parents Good Admonitions, ran away from them, and joyned himself to bad Company. Thus he added to his own Evil Inclinations, and was trained up among his Companions, in getting Money by Slight of Hand, in Picking Pockets, till he adventured to rob Men of their Hats in the Street. He would not take former Warning, nor acknowledg his Consorts but said, That it repented him he left his

2. Taken from A *True Account of the Behaviour, Confession and Last Dying Speeches of the 8 Criminals that were Executed at Tyburn on Monday the 26th of January, 1690.*

Fathers Imployment, and that he was disobedient. But if he might be spared he resolved to amend his evil life. . . . Nicholas Carter, the Boy, desired all Young People to take timely warning by his so sudden a Death, acknowledging withal, That he had been used to pick Pockets all his days, &c. . . . they were turned off [hanged].
Feb. 18, 19, 20.

Thomas Jones a Boy . . . tryed for breaking the House of Thomas Kittle . . . and taking away two Silver Spoons, value 12s. apiece . . . found Guilty. [Sentenced to death.]
Feb. 26, 27, 28.

Philip Clarke, a Boy, was tryed for stealing a parcel of Gloves and 60 Yards of Filleting, from John Carlton. The Boy being seen to go out of the Shop with the Gloves under his Arm, was presently stopt. Notwithstanding his denial of the Fact, he was brought in Guilty to the value of 10d. [Sentenced to be whipped.]

Robert Harlow, a little Boy, was tryed for stealing a Cloth Gown value 10s. 3 stuff Peticoats 3s. from Matthew True, on the 16th of February last. The Boy was an Apprentice near to Trues, and let a Man into the house in the Night time; which he confest before the Justice of Peace when apprehended, but deny'd the Fact upon his Tryal. He was found guilty to the value of 10d. [Ordered whipped.]
May 1, 2.

Lawrence Noney, a black Boy, was Tryed for stealing a Leading Staff, having a Silver Head on it weighing 19 ounces, value £4 15s. on the 16th of March last, from the Honourable Company of Haberdashers, London, out of their Hall; which the Boy did confess to have taken way, by breaking open the Door with a pair of Tongs. But he denied it upon his Tryal. It was further evidenced, that part of the Head was found in his Pocket, which was proved very plain. But the Company having the Head again, he was found Guilty but to the value of 10d. [He was sentenced to be whipped from Newgate to the Royal Exchange.]

William Gravestock, a Youth, was Indicted for shooting one Mary Feney, a Girl, with a Pistol Bullet upon her Right Arm, giving her a mortal wound 4 Inches deep, of which she immediately Dy'd. The Boy said, he did not think the Pistol was Charged, for that he lookt in the Pan and saw no Powder, and did not intend Mischief against the Girl; so he was found Guilty of Manslaughter. [Sentence: William Gravestock order'd to bring in his Pardon in course.]

William Carter a little Boy, about Ten Years of Age, was Indicted for stealing on the 29th of March [1690], two Gold Rings

value 30s. a piece of Coined Gold 20s. and 36s. and 10d. in Money, the Goods and Money of Martha Gill. It was fully proved, so he was found Guilty. [Sentenced to be burnt in the hand.]
July 17, 18.

Rebeckah Cook, and Sarah Tomson, a Couple of young Girls, were both Indicted for stealing on the 20th day of *June* last, 50 Yards of Silk Stuff, value 40s. the Goods of *Thomas Chamberlain:* It appeared that one Elizabeth Burzey was the Receiver, but was gone away, and did sell the Stuff for 30s. to one *Margaret Woodborne,* as their Confessions before the Justice did testifie, they both deny'd it, but however the Jury found them both Guilty, to the value of Nine Shillings. [They were sentenced to be burnt in the hand.]
Sept. 3, 4, 5.

Susannah Tyrrell, a Girl about ten Years Old, was Indicted for stealing two Gold Rings, value 21s. and 14s. in Mony, on the 25th of August, from Rachel Sturdy. The Evidence was, That she confest, That one Elizabeth Sallowes (now in Newgate) did give her a Key to open the Door, and bid her steal away the Rings and Mony; all which was plainly evinced, and the Girl did own that Sallowes set her a work. So that upon the whole, she was found guilty to the value of 9s. [She was ordered to be transported.]

[One James Arden enticed Richard Eaton, a Boy to rob his Master of Gold and Money to the value of £24. Both were found guilty. The boy was sentenced to be transported.]
Oct. 15, 16, 18.

[Constance Wainwright, aged 16 Years, was condemned to death for stealing a Silver Tea pot and some other things. She was reprieved, but later re-sentenced to death[3] for setting fire to Newgate Prison.]

1691
Jan. 15, 16, 19.

Edward Blewet, a Boy, was Tried for Stealing £4. in Mony, from *Robert Falconer* of *St. Michaels Cornhill,* on the 22d of December. The Boy was Wm. Falconer's Apprentice, whom he took upon liking out of meer Charity, the Boy coming as a Begger to the door; but after he had been there about Six Weeks, he took the Key out of his Masters Breeches, and unlockt the Drawer where the Mony lay, and went away with it; and within two or three hours

---

3. *A True Acc't of the Behaviour, Confession, and Last Dying Speeches of the Criminals that were Executed at Tyburn on . . . the 24th of October, 1690,* p. 2.

after, the Boy was met upon *London Bridge* with the Mony about him, all which the Boy had confest before his Tryal; and had nothing to say for himself, so he was found guilty. [He was ordered to be transported.]

April 22, 23, 24, 25.

John Symons, a Boy, was tryed for stealing 35 yards of Printed Stuff, from Mr. Overton in *Lumbard-Street*, value 30s. The Stuff was found upon the Boy, and he was seen to go into the Shop and take it away, so he was found Guilty of Felony. [Sentenced to be burnt in the hand.]

Sept. 9, 10, 11, 12.

Elizabeth Smith, a Girle, was Indicted for that she together with one Alice Merser, not taken, did Rob one Henry Hartis, about *Whitsuntide* last, of a Hair Camblet Cloak, value £4. a Cloth Coat, value 40s. a Waistcoat value 15s. a Hood, value 7s. a Petty coat value 5s. The prisoner and the other, *viz.* Merser were Lodgers in the Prosecutors House, and run away with the Goods. The Cloak the prisoner had pawn'd to a Broker, one *Bench;* the prisoner having little to say, she was found Guilty to the value of 9s. [There were two Elizabeth Smiths—one was sentenced to be whipped and the other to be burnt in the hand, so that the sentence in the above case is uncertain.]

Thomas Ross, the Boy, Convicted last Sessions for Publishing the two Libels . . . was ordered to be set in the Pillory according to the intent of his Sentence last Sessions.

1692

June 29, 30-July 1.

Edward Kallaway, a Boy of the Parish of Little All-hallows, was Indicted and Tryed for Stealing Eight pairs of Mens Wosted Stockings, (on the 28th of May last past,) value 25s. the Goods of Frances Crompton, Widow, who swore that the Stockings were put to be Colour'd at a Dye-house, where the Prisoner stole them, and the Goods were found in his Breeches; The Prisoner could say nothing, but that he found them at the Dye-house Door in Thames street, and that he belonged to the Blew Coat-Hospital, he was not able to vindicate himself; So he was found Guilty of Felony. [He was sentenced to be transported.]

1693

April 26, 27, 28, 29.

Walter Stephens, a young Youth, was Indicted for Felony, in secretly Stealing from one Mr. Beacon on the 14th day of *March* last, a Sword with a Silver Handle, value 40s. Mr. Beacon was going along *Lombard-street* and the Prisoner was near him when he mist his Sword, which dropt upon the ground; but the Prosecutor said he could not Swear he was the Person that took it from his side; but another Witness proved that the Prisoner dropt the Sword, &c. he was found Guilty of Felony. [He was sentenced to death.]

Mary Williams and Elizabeth Burkin, two young Girls, were both Tryed in one Indictment for secretly stealing from Esther Burnham Wife of Henry Burnham 5s. in Money. On the 14th instant Mrs. Burnham was going along the Street, and Burkin's Hand was seen diving into her Pocket; but she had conveyed what Money she found to another Person that run away, and nothing was found about either of the Prisoners; they both denied the Fact, but they were known to be old Offenders, tho very young; they were both found guilty of Felony. [Both received sentence of death.]

Mary Middleton, a Child, aged about seven or eight years, was arraigned for stealing from Mr. *Thomas Nichols,* Sollicitor at Law, two Silver Spoons, value 10s. one Allamode Scarf, value 14s. a Snuff-Box, value 5s. a Muslin laced Head-Dress, value 6s. to which she pleaded guilty [She was sentenced to be burnt in the hand.]

Robert Johnson, a young Lad, was Tryed for breaking the House of one Robert Combes in the Night-time of Stepney, on the 17th of January last, taking away 46 yards of Lute-string Silk, value £17. a Silver Cup £5. and seven Spoons, value £3. He confest the Matter; but the House was not broken, so he was found guilty of Felony only. [He was ordered into Their Majesties' Service.]

May 31-June 1, 3.

Challis Searl a little Youth, Aged about 12 Years, was tried for Felony in picking the Pocket of a Person unknown in Fleet street of 3s.6d. There was no Evidence against the Boy, but his own Confession before the Justice, where he said that one Constantine being with him in the Croud in Fleet street the day Captain *Winter* was Executed, he bid him pick a Gentleman's Pocket; there were several Neighbours who appeared for the Prisoner, that declared that the Boy was not given to any ill disposition, never guilty of pilfering nor stealing, and that he went constantly to School, as was Attested by the School master to whom he was a Scholar in Fetter-lane; he was acquitted.

Richard Merrick, a Boy, and Joseph Sarner, were both indicted for stealing 17 Weather Sheep value each 20s. the Goods of *Edward Waldoe,* Esq., of *Harrow on the Hill,* and a Mare price 25s. from *Moses Edling,* of the same Parish; the Boy was found upon the back of the Mare. . . . Merrick [was found guilty] both of Sheep and Mare. [Merrick received sentence of death.]

Morris Morris, a young Youth, was tried for stealing 800 Half-pence and Farthings, the Goods of *John Locker*. The Boy was left in Locker's Shop in Leaden-hall, being wont to go of Errands for her, she did not mistrust him, but he took away the Farthings, and when he was before the Right Honourable the Lord Mayor of London he confest to have taken them, and that he and another Boy were to divide them the next morning; he was found guilty of Felony to the value of 10d. [He was sentenced to be whipt.]

John Earl a Youth, was indicted for killing one William Prosser in the Parish of St. Mary Savoy on the 25th of May last, giving him a Mortal Bruise on the left part of the Head, of which he instantly died. The matter upon Evidence appeared thus, the Parish Boys abovesaid and St. Clements Boys were going in Procession, and they fell out, and the Prisoner was seen to knock the said Prosser down with a Stick, holding it in both Hands. The Surgeon said that the deceased's Skull was broke, which put him into a Feavor and Convulsion, of which he died. The Prisoner called some Youths, who gave account of the matter of Fact, how that the Prisoner was pursued by the Boys, and put to great extremity to save himself from the danger, so he was found guilty of Manslaughter. [He was sentenced to be brunt in the hand.]

July 13, 14, 15, 17.

Leonard Cooper, a Youth about 11 or 12 years of Age, was tried for stealing 10 pound weight of Tobacco from Thomas Walker of St. Dunstan's in the East; the Prisoner was found in the Warehouse with the Tobacco in his Apron, and another Boy that was with him got away, by reason the Skirt of his Coat rent off; this was fully proved by two Witnesses: He was found guilty to the value of 10d. [No sentence listed.]

John Cook, a Boy of about 12 years of age, was tried for Felony and Burglary, in breaking the House of Thomas Nichols of Shan-dois-street, with an intention to steal his Goods; the Boy was found in the House, but he did not break into the House; Mrs. Nichols declaring that the Door was left open. The Boy confest that there were four more that intended to have robbed the House besides him; he was acquitted.

December 6, 7, 8, 9.

Thomas Powel, a Youth, was tried for stealing Two Ship Masts, val. £3. 10s. the Goods of Mr. *James King;* which he Stole from off Mr. King's Wharf at Horslie-Down: The Prisoner alledged that a Waterman Stole the Masts, and gave him Half a Crown to Convey them to Queenhithe; which was but a feigned story; he was found guilty to the value of 10d. [He was ordered whipped.]

1700
May 24.

John Hatchman, aged 15 Years, Convicted for the same [Burglary], Confest his Crime, and said that Titt meeting him in Southwark made him Drunk, and then brought him along with them to break open the House. He denyed he ever was concern'd with such Persons any more, and Promises if he be Transported, to lead a better life for the future. . . . [At the scaffold] John Hatchman wept very much and confest his Crime. . . . After that the cart drew away, they were turned off.[4]

1702
Jan. 15, 16, 18, 19.

Joseph Tose, alias Towse, a little Boy, of the Parish of St. Leonard Shoreditch, was indicted for feloniously Stealing a silver Watch, and a Blood-stone Necklace, and divers other Goods of John Trotter, on the 10th of *December* last. The Prisoner upon his Tryal did not deny the Fact; the Jury considering the Tenderness of his Age, found him guilty to the value of 10d. [He was ordered to Sir Robert Clayton's Workhouse.]

1712
Dec. 10, 11, 12, 13.

Samuel Brown (a Boy) of the Parish of St. Giles's Cripplegate was indicted for stealing a Callicoe Handkerchief, valued Eight Pence, from Christopher Stevenson. The Prosecutor swore, That being in a Crowd in Moor-fields, the Prisoner pick'd his Pocket, and put the Handkerchief into his Bosom, which he took upon him. The Prisoner said he found it upon the Ground, though he confess'd it before Justice Manlove. The Jury found him Guilty to the value of 10d. [He was sentenced to be whipped.]

1733
Oct. 5, 6, 7, 8.

Elizabeth Ran, (a little Girl) was indicted for stealing a silver Spoon, two Aprons, four Mobs, twenty Guineas, and twenty-one Shillings, the Goods and Money of *Stephen Freeman*, in his House, Nov. 24. *Stephen Freeman* [testifies]. The Prisoner was my Apprentice, her Work was to make Shoe-maker's-Pegs. She had run away from me several times, and therefore, as I was to go over the

4. John Allen, *A full and true Account of the Behaviours, Confessions, and last Dying Speeches of the Condemn'd Criminals, that were Executed at Tyburn, on Friday, the 24th of May, 1700.*

Water, I set her to work in the Kitchen, lock'd the Door, and went out. I return'd about 6 at Night, and the Prisoner was not to be found, my Drawers were broke open, and my Money and Goods gone. On the Friday following, a Neighbour met her in Cannon-Street, and brought her home to me. I ask'd her, what it was she broke open the Drawers with? Why, what shoud I open them with, says she, but with a Chissel? I ask'd her, what she had done with the Money and Goods? She own'd she had taken three Guineas; but said, she had been to the Prisoners in Newgate, and they had got them from her. They found her Guilty. [She was sentenced to death.]

Sarah Lacy, alias Long, and Elizabeth Hopkins, (a Girl) were indicted for stealing a pewter Dish and a pewter Tankard, the Goods of Benjamin Fletcher, November 27. Lacy acquitted, and Hopkins guilty. [She was sentenced to be transported.]

Elizabeth Murray, (a little Girl) was indicted for stealing two Gold-rings, value 24s. and a Tea-spoon, value 1s. the Goods of Richard Eld Walker, Nov. 16.

Mr. Walker [testifies]. The Prisoner was my Servant, she took the Goods out of a Drawer, and went away. She was found again in Holbourn, with 8s. in her Pocket; she confess'd the Fact, and carry'd me to Robert Pardy, a Pawn-broker, at whose House I found the Goods.

Robert Pardy [testifies]. This Girl brought the Rings and Spoon to me, and said her Mistress wanted two Guineas and 4s. upon them; I told her, that was more than they were worth. Then she would have had 30s. upon them; I ask'd her where her Mistress liv'd? She said in Monmouth-Street, and dealt in Shoes, and wanted Money presently, to buy a Bargain, and so I lent her 25s.

Court. You did? And would you offer to take such Goods of such a Child?—Sir, before you go out of Court, find me Security for your Appearance next Sessions, or I'll commit you. Guilty. [She was sentenced to be transported.]

Hester Bray, (a Girl of 13 Years old) was indicted for privately stealing a Gold-Watch chain, value 35s. the Property of George Oliver, in his Shop, November 20. Guilty of Felony. [She was sentenced to be transported.]

1734
Jan. 16, 17, 18.

[Henry Werrel, or Worrel, a Boy, along with one Henry Tilson was charged with breaking and entering a House and stealing certain goods which were specified. Both were found guilty and were sentenced to death.]

May 30, 31-June 1.

[John Jones, a Boy, was found guilty of stealing a Wig and a Wig-box. He was sentenced to be transported.]

Samuel Cooper, William Bellers, and Thomas Smallwood, 3 Boys, were indicted for stealing a Coat, Waist Coat and Breeches, 2 Shirts, 2 Shoes, 2 Buckles, a Hat, a Handkerchief, 5 silver Buttons, a silver Head of a Cane, a Handle of a Knife, 2 Guineas, and 9s. the Goods and Money of *John Williams,* in the House of Lawrence Neal, May 21.

David Jenkins, a Boy (who lodged in the House where the Prisoner liv'd) depos'd, that himself and the 3 Prisoners, forc'd the Lock of the Prosecutor's Door, broke open his Box, and took the Goods and Money, and that he was stopt in offering the silver Buttons to Sale. But there being no other Evidence against the Prisoners, and several appearing to their Characters, the Jury Acquitted them.

Thomas Coles, a little Boy, was indicted for stealing 2 silver Spoons, and a Brass Candlestick, the Goods of *William Webster,* May 13. The Prisoner was an Errand-boy to the Prosecutor. The Spoons being mist he was examin'd, and confest he had taken them, and pawn'd them, one for a Shilling, and the other for 8s. at Wybourn's, the 5 Roses on Saffron-hill. And the Court order'd William Kay (the Pawnbroker's Man) who receive the Spoons of the Boy, to be taken into Custody. [The boy was sentenced to be transported.]

William Banks, and Thomas Rose, 2 little Boys, were indicted for stealing a Bell-metal Mortar, the Property of John Westal, May 16. Guilty. [Both were sentenced to be transported.]

Charles Thomson, a little Boy, was indicted for stealing a Gold-Ring, and a French Six-Pence, May 2. . . . Thomson guilty. [He was sentenced to be transported.]

Sept. 11, 12, 13.

Thomas Armson, a little Boy, was indicted for stealing a Guinea, three half Guineas, half a Moidore. and £8.2s. the £8.2s. the Money of *William Ward,* in the House of William Newman, in the Parish of Harrow. Sept. 6.

William Ward [testifies]. I live in *William Newman's* House, where the Prisoner had work'd a Week; I miss'd the Money in my Chest on *Friday* Afternoon. I suspected the Prisoner, and charg'd him with taking it. He at first deny'd, but afterwards confess'd it;

and pull'd part of it out of his Pocket. He said he had laid out the rest, which was £4. in buying a Horse, and some Clothes at *Watford;* tho' it was then but 7 Hours since he stole it. I found £7. 13s. upon him, and I got the Money again for the Horse, but 36s. was quite lost.

William Newman [testifies] The Boy had been a Haymaking and I took him in last *Wednesday* was a Week, to look after my Cows. On *Friday* morning he went to fetch the Cows, but did not come back. The Prosecutor came home, and miss'd his Money; upon which I sent a Man and Horse after him, and he was taken at *Watford.*

Prisoner [testifies] An *Irishman* (a Haymaker) told me where the money lay, and bid me take it.

The Jury found him Guilty. [He was sentenced to death.]

Jane Hacker, a Girl, was indicted for stealing 3 Yards and a Half of Callico, and 5 Guineas, the Goods and Money of Thomas Bocock, July 29. Guilty 4s.10d. [She was sentenced to be transported.]

1734/5
Jan. 16, 17, 18, 20.

Peter Votiere, a Boy, was indicted for stealing 14s. the Money of *John Cave,* and 5s.6d. the Money of John Hyat, January 10. Guilty 10d. [He was sentenced to be transported.]

1735
Feb. 26, 27, 28-Mar. 1.

William Cummins, a Child, and Mary Cummins his Mother, were indicted, the Boy for stealing twelve Yards of Silver Lace, value £4.10s. the Goods of *John Beckwith,* and the Mother for receiving the same knowing it to be stolen, Feb. 1.

It appeared that Will Cummins was the Prosecutors Errand Boy, and the Lace being mist, he was taken and confest the Fact, and said his Mother enticed him to steal the Lace and received it from him. The Jury found him guilty to the value of 10d. and acquitted his Mother. [He was sentenced to be transported.]

April 16, 17, 18, 19.

John Smith, a Boy, was indicted for privately stealing four Yards of Printed Linnen, value 5s. the Goods of Isaiah Flureau, in his Shop, March 21. Guilty 4s.10d. [He was sentenced to be transported.]

May 22, 23, 24.

Charles Simmonds, a little Boy, was indicted for privately stealing a Handkerchief, value one Shilling and six Pence, from the

Person of *Jeremy Lucas,* April 24. Guilty 10d. [He was sentenced to be transported.]

July 11, 12, 13, 15, 16, 17.

Mary Wotton, was indicted for stealing twenty seven Guineas and a half, and four Shillings and six Pence, the Money of John Easton, in the House of Thomas Foxly, September 2.

John Easton [testifies]. This Girl was put Apprentice by the Parish to my Wife.

Court. How old is she?

John Easton. She is Ten next February; she had lived with us thirteen or fourteen Months. My Wife and I went out in the Afternoon; I returned first about six in the Evening, and the Girl was gone. I did not search the Drawers till my Wife came home; she had run away once before, but did not steal anything then. We found the Drawers broken open and mist the money.

Mrs. Easton [testifies]. There was twenty-nine Pounds in a Spice Box in my Drawers in Mr. Foxley's House. I went out and left only the Girl in my Room, when I returned the Girl was gone, my Drawers broke open, and the Money taken away. She was found in Rag-Fair, she owned she took the Money, and said at first, that she put it in her Bosom, and sat all night in Moor-lane, and there a Man came and took it from her—Then she said a Woman took it out of her Apron, and at another time she told me that she gave it to a Girl who was to go out of Town with her.

The Jury found her Guilty. [She was sentenced to death.]

1738

Jan. 12[5]

On *Thursday, January* the 12th, Report was made to his Majesty in Council of the Eighteen Malefactors under Sentence of Death in the Cells of *Newgate.* When

Charlotte Gregg, a little Girl, convicted of stealing Money to the Amount of £21 9s. 6d. in the House of *Ann Howell, October* 8 [and two other condemned prisoners] received his Majesty's most gracious Reprieve.

1758

Dec. 7, 8, 9.

[Thomas Lyon, a Boy between 12 and 13 years old, for stealing a watch, was sentenced to be transported for seven years.]

5. Taken from *The Ordinary of Newgate, His Account of the Behaviour, Confession, and Dying Words, of the Malefactors Who Were Executed at Tyburn on Wednesday the 18th of January [1738],* p. 3.

34

1760
July 9, 10, 11.

John Drake, was indicted for stealing 7s. in money, numbered the property of William Christopher, May 30.

Ann Christopher [testifies]. I live at Limehouse, my husband's name is William; the prisoner is between 13 and 14 years of age, we took him apprentice out of the Workhouse, to go on errands and draw beer [evidence given shows that the money was found on the boy, who said nothing in his defence]. Guilty. [He was sentenced to be branded.]

1783
December.

[John Hudson, a child nine years old, sometimes a chimney sweep with both parents dead, was tried for housebreaking. He was acquitted of the capital charge, but convicted of felony, and sentenced to be transported for seven years. The judge said in the charge to the jury—"His confession, I think, should not be allowed, because it was made under fear. It would be too hard to find a boy of his tender age guilty of the burglary."][6]

1814
February 16.

Five children of from eight to fourteen years of age were condemned to death—viz., Fowler, age 12, and Wolfe, age 12, for burglary in a dwelling; Morris, age 8, Solomons, age 9, and Burrell, age 11, for burglary and stealing a pair of shoes![7]

1835
April.

[John Murphy, aged 13, and Peter Conolly, aged 14, for picking pockets in Holborn, were sentenced to transportation for seven years.]
June.

[A Boy, aged 12, for stealing a coral necklace and a watch, was sentenced to transportation for fourteen years.

George Johnson, aged 10, for stealing a gold ring, a brooch, and other articles of jewelry was sentenced to five days imprisonment, and then to be given up to his aunt.

A number of boys between the ages of 10 and 14, convicted of

6. *Select Criminal Trials at Justice Hall in the Old-Bailey* (Durham, 1810), pp. 379-82.
7. Willam Tallack, *Peter Bedford, the Spitalfields Philanthropist* (London, 1865), p. 16.

picking pockets and stealing handkerchiefs, were promised "as a reward for their dexterity, a voyage to New South Wales."]
November.

[Three boys, aged 12, 12, and 13, convicted of stealing, were sentenced to seven days imprisonment. Another boy, aged 12, for stealing a pocket-handkerchief was sentenced to seven years transportation.

Thomas Fisher, aged 11, for breaking into the dwelling-house of John Ennies, shoe-maker, of Whitechapel, and stealing a bag and 10s. was condemned to death.]
December.

Alfred Davis, Joseph Williams, and William Bull, three little urchins, not more than 12 years of age, were indicted for stealing three silk handkerchiefs, the property of a laundress named Hare. Davis three months imprisonment; Williams and Bull, seven days each, and to be once privately whipped.

1836
January

James Lynch, aged 9, for stealing a handkerchief from the person of Mr. Henry Harris, in Farringdon Street—7 years transportation.

John Johnson, aged 9, who had been tried before, was convicted of stealing a till, containing upwards of £1 . . . 7 years transportation.

Quaker Children in Bristol Put in the Stocks and Whipped, 1682

Joseph Besse, *A Collection of the Sufferings of the People called Quakers, for the Testimony of a Good Conscience* . . . (London, 1753), Vol. I, p. 66 (UNC Lib.)

Bristol, 1682.

On the 7th of the Month called *July*, they disperst the Meeting which then consisted chiefly of Children; for the Men and Women being generally in Prison, the Children kept up their Meetings regularly, and with a remarkable Gravity and Composure. . . .

On the 16th *Tilly* caused five of the Boys to be set in the Stocks three Quarters of an Hour. On the 23rd eight of the Boys were put in the Stocks two Hours and an half. . . .

On the 3rd of the Month called *August, Tilly*, with a small Faggot-stick, beat many of the Children, but they bore it patiently and cheerfully. On the 6th he beat some of them with a Whalebone-stick, and sent four Boys to *Bridewell*, who were released in the Evening with Threats of Whipping if they met together again. On the 13th *Helliar* [constable] . . . sent eleven Boys and four Girls to Bridewell. . . . The Boys and Girls were mostly from ten to twelve Years of Age. . . .

Children as Debtors in Halifax Gaol, 1691

Moses Pitt, *The Cry of the Oppressed* . . . (London, 1691), pp. 82-83 (Brit. Mus.) Illustrated with copper plates.

[The author, a bookseller, imprisoned for debt, describes his experiences in gaol. He tries to raise enough money while in gaol to finance through Parliament an Act for Relief of Debtors. He writes to the prisoners in sixty-five other prisons, explains his plan, and requests their help, including their accounts of their own sufferings in gaol. Most of the pamphlet is made up of the replies received, recounting many abuses. Illustrations include "Debtors in a Dungion 9 foot under Ground"; "A Debtor Thumscru'd and Iron Pothooks about his neck"; "Debtors Wives and Daughters attempted to be Raveshed by Goalers," etc.]

A FURTHER ACCOUNT OF THE CRUELTIES COMMITTED IN HALLIFAX-GAOL IN YORKSHIRE

. . . there has been Committed to this said Gaol several Children, both Boys and Girls, for Debt, some of which have been not above Fourteen Years of Age, and some of them under the said Age, and there kept till they have been ready to starve; and both the Attorneys and Gaoler have said, that they could not take their own Bail, because they were under Age; and by these ways and means did oblige these poor Children to work for their said Creditors, till they had paid their said Creditors the said Debts they had Impos'd upon them . . . there is no Allowance of Victuals, or Money, from the Town, or County; nor no Basket, or Begging-place. . . .

Sixth of June, 1691.

A Mother and Her Eleven-Year-Old Daughter Executed for Witchcraft, 1716

Philopatris Varvicensis (Samuel Parr); *Characters of . . . C. J. Fox* . . . (London, 1809), pp. 370-71 (Hist. Soc. Pa.)

Yet so far did he share in the credulity of his contemporaries about witchcraft, that in the Suffolk Sessions of 1664 he not only condemned two widows of Leystoff, but suffered judgement to be executed upon them . . . the two women were hanged.

I know not that Judge Powel was a weak, or a hard hearted man. But I do know that in the Augustan age of English literature and science, when our country was adorned by a Newton, a Halley, a Swift, a Clarke, and an Addison, this Judge in 1712 condemned Jane Wenham at Hertford, who in consequence perhaps of a controversy that arose upon her case, rather than from any interposition of Powel, was not executed; and that four years afterwards he at Huntingdon condemned for the same crime [witchcraft] Mary Hickes and her daughter Elizabeth, an infant of eleven years old, who were executed on Saturday the seventeenth of July, 1716. At the beginning of the same century, of which English philosophers and English scholars talk with triumph, two unhappy wretches were hung at Northampton, the seventeenth of March, 1705; and upon July the 22nd, 1712, five other witches suffered the same fate at the same place. The Judges who tried them might be very wise and upright men. But they were terrified at witchcraft, and employed all the wholesome severities which the laws had provided against it. We are no longer scared at witchcraft. But can it be said that we are none of us subject to unreasonable and excessive prejudice against other offences, real or supposed?

Discipline in a Charity School at Greenwich, 1724

> *An Account of Several Work-Houses for Employing and Maintaining the Poor . . . As Also of Several Charity-Schools for Promoting Work, and Labour* (London, 1725), pp. 24-26 (UNC Lib.)

A Letter from a Gentleman at Greenwich, to his Friend at London, concerning the Girls School of that Place.

Greenwich, May 4, 1724.

Sir,

In the Year 1700, several Charitable Ladies of this Town, join'd their Subscriptions for setting up a School for Teaching and Cloathing 30 Girls. . . .

In 1716. The School was in such Reputation that the Trustees were enabled, by a Collection at the Church-Doors, to augment the Children from 30 to 40. And the Collection has been yearly continued ever since for keeping up that Number: So that since the School was first set up, about 200 Children have gone out to Services in private Families; and no sooner is there a Vacancy in the School, but Interest is made by Poor Parents to get another in; so pleas'd are they with the Management of it, tho' at first, they were much averse to it.

Before an Account is given of the Method of Employing them, it will undoubtedly be acceptable to you, to be inform'd of some of the Methods us'd in Governing this School. The Trustees for directing it, wisely judging that Shame might have a better Effect on the Minds of their own Sex, than Fear; have order'd the Mistress to punish them rather with what may excite their Modesty, than their Dread of corporal Punishment. In order to this, the Names of the Children are all enter'd on a Table, hung up in the School; against each Name there are seven Holes, with a Peg in the first of them. When a Child commits a Fault, the Peg is remov'd one Hole from her Name, and she is admonish'd accordingly. Upon the second Offence, she is led up to the Table; and, upon removing the Peg to another Hole from her Name, admonish'd again, with an Injunction to get a Psalm, or a Piece of a Chapter by Heart, which the Child must take Care to do, or the Peg is carried on to a fourth or fifth Hole, by which she is look'd upon as a high Criminal upon Record in the School, till some Atonement by Task, or otherwise, has prevail'd with the Mistress to remove the Peg back again, and to wipe out all past Faults.

If the Hearts of the Children are not melted by this Usage, the Mistress proceeds to greater Severity, by pinning a Horn-Book, or a Rod upon the Child, according to the Nature of the Offence: But for high Crimes, such as profaning God's Name, Lying, or Pilfering, they are dress'd up in a Fool's Cap and Coat, and made to sit in the middle of the School for an Hour or more, which they have in great Abhorrence. And if they have pilfer'd of any Person out of the School, they are made to go publickly in that Dress, and ask Pardon of the Person offended, which they do with great Reluctance; but this they rather do, than be turn'd out of the School, as they must be, if they don't comply with the Rules of it.

Thus the Mistress has seldom Occasion to proceed to severer Punishments, and the Children acquire under this Discipline such a Tenderness of giving Offence, as, through God's Grace, may remain with them ever after; and where they have been put out, the Modesty and Dutifulness with which they serve, has very much recommended them.

The Mayor of London Orders Constables to Take up Vagrant Children, 1732

Mayors Proclamation, November 28, 1732 (Brit. Mus.)

This Court taking Notice, that divers Poor Vagrant Children are suffered to skulk in the Night-time, and lie upon Bulks, Stalls, and other Places in the Public Streets of this City, whereby many of them perish by the Extremity of the Weather, and other Inconveniences ensue. Therefore to prevent the same for the Future, This Court doth desire the several Aldermen of this City to call before them the several Constables and Beadles within their respective Wards, and to give them strictly in charge, that if they or any of them shall find any poor Vagrant-Child, or Children, or others, lurking in the Publick Streets of this City in the Night-time, that they immediately apprehend such, and secure him, her or them, in their Watch-house, or some other convenient Place, until they convey them before some Justice of the Peace for this City and Liberty thereof, that they may be examined and sent to the Places of their Legal Settlements, or otherwise disposed of according to Law. And if any Constable, Beadle, or other Officer, shall be found negligent or remiss in his Duty, and shall suffer such poor Child, or Children, or others, to be vagrant, or lie in the said Streets, without obeying this Order as aforesaid, such Constable, Beadle, or other Officer, shall be punished for such his or their Neglect with the utmost Severity of the Law. . . .

Black-Guard Children in the London Workhouse, 1739

Sir William Maitland, *The History of London, from its Foundation By the Romans to the Present Time . . . In Nine Books* (London, 1739), Act. Parl. 14 Car. II (Brit. Mus.)

By an Act of Parliament made in the Year 1662 for the Relief of the Poor, the Governors of this House (which is partly an Hospital, and partly a House of Correction) were constituted a Body Politick and Corporate, by the Name of *The President and Governors of the Poor for the City of London;* and by that Name, without a Licence of Mortmain, to purchase, or receive Lands, Tenements, &c. to the Amount of Three thousand Pounds *per annum;* by which it seems that the Parliament were confident of the Success of this Undertaking, by imagining that the Citizens would readily and largely contribute for the Encouragement of so great and laudable a Design.

The Government of this Corporation consists of the Lord Mayor, who is always President; together with a Vice-President, all the Aldermen, and Fifty-two Commoners, who were at first appointed by the Common Council, *anno* 1698, and who, by the money given by the Common Council, and the charitable Benefactions of well-dispos'd Citizens, found themselves not only in a Condition to fit up and finish a spacious Building in *Bishopsgate-street without,* for the Entertainment of the greatest Objects of Commiseration, but likewise to receive into the same a great Number of the said miserable and unhappy Vagrant Orphans, known by the infamous Name of the *Black Guard;* and whose Parents being dead, were reduc'd to the greatest Extremities; and being destitute of Relations, Friends, and all the Necessaries of Life, were become the Pest and Shame of the City, by pilfering and begging about the Streets by Day, and lying therein almost naked in all Seasons of the Year by Night.

Of this Sort of wretched and piteous Objects, there were in this House in the Year 1704. Three hundred and Sixty-eight, who were fed, cloath'd and taught, both in the Principles of Religion, and to work toward their Support, whereby, instead of being a common Nusance to, they were render'd of Service to the Publick; and who otherwise would have been brought up in the greatest Wickedness, the Consequence whereof, is generally an ignominious Death. Besides this great Number of Children, there were at the same Time maintain'd and employ'd in this Workhouse, Six hundred and Fifty-three Vagabonds, sturdy Beggars and other idle and disorderly Persons, many of whom being inur'd to Labour, were enabled to get their Bread in an honest Way, and without being burdensome to the Publick. Of the former, One hundred and Sixty-one were put out Apprentices in the same Year; and of the latter, Six hundred and Nine were discharg'd: The happy Effects whereof soon after appear'd by a Representation of the Grand Jury, at Justice Hall in the *Old Bailey,* wherein they set forth to the Court, that during their Attendance that Session, they had not had any of the above nam'd young Criminals brought before them, who formerly, by their Numbers, used to take up half their Time; which they were of Opinion was intirely owing to the laudable and indefatigable Zeal of the Governors of the *London Workhouse,* who had so carefully provided for those distress'd and miserable Objects. Yet, however useful this Foundation has prov'd to the Publick, the Citizens seem not to have the same Regard to it, as they have to those of the City

Hospitals, by their not extending their Charity to this, in proportion to them. Probably this Coolness arises from an Aversion they have to Force, in being compell'd by the Common Council to contribute towards its Support; whilst, in regard to the Hospitals, they are left to Act according to Discretion.

Be that as it will, I am certain no Charity can be better bestow'd, than on the helpless and miserable Objects before us, who seem to have a Claim to it previous to all others, by reason of their Age and most deplorable Circumstances. But the Citizens withdrawing their Contributions, this great and truly good Work, is very much decreas'd, as will appear by comparing the above with the following Account. And for want of a proper Fund for its Support, 'tis like to be intirely lost, to the great Dishonour of the City, whose Streets were never more pester'd with such deplorable Objects than at present; many of whom, to the great Scandal and Reproach of the Citizens, having neither Friends, or Abode, go about naked, and in the utmost Extremity by Night, seek Shelter under Bulks and Penthouses in the Rigor of Winter; whilst many of their fellow Creatures, who enjoy all the good Things of this Life, seem to regard them without the least Commiseration: While their domestick Brutes (Lap-Dogs, Cats, &c.) are dandled and pamper'd after the most delicate Manner, and soft Cushions, or other downy Beds carefully laid, to repose their irrational Darlings on. . . .

The poor Children in the *London Workhouse,* as already hinted, are not only taught the Principles of the Christian Religion, and to read, write and account, but likewise at certain Hours to spin, knit and wind Silk, to inure their young Hands early to work, which also contributes something toward their Support. But the Vagrants, Impostors and sturdy Beggars that are committed to this Place, have no other Allowance than what they earn.

The Officers and Servants belonging to this House, are, Four Physicians, who attend alternately Monthly, *gratis,* a Secretary, or Clerk, a Steward, Minister, Surgeon, Writing-Master, Keeper, Porter, Messenger, Master of the Work, School-Mistress, Nine Teachers, first and second Matron, the Cook and Under-Cook, Eleven Nurses, Singing Master, Two Hemp Dressers, Shoemaker and Taylor.

The annual Charge for the Support of this Workhouse, by the Account of its Disbursements in the Year 1732 appears to be One thousand Nine hundred and Seventy-two Pounds Ten Shillings and Six-pence.

To what has been said, I shall subjoin a Septenary Account of this House, whereby the Reader, by comparing it with that of the

A Septenary Account of the London Workhouse

	Children				Vagrants			
Years	Admit.	Put. Ap.	Buried	Rem.	Com.	Disch.	Buried	Rem.
1728	61	40	8	189	685	676	8	72
1729	33	43	9	170	515	545	7	35
1730	32	69	4	129	305	304	2	34
1731	57	49	2	135	315	313	0	36
1732	48	45	3	135	367	367	1	35
1733	53	44	5	139	445	418	2	60
1734	23	49	2	110	250	280	1	29
TOTAL	307	339	33	1007	2882	2903	21	301

Year 1704 above specify'd, will find how greatly this Foundation is impair'd.

The Legal Status of Delinquent Children as Illustrated by the Case of a Ten-Year-Old Boy Murderer, 1748

Anon., *The Laws Respecting Women . . . Also, the Obligations of Parent and Child, and the Condition of Minors. In Four Books* (London, 1777), pp. 429-32 (Brit. Mus.)

BOOK THE FOURTH OF THE LAWS CONCERNING PARENTS AND CHILDREN, AND THE INTEREST OF MINORS

CHAP. V. OF INFANTS, OR MINORS . . . LEGAL RESTRAINTS LAID ON INFANTS

In criminal cases an infant of the age of fourteen may be capitally punished for any capital offence, but under the age of seven he cannot. The period between seven and fourteen is subject to much uncertainty. For the infant shall, generally speaking, be judged *prima facie* innocent; yet if he was *doli capax,* and could discern between good and evil, at the time of the offence committed, he may be convicted, and receive judgment and execution of death, though he hath not attained to years of puberty or discretion. A remarkable instance of this kind we have in the case of William York, a boy of ten years of age, who was convicted at Bury summer assizes in 1748, before lord chief justice Willes, for the murder of a girl about five years of age, and received sentence of death. But the chief justice, out of regard to the tender years of the prisoner, respited execution, till he should have an opportunity of taking the opinion of the rest of the judges, whether it was proper to execute him or not, upon the special circumstances of the case, which he reported to the judges as follows. The boy and girl were parish children, but under the care of a parishioner, at whose house they were lodged and maintained. On the day the murder happened, the man of the house and his wife went out to their work early in the morning, and left the children in bed together. When they returned from work the girl was missing, and the boy being asked what was become of her, answered, that he had helped her up, and put on her clothes, and that she was gone he knew not whether. Upon this, strict search was made in the ditches and pools of water near the house, from an apprehension that the child might have fallen into the water. During this search the man under whose care the children were, observed that a heap of dung near the house had been newly turned up; and upon removing the upper part of the heap he found the body of the child, about a foot's depth under the surface, cut and mangled in a most barbarous and horrid manner. Upon this discovery the boy, who was the only person capable of committing the fact, that was left at home with the child, was charged therewith, which he stifly denied. When the coroner's jury met, the boy was again charged, but persisted still in denying the fact. At length being closely interrogated, he fell to crying and said he would tell the whole truth. He then said that the child had been used to foul herself in bed; that she did so that morning, (which was not true, for the bed was searched, and found to be clean); that thereupon he took her out of the bed, and carried her to the dung-heap, and with a large knife, which he found about the house, cut her in the manner the body appeared to be mangled, and buried her in the dung-heap: placing the dung and straw that was bloody under the body, and covering it with that that was clean; and having so done, he got water, and washed himself as clean as he could. The boy was the next morning carried before a neighbouring justice, before whom he repeated his confession, with all the circumstances he had related to the coroner and his jury. The justice very prudently deferred proceeding to a commitment, till the boy should have an opportunity of recollecting himself. Accordingly he warned him of the danger he was in, if he should be thought guilty of the fact he stood charged with, and admonished him not to wrong himself; and then ordered him into a room where none of the crowd that attended should have access to him. When the boy had been some hours in this room, where victuals and drink were provided for him, he was brought a second time before the justice, and then he repeated his former confession: upon which he was committed to gaol. On the trial evidence was given of the declarations before mentioned to have been made before the coroner and his jury, and before the justice: and of many declarations to the same purpose, which the boy made to other people after he came to gaol, and even down to the day of his trial. For he constantly told the same story in substance, commonly adding, that the devil put him upon committing the fact. Upon this evidence, with some other circumstances tending to corroborate the confession, he was convicted. Upon this report of the chief justice, the judges having taken time to consider of it, unanimously agreed; (1) That the declarations stated in the report were evidence proper to be left to a jury; (2) That supposing the boy to have been guilty of the fact, there are so many circumstances stated in the report, which are undoubted tokens of what lord chief justice Hale somewhere calls *a mischievous discretion,* that he is certainly a proper object for capital punishment, and ought to suffer. For it would be of very dangerous consequence to have it thought, that children may commit such atrocious crimes with impunity. There are many crimes of the most heinous nature, such as in the present case, the murder of young children, poisoning parents or masters, burning houses, and the like, which children are very capable of committing, and which they may in some circumstances be under strong temptations to commit; and therefore though the taking away the life of a boy of ten years old may savour of cruelty, yet as the example of this boy's punishment may be a means of deterring children from the like offences; and as the sparing this boy merely on account of his age will probably have quite a contrary tendency, in justice to the public the law ought to take its course, unless there remaineth any doubt touching his guilt. In this general principle all the judges concurred. But two or three of them, out of great tenderness, and caution, advised the chief justice to send another reprieve for the prisoner, suggesting that it might possibly appear on further enquiry, that the boy had taken this matter upon himself, at the instigation of some person or other, who hoped, by this artifice, to screen the real offender from justice. Accordingly the chief justice did grant one or two more reprieves: and desired the justice who took the boy's examination, and also some other persons in whose prudence he could confide, to make the strictest enquiry they could into the affair, and make report to him. At length receiving no further light, he determined to send no more reprieves, and to leave the prisoner to the justice of the law at the expiration of the last. But before the expiration of that reprieve, execution was respited till further order, by warrant from one of the secretaries of state. And at the summer assizes 1757, he had the benefit of his Majesty's pardon granted to him upon condition of his entering immediately into the sea service.*

Any new felony created by act of parliament, is not construed to extend to infants under fourteen years of age, but binds them at that age†. . . .

[A more detailed account of this sensational case may be found in the *Gentleman's Magazine,* Vol. XVIII (May, 1748), p. 235. At the end of this article the editor of the *Magazine* comments—"Judge Hales order'd a boy of the same age to be hang'd, who burnt a child in a cradle."]

Discipline of English Children of the Upper Middle Classes, 1753

James Nelson, *An Essay on the Government of Children, Under Three General Heads: Viz. Health, Manners and Education* (London, 1753), pp. 163-64, 174-77, 179-80, 182, 192, 197, 199, 201, 203, 205, 208, 215-16 (editor's lib.)

[A rambling, discursive essay by an apothecary whose ideas of child discipline are conditioned by the difficulties he has experienced in getting the pampered, spoiled children of the well-to-do classes to take disagreeable medicine when they are sick.]

In the Government of Children Parents should be obstinately good; that is, set out upon right Principles, and then pursue them with Spirit and Resolution: otherwise their Children will soon grow too cunning for them, and take the Advantage of their Weakness.

Severe and frequent Whipping is I think a very bad Practice; it inflames the Skin, it puts the Blood into a Ferment, and there is besides, a Meanness, a Degree of Ignominy attending it, which makes it very unbecoming: still there may be Occasions which will render it necessary; but I earnestly advise that all the milder Methods be first try'd. A coarse clamorous manner of enforcing Obedience is also to be avoided; it is vulgar, and nothing vulgar should be seen in the Behaviour of Parents to their Children, because through the Eyes and Ears it taints their tender Minds: still,

* Fost. 70.
† 1 H.H. 706.

let Parents make their Children both see and feel the Power they have over them.

If a Child is passionate and wilful, a Look, or a little Tap on the Hand, will, without hurting it, sometimes suffice to convince it that it is doing wrong; and will often cure the Fault, or at least keep it under. A Child, in a perverse Mood, throws down its Playthings; if they are taken up fifty times successively, they are still thrown down as long as the Spirit of Contradiction lasts; now the Remedy here should be to take them away; or by a serious Countenance shew you are displeased; and the Child will very probably not only soon be quiet, but be less prone to do the like another Time. I have seen Children that could not speak, distinguish perfectly those who were disposed to spoil them, from those who were not; scratch Faces, break China, and play the tyrant over all who humour'd them, and yet not offer to lift a Finger against those who did not. By all means let Children be play'd with, and have every Amusement; but great care must be taken to distinguish Play from Mischief; innocent Freedom, from a growing Perversity. . . .

The first Rule Parents are to lay down to themselves is, never to deceive their Children; for surely those who are to teach them never to be deceitful, cannot but be very unfit Persons to deceive them themselves: nor does this square with the Practice of quibbling down a Dose of Physic, under a thousand Shifts and Turns, and even manifest Falshoods. The next Rule is, to avoid the Practice of Bribes. Children should be taught to know that their greatest Happiness is their Parents Love; therefore the Custom of giving them Sugar-Plumbs, Cakes, Toys, or Money for every thing they take, is grievously wrong: it gives them a Fondness for improper things; it gives them a restless Desire for every new Bauble; and above all, it gives them an early Meanspiritedness; an odious Selfishness; a Desire of being paid for every thing they do.

At the same time that I recommend to Parents never to call things by wrong Names, never to attempt imposing on a Child's Senses or Understanding, or to force down Medicines with Bribes; so I also recommend, that they avoid Harshness and Violence, unless pressed to it by great Necessity; but this Caution is almost needless after what has been said: for with the Method proposed, it requires no more than to approach the sick Bed with, Come, my Dear, take your Dose; if the Child says, it is nauseous, grant it: but at the same time say, We do not take Medicines for Pleasure, but to make us well: if it declines it, urge how wrong it is to dwell on what would be gone in a Minute; and if any Difficulty still remains, inform it, that it is not for your Sake you urge it, but its own; and that while you are doing all you can to restore it to Health, you must, and will be obeyed. At intermediate times, let Parents, by a fond, engaging Behaviour, convince their Children how tenderly they love them; let them frequently mingle with them in their little Plays and Sports; and let them sometimes overlook Trifles, that they may have more Influence in Matters of Moment.

Lord *Hallifax* observes, that the first Impressions Children receive are in the Nursery; whence he infers, that Mothers have not only the earliest, but the most lasting Influence over them.

That the first Care of Children, and many of the most tender Offices they require, are the Mother's Province, is an undoubted Truth; but when the forming their Manners is under Consideration, the Influence of both Father and Mother should, if possible, be equal; at least it is necessary that Parents go hand in hand, and not counteract one another in the Government of them.

Parents should make it a Rule to themselves, never to shew to their Children, both at once, the Marks of extreme Anger, or excessive Fondness; but when a Child has done such a Fault as demands of the Father to affect great Severity, let the Mother put on an equal Share of Lenity and Compassion mixed with Grief: and so on the reverse. . . .

If a Child is to be reformed of any peevish or passionate Behaviour, what Effect can Correction have on him, if given by a Parent delivered over by his own Passions to all the Fierceness of a Brute? It may make him hate the Correction, but can never make him hate Faults, the opposite Virtues to which he sees not the least Example of in his Corrector. . . .

Parents then should seriously acquaint themselves with their own Tempers, and mutually consent and agree on the Methods of regulating their Children; never to reward or punish, seem angry or pleas'd, but by Concert; and above all, never to correct while in a Passion, nor reward till the fond Fit be over. . . .

Yet Parents must be extremely cautious never to differ about the Government of Children in their hearing; it does incredible Mischief; but particularly, it alienates them from their Duty; and weakens the Authority of the Parents on one Side at least, if not on both. . . .

Parents should give their Children an early and an ardent Love of Truth; in order to this, it is not sufficient that they give them Precepts, they must add Example too. There is no Vice more dangerous, none more odious, than a Habit of lying; and yet none more common. But what is stranger still, Parents themselves are often the Persons who teach it them. . . .

Parents should encourage in their Children a lively chearful Disposition; but quite pure, and unmixt with Vice, however distant. In order thereto, they should never suffer them, for any Consideration, to utter an indecent Word, or commit any irregular Action which has the least bad Tendency; but above all, Parents must be careful themselves, never to say or do any thing in their Presence that they ought not to hear or see. . . .

But besides the nicest Care with regard to Words, Parents, as I have observed before, should be greatly circumspect in their Actions. Nothing gross or indecent should be done in their Sight; a Mother should by no means appear too much undressed in the Presence of her Son; nor a Father in that of his Daughter; for these and many other Things, though in themselves innocent, are not allowable; they give Boys a boldness which borders on Impudence; and they are apt to wean Girls from some Degree of that Modesty they ought so carefully to preserve.

I cannot but recommend, what I doubt very few will comply with, that Boys and Girls, even when Infants, have not only separate Beds, but, wherever it is practicable, always lie in separate Rooms: nor should they ever be exposed naked to one another, or the least wanton Curiosity be permitted: the Eyes and Ears convey Corruption to the Mind; and we cannot begin too soon to shut up every Avenue to Vice. . . .

At the same time that Parents are industrious to make Children obedient to themselves, they must teach them to consider every one as an Individual of Society, and give them a deep sense of the Necessity of good Behaviour to all, whatever be their Circumstances or Condition. In every Family there are particular Obligations which Children must be taught to distinguish, and to reduce to Practice. Next to their Parents, Children owe to all senior Relations, Respect and Duty; to their Brothers and Sisters they owe not only a tender but an unalterable Affection; and all of more distant Kin have a claim of Respect which cannot be refused them. Yet all this is but little, if compared with the universal Demand Mankind have on one another. We cannot without Injustice deny Virtue and Merit our Esteem; old Age is venerable, and to refuse the Honours due to it, is a Degree of Impiety; Obligations demand Gratitude; Misfortunes call for Friendship and Compassion; and even Vice and Folly demand our Pity and Concern, nay more, demand our Endeavours to remove them. But among the various Situations in Life, that which most requires the Care and Attention of Parents is, the teaching Children a due Regard to People in Poverty and Distress. It does not cost much pains to give Children a proper and becoming

Behaviour to their Betters and Equals; but to persuade them to maintain a considerable Degree of Respect to Inferiors, or to those in disadvantageous Circumstances, is an arduous Task; still it may and ought to be done. Nothing so humanizes the Soul, nothing so strongly proves the Man, as sympathizing with, and relieving the Distresses of our Fellow Creatures: 'tis then the Duty of Parents never to let their Children speak or act with the least Degree of Rudeness to the lowest among Mankind; never to let them divert themselves with their Rags or Misfortunes; but on the contrary, they should sometimes furnish them with Money or other Things, that the Relief they design to give the Needy may pass through their Hands: and at the same time imprint this Truth on their Minds; that he who is thus reduced to ask, is often far more deserving than he who bestows.

Another indispensable Duty of Parents to their Children is, that they teach them never to dare to sport with the natural Defects of others. . . .

Another Caution equally necessary is, that Parents utterly avoid all Distinction of Favourites among their Children. Sometimes the Father has his Darling, and the Mother her's; sometimes they both dote on the same Child, and neglect the rest. Again, it is frequently observed, that Mothers are extravagantly fond of the Boys, and either treat the Girls with a visible Indifference, or grossly neglect them, they know not why. . . .

If then Parents really intend the Good of their Children, they must with the utmost Resolution throw off all Partiality; if not, 'tis more than probable it may greatly injure, or even undo, a whole Family. The Darling is liable to be ruined thro' Indulgence; the rest, thro' Neglect and Ignorance. Children, by this unequal Treatment, conceive a Hatred to one another, and often to the Parents themselves, which perhaps lasts as long as their Lives. But besides that this injurious Treatment debases their Minds, it is productive of many dreadful Evils; for hence proceed, not only inveterate Malice, but Confusion, Law-suits and Poverty; and hence too proceed rash, precipitate, and disgraceful Marriages; with many other Calamities, which it would require a Volume to enumerate. . . .

Parents should be particularly careful not to dispirit their Children; which undoubtedly will have a bad Influence on their whole future Conduct. There is a Degree of Courage to be maintained that is not only graceful, but absolutely necessary to carry us thro' Life, which Parents therefore must not destroy. . . .

But here Parents must be very careful to distinguish false Courage from true, imaginary Evils from real: let there be no trembling about Hobgoblins, or dark Holes; no Stories of Apparitions, to raise Terror in the tender Minds of Children: Parents should never mention these things to them, nor, if possible, suffer any body else to do it; unless it be to laugh at, and expose the Folly of them.

Nothing can be a greater Weakness than the creating or cherishing these Fears in Children: nay how senseless a thing is it to make them afraid of a dark Room, a Chimney-sweeper, or whatever else can impress a groundless or an unjust Fear on them, for more or less they feel it their whole Lives, and by that Means are oftentimes made very miserable. Children, as soon as they can distinguish, should be taught to look, and move, and speak with Courage; and, as they grow up, they should be put frequently in the way of exercising it, whereby many natural or acquired Weaknesses will be conquered: such as, a Fear of the Water, Riding, and innumerable other things, which Parents should by every Means endeavour to prevent or remove: taking along with them this Caution, not to treat Children, whose Spirits are naturally weak, with the same Freedom they do the more robust; nor ever rashly expose them to real or imminent Dangers.

Children of the London Poor, 1753

Saunders Welch, *A Letter Upon the Subject of Robberies, Wrote in the Year 1753.* [This letter, reprinted from the *London Chronicle* appears as an appendix to Welch's *A Proposal to render effectual a Plan, to remove the Nuisance of Common Prostitutes from the Streets of this Metropolis &c.* (London, 1758), p. 54] (editor's lib.)

[CHILDREN OF THE POOR]

Another cause of robberies I apprehend to be, the want of provision for maintaining and educating in good principles, and habits of industry, the children of the Poor.

The children of the Poor may be reduced to three classes:

1. The families of the Industrious, too numerous for their parents to maintain with decency, much less to provide for their education in good principles, or labour suitable to their tender age.

2. The children of the extravagant dissolute Poor. These are indeed miserable; for so far are these wretches from taking proper care of their offspring, that they themselves encourage and instruct

their children in the pilfering trade, and are ready to receive whatever they steal.

3. Orphans of the Poor, left destitute and friendless from the age of seven years to that of fourteen: unnoticed, and unrelieved by parish officers, they are left to wander under the cruel alternative of begging, stealing, or starving.

What other consequences can arise to the Public, from children turned adrift in a town wicked as this, with minds untutored, and pinched by necessity, but a constant supply of pick-pockets, pilferers from shops, and instruments in the hands of greater villians to lie concealed in houses till the dead of night, and then let them in to plunder, perhaps murder an innocent family? Children thus bred up in sloth and nastiness until seven years of age, at the time when education and habits of industry should commence, become thieves by necessity; and, if they are bold and daring, if they escape transportation, or being cut off by disease and rottenness, turn street robbers, and perhaps murderers. The sacred name of God is no otherwise known to them, but by dreadful execrations; and religion is first taught them by the Ordinary of Newgate.

If I am rightly informed, in our manufactory towns children cease to be a burthen to their parents at less than seven years of age: and sure little need be said of the necessity and utility of some hospital to receive these innocents, educate and employ them: when instead of their being a dreadful nusance to society, as they now are, such a foundation would prove a seminary of excellent servants to the Public.

The Marine Society Apprentices Vagrant and Delinquent Boys to Sea Service on Warships, 1756

[A] Jonas Hanway, An Account of the Marine Society . . . from the Commencement of July 1756, to September 30, 1759 . . . (6th Ed.; London, 1759) (editor's lib.)

[One of the earliest private agencies in London to become interested in reclaiming delinquent boys was the Marine Society, established in 1756. No single individual can claim the undisputed honor of founding this Society, but Jonas Hanway, an eccentric London philanthropist, and Sir John Fielding, blind magistrate, both contributed substantially of their services in getting the infant Society started and in smooth working order.

England at this time was at war with France and Spain, and

needed greatly to increase its naval forces. At this juncture the Marine Society was organized with the primary object of encouraging recruits for the Royal Navy, first by outfitting landmen with suitable clothing for sea service (the navy had no regular uniform at this time), and second, by sending stout, active boys, properly clothed, between the ages of thirteen and fifteen, to serve on board the King's ships, as servants to the captains and the other officers. It was expected that these boys after getting a taste of sea life would remain in the service as active sailors. The Society announced it would take no runaway apprentices, nor boys running away from home without their parents' knowledge. Since three thousand boys were needed however, the Society could not be too rigid in its requirements, as regards social status and conduct record. Young vagabonds from the city streets, who were not "defective in *sight, or lame, dwarfish,* or laboring under any *chronical* distemper" (p. 36) were regarded as fair subjects for recruiting. Magistrates were encouraged also to commit delinquent boys to the Marine Society, rather than send them to prison (p. 111). Even after boys were committed to prison they sometimes were released to the Society, which was proud to claim that by checking these young vagabonds "in the *dawnings* of *iniquity, Tyburn* might be left a *desert.*"

After being collected from the streets or prisons, the boys were clothed in a special uniform at the offices of the Society, and were examined and treated for itch, fever, or other curable distempers. Boys with foul, bushy hair, had to have their hair cut off, and their heads washed with brandy as a disinfectant. They were housed and fed until a sufficient number had accumulated, when they marched in a body through the country, or were transported, to the nearest port of embarkation.

From the time of the establishment of the Marine Society in 1756 until the close of the war in 1763, this "nursery of seamen" fitted out 5174 poor boys as servants to officers in the Royal Navy at a cost of nearly £24,000. Between 1763 and May 1769 the Society suspended operations. It appears, however, that an English merchant adventurer, residing in Hamburgh, was so favorably impressed with the usefulness of the Society that in 1763 he left to it a legacy valued at about £18,000. This sum was tied up in legal suits for several years, and when the estate was finally settled, the portion allotted to the Marine Society was sufficient to yield an income of about £300 per year. According to the terms of Mr. Hicks's will, this sum was to be spent in time of war in fitting out boys as servants to naval officers; but in time of peace it was to be used as follows:—half of the sum, £150, was to be spent in fitting out boys as apprentices to owners and masters of ships in the merchants service and coasting vessels, and the other half was to be spent in placing out poor girls to honest trades, usually domestic service. The Society was incorporated in 1772, and has been engaged continuously since that time in training boys of good character for the sea service. It was only in the first few years of its existence, however, that the Society was interested in reclaiming delinquent boys.

Hanway's rambling, repetitive and moralistic style does not lend itself easily to extensive quotation.]

> [B] Sir John Fielding, *An Account of the Receipts and Disbursements Relating to Sir John Fielding's Plan, for the Preserving of distressed Boys, by sending them to Sea, as Apprentices in the Merchants Service . . . and a Short Account of the sending Boys on board Men of War . . . in the Year 1756 . . .* (London, 1771?) (Brit. Mus.)

. . . In the latter end of the year 1755, it appeared, that there were a vast number of wretched boys, ragged as colts, abandoned, strangers to beds, and who lay about under bulks, and in ruinous empty houses, in Westminster, and its environs. The removal of this evil, at first seemed insuperable, until Heaven inspired the thought of their preservation, by sending them to sea, and cloathing them by public subscription; which arose as follows:

In January, 1756, his Majesty's ship the Barfleur, of 90 guns, being in want of captain's servants, that is to say, boys, for every man of war is allowed four boys to every 100 men on board, whose pay the captain receives, allowing them 40 shillings a year for cloaths; so that the boys' pay is absolutely a part of the captain's; and was intended to be so, in order that the captains might take care to have such a number of boys on board, by way of nursery for seamen: and these boys are, therefore, called captain's servants: besides which, every other officer on board, is allowed one or more of these boys, according to his rank, on the same footing with those belonging to the captain. And as long as this regulation, and the above, relating to merchant ships are duly regarded, there never will be wanting a succession of seamen to supply the Navy. The Barfleur was at this time commanded by Lord Harry Pawlett, now Duke of Bolton, who wrote to Sir John Fielding to procure him 30 boys, which his lordship cloathed at his own expense. And as Sir John had been at sea himself, and was well acquainted with the station of captain's servants abovementioned, he began to think that this would be an excellent provision for the numberless, miserable, deserted, ragged, and iniquitous pilfering boys, that at this time shamefully infested the streets of London. But the great difficulty was to get them cloathed, and cured of the various distempers which are the constant consequences of poverty and nastiness. To effect this, he put a paragraph into the papers, stating their miserable situation; which struck so strongly on the sensible minds, and generous hearts of the English, that in the space of six months, the sum of £600. and upward, was paid into the hands of that magistrate, for the above purpose; by which means the Navy was at once supplied with four hundred young recruits, from fourteen to eighteen years of age; and our streets were cleared from swarms of boys, whose situation made them thieves from necessity; though many of them were unhappy enough in parents who subsisted from the felonies their children committed, not only by their consent, but, what is still more shocking, by their tuition. About July, 1756, Mr. Hanway struck with the great utility of this scheme, to which he had originally subscribed, collected a number of respectable merchants, and other persons of rank, together, and, to use his own expression, adopted this Plan, under the name and title of the Marine Society, with intent to cloath men and boys for the sea.

This excellent society soon increased in its members, and in its subscriptions; and Sir John Fielding's subscriptions being nearly exhausted in this service, and there being still a great demand for boys for the Navy, and being unwilling to occasion confusion by keeping open two subscriptions for the same purpose, immediately joined this generous body; and from that time all the little interest Sir John had with his friends, acquaintance, or the public, he employed to promote the success of this glorious undertaking; and paid his future subscriptions, which were very considerable, to that society; which soon became so much the object of universal respect, attention and encouragement, that from February 1756, to the end of the war, there has not been less money subscribed, including the £610 Sir John received while he carried on the scheme of boys himself, than £30,000 by means of which generous subscriptions, upwards of 4000 boys have been cloathed and sent on board his majesty's ships, besides which, they have cloathed upwards of 5000 young fellows, to go on board the fleet: so that by this admirable institution, near 10,000 hands were sent into the Navy, without putting the Government to one shilling expence. And it is remarkable, that very few or any of these boys, have since appeared in a criminal light before Sir John Fielding.

[C] *The Bye-Laws, and Regulations of the Marine Society, incorporated in MDCCLXXII* . . . (London, 1772), pp. 42-43 (editor's lib.)

1. Such boys as are literally in a vagrant state, of whom some are recommended by magistrates, either as found wandering, or as guilty of some petty offence.

2. Those who live chiefly by begging, or seldom do any work, but appear in filth and rags, and sometimes half naked.

3. Some who have occasionally earned their bread by going on errands, or in markets, brick-kilns, glass-houses, or by hackney coachmen, draw boys, and such like.

4. The sons of poor people who have numerous families; or such as, upon enquiry, are in too great a state of indigency to provide any clothing or bedding fit for the sea; so that such boys, whatever their inclinations may be for a sea life, are not likely to be accepted by any master, but by the means proposed by this Society.

5. Boys whose parts have been wrong cast, being so contrary to their genius, that they are more inclined to hazard their necks, than to live a sedentary life. . . .

Sir John Fielding Establishes a House of Refuge for Orphan Girls, 1758

> Sir John Fielding, *A Plan of the Asylum; or, House of Refuge for Orphans and Other Deserted Girls of the Poor in this Metropolis* (London, 1758), pp. 4-10 (editor's lib.)

INTRODUCTION

Whoever has long acted as a Magistrate in this Metropolis, must have observed, that the Body of the neglected Sons of the Poor, Gaming in Public-Houses, and the very low Bawdy-Houses are the constant Fountains that furnish the Courts of Justice with Offenders, and the Place of Execution with Victims.

Enough has been said of the former of these, and the Evil being considerably lessen'd the latter is proposed to be the Subject of what follows; as it seems to be as material an Object of the Police as any whatever; for, in these Brothels, the Apprentice and Journeyman first broach their Morals, and are soon taught to change their Fidelity and Integrity for Fraud and Felony; here the Tradesman, overcome with Liquor, is decoy'd into a Snare, injurious to his Property, fatal to his Constitution, destructive to his Family, and which frequently puts a Period to his Peace of Mind.

1. Several footnotes omitted.

Relieving Industry in Distress, preserving the Deserted, and reforming the Wicked and the Penitent, are the acceptable Employments, the favourite and advantageous Delights of those Minds, which are happy enough to have a good Heart for their Prompter. There is indeed abundant Reason to believe, that these Pleasures have been fully enjoy'd by those who have subscribed towards cloathing friendless and deserted Boys to go to Sea. And it is to be hoped, that the Public in general, we well as the particular Objects of that Charity, have reap'd some Advantages from those Subscriptions.

And I shall now beg Leave to present to the Public a Body of Fellow-Creatures, equally distress'd with those who have been the Objects of the above mention'd Benevolence; and which may, and will, I hope, be made of equal Use to their Country.

The Preservation of the common People, in all States, is highly deserving Attention; for, from this Fountain, your Manufactures, Fleets, Armies, and domestic Servants, are supplied: And in Country Villages this Task is easy, as Temptations to Vice are more rare, and most Parishes employ their Inhabitants. But in such a populous City as is the Metropolis of this Kingdom, numbers of Persons may be idle, numbers of Children may be deserted, who are capable of Employment, without ever being perceived by the Public, till their Crimes have made them the unhappy Objects of public Justice.

For the Truth of which Assertion I refer to the Sessions-Paper, and Kalendars for the Years 1755 and 1756, when Gangs of friendless Boys, from 14 to 18 Years of Age, were transported, indeed, I may say by wholesale, for picking of Pockets and pilfering from Shops.

And as these deserted Boys were Thieves from Necessity, their Sisters are Whores from the same Cause; and, having the same Education with their wretched Brothers, generally join the Thief to the Prostitute.

This brings me to that completely wretched, distempered, deserted, pitiable Body of whom I mean to speak; whose Sufferings have so often made my Heart ach, and whose Preservation I now so ardently wish to accomplish. And indeed, I think, I have great Reason to indulge these my Wishes, as I flatter myself I have hit upon a Plan that will as effectually preserve these deserted Girls from Infamy and Distress, and make them happy in themselves, and useful Subjects at Home, as that which has preserved so many of their Brothers, and made them useful Abroad.

But before I speak of my Plan, I will endeavour to shew from what Fountain it is, our low and infamous Bawdyhouses, which furnish our Streets with thieving, distempered Prostitutes, are supplied.

Infinite are the Number of Chairmen, Porters, Labourers, and drunken Mechanics in this Town, whose Families are generally too large to receive even Maintenance, much less Education, from the Labour of their Parents; and the Lives of their Fathers being often shortened by their Intemperance, a Mother is left with many helpless Children, to be supplied by her Industry; whose Resource for Maintenance is either the Wash-Tub, Green-Stall, or Barrow. What must then become of the Daughters of such Women, where Poverty and Illiterateness conspire to expose them to every Temptation? And they often become Prostitutes from Necessity, even before their Passions can have any Share in their Guilt.

And as Beauty is not the particular Lot of the Rich more than the Poor, many of the abovementioned Girls have often great Advantages of Person; and whoever will look amongst them will frequently see the sweetest Features disguised by Filth and Dirt.

These are the Girls that the Bawds clean and cloathe for their wicked Purposes. And this is done to such a Degree, that on a search Night, when the Constables have taken up near forty Prostitutes, it has appeared on their Examination, that the major Part of them have been of this Kind, under the Age of Eighteen, many not more than Twelve, and those, though so young, half eat up with the foul Distemper.

Who can say that one of these poor Children had been a Prostitute through Viciousness? No. They are young, unprotected, and of the female Sex; therefore become the Prey of the Bawd and Debauchee.

Here I cannot help mentioning a Misfortune; nay, I may say, a Cruelty, that often happens to these deserted Children, and I believe the Offenders as often go unpunished; for the maternal Tenderness of their Mothers is either starved by their Necessities, or drowned in Gin; and, for a Trifle, conceal and forgive an Offence which our Laws have made Capital. And I have sometimes seen Mothers, but indeed they ill deserve that Name, who have trepanned their Children into Bawdy-Houses, and shared with the Bawd the Gain of their own Infant's Prostitutions. And scarce a Sessions passes without Indictments being found against Porters, and such low Sort of Men, for ravishing the Infants of the Poor. But, as I said before, I am afraid more of these Offences are concealed from the Magistrate than are brought to Light. Who can behold this Havock on Youth and Innocence, and not be shocked with their pitiable Case? And who can feel for them without being warmed with a Desire of affording them Protection, and rescuing these help-less Lambs from the Hungry Jaws of such ravenous Wolves?

To preserve these Objects, is my princi[pal]-View in what I shall hereafter propose; though I am persuaded if I can succeed in this Work of Prevention, there will be at least fewer to repent; for Evils of all kinds in public Societies are only to be cured by being prevented: Remove the Cause, and the Effect must cease. The skilful Surgeon, indeed, when applied to too late, finds Amputation of a Limb absolutely necessary to preserve the whole Body; which very Limb might itself have been preserved, had the same Skill been earlier applied: and *Venienti occurrite Morbo,* is as good a Maxim in Politics as in Physic.

The only Difficulty I see in putting this Plan in Execution, is, the first Expence: for, I hope, in a very few Years, it will not only sup-port itself, but prove a constant Nursery for a Body of useful Domestics, much wanted in this Town.

And as the Evil it proposes to remedy, is grown to a most obnoxious Height, and the Wretches that occasion it are the Objects of universal Compassion, I doubt not, but it will receive an En-couragement proportionable to the Public's Opinion of it's Utility; nor do I fear, but that in these my Endeavours, I shall be honored with the kind Attention, the friendly Approbation, and the generous Assistance of the Ladies, whose tender Feelings will give them a much juster Idea of the Sufferings of these poor Creatures than any Thing the warmest Imagination can suggest; for really some of their Cases, as *Shakespear* says, beggar all Description.

[The author proceeds to outline his plan for establishing a public laundry for training deserted girls and those without means of sup-port, and afterward placing them as domestic servants in suitable homes. This House of Refuge situated near Westminster Bridge on the Surry-Side was opened in May 1758, and was supported by public subscription. The description of the first young girls ac-cepted follows:]

Mary Kirton, nine years of age, the child of a poor woman left in great distress by her husband, and no relief from the parish, where she resides.

Jane Gripton, twelve years of age, an orphan, hitherto main-tained by a stranger, and no parish relief.

Sarah Blackmore, eleven years of age, a foundling, hitherto maintained by a stranger.

Sarah Carpenter, eleven years of age, a child in the utmost distress, and no relief from a parish.

59

Sarah Gelder, twelve years of age, the child of a father very infirm, and no parish relief.

Mary Wood, eight years of age, the child of a widow in great distress, with a large family, and without any parish relief.

Mary Purdue, ten years of age, the child of a poor woman, deserted by her husband, and no parish relief.

Elizabeth Hoare, eight years of age, an orphan in great necessity.[1] . . .

Blackstone on the Criminal Responsibility of Children under the Common Law, 1769

Sir William Blackstone, *Commentaries on the Laws of England: In Four Books* (London: Murray, 1857), Vol. IV, *Of Public Wrongs,* p. 19 (editor's lib.)

CHAPTER II OF THE PERSONS CAPABLE OF COMMITTING CRIMES

. . . Infants, under the age of discretion, ought not to be punished by any criminal prosecution whatever.* What the age of discretion is, in various nations, is matter of some variety. The civil law distinguished the age of minors, or those under twenty-five years old, into three stages: *infantia,* from the birth till seven years of age; *pueritia,* from seven to fourteen; and *pubertas,* from fourteen upwards. The period of *pueritia,* or childhood, was again subdivided into two equal parts: fro n seven to ten and a half was *aetas infantiae proxima;* from ten and a half to fourteen was *aetas pubertati proxima.* During the first stage of infancy and the next half stage of childhood, *infantiae proxima,* they were not punishable for any crime.† During the other half stage of childhood, approaching to puberty, from ten and a half to fourteen, they were indeed punishable, if found to be *doli capaces,* or capable of mischief; but with many mitigations, and not with the utmost rigour of the law.‡ During the last stage (at the age of puberty, and afterwards), minors were liable to be punished, as well capitally as otherwise.

The law of England does in some cases privilege an infant, under the age of twenty-one, as to common misdemeanors, so as to escape

1. An Abstract of the Proceedings of the Guardians of the Asylum, or House of Refuge, for Orphan Girls . . . [London] June the 16th, 1760, p. 11-12.
* 1 Hawk. P. C. 2.
† Inst. 3, 20, 10.
‡ Ff. 29, 5, 14, 50, 17, 111, 47, 2, 23.

fine, imprisonment, and the like: and particularly in cases of omission, as not repairing a bridge or a highway, and other similar offences;* for, not having the command of his fortune till twenty-one, he wants the capacity to do those things which the law requires. But where there is any notorious breach of the peace, a riot, battery, or the like (which infants, when full grown, are at least as liable as others to commit), for these an infant, above the age of fourteen, is equally liable to suffer as a person of the full age of twenty-one.

With regard to 'felonies,' the law is still more minute and circumspect, distinguishing with greater nicety the several degrees of age and discretion. By the ancient Saxon law, the age of twelve years was established for the age of possible discretion, when first the understanding might open;† and from thence till the offender was fourteen, it was *aetas pubertati proxima*, in which he might or might not be guilty of a crime, according to his natural capacity or incapacity. This was the dubious stage of discretion; but, under twelve it was held that he could not be guilty in will, neither after fourteen could he be supposed innocent, of any capital crime which he in fact committed. But by the law, as it now stands, and has stood at least ever since the time of Edward the Third, the capacity of doing ill, or contracting guilt, is not so much measured by years and days, as by the strength of the delinquent's understanding and judgment. For one lad of eleven years old may have as much cunning as another of fourteen; and in these cases our maxim is, that "*malitia supplet aetatem.*" Under seven years of age, indeed, an infant cannot be guilty of felony,* for then a felonious discretion is almost an impossibility in nature; but at eight years old he may be guilty of felony.† Also, under fourteen, though an infant shall be *prima facie* adjudged to be *doli incapax;*‡ yet if it appear to the court and jury that he was *doli capax*, and could discern between good and evil, he may be convicted and suffer death. Thus a girl of thirteen has been burnt for killing her mistress: and one boy of ten, and another of nine years old, who had killed their companions, have been sentenced to death, and he of ten years actually hanged; because it appeared upon their trials, that the one hid himself, and the other hid the body he had killed, which hiding manifested a consciousness of guilt, and a discretion to discern between good and evil.§ And there was an instance in the last century where a boy

* 1 Hal. P. C. 20, 21, 22.
† LL. Athelstan; 1 Thorpe, 199.
* Mirr. c. 4, § 16; 1 Hal. P.C. 27.
† Dalt. Just. c. 147.
‡ *Rex v. Owen*, 4 C. & P. 236.
§ 1 Hal. P.C. 26, 27.

of eight years old was tried at Abingdon for firing two barns; and it appearing that he had malice, revenge, and cunning, he was found guilty, condemned, and hanged accordingly.* Thus also, more recently, a boy of ten years old was convicted on his own confession of murdering his bedfellow, there appearing in his whole behaviour plain tokens of a mischievous discretion; and, as the sparing this boy merely on account of his tender years might be of dangerous consequence to the public, by propagating a notion that children might commit such atrocious crimes with impunity, it was unanimously agreed by all the judges that he was a proper subject of capital punishment.† But, in all such cases, the evidence of that malice which is to supply age, ought to be strong and clear beyond all doubt and contradiction.

William Smith and John Howard Deplore the Jail Confinement of Children, 1776-1777

[A] William Smith (M.D.), *State of the Gaols in London, West-minster and Borough of Southwark* (London, 1776), pp. 62-63 (Brit. Mus.)

To suffer children to remain in gaol is very impolitic for many reasons; besides crouding the house unreasonably, it not only corrupts their morals, but injures their health, stops their growth, hurts their looks, and endangers their lives. . . .

Parents sometimes suffer an extravagant son to be some time confined in gaol, in order to reclaim him. This is a very dangerous and erroneous practice. Satan will rebuke sin when reformation of manners is brought about in a gaol.

[B] John Howard, *The State of the Prisons in England and Wales* (Warrington, 1777), pp. 15-16, 21 (editor's lib.)

The evils mentioned hitherto affect the *health* and *life* of prisoners: I have now to complain of what is pernicious to their *morals;* and that is, the confining all sorts of prisoners together: debtors and felons; men and women; the young beginner and the old offender. . . .

Few prisons separate men and women in the day-time. In some counties the Gaol is also the Bridewell: in others those prisons are contiguous, and the yard common. There the petty offender is

* Emlyn on 1 Hal. P.C. 25.
† Foster, 72.

committed for instruction to the most profligate. In some Gaols you see (and who can see it without pain?) boys of twelve or fourteen eagerly listening to the stories told by practised and experienced criminals, of their adventures, successes, stratagems, and escapes.

... Multitudes of young creatures, committed for some trifling offence, are totally ruined there. I make no scruple to affirm that if it were the wish and aim of Magistrates to effect the destruction present and future of young delinquents, they could not devise a more effectual method, than to confine them so long in our prisons, those seats and seminaries (as they have been very properly called) of idleness and every vice.

Lewd Ballads and Prints Corrupt the Young, 1778

William Smith (M.D.), *Mild Punishments Sound Policy; or Observations on the Laws Relative to Debtors and Felons . . .* (London, 1778), pp. 44-45, 48-49 (Goldsmiths' Lib.)

... Even the ballad singers and street musicians are useful in their spheres to promote vice. . . .

Observe who listen to and buy those lewd ballads, and you will find that young people of both sexes, particularly apprentice boys, servant maids, and gentlemen's servants, are the purchasers. They read them with the greatest avidity, and thereby poison their morals, by affording fuel to their turbulent passions. . . .

Our print shops lend their assistance to promote vice. The indecent custom of exposing to view, in shop-windows, lewd and infamous prints, is of late become so flagrant, as to be a real nusance and insult to the modest part of the public. These prints instil the most dangerous poison into the minds of the youth and seduce them into the ways of vice, by exposing to their view, in the most open and conspicuous manner, scenes only fit for a brothel. Such a scandalous nuisance should be checked; and if the magistrates do not put a stop to it, every lover of decency has the means in his own hands, by breaking the windows where such sights are presented.

A Juvenile Court in Children's Fiction, 1786

Master Tommy Littleton (Secretary to the Court), *Juvenile Trials for Robbing Orchards, Telling Fibs, and other Heinous*

Offences. Embellished with Cuts (London: Printed for T. Carnan, in St. Pauls' Church-yard, 1786) (Brit. Mus.)

[This popular little work of children's fiction which appeared in several editions in England and in America is an early example of student self-government. Accordng to Rosenbach's *Early American Children's Books,* 1933, it was entered by T. Carnan at Stationers' Hall on Dec. 18, 1771, but was probably of much earlier date. The earliest edition in the British Museum is that for 1786. Two American editions are known, Boston, 1797, and Philadelphia, 1801. In early editions a detailed account of five trials is presented, but in the Boston edition, 1797, there is a sixth trial attributed to Dr. John Aiken. On the back of the title page of the Boston edition is the statement, "This," says Dr. Aiken, "is a very pleasing and ingenious little work, in which a Court of Justice is supposed to be instituted in a School, composed of the scholars themselves, for the purpose of trying offences committed at School." It is interesting to speculate on whether the juvenile juries of the early Boston House of Reformation and of the New York House of Refuge were inspired by this little book.]

DIALOGUE BEETWEEN A TUTOR AND GOVERNESS, BY WAY OF
INTRODUCTION

Tutor. It is much to be lamented, that perversity shows itself so early, as we generally find it does in growing children; and this is principally owing to the overindulgence of parents, who can not persuade themselves to curb them in their infancy, hoping that, when they grow up, reason and prudence will point out to them their errors; but this is a fatal mistake. Children begin to think much earlier than people generally imagine; and were there [their] inclinations and passions to be checked on their first appearance, the matter would not be difficult. For want of strictly adhering to this rule, the tutor has frequently more to do, to keep order in his school, than he has to instruct them in the sciences. Feuds and contentions are continually arising among them, which always take off their attention from learning.

Gov. I am inclined to believe, could we think on any method which would prevent these bickerings among them, everything would then go on smoothly. We must find out some other kind of punishment for offenders of that nature, than what we make use of at present. The rod and the cane had better be laid aside; and, if we can bring them to a sense of their errors, either by inflicting on them some kind of disgrace, or depriving them of any particular object that pleases them, I shall then begin to hope for success.

Tutor. I have long had it in my mind to establish among them a kind of equitable court, in which one of the young gentlemen should sit as a supreme judge. He should hear all complaints against anyone who should be accused of telling fibs, taking from another that which did not belong to him, and such other offences; but, above all, he should be particularly severe against domestic cabals, I mean quarrels among themselves. Their punishments should extend only, on slight occasions, to the depriving them of cakes and fruit for a time, which should be limited in proportion to the degree of their crimes. When any of them were found guilty of being turbulent, quarrelsome, and seditious, sentence should be given against them, that no one should presume to speak to them for a certain time, under particular penalties.

Gov. I am inclined to think this method of treating them would have a proper effect. When they are corrected by the hands of their governor, it is no sooner over than forgotten, and their companions immediately crowd around them, to console them under a misfortune, which they know not how soon may be their own case; but when they are made judges of their own cause, with respect to harmony among themselves, it will become the interest of everyone to abide by the general determination, and the shame of being condemned by their own companions may have far greater effect on them than any other kind of correction possibly can. But how will you prevent abuses in this new mode of administration?

Tutor. I will assemble all the little ones of both sexes together; I will tell them of my intended regulation, and will propose to them, that they themselves shall chuse a Lord chief justice, whom they shall invest with the power of hearing complaints, examining witnesses, and giving judgment thereon. If the major part should be at any time dissatisfied with this decree, then an appeal shall lie open to me. And the better to prevent litigious suits; if any complaint shall appear to have been made out of either wantonness or ill-will, such complainant shall be severely fined; as shall all such who shall give false or partial evidence; of all crimes, this last shall be deemed the worst.

Gov. I see very plainly you have Master Meanwell in view to fill this high and important office. For my part, I could wish Miss Sterling had some share in this administration of justice; besides, I think it is nothing unreasonable, that young ladies should be tried by one of their own sex; and, where the matter is doubtful, that I likewise might be appealed to.

65

Tutor. This, Madam, is a little out of the usual method of judicial matters: however, I am contented that you should share with me the cares and honours attending the management of this little flock. I will go and instantly propose Meanwell to their choice as judge; at the same time, I will propose Miss Sterling to the young ladies.

Gov. I am obliged to you, Sir, for your ready agreement to my proposal; and, so long as we go hand in hand in our important undertakings (for surely the education of children is a very material one) there is no fear of success. . . .

JUVENILE TRIALS

TRIAL THE FIRST

The governor instantly called all his scholars together, and thus spoke to them: "My little pupils, as well young ladies as gentlemen, I consider myself as a shepherd, and you as the little flock over whom I am placed by your parents. It has always been my study to keep harmony and good temper among you, at best to endeavour at it; to give you a taste of solid learning, virtue, and morality; and to inspire you with such notions, as, when you shall arrive at an age in which you shall quit this place, you may launch forth into the world with such happy dispositions, as may direct you how to keep clear of those fatal rocks, on which the giddy and the thoughtless are often wrecked, But, alas! in spite of all my endeavours I have the unhappiness to find you still quarrel among yourselves; you tell fibs, rob orchards, and are guilty of other irregularities, which are committed only by naughty and disobedient children.

"Correction is, of all things, the most displeasing to a fond and indulgent tutor, who would wish to subdue your passions, rather by reason than force. With this view, I am desirous of establishing among you a court of Inquiry, at the head of which I would recommend you to place, as chief justice, Master Meanwell; his character is well known among you, and, as he is present, I will save his modesty the blush by hearing his virtues recounted to his face. The choice, however, of your judge shall be left to yourselves. That he may not have it absolutely in his power to decide just as he pleases, on every complaint which shall be made, I would recommend the following mode of proceedings:

"When any one among you has committed an offence, such as shall be deemed worthy of punishment, complaint may be made thereof to the judge, who shall examine the complainants on their

66

word of honour. And here I must observe, should any one spitefully lay a false charge to another, or give false evidence in Court, they shall be deemed guilty of the most capital offence, and punished accordingly. If the judge shall deem the complaint a just one, though only of a very trifling nature, then he shall send for the party accused, inquire into the matter himself, and, if he finds the charge is true, and the accused is sorry for his crime, then he shall content himself with reprimanding him, and ordering his secretary to make a minute thereof in a book kept for that purpose; but shall not, of himself, have any power to inflict punishments.

"If the party accused should be obstinate, or be found culpable a second time, then the judge shall order his secretary to give notice for trial the next day in the Great Hall, which shall be open to every one during the course of any judicial proceedings. The accused (who shall be obliged to keep his chamber till the trial is finished, and the judgment given, excepting the time he is at the bar before his judges) shall have notice to prepare for his defence, and to name any six, by whose judgment he will abide; if the prisoner is a female, then so many young ladies. If the accused should think the punishment too severe, or the jury shall bring it in *special*, then I will determine it.

"That the young ladies may not complain of having a young gentleman for their judge, I would propose Miss Sterling to determine the differences. . . .

[Several days later at a public trial attended by the scholars as well as by people in the neighborhood "Master Billy Prattle was brought before judge Meanwell, charged with the high crime of robbing an orchard." The evidence was overwhelming, and the jury brought in a verdict of guilty, with a recommendation to clemency, which was granted upon the defendant apologizing to the owner of the orchard, etc.

The form of procedure in this as well as in subsequent trials was the same as for adults, with a strong leaning toward leniency if the offender repented and promised to do better.]

Public Asylums Proposed for Children of Convicts and for Other Neglected and Destitute Children, 1786

Hewling Luson, *Inferior Politics: or, Considerations on the Wretchedness and Profligacy of the Poor . . . On the Defects in the Present System of Parochial and Penal Laws . . .* (London, 1786), pp. 79, 91-92, 110 (editor's lib.)

From the moment that a man, who subsists himself and family by labour, is apprehended on a criminal accusation, to the time of his acquittal, the Legislature are *bound,* no less by equity than good policy, to maintain that family whom they have thus bereaved of their proper and natural support. . . .

Another, still more powerful and extensive in its operation, is the total disregard of the unhappy widows and orphans of those wretches who die by the sentence of the law! What can be more unjust, impolitic, or inhuman! When twenty criminals were lately hanged at once, it is probably twice that number were *destined* to future execution, if the present system of sanguinary punishment be not abolished. The widows and children of these convicts, though supported by the wages of iniquity, are perhaps innocent themselves; the *infants* are certainly so. But how should they possibly continue in that state? Neglected by that society whose laws have bereft them of their support, to whom should they apply for subsistence but to the *associates* of their late unhappy parents? And by these they *will* be received and maintained, and instructed in the early rudiments of that calling by which they are in future to be supported. Thieving is now become a *science;* and no sooner are these outcasts of the community arrived at an age to be capable of distinguishing good from evil, than they are systematically trained up to it by the most industrious and able proficients. . . .

Long before other children have finished the common school-education, to fit them for their employment, this unhappy orphan is an *adept* in his profession; before his equals in age can read a lesson with tolerable fluency, the infant thief can pick a pocket with wonderful dexterity; and the transition, from this beginning to higher exploits, is rapid and easy. . . .

When . . . hundreds of wretched children are thus annually trained up, by their abandoned parents, to a life of misery, beggary, prostitution, or plunder, can it be a subject of astonishment that robberies are daily increasing? Surely it is a duty incumbent on the legislature to *save* these innocent victims from infancy and ruin, by taking them from parents who thus violate the trust reposed in them, and pervert, to the worst of purposes, that authority which the laws have too long allowed them to abuse. Let *these* children, as well as those whom the sentence of the law deprives of their parents, be taken under the protection of the public, and placed in some asylum, where similar maintenance, employment, and instruction, may be provided for them. . . .

Transportation of Delinquent Children from England to Australia, 1787-1797

The Report of the Select Committee Appointed by the House of Commons, Relative to the Establishment of a New Police in the Metropolis, etc. (London, 1799), p. 132 (editor's lib.)

SUPPLEMENT (M. 2.)

List of Convicts Sent to New South Wales and Norfolk Island, from 1787 to 1797 inclusive; viz.

Years	Men and Women	Children
1787	778	17
1789	1,251	22
1790	2,029	9
1791	408	11
1792	412	6
1794	82	2
1795	133	3
1796	279	13
1797	393	10
	5,765	93

Transportation of Delinquent Children to Australia—Confinement on the Hulks, 1812-1817

Hon. Henry Grey Bennet, M.P., Letter to Viscount Sidmouth, Secretary of State for the Home Department, on the Transportation Laws, the State of the Hulks, and of the Colonies in New South Wales (London, 1819), pp. 10, 23, 31, 36, 38 (Harvard Law Lib.)

[JUVENILE OFFENDERS TRANSPORTED TO AUSTRALIA, 1812-1817]

I am not able to find in these returns [to the House of Commons] any account of the ages under twenty-one years of the convicts prior to January, 1812; but from that period to January, 1817, 780 males and 136 female convicts were transported under that age, of whom 5 were infants of 11, -7 of 12, -17 of 13, -32 of 14, and 65 of 15 years of age. . . .

After having pined and rotted in their respective county gaols for a given portion of time, which varies from three months to as many years, the prisoners are removed on board the different hulks designed for their reception; there are various modes of transport; some are chained on the tops of coaches; others, as from London, travel in an open caravan, exposed to the inclemency of the weather, to the gaze of the idle and the taunts and mockeries of the cruel. . . . Men and boys, children just emerging from infancy, as young in vice as in years, are fettered together, and . . . paraded through the kingdom,—they are besides generally fettered in the cruelest manner. . . . Some years back I saw in the Compter of the City of London, a considerable number of convicts who were on the road to the hulks. Among them were several children all heavily fettered, ragged and sickly, and carrying in their countenance proofs of the miseries they had undergone. . . .

[Boys on Board the Hulks]

On board the Leviathan [out of a total of 500 convicts] were 35 convicts under 20 years of age, a boy of 13 was the youngest. . . .

On board the Retribution, the wards were better ventilated than in the other ships,—they contained in the whole 552 prisoners, and the following is a list of their respective ages and sentences:

> Boys under 15 years of age for life. . . . 8
> Ditto, for 14 years. . . . . 6 } Total 37
> Ditto, for 7 years. 23

. . . On board this ship were 37 boys confined . . . and not working on shore [with the men]:—they are employed as tailors, shoemakers, coopers, carpenters, bookbinders, etc. . . . Among these boys were two little infants from Newgate of nine years of age. . . .

The Philanthropic Society in London Opens an Institution for the Offspring of Convicts and for Other Destitute and Delinquent Children, 1788

[The Philanthropic Society was first suggested and introduced to the public by Robert Young, Warwick-Court, Holborn, in London. Although a contemporary magazine described the Philanthropic Society as an extension of the Marine Society, it is apparent from the early reports that it was regarded as an entirely new charity, "as an experiment; and as a record to posterity of what is possible to be done for the good of mankind." As set forth in an early pamphlet, and probably published by its own press, the Society was established "for the Prevention of Crimes, and for a Reform among the Poor; by training up to Virtue and Industry the Children of Vagrants and Criminals, and such who are in the Paths of Vice and Infamy." The President of the new Society was the Duke of Leeds, while Robert Young served as "Intendant and Treasurer." It was supported by subscriptions and donations, and frequent appeals were issued for funds, with lists of subscribers and donations, and sometimes short descriptions of the children aided. Though originally located at Cambridge Place, Hackney, by 1792 the Society moved to St. George's Fields in Southwark to a piece of ground leased to the Society by the City of London. The Institution took both boys and girls, not from London alone, but from other parts of the country as well. The Society ceased to take girls in 1845. Due to its crowded situation in London, and its inability to provide agricultural training, the institution was moved to Redhill, Surrey, in 1849, where on a 133 acre tract (later increased to 350 acres) it became a farm school patterned after the French agricultural colony at Mettray. Under Rev. Sydney Turner, its resident chaplain and chief administrative officer at Redhill, the institution played a prominent part in the movement to establsh reformatories and industrial schools in the 1850's. It is still in operation as a highly successful "Approved School" for boys.

Robert Young is known to have written the *Second Report of the Society,* 1790, which sets forth with rare sociological insight the philosophy and ideals of the Reform. In 1792 he wrote a pamphlet describing the establishment of an *Asylum for Industry* designed to rescue youth discharged from gaols, female prostitutes, seamen and soldiers in want, vagrants, and the unemployed in London. A rare and valuable, but little known document, in the history of social science is Young's *Gnomia,* or the *Science of Society,* published in 1801.]

[A] *First Report of the Philanthropic Society: Instituted in London, September, 1788, for the Prevention of Crimes* (London, c. May, 1789), pp. 2, 5, 6, 14-17, 20, 22, 26, 33, 44, 49, 56 (Brit. Mus.)

[Failure of the Poor Law to Provide Adequately for Destitute Children]

The plan of this institution is almost or altogether new: it is therefore expedient, not only to state the reasons for deviating from the forms of other charitable establishments, but also with freedom to point out those errors in them which in this have been the great object to avoid.

The society is formed rather on principles of police than of charity. . . .

The legal provisions for the poor, the establishments supported by voluntary contributions, the alms given to beggars, and the private donations of individuals, make together a sum surpassing belief—much of this bounty is annually employed in the support, and consequently in the reward of idleness. . . .

The great defect of the poor laws we judge to be their want of discrimination between merit and demerit, amounting virtually to the discountenancing of honest industry, and rewarding of indolence and vice. . . .

Those children, whose parents cannot provide for them, are children of the state. . . .

By the creed of an overseer the number of births is the standard of the nation's decay, and the command to increase and multiply, was given as a scourge to mankind. A breeding poor woman is detested, by him, as the plague, and fines and persecutions are the lot of those who bring into a parish, children likely to have the state for their parent. Families are hunted from one district to another, as if a reward was offered for their heads. The wolves, which formerly infested this country, were not so abhorrent to the villagers as the poor now are to parish officers.* There are a variety of circumstances which render the settlement of a poor person liable to litigation. Each parish rejects on the smallest pretext they can find, and the miserable wretch starves, between a divided claim to support, from two or more funds. A beadle has been seen to drag a dying man in the streets across the way into the boundaries of another parish, to rid his own of the charge of his burial; and there has left him to perish. From the difficulties thrown in the way of obtaining parish relief it happens that thousands of destitute children are left exposed to the worst examples, and compelled by hunger to commit depredations on that public, who from

* To the general representation there no doubt are particular and honourable exceptions.

being their natural and legal protectors, have abandoned them to the rigors of their fate. . . .

Our attention is next demanded to the management of those destitute children, whose settlements being unequivocal, are admitted to parochial benefits. The same principle pervades every part of the system. Children are considered in the false and narrow light of burthens on a parish. . . .

The parish officer feels himself not as he ought to do, the agent of the state, having a portion of its subjects committed to his care, but as appointed by his parish to reduce the burthens of the poors maintenance; and if he does not succeed in diminishing the tax on his parishioners, he, at least generally takes care that the poor are not encouraged to expect too much from the support appointed them by law. The expence, time, and trouble, of maintaining children, being considered as entirely sunk, is conducted on the most confined scale, and notwithstanding that the amount of the poor rate through the kingdom is prodigious, the children of the state are brought up in circumstances of apparent indigence, but one degree superior to those children who are abandoned to a vagrant life, and who virtually have no parent at all. The most economical maintenance and speedy riddance of them are the grand arcana they study, while the care of their morals, and the formation of their characters, are the most remote from any plan of conduct they adopt. . . .

It is no doubt to supply, in some measure, the defects of the parochial system, that so many benevolent institutions supported by voluntary donations, are become the boast of this country. . . .

Every child, brought up in the resort of vicious and profligate people must almost inevitably imbibe the contagion of moral turpitude, and become an enemy to those laws on which the general good depends. Lying is the first lesson of their tongues, and theft the first exercise of their hands; every object they see is at war with decency, and every impression they receive is a vice.

These children, from their lost condition, are first in their claims upon humanity; and become, from the vices in which they are growing up, the most important object of police; Them, the plan of the Philanthropic Society is framed to restore to civil community, to their proper condition as men, and to the right knowledge of their God.

It was not the design of the present institution to augment that general sum of charity, which is considered, as being already too great, and as injurious not only to the community at large, but to the poor who receive it. It was proposed to establish a fund, not to be sunk in gratuities without any return, nor to be a perpetual current from the purses of the rich to the miseries of the poor, there to stagnate, and keep alive, rather than relieve, their wants.

The object in short was to unite the spirit of charity with the principles of trade, and to erect a temple to philanthropy on the foundation of virtuous industry. . . .

In the choice of employments for a class of people, who, from time immemorial, have subsisted on the labour of others, it has been a fundamentaal maxim to guard against injuring any of the present classes of working hands. If on account of giving employment to a vagrant, any honest man be turned out of bread, no good is done to humanity, or to the state.

To prevent this evil, the wards of the society are to be employed, primarily, in the produce of such things as they will consume.

As they will, in all respects, enjoy comforts, to which they were strangers before, their altered state of life will create a new market for the produce of labour, and for that market their own labours are the most proper source of supply.

The society began their purpose with children, not exceeding five or six years old; this threw back the prospect of any benefit from their labours, to a period too remote to gratify the desires of those who were anxious to see their plan mature, in their own time, and under their own guidance. Children of nine or ten years old came under their notice, and they felt it a duty not to consign such to ruin, wiithout affording them a chance for salvation.

The same motives led to an acceptance of children of twelve or fourteen, and they were regarded as affording a valuable expriment upon which to ground the future line of conduct. The result was equally favourable to humanity, and to the interests of all parties. The mischiefs many had feared from the evil habits children of so ripe an age must have contracted in bad company, and a vagrant life, were found within the power of seasonable correction and good government to prevent. The basis of this happy reform, was their preference of the situation to which they were admitted, before that from which they were taken; the threat of being returned to it, was more terrible to them than correction: by this means an absolute ascendency was gained over them, and the dominion of virtue and good order was established. Those who had been gained over, were instrumental in the conquest of others; and the vices of a new comer, instead of contaminating the older wards, yielded to the influence of their reformed manners. Individual dispositions, however adverse in themselves, falling into a regular current of virtuous habits, mingle with the stream, and unite with it of course.

In every step of this procedure, the fears of great numbers who were acquainted with the design, foreboded disappointment, and kept them back from embarking in its support. Nothing could satisfy those fears, but facts which should speak for themselves. They feared that abandoned people would not consent to their children being made good members of community; that they would entice them away from the society's care—visit them—inspire them with evil inclinations; and by their intercourse, defeat the purposes of the charity: they contemplated the enormity of the corruption of the poor, and the ill success of the means which had hitherto been tried. The enemy appeared in full view; but they could not as yet see, nor confide in, the resources which were looked to for his defeat.

In fine, the plan was considered altogether as the pinnacle of romance, and adjudged to be practised in the city of Utopia, or the Arcadian fields.

Few were found who, as an abstract proposal, would hazard their names in its support; and had its promoters waited for the collection of a considerable fund, and the sanction of a numerous body, before they had commenced their undertaking, it is probable it would have remained ever unattempted. . . .

A single child was first put to nurse, to which several more were soon added; when the number amounted to twelve, a small house of 10 pounds per ann. rent was hired, in a situation, where more could easily be obtained as they might be wanted. A matron was placed there to superintend the household concerns, and the government of the wards; such of them as were capable, were employed in knitting stockings, and weaving of lace and garters.

A second house was soon hired; and presently a third; the number of wards was encreased to twenty; and among them were several from ten to fourteen years old. The boys and girls were now separated. A shoe-maker was placed in the second house, several of the elder boys began this necessary branch of manufacture, and already the whole seminary is supplied with shoes made within itself.

In the third house is a taylor, who has a certain number of wards under his tuition. It is intended that all shall learn knitting, spinning, or some such employ as may be useful to them in old age and infirmity.

Agriculture is the grand source to which the society looks for employment for their Wards. Agriculture, man's natural labour, and the primary spring of riches, of health and of happiness.

Our populous cities and towns are already too much crowded

with manufacturers, mechanics, and menial servants, who flock from all parts of the country. To preserve the just balance, let us then, send to wholesome air and exercise, the miserable wretches who are now perishing upon dunghills in London, and form them a hardy race of husbandmen, from the waste of society, to populate and cultivate the waste and barren parts of the country.

The mode of living is in distinct houses, as separate families. A manufacturer has a house for himself and his wife, if married, and a certain number of wards, whom they are to regard as their own children. In these respects, the design is to approach as nearly as possible to common life.

They have two banyan days every week, or days when meat is not allowed. Their beds are laid on a kind of wicker hurdle, which is removed in the day time to gain room for work. Utility only is consulted in every arrangement, and as the wards are forming for the humble station of labourers, it is thought an important care not to accustom them to conveniences and indulgences, of which afterwards they might severely feel the want.

They have regular hours for every avocation; and prayers in the established form of worship every morning and evening. To preserve good order, and to give them ideas of services to each other, certain wards are appointed daily as stewards for domestic offices; these lay and remove the cloth, and wait on their companions at table. They are called to every different exercise by the ringing of a bell. Each master or mistress keeps a day book of their children's conduct, minuting down any fault or desert that is proper to be noticed. This day book is an index to the character, and a most powerful instrument of forming it to good. The calendar of their faults is termed the *black book,* and the disgrace of being on this list, is more dreaded by them than a chastisement.

They are governed rather by the influence of rewards than punishments; to be omitted in the former keeps the same distinction between merit and demerit as being included in the latter, while the one exalts and the other debases the mind.

At certain times they are called together, the book of character read and commented upon, and praise or blame publicly bestowed.

To the most distinguished there is given weekly, a ticket or testimony of good behaviour, and they are taught to consider these tickets as treasure, which they are to be diligent in accumulating.*

Of late, few have been on the black list, and all have received these tickets. Already these poor children, who a few weeks since

* This idea was adopted from the practice of Mr. Raikes of Gloucester Institutor of the Sunday Schools.

were loathsome spectacles in the streets, with misery and the gallows before their eyes, are not a little superior in behaviour and disposition to the greater part of those, who belong to the body of honest and industrious poor. So easily are youthful minds, made to receive the impressions either of virtue or vice; and so certainly might the charity-poor, of every kingdom, be made patterns for all the other classes of citizens.

A practical school of morality constitutes a very essential part of the society's plan; of this, the foregoing regulations form but an inconsiderable portion, and time and circumstances have not as yet permitted it to be carried further into effect. . . .

INCIDENTS

Important information is often to be gathered from incidents in themselves trivial, and is better conveyed by a recital of the circumstances than by abstract moral reflections.

Almost all the younger wards have given proofs of their origin by little thievish practices. On first coming to their nurses it was common, at night, to find their pockets crammed with trifles, which they picked up about the house. This disposition, the germ of future mischief, was in general, easily subdued. The elder children discovered less of it, being more capable of judging of their new circumstances, of the certainty of detection, and the inutility of success: the inclination in general appeared to cease with the occasion.

Dismissal from the society's care has always been held out, both to parents and children, as a punishment for ill behaviour. A girl had told a wilful lie, for which she was whipped; she declared she would go away, and those about her thought it necessary to watch her, lest she should escape. This gave a dangerous consequence to the girl, and turned the society's threat on itself. To correct this evil, the children were called together, and informed that the girl had deserved dismissal for telling an untruth, but in lenity to her had only been punished with a whipping; but that having presumed to threaten to go away, and thereby showing herself insensible of the society's bounty to her, she must immediately be discharged as a necessary example to the rest. Her rags, which were preserved on purpose for such occasions, were put on her, and she was ordered to take immediate leave of her companions, and depart. This produced a most affecting scene. The girl bid a faint good bye; the rest echoed "good bye" in most melancholy tones, and with tears trembling in several of their eyes; she did not, however, offer to stir; and, on her being pushed to the door, one of them burst into a loud lamentation—he was her cousin—and there was a general intercession for her permission to stay; she did not know, they said, when she was well used; they hoped she would behave better in future. She was desired to kneel and ask forgiveness—she did so—and thus the affair ended.

One of the boys was of a disposition uncommonly mischievous; he had not been long with his nurse before he struck a companion on the head with a brass candlestick, seized the poker, and used the most violent imprecations in his passion. After a severe flogging for his conduct, he, notwithstanding, kneeled down to beg that he might not be sent away. This has been the most troublesome boy of the whole number, but by proper admonitions and seasonable rewards, as well as timely punishments, he is now brought to be one of the most useful members of our little community. . . .

Mode of Obtaining Children

The friends of the institution visit the places where the objects of it reside. They find there undescribeable misery, which no friendly hand had reached, nor pitying eye had seen. The most abominable filth renders their habitations to the last degree offensive; swathed with rags, and begrimed with dirt, the traces of the human figure, in them, are almost lost; a person cannot go up stairs without apprehending danger to his limbs; an empty apartment, or at best, furnished with a broken chair, and a bundle of rags for a bed, is their wretched residence, for which the miserable tenant pays a shilling a week to some landlord, but a few degrees advanced above themselves. Sometimes there are two or three in a room. Begging and stealing are their ordinary means of subsistence; drunkenness, lying, quarrelling, profaneness and prostitution, are their manners and way of life. The springs of honest industry, in their minds, are wholly unbent; they neglect the little comforts, or alleviations of misery, they might procure by their own exertions; and either abandon themselves to despair; or vainly endeavour to drown the sense of affliction, by plunging themselves more deeply in oaths, intoxication and debauchery. Thus the promoters of this charity seek acquaintance with wretchedness in its last and lowest stages: They converse with these forlorn people on their way of life, and on the vileness of their condition, and point out the means of relief through the bounty of the society. On these occasions, they are witnesses to blessings from lips accustomed to utter only blasphemies; they hear the name of God invoked with praise, in places where it had been known, only as a mode of cursing their neighbours; and they have seen the frames of men and women, on contemplating the plan of the society, agitated with emotions of gratitude, which they knew no language to express. FROM THESE PLACES THEY PROCURE CHILDREN, WITH THEIR OWN AND THEIR PARENTS JOYFUL CONSENT.

All applications on the behalf of children who are not resident in some such places of extreme debasement, are received with caution and jealously. It is rarely that the last stage of misery, allied with vice, can be *recommended* to charity. An acquaintance with this class of people is only to be had by painful researches, in which few will engage; and to receive such objects as, in the ordinary course, have friends to intercede for them, would be to defeat the plan of the society, and leave undone that great work, which is its peculiar distinction and boast. . . .

It will be learned, with pleasure, that the example of this society has been already followed in other places. A similar institution bids fair to be established in Wales, by the exertions of George Hardinge, Esq. M. P. one of the Judges there, and a Vice-President of this society; and the Governors of the poor at Birmingham, have set on foot a plan of the same kind.

From such happy beginnings, co-operating with a general spirit of reform and diffusion of just sentiments, that every where appears; particularly from the good effect of Sunday schools, on the poor of a less depraved description than those for whom the present plan is designed; the most flattering prospects present themselves, that human nature will at length assert her rights, society learn its true interests, and the sum of happiness be augmented beyond what has been known in any former period of the history of mankind.

> [B] *The Philanthropic Society, Instituted September, 1788, for the Prevention of Crimes* . . . [London, *c.* September, 1789] pp. 4-6, 8, 15-16 (editor's lib.)

The first year of the *Philanthropic Society* has now passed; and during that interval the circumstances and prospects of this infant establishment has undergone a very material change. . . .

Within the first six months, the funds, with the aid of two liberal donations of 100 guineas from the President [The Duke of Leeds], and 100 pounds from the Earl of Egremont, served only for the admission of nine wards. In the last half-year, thirty-six were added—The whole number is forty-five wards at the expiration of the first year.

As the plan of the institution has no parallel, so such a growth, in extent and in public esteem, is without example. . . .

Those forty-five children who are now in this institution would, almost to a moral certainty, have been numbered among the pests and annoyers of society, among the heirs of misery, or victims to the law. On the contrary they have already entered upon the path of virtue, and are tasting the comforts, of that industry by which they will soon become useful to the state. These owe their preservation from ruin, temporal, and perhaps eternal, mediately, to the bounty of the present List of Subscribers [about 400 names listed on pages 9-13]. . . .

The institution supported by this society is named *The Reform.* In this seminary are, or are intended to be taught, all the most simple and useful arts of life. In particular, the moral and social virtues are cultivated by a regular system of exercises and encouragements. To give time for this plan to produce a lasting effect, the wards are apprenticed to the Society: they will, thus, continue under its care till the age of twenty-one; at which period it may be hoped that good habits will be confirmed. . . .

As an *Instrument of Police,* cooperating with the Law, it strikes an unerring and effectual blow at the root of vice; it cuts off the succession of evil from the old to the young, and destroys its existence by leaving it no inheritors. It is therefore to be preferred before an increase of judicial penalties, not only inasmuch as prevention is easier than remedy, but because punishments have proved ineffectual, while the salutary operation of these means is indubitable and certain. . . .

MANUFACTURE

The institution already begins to show the fruits of industry. There are now carrying on a manufactory for carpenters work; another for taylors; a third for shoe-makers; garters are wove; and plain-work done. In each of these, more work may soon be performed than the seminary will require for its own consumption; the surplus will therefore be employed for the benefit of the Fund. . . .

As soon as a suitable spot of ground can be obtained, the *New Wards* will be employed in *Agriculture,* in a reliance upon Public Support. . . .

NAMES AND DESCRIPTION OF CHILDREN RECEIVED UNDER THE CARE OF THE SOCIETY

Roger, John, and Michael Connor.—Their father is now under

sentence of death in Newgate.—Their mother lives in Carrier-Street; a place where few but persons of the most abandoned character reside.

Mary B—, aged about five years.—Her mother is now a prisoner in Newgate, under a charge of felony.

Mary Connor, aged about five years. The daughter of a drunken wretch, who was bringing up her child among the most abandoned characters. . . .

John Fletcher.—His father is a convict on board the hulks at Woolwich, and his mother a vagrant woman.

Samuel Grub.—His mother is a miserable wretch, living in Hog-Yard; Liquor-Pond-Street, and was bringing her child up to vagrancy and ruin. . . .

William Marlove.—An orphan; his mother dying about three months ago, he was turned out of doors, since which time he has had no home; has lived in the streets, and slept under a Butcher's shambles in Fleet-Market, without bed or covering. . . .

Jane Windsor, aged nine years.—Her father is a penny Barber, a notorious drunkard, who with his wife and four children, all sleep in one small bed.

Margaret Bell, aged thirteen years.—Deserted by father and mother, found begging about the streets and selling matches.

William Colton, aged seven years.—His father and mother are beggars, and being Americans, can claim no relief from any parish. . . .

Henry Jones, aged ten years.—Has no father, his mother gets a poor living by crying matches or flowers about the streets, and was bringing the boy up a beggar.

> [C] *Second Report and Address of the Philanthropic Society . . .*
> *Containing Remarks upon Education, and Some Account of the*
> *Methods Adopted in the Reform for Cultivating Virtuous Dis-*
> *positions and Habits in the Wards of the Society* (2nd Ed.;
> London, 1790), pp. 41-42, 43, 51-57, 59 (Brit. Mus.)

[THE SCHOOL OF MORALS]

It must be admitted, that in civil society something more is required to fill any sphere with credit and usefulness than a mere negative character; some positive good is necessary. Punishments which at best are intended only to suppress vice, cannot effect that end, cannot form men, even negatively good, much less give rise to real virtues, to which they do not pretend. . . . The seeds of virtue should therefore be planted, and the harvest cherished with indefatigable care to guard against the weeds and tares that threaten to check its growth. The mind should be exercised in the social character; the qualities wanted in the man should be called forth in youth, put on trial, brought under government, directed to their end, and confirmed by habit. . . .

Men do not bow in a gay circle, nor destroy a fellow-creature in war, without having passed years of probation: yet they enter upon the highest concerns, infinitely more important and more difficult; become masters, husbands, fathers, guardians, or statesmen, without having taken a single preliminary lesson to initiate them in their duty?

. . . Rewards given to children are to be considered principally as tokens of this esteem of the world. The infant mind requires such sensible evidences, as the mediums of impressing the more refined sentiment. The sugar plum may be grateful to the palate; but it is doubly so when given with a smiling face, as a testimony of approbation. This latter impression will remain when the flavour of the sweetmeat is gone. Badges, or distinctions in dress, calculated to please the eye, are, in common, to be preferred before money, or any thing which is soon consumed, because their effect is more lasting. The rewards which hitherto have been bestowed upon the children of the Reform have been such, that they could be valuable as tokens of esteem only. They are tickets, as testimonies of good behaviour. They consider these as treasure; they have been known to prefer them before money, and they always carefully reckon up and compare the number each possesses.

The first part of the School of Morals at present in practice is a Day-book, kept in every house by the several masters and mistresses, as a record of faults and virtues, in their daily manners, occupations, and intercourse with each other. This record gives to their actions a sort of perpetuity, the idea of which operates with wonderful force as an incentive to a laudable and a preventative of an improper conduct. Those who would despise a flogging, are kept in awe by the Black Book, (as the calendar of faults is named); and this simple mean has already produced an astonishing effect in the manners of these children, and almost removed every trace of their former evil propensities.

From these several day-books the materials are collected into one common book, in the form of a ledger, in which an account is opened with every ward; he being made debtor to his faults, and creditor by his praise-worthy actions.

Every Sunday evening, between the hours of six and eight, the School of Morals is opened: in this school an officer, called the

Regulator, presides. He explains to the children the nature of faults and virtues, as they tend to their happiness or misery, in a simple manner, and with familiar exemplifications, suited to their capacities. He then distributes rewards and punishments.

These consist chiefly in tokens of honour or disgrace. Those against whom no faults worthy of notice are alleged for the preceding week, have a ticket, expressive, generally, of good behaviour. These tickets are preserved for each proprietor. Those who are found guilty of slight faults only, are punished merely with the deprivation of one or more tickets. Faults of a more serious kind, or frequent repetitions of slighter faults, are noticed by badges of disgrace, which are to be worn till a certain term of good behaviour shall purchase their removal. Chastisement is as rarely bestowed as possible, and is performed with solemnity in public. Every transaction, either of reward or punishment, of these weekly schools, is registered. . . .

To give effect to this Register of weekly prizes and penalties, an annual day of account and retribution is proposed to be held: on this day, those who have been for the preceding year distinguished by their most uniform good conduct, or their most eminent merit, are to be rewarded by some badge of honour, to be worn as a constant incitement to others to attain a similar recompence. On this day also, penalties of a more permanent and serious nature are to be adjudged to faults and crimes which have accumulated on the Weekly Register, or are transferred to this more solemn day of appeal. . . .

In order to produce the occasions of virtue, the first and fundamental thing is to impress clear ideas of what emotions and feelings are virtuous, and particularly what are the virtues intended for them to learn, and what the contrary vices to shun.

To this end, there is placed in the schoolroom a catalogue of what they are to practise, and what to avoid; in the following manner:

Industry,	Idleness,
Speaking truth,	Lying,
Honesty,	Dishonesty,
Piety,	Impiety,
Obedience,	Disobedience,
Good temper,	Ill temper,
Kindness,	Cruelty,
Decent language,	Immoral language,
Gratitude,	Ingratitude
Contentment	Discontent

These are considered as the qualities most adapted to the comprehension and use of the multitude, and most essentially necessary in life. There are other more refined virtues and qualities of different casts, suited to particular situations and to higher ranks; but even of them these must inevitably form the basis.

The first row, or the Virtues, are painted in a gold letter on a white ground; the other in red upon black. Such trivial distinctions are not unworthy of attention. A short explanation of these virtues, suited to their tender capacities, is given to each ward; and they are catechised upon this book—not in the way of getting by rote set answers to certain questions, but by answering questions in their own manner, to ascertain how far they understand what they have read.

The occasions, exercises, and trials of virtues, are various, according to the nature of the virtue. . . .

This second department of the School of Morals consists, therefore, in placing the wards under circumstances which will give occasion to the exercise of the several virtues designed in particular to be cultivated.

An account of the methods by which this purpose is to be attempted, is reserved for future Reports. . . .

[D] *An Address to the Public, from the Philanthropic Society. To Which are Annexed, The Laws and Regulations of the Society, Etc.* (London: 1792), pp. 8-13, 25-26, 29 (editor's lib.)

. . . The Philanthropic Society aims at the prevention of crimes, by removing out of the way of evil counsel and evil company those children who are in the present state of things destined to ruin: in a word, to educate and instruct in some useful trade or occupation the *children of convicts,* or such other infant poor as are *engaged in a vagrant or profligate course of life.* . . .

To carry into effect these desirable purposes, it is the first business of the Society to select from the haunts of vice, profligacy, and beggary, such objects as appear most likely to become obnoxious to the laws, or prejudicial to the community; this task is committed to four Visitors appointed quarterly from the Governors at large, subject to the inspection and controul of the Committee; and in the execution of this duty, the assistance of the Magistrates, the Clergy, and all who are interested in the promotion of good morals and good government is most earnestly requested.*

*To those who may conceive that this Society is in any degree anticipated by the liberal provison, which is made throughout the kingdom for the poor, or

For the employment of the children, several houses are supported in a temporary situation in *St. George's Fields;* in each of these houses a master workman is placed for the purpose of teaching the children some useful trade. The trades already established are those of a Printer*, Carpenter, Shoemaker, and Taylor: the girls are at present educated as menial servants. A steward resides upon the spot to keep the accounts, distribute the provisions, &c. and the whole is under the care of a Chaplain superintendent, (to be also resident near the spot) who sees that the workmen do their duty, and instructs the children in religion and morals.

It is the intention of the Society, as soon as their funds will admit, and other circumstances prove favourable, to employ a considerable number of hands in the different branches of agriculture; and occasionally to send others, under proper directions, to cultivate waste lands, or to assist in carrying on useful and laborious manufactures in different parts of the kingdom.**

The Society is under the direction of a President, eight Vice-Presidents, a Treasurer, a Secretary, a Chaplain superintendant, and a Committee of twenty-four members chosen by the Society at large. Besides these, there are four Visitors chosen quarterly, and three Auditors of Accounts, the nature of whose respective offices will be better understood by referring to the Laws and Regulations. The Committee meet every Friday, at eleven o'clock, precisely, at the St. Paul's Coffee-house, in St. Paul's Church-yard. . . .

Among this number [of children] are to be found many, who, though young in years, were yet old in iniquity. There are amongst them boys who have been guilty of felonies, burglaries, and other

---

that any part of this plan might be adopted in our workhouses, the reply is obvious. The overseers of the poor do their duty, if they receive every *application* for relief: our business is with those chiefly who do *not apply*. It is the part of the Society to inspect the abodes of profligacy and dishonesty, to *find out* the proper objects, and to *allure* them from their evil habits and connections by peculiar advantages, and peculiarly good treatment.

* The trade of the Bricklayer has been discontinued, because as the buildings in the late situation of the Reform near Hackney were completed, the boys could not be employed, unless they went out to work, by which means they would have been removed from inspection, and greatly endangered in their morals by mixing with various characters, and frequently resorting to public houses. On mature deliberation, therefore, it was resolved to discontinue, at least for the present, the trade of the Bricklayer, and to take up that of the Printer, as there were printing-materials belonging to the Society, and as the boys might be employed in this both usefully and profitably.

**Some of the younger children of both sexes, whose labour could be productive of little benefit to the Institution, have lately been sent to work in a WORSTED MANUFACTORY, near Nottingham, conducted by the Revolution Mill Company, and are placed under the immediate protection of a gentleman of known humanity and benevolence.

crimes. Yet, singular as it may appear, these very children are now become no less remarkable for industry, decency, and obedience, than they formerly were for the contrary vices.

They appear all cheerful and happy. They are scarcely ever found guilty of profaneness or any irregularity of conduct. . . .

A CONCISE DETAIL OF A FEW OF THE CHILDREN WHO HAVE BEEN RECEIVED INTO THE REFORM

There are at present upwards of 90 children, male and female, in the Reform, among these are several who have been taken from prisons; several who have been rescued from the retreats of villany, and the haunts of prostitution. The following select ACCOUNT *of some few of the objects who have been admitted, will best illustrate the nature of the institution, and recommend it to the attention of a benevolent Public.*

In this account the names of the children are carefully concealed, because it would be cruel to brand them with their parents' crimes, or to record those faults of their own, which were once committed from necessity, but are now atoned for by amendment.

—— and ——. An unhappy female in Newgate was sentenced to be transported to Botany-Bay for 14 years. Her husband was dead, and she had no friend in the world to take the charge of two poor children, a little boy and girl, who were wandering desolate about the streets. Two of the Visitors went to this unfortunate mother. Her great concern was for these unprotected children; and the only comfort she could receive was to know that they were admitted into the Reform. Before she sailed for Botany-Bay, she was indulged with an interview with them in the presence of proper officers of the Reform, when few can conceive the violence of her emotions, or the warmth of her gratitude to the Society.

—— His father is a drunken brutal fellow, who occasioned the death of one child, by turning him in his mother's arms out of doors in severe weather; the boy a vagrant in the streets, almost naked.

——, was in so complete a state of vagrancy that he had never slept in a bed for two years previous to his admission into the Reform: he is now as singular for his industry and obedience. . . .

—— 12 and —— 13. Had wandered about the country, with their vagrant mother, from their infancy, subsisting by beggary and plunder. She deserted them about four months before their admission, during which time they were taken up by some parish-officers, cloathed, and sent to London. They came to the Reform and begged to be received.

86

——. A friendless and fatherless boy, whose sole maintenance for three years was the casual employments of the public streets. He was apprehended for a theft, and recommended to the Society's care by Sir Sampson Wright.

——. An orphan who came up out of the Country; knows not his parish; was found begging and almost naked in the streets.

The greater number of the boys and girls when admitted were deplorably ignorant. Very few knew their letters: but now they have made such a progress in reading, that many of the boys and almost all the girls can read a chapter in the Bible, and the rest have made a proportional progress according to the time they have been learning. This must be considered as no small advancement, when it is known that the only time allotted for this purpose is a Sunday evening school, after the children have been twice at church: and a short interval between their working hours and bed-time, in which they are obliged to learn the lesson appointed for the week.

The Society gratefully acknowledge the kind indulgence of several Clergymen in favouring them with their churches or chapels, and the essential service received from the benevolent exertions of others in ably pleading their cause before the Public. They doubt not but these distinguished favours will continue and multiply while they assiduously labour to promote the general good, to combine economy, instruction, and industry, together in promoting the reformation of the children of the Criminal poor.

The benefits of this institution are not confined to the metropolis and it's environs. Children have been recommended by Magistrates and others from various parts of the country, and have been admitted as proper objects.

> [E] *An Account of the Nature and Views of the Philanthropic Society* . . . (London, 1799), p. 8 (editor's lib.)

[SUPERVISION AFTER RELEASE][1]

Till after seven years (the usual term of apprenticeship) had elapsed, it could not be expected that any *succession* of objects would take place to make room for others; but at the anniversary, in April, 1796, were exhibited the *first fruits* of this noble Institution, when *four young men,* who had completed their term of servitude within the Reform, were presented to a very numerous and respectable assembly, *regenerated* in their morals, complete

1. During the year 1798 rewards for good behavior to children in the Reform amounted to £ 64-14s.-3d. Apprentice-fees, Indentures, and Gratuities to Girls for their good behavior in Service totalled £ 24-13s-0d.

masters of their business, and useful members of society. Others, in a similar way, have annually gone forth into the world with character and abilities to acquire their own livelihood; and at this time there are now serving their apprenticeships to the masters within the Reform, no less than 54 boys, who, there is every reason to expect, will go out under the same advantages. Several also have had their indentures assigned over to masters without the Reform, who have applied for them, and continue to express satisfaction with their behaviour.

In order to extend the benefits of the Institution to a still greater number of objects than the funds will enable them to maintain within the Reform, the Committee endeavour to obtain masters out of the Reform for those boys that have become entitled to good characters, by paying an annual sum with each for the two or three first years of their apprenticeship; and propose to distribute rewards to such of *those* boys who behave well, either at the end of their several apprenticeships, or at any intermediate periods, when they appear to merit them. And they continue the protection of the Society to all boys so placed out, putting each of them under the *guardianship* of some *one* of the Committee, or Governor of the Society, whose residence near the boy and his master may enable him to watch over the conduct of each towards the other. . . .

[F] *An Account of the Nature and Present State of the Philanthropic Society* . . . (London, 1804), pp. 11, 13, 15, 17, 21 (Brit. Mus.)

[Five boys under sentence of death were accepted by the Society to prevent their execution-Children were seldom taken younger than eight or nine or older than twelve- Investigations were made of all applications. If the Society was unable to take an applicant his name would be placed on a waiting list, but admissions were not necessarily taken in order of listing- Emergency cases could be given the preference.]

The Society has for the reception of the children taken under its care, an house at Bermondsey, called, "the Reform," and a large manufactory, in St. George's Fields, for the boys;—and a spacious building, adjoining to the manufactory, for the girls.

All boys admitted on account of own delinquency, are sent in the first instance to the Reform. This very important addition to the Society's establishment, was made in 1802, partly in consequence of the inconvenience and impropriety of placing such as were criminal, amongst those, who had not been received as guilty of any crime, and partly from the necessity of keeping boys of the former description under a stricter superintendence, and in more close confinement, than was consistent with the regulations of a manufactory. . . . [After being in the opinion of the Chaplain] "sufficently reformed" they are transferred to the manufactory, and placed on the same footing with the rest of the boys there. . . .

The profits of the trades [carried on in the manufactory] . . . are considerable . . . a portion of the boy's earnings is appropriated, by way of reward, to such of them as are industrious, part of which is paid immediately, and the remainder* reserved for their use, till they have served out their apprenticship, and cease to belong to the Society. The boys of the Manufactory are not always confined within their own walls, but are occasionally allowed to carry out parcels, and treated like other apprentices, or the boys in great schools. . . .

The Manufactory will be shown to any respectable person, who may chuse to visit it; and the Committee will be obliged to those, who will take the trouble of inserting any remarks or observations, which may occur on what they see there, in the Superintendent's journal, or communicate them to the Committee.

. . . .The Committee have adopted the plan of apprenticing out some of the best behaved boys to tradesmen of good character with an handsome premium; the apprentices so put out, are however still considered as under the care of the Society; the conduct and situation of each of them is inquired into from time to time, and regular reports of the result of such inquiries are laid before the Committee once a quarter;—they also become entitled, on appearing before the Committee with satisfactory testimony of their good behaviour, to certain rewards, at stated times during their apprenticeship, or at its conclusion.

The girls are placed in a building contiguous to the Manufactory; but all intercourse between them and the boys is effectually prevented by a wall of considerable height. They are in general the offspring of convicts, such only being received in consequence of their own misconduct, as may have been guilty of a single act of dishonesty, or have misbehaved at a very early age;—for the Society, having no means of separating the two classes of females from each other, are obliged to act with great caution in their

* A boy, who had received his indentures in March last had then due to him £20-14s. for the portion of his earnings laid by for him while he had been in the Manufactory;—there are others, whose apprenticeships are not yet expired, whose rewards at present amount to from 10 to £15.

admissions of such as have been criminal: whenever therefore there is reason to apprehend from the age or former course of life of the female, on whose behalf application is made for admission, that habits have been contracted, or a knowledge of vice acquired, which would render her a dangerous associate for those whose minds are uncontaminated, she is of necessity deemed inadmissible. The girls are brought up for menial servants; they make their own clothing, and shirts for the boys, and wash and mend for the Manufactory;—besides which, their earnings in plain work have for the last two years been considerable:—when of proper age they are placed out, at low wages, in respectable families, and receive rewards for good behaviour, at the end of the first and second years of their service.

[Visits of ladies, and their suggestions, are welcomed]

. . . The number of children within the Society's walls at present are, 110 boys (of whom 18 are in the Reform, and 92 in the Manufactory), and 49 girls; there are also 20 apprentices serving masters out of the Manufactory, but still under the protection of the Society, as before stated, all of whom have been put out since the month of April, 1801, when the present system of apprenticing was adopted.

Description of Some of the Children Admitted in 1803

[Names of children omitted with reasons for same.]

A Boy, aged about 12,—was tried and capitally convicted for house-breaking, at the assizes at Oxford; he received sentence of death, but was recommended to mercy by the Judge, through the humane interposition of Stephen Lushington, Esq. His Majesty was graciously pleased to grant him a pardon, on the Society's engaging to receive him. This unfortunate boy was turned out of doors by a man who had married his mother; he then wandered about the country with a party of vagrants for some time, till, by their instigation, he committed the offense for which (unless this Society could have received him), he would probably have suffered.

A boy, aged 14,—convicted of felony, at the County Sessions of Stafford, and recommended by desire of the magistrates, by the Honourable Richard Ryder.

A boy, aged 10,—had stolen a metal watch: on account of his youth it was thought more proper to put him under the care of this Society than to carry him into a court of justice.

Home Investigation of a Juvenile Delinquent by a Constable upon Order of a Magistrate, 1790

The Gentleman's Magazine (February, 1790), p. 173 (UNC Lib.)

January 26 [1790]. A boy under ten years of age was brought before the Magistrates in Bow-Street, and on the oath of Elizabeth Bamber charged with stealing half a guinea. Mrs. Bamber, who keeps a grocer's shop in Russel-street, Bloomsbury, saw the boy, from her back parlour, reach something to two children from behind the counter, who instantly ran away; but the boy, who said his name was George King, being seized, confessed he had taken the money, and that his accomplices had made off with it; he said, farther, that about three years ago he had the misfortune to lose both father and mother, and that ever since he has lived by pilfering and stealing. Being asked where he lodged? He said in a cellar in St. Giles's, where fourteen or fifteen boys of different ages assemble, and pay two-pence a night each for their lodging. A constable being dispatched by the magistrate to examine the lodging, reported, that what the boy had said was true; that the cellar where they all lay was filthy beyond description; and that the fellow who rented the cellar got a livelihood by letting it. The magistrate lamented that he was under the necessity of committing the boy for trial; and that, if no provision can be made for these deserted children at home, it surely is charity to send them abroad, where they may be usefully employed.

Harmful Effect of Indecent Publications, 1790-1792

[A] *Memoirs of an Unfortunate Young Lady; which appeared in Numbers IV, V, and VI of the Citizen: Published in The Bristol Mercury* . . . (Bristol, 1790) (Brit. Mus.)

[This touching and convincing autobiography is dated "Bristol, May 11, 1790" and is signed "A Female Penitent." "The public may be certified that this is a true account of an unhappy young woman—though somewhat corrected and improved." She attributes her downfall to two older girl companions.]

. . . [My companions] were great readers—and procured for themselves, and lent to me several books that were TOO BAD indeed, and had the most ruinous tendency. To mention their titles is needless, and might be injurious to any who may see this account.

I do not know whether or not the keepers of Circulating Libraries let out such books at this time—but I am sure that such poisonous trash were then to be borrowed, though at some extraordinary prices, for I was sometimes sent to procure them. . . . I doubt not that almost so many girls have been seduced by books as by men. These companions of mine were indefatigable in procuring a continual supply of such infernal volumes, and in imparting and conversing about them to me. Infamous song books, histories, memoirs, trials, plays, and jest books were poured in upon me. In time we all became inured to the most improper conversation and to a freedom and boldness of behaviour that made us noted and censured by our acquaintance, and the whole neighborhood. . . .

> [B] *The Evils of Adultery and Prostitution; with an Inquiry into the Causes of their Present Alarming Increase, and Some Means Recommended for Checking their Progress* (London, 1792), pp. 48, 51, 53-54 (Goldsmiths' Lib.)

[This anonymous author, if not a clergyman, was a man of high principles and religious convictions. The first chapter describes the evils of prostitution, to society, as well as to the direct participants. Chapter two takes up the causes, and chapter three the remedies. It is ably written with references to Roman customs, Biblical allusions, etc.]

PART II. CAUSES OF THE PRESENT ALARMING INCREASE OF ADULTERY AND PROSTITUTION

[The profligate and debauched manners of men of rank and fortune, and the rage for pleasure characterizing women of all classes, are given as two leading causes of increase in vice.]

But a third cause is the ready circulation which is given to this vice. The daily papers are constantly retailing connections of this kind; and thus they become the vehicles of vice from the center to the most distant corners of the kingdom. They are told as articles of news, and as common occurrences, which excite neither surprise nor detestation. . . . The present practice of circulating so fully and so speedily, every article of this kind, is a poison to the youth, and indeed pollutes every age. Adultery and elopements constitute a material part of our news, and, being commonly retailed with numerous and minute circumstances, help to inflame the passions, and to abate our horror for the crimes. No paragraphs are more greedily read, than those which relate to business of this kind.

But, not content with making them an article of news, you have frequently the whole trials for adultery and rapes published at full length, with every circumstance belonging to them. . . . The alarming length to which such impudent writings are carried, loudly calls for the interposition of parliament. . . .

A fourth cause of the profligacy of the present age, is that mass of novels and romances which people of all ranks and ages do so greedily devour. This is a new species of entertainment, almost totally unknown to former ages. . . .

Novels have an unhappy effect on the rising generation; they debauch the morals, and they corrupt the taste. Were there only an equality of chances in favour of morals, this might stand as an apology for these writings: but the fact certainly is, that where one is instructed, one hundred are poisoned. . . . But the worst effect: Novels dress out vice in pleasing colours, gild over all its deformities, and thus insensibly instil the deadly poison into the thoughtless and unwary heart. The dissipated rake, who glories in his debaucheries, is painted often as humane, generous, and benevolent; whilst the heedless female, for the sake of these accomplishments, forgets his want of principle, his diseased body, and his rotten heart. This kind of employment is worse than idleness. Many young girls, from morning to night, hang over this pestiferous reading, to the neglect of industry, health, proper exercise, and to the ruin both of body and of soul. And this pernicious practice is not confined to girls only of fortune, but extends to every age and rank; and there are instances even of servant girls who are well acquainted with all the fashionable romances. Full of the romantic ideas that they collect from such books, they long to copy the manners, and to share the fate of some of their favorite heroines. . . .

Sale of Obscene Books and Prints to English School Children, 1803

Part the First, of an Address to the Public, from the Society for the Suppression of Vice, Instituted, in Iondon, 1802 (London, 1803). (Brit. Mus.) and Part the Second, containing on Account of the Proceedings of the Society, from its Original Institution (London, 1804), pp. 15, 19-21 (Brit. Mus.)

[The Society was established after a Royal Proclamation "For the Encouragement of Piety and Virtue, and for preventing and punishing of Vice, Profaneness, and Immorality." The objects of the Society were stated as assisting magistrates in enforcing existing laws for the regular observance of the Lords Day; the suppression of blasphemous, licentious and obscene books and prints; the preventing of frauds, in selling by false weights and measures; the protecting of female innocence, by the punishment of procurers; correcting the complicated evils resulting from lotteries; the reforming of excesses committed in riotous and disorderly houses, brothels and gaming houses; the punishing of breaches of the peace, profane swearing, libelling, and cruelty to animals. Societies of similar design known as Societies for the Reformation of Manners, etc. were established in the early part of the reign of William and Mary, in the latter part of the seventeenth century.]

BLASPHEMOUS, LICENTIOUS, AND OBSCENE BOOKS AND PRINTS

. . . The information on which the Society have acted, in this branch of their exertions, has been derived from different sources; it has been generally supported by the confession of the offenders themselves, and the testimony of others connected with them; and it has been confirmed upon the strictest investigation in courts of justice. It appears that the traffic in question is very extensive, that it does not merely afford a precarious subsistence to a few hawkers and pedlars, but that some foreigners, of apparent respectability, and and of no inconsiderable property, are engaged in it: and it is by no means confined to the Metropolis, but, by a regular and established intercourse, is conveyed through a great part of the United Kingdom.

From a respectable quarter the Society derived the information that a considerable house, consisting of several partners, employed about thirty persons, who went from place to place, generally two in company, ostensibly dealing in looking glasses, and other articles of fair trade; but vending, whenever they could, indecent prints, watch-papers, and other articles of a like kind- and that two artists,* of whose names and residence the Society are in possession, were in the habit of designing and engraving many of the plates.

The following particulars were obtained by a member of the Committee who had an opportunity of conversing with one of these itinerant print-sellers, who, during the last summer infested Brighton and its vicinity. He was plainly told that they all belonged to a partnership, which carried on the trade of obscene books and prints in London, that there were twelve in number, who travelled the country, being supplied with goods by the partners in town; that when their stock was exhausted, they received a fresh supply

---

* Not only etching, engraving, and drawing, but sculpture and modelling, and particularly the latter, are also abused to the odious purpose of corrupting the minds of youth. Of the existence of this practice, the Society have conclusive evidence.

by the waggon, wherever they might happen to be; that four of them were then on their route at Brighton, and had been for the last three months in that neighborhood; that they intended to remove to Maidstone, and thence to London; that at other times they had been at York and Manchester, and at many other inland towns; that the other eight itinerant partners were then in Norfolk and Suffolk—that their mode of travelling was generally in parties of two, and sometimes singly; but that all of the same party met once in every week, at a town previously agreed on among themselves: that the partners in London designed many of the articles of prints and pictures; that the itinerants also dealt in telescopes, and were in the habit of visiting schools, where they sold many prints and pictures to youth of both sexes. Being asked how he gained admittance into schools, as the heads of them were circumspect and vigilant, he smiled, and significantly said, he knew how to get in. . . .

Information of a similar nature, strongly corroborating the above, was obtained from a person who had himself been connected with these men, by supplying them with frames, and other articles of trade. He stated, that many of those engaged in this traffic were itinerant Italians, who were employed as agents by persons in London; that the articles in which they dealt were sent to them by the waggon, and sold by them at the same price at which they received them; that at Newcastle he knew of six Italians who made *that* town their principal place of residence, receiving a constant supply of prints from London, and dispersing them over the neighbouring country; that he had frequently been in company with them when they settled their accounts; that he had often heard them say they had sold obscene prints at Boarding Schools through the medium of servants; that he had known them absent from their lodgings at Newcastle for a week together, but that they always returned to the same place.

Evidence has also been procured, that some apparently respectable houses, consisting principally of foreigners, are concerned in supporting this itinerant trade, by supplying the hawkers engaged in it with the goods which they carry about the country. And, considering the number of these hawkers who meet the eye of the traveller, and also that, according to the confession* of the parties themselves, many of them are entirely supported by the sale of

* From one of the persons who had been connected with these itinerants, by supplying them with frames, &c, it appeared that their number in the kingdom was about *six hundred*; one of them, indeed, informed a person employed by the Society that there were *eight hundred* of them; this number may possibly be exaggerated, but that they are alarmingly numerous cannot be doubted. . . .

these articles, it must appear that the trade in question is carried on to an extent which affords just cause for the most serious apprehension to every friend of society.

To the above statement the Society have further to add, that the diffusion of this subtle poison is not confined to men, but that females are also engaged in the same deadly work. It has been discovered that women infest the neighbourhood of the Metropolis, who circulate the very same kind of books and prints as the itinerants above-mentioned; and that, under the pretext of purchasing cast-off clothes from servants, or of vending some trifling articles, they gain admittance into female boarding schools, where they find means to carry on their pernicious traffic without suspicion or interruption.

[Many obscene prints were imported from the continent. The mistresses of boarding schools and head masters of public schools were warned by the Society through letters of the dangers of admitting itinerant peddlers. Several peddlers through information supplied by the Society were convicted and received sentences of from six months to two years imprisonment and the pillory.]

The Refuge for the Destitute, London, Relieves Children Discharged from Prisons, 1804-1832

[A] *The Annual Report of the Refuge for the Destitute, for the Year 1832* . . . (London, 1833), pp. 17-23 (Yale Univ. Lib.)

A SHORT PREFATORY ACCOUNT OF THE INSTITUTION

The Refuge for the Destitute, Hackney Road [For Females] and Hoxton, [For Males] was founded in the year 1804, with the design of counteracting the progress of youthful delinquency, by providing an asylum for young persons of both sexes, who, having been discharged from prison or the hulks, or having forfeited their character by dishonest practices, are desirous of returning to the paths of industry and rectitude.

To youthful delinquents of this class, the Refuge for the Destitute opens its doors, and affords those means of instruction and reformation which are suited to their deplorable condition. Within its walls they are for a season withdrawn from the allurements of temptation, and the polluting influence of evil associates. They are taught to look with abhorrence on their former habits of life, and, as far as human teaching is effectual, to adopt those of religion, industry, and subordination. They are employed in useful occupations, as shoemaking, tailoring, laundry work, needle work, household business, &c.

"Repentance towards God, and faith toward our Lord Jesus Christ," are daily set before them, as the only sure basis on which to ground their resolutions of permanent amendment. And after remaining a certain time, varying from one year to two and a half in this asylum, and conducting themselves conformably to its rules, these youthful penitents are restored to society with reformed characters, and, in many instances, there is reason to believe with renewed hearts; and are either sent home to their friends, provided with reputable situations or apprenticed to respectable tradesmen at the expense of the Establishment.

[B] [Second] *Report of the Committee of the Society for the Improvement of Prison Discipline and for the Reformation of Juvenile Offenders, 1820.* (London, 1820), pp. xxviii-xxix, 2-4 (Brit. Mus.)

An arrangement was . . . made with the Committee of the "Refuge for the Destitute" by which a part of the premises of that Institution were fitted up, at the expense of the Society for the Improvement of Prison Discipline, &c. This temporary asylum was opened in June 1818, when several distressed individuals, discharged from different prisons, were admitted, till they could be satisfactorily provided for, either by procuring them suitable employment, by furnishing them with working tools and decent clothing, by reconciling them to their friends, or, in the failure of other relief, by passing them to their legal settlements.

The total number of persons thus admitted has been 210; of whom 177 have been provided with employment, restored to their friends, or passed to their respective parishes; 13 remain in the Establishment; 20 have absconded, or have been dismissed for improper conduct . . . a very large proportion have conducted themselves with the strictest propriety. . . .

[CASES OF CHILDREN IN THE TEMPORARY REFUGE]

3. W. R. age 15, committed to Newgate for stealing a loaf of bread, which he was induced to take, to keep himself from starving, was sentenced to be flogged and discharged; placed in the Temporary Refuge for three months, and provided with a situation in a reputable family, where he has behaved with much propriety. . . .

17. M. M. a girl, 8 years of age, was found in solitary confinement in one of the prisons in the metropolis. She had been

committed for one month, on a charge of child-stealing. It appeared the parents had driven this girl into the streets, to beg, sing ballads, or sell matches, and whenever she went home without money she was severely beaten and turned out of doors. This cruelty had probably induced her to entice a little child from its home, with a view to take off its clothes, in attempting which she was detected. The time of imprisonment being just expired, she must have been turned into the streets, helpless and destitute, if the visitors had not placed her in the Temporary Refuge. Her conduct there was satisfactory, and she has been placed at a respectable manufactory in the vicinity of the metropolis.

[C] *Fifth Report of the Committee of the Society for the Improvement of Prison Discipline, etc.* (London, 1823), p. 70 (Brit. Mus.)

[RELIEF OF BOYS DISCHARGED FROM PRISON]

In the course of the last year, the Committee have continued to extend essential relief to distressed boys, on their discharge from the prisons of the metropolis, who have expressed a desire to abandon their criminal courses. There are few situations of such entire destitution as that of a boy thus circumstanced. His character is lost: friendless and without protection, he has no means of obtaining employment, or of procuring subsistence. It is not long since that eight boys were released on the same day from Newgate. The Court had sentenced them to be flogged; and the sentence was, as usual, carried into effect on the day of their discharge. The boys were then immediately turned into the streets with their backs sore from the flagellation, and in such a state that two of them who were received by the Committee into the "Temporary Refuge," were obliged, immediately on their admission, to be placed in the infirmary; one of them, a lad of fifteen, having received seventy lashes.

[Other annual reports of the Society contain accounts and case studies of children released from prison who were helped by the Temporary Refuge.]

[D] *The Annual Report of the Refuge for the Destitute, for the Year 1832* . . . (London, 1833) (Yale Univ. Lib.)

[THE REFUGE FORCED TO CLOSE IN 1832]

During twenty-seven years that the Refuge has been open to the public, upwards of *four thousand one hundred* juvenile outcasts have received maintenance and instruction within its walls, many of whom are now respectable members of society, and some are *subscribers* to that institution by which they were early rescued from destruction. It is distressing, however, to be obliged to add, that the number of young applicants for relief, against whom, on account of *want of funds,* the Refuge has been obliged to shut its doors, has amounted to considerably more than six thousand, and may be calculated at not less than three hundred annually. . . .

The Funds whereby the Refuge for the Destitute is maintained arise out of annual subscriptions, donations, legacies, and collections after sermons.

For some years they have also been indebted to his Majesty's Government for an annual grant.

Children in Newgate Prison, London, 1813-1817

> Hon. H. G. Bennet, *A Letter to the Common Council and Livery of the City of London, on the Abuses Existing in Newgate; Showing the Necessity of an Immediate Reform in the Management of that Prison* (London, 1818), pp. 9, 46-47, 56-57, 62-63 (Brit. Mus.)

The keeper of Newgate never attended divine service; and the ordinary did not consider the morals of even the children, who were in Prison, as being under his care and attention. *No care was taken to inform him of the sick, till he got a warning to perform a funeral.* There was no separation of the young from the old, the children of either sex from the hardened criminal. Boys of the tenderest years, and girls of the ages of ten, twelve, and thirteen were exposed to the vicious contagion, that predominated in all parts of the Prison; and drunkenness prevailed to such an extent, and was so common, that, unaccompanied with riot, it attracted no notice.*

. . . During the first three years of the period above referred to [i.e. 1813-15 inclusive], forty girls and two hundred and eight boys, under fifteen years of age, were committed to Newgate; and from the 1st of January, 1816, to the same day, 1817, eighty-five girls, and four hundred and twenty-nine boys, under twenty years of age, were confined in that Prison; and thus were more than five hundred young persons exposed last year to the contamination of the Prison System of the metropolis, and by much the greater proportion of them were associated with old offenders, and hardened delinquents.

* Commons' Report and Evidence, 1814.

I contend, that the public have a right to demand from the magistrates so to construct their Prisons, that of the children, the innocent at least, should not be made criminal by example and education. . . .

THE CONDEMNED CELLS

There are fifteen condemned cells in Newgate, each nine feet long by seven wide, furnished with one barrack or bedstead; and in which . . . two persons *may* lie. These cells were originally constructed for the solitary confinement of those who were condemned to death, in the period between their sentence and its execution. From their size, it is evident they were not designed to hold more than one person; and yet two are almost constantly confined there, and very often three. . . . On the 20th December last there were twenty-seven capital convicts in them. . . . Of the twenty-seven convicts, fifteen were under twenty years of age; and two of them infants of the tender years of thirteen and nine, who were both capitally convicted of highway robbery on the person, and by the evidence of a child of six years of age.

It must be remarked here, first, that about one in ten or twelve of the persons capitally convicted are executed: and, secondly, that sometimes three, four, and even six months elapse before their fate is determined. . . .

[The Prison Committee of Magistrates] . . . came to a resolution to place all the boys (*infants* as well as *children*), who were convicted, *ironed,* in the cells with the most hardened and guilty malefactors, there to remain, unless removed by the special order of the Prison Committee. . . . Accordingly, the first result of this inhuman and irrational order has been the placing of two children, infants in mind as well as body, ironed, in the same cell with another man. The good sense and humanity of Mr. Brown, the keeper, have instructed him to place them with a well-conducted and orderly convict; but they are still exposed to the conversation of all around them during the day; and if the cells, as is often the case, had been filled with persons of the most depraved habits and character, with these the children must have passed sixteen hours out of the twenty-four.

Children in Irons in the Bristol Gaol, 1815-1818

[A] John S. Harford, *Considerations Upon the Pernicious Influence of the Bristol Gaol, both in Relation to the Health and*

Morals of the Prisoners Confined Therein . . . Bristol, 1815,[1]
p. 23 (Brit. Mus.)

The Author of these Pages witnessed within the walls of the Gaol only a few days ago, a most affecting case. . . . He saw the irons put on a little boy only ten years old, who had just been brought into Prison for stealing a pound and a half of sugar (as the Gaoler stated) and carrying it to some iniquitous person, who was in the habit of encouraging young depredators in such practices. As soon as the irons were put on this little fellow, he was introduced into the Felons' court, which was crowded with a set of wretches, several of whom are said to be among the most abandoned of the class of Felons. Sad to say, there were four other young lads, mingled in the crowd—In what state of mind will these young offenders emerge from such society? Shall evils like these be still perpetuated?

[B] Thomas Fowell Buxton, *An Inquiry, Whether Crime and Misery Are Produced or Prevented, by our Present System of Prison Discipline* (2nd Ed.; London, 1818), pp. 155-56 (editor's lib.)

[Bristol Jail] In this yard is to be seen vice in all its stages; boys intermingle with men; the accused with the convicted; the venial offender with the veteran and atrocious criminal. Amongst a multitude of persons, whom the jailer described as having no other avocation or mode of livelihood but thieving, I counted eleven children,—children hardly old enough to be released from a nursery—hardly competent to understand the first principles of moral obligation—here receiving an education which, as it must unfit them for every thing useful, so it must eminently qualify them for that career which they are doomed to run. All charged or convicted of felony, without distinction of age, were in heavy irons—almost all were in rags—almost all were filthy in the extreme—almost all exhibited the appearance of ill health. The state of the prison, the desperation of the prisoners, broadly hinted in their conversation, and plainly expressed in their conduct—the uproar of oaths, complaints, and obscenity—the indescribable stench—presented together a concentration of the utmost misery with the utmost guilt—a scene of infernal passions and distresses, which few have imagination sufficient to picture, and of which fewer still would believe, that the original is to be found in this enlightened and happy country.

1. Alderman Wood of London who made a general survey of the gaols of England is reported (p. 38) to have said that the Bristol gaol was *the worst* he had seen. At night the felons slept in a damp, unventilated dungeon eighteen steps below the surface.

First Survey of Juvenile Delinquency in London, 1815-1816

Report of the Committee for Investigating the Causes of the Alarming Increase of Juvenile Delinquency in the Metropolis (London, 1816), pp. 5-10, 21-27, 29 (editor's lib.)

London, 18th May, 1816.

REPORT
&C. &C.

It is now about twelve months since the exertions of a few individuals were directed to the investigation of the cases of several boys, who had been convicted of capital offences. In prosecuting these inquiries, it was found, that Juvenile Delinquency existed in the metropolis to a very alarming extent; that a system was in action, by which these unfortunate lads were organized into gangs; that they resorted regularly to houses, where they planned their enterprises, and afterwards divided the produce of their plunder. These facts having been made known, a public meeting was convened, at which, after a due consideration of the subject, a Society was formed, the object of which was to obtain every possible information respecting the nature and causes of the evil in question, in order to ascertain the most efficient means of removing or diminishing it. It was considered, that such as Association should not confine itself to inquiry alone, but, that where relief could, with propriety, be extended to youths disposed to return into the paths of virtue, every assistance should, in such cases, be afforded.

Such was the origin of this Society. To accomplish its designs it was determined, that the prisons of the metropolis should be regularly visited by sub-committees appointed for that purpose, the youths in confinement separately examined and privately admonished, the evil consequences of their conduct represented to them, and every persuasive used for their recovery which kindness could suggest. It was thought particularly desirable that these boys should be made to feel, as much as possible, not only the danger of their own condition, but also that of their former associates in guilt; in order that, from a regard for the welfare of their late companions, the boys who were in confinement might be induced to give information respecting them. It was deemed adviseable that these lads should be sought out and examined as circumstances would permit, and that no opportunity should be lost of impressing on their minds the hideousness of vice, and of contrasting it with that happiness and peace, which religion only can ensure.

Questions calculated to obtain the necessary information were framed. The metropolis was divided into districts, and sub-committees appointed respectively.

In conformity with these arrangements, the Society was rapidly put in motion. A list of 190 boys, the friends and associates of youths confined in Newgate, was soon obtained: these names were divided among the visitors; reports were speedily produced and recorded in a ledger provided for that purpose. Further lists of associates have, from time to time, been received from that prison only, containing upwards of seven hundred names.

These lists having been procured from boys in confinement, the accuracy of such documents was justly questionable; more especially, as a pecuniary inducement was deemed needful in the first stage of the business. Notwithstanding the suspicion that naturally accompanies information derived from such a source, and under such circumstances, the instances have not been many, in which the accounts received have, upon investigation, proved incorrect.

When the labours of the Committee were in their infancy, they anticipated difficulties: nor were their apprehensions unfounded. Besides the awkwardness arising from the nature of the pursuit, the Committee were not able, on all occasions, to convince the parents of the children whom they visited of the correctness of the motives which animated the Society; and, in such cases, of course, but little information could be obtained. In attending, also, at the prisons, the Committee frequently had no suitable opportunity of examining or admonishing the offending youths; and, if at any time favourable impressions were excited on their minds, the visitors had the mortification to reflect, that such feelings could be but transitory, as the boys were doomed to mix with characters the most atrocious; in a society, where the first risings of penitence would be repelled by mockery, and the name of religion treated as a jest. But, for these considerations, the Committee would doubtless have been in possession of a larger body of facts. They are, however, of opinion, that sufficient evidence has been collected to enable them to ascertain the causes in which the evil originates. The information which has been obtained may be generalized in the following order:—

1st. That, although the judgment which the Committee are able to form, relative to the extent of Juvenile Delinquency is very indefinite, there is reason to believe, from their inquiries, that there are some thousands of boys under seventeen years of age in the metropolis, who are daily engaged in the commission of crime.

2ndly. That these boys associate with professed thieves of mature age, and with girls, who subsist by prostitution.

3dly. That such characters frequent houses of the most infamous description, where they divide their plunder, and give loose to every vicious propensity.

4thly. That the following appear to be the principal causes of these dreadful practices:—

The improper conduct of parents.

The want of education.

The want of suitable employment.

The violation of the Sabbath, and habits of gambling in the public streets.

5thly. That, in addition to these primary causes, there are auxiliaries which powerfully contribute to increase and perpetuate the evil:—These may be traced to, and included under, the three following heads:—

The severity of the criminal code.

The defective state of the police.

The existing system of prison discipline. . . .

The severity of the criminal code, which inflicts the punishment of death on upwards of two hundred offences, acts very unfavourably on the mind of the juvenile delinquent; for, while the humanity of the present age forbids the execution of the greater part of these laws, the uncertainty of their operation encourages the offender to calculate, even if convicted, on a mitigated punishment. But if the laws have no tendency to prevent crime, it is truly shocking to witness the direct facilities which the vicious inclinations of the delinquent receive from the system on which the police of the metropolis is now conducted. The sum to which the officer is entitled on the conviction of a prisoner, for the most aggravated of the capital offences, is forty pounds. The practice of holding out rewards for the apprehension of criminals, in proportion to the enormity of their guilt, stimulates the officer to overlook the minor depredations of the incipient thief; and often might the youth be early arrested in his course, but for the principle on which it becomes the interest of the officer, that the young offender should continue in iniquity until he attains maturity in crime. The encouragement which the officers of police give to those pestiferous haunts, termed *"flash houses,"* to which thieves are accustomed to resort, is a very serious evil. In these nurseries of crime are to be found the most experienced and notorious thieves; boys and girls, from nine years of age; women of the most profligate description; associating indiscriminately, and mixing with the very men, who are employed for the preservation of public morals.

The Committee, in prosecuting their inquiries, have frequently visited the prisons of the metropolis. This part of their duty has often proved to them painful and heart rending. The mere sight of so many youths, under such circumstances, whose talents, if properly directed, would have qualified them to become valuable members of the community, is in itself sufficient to inspire the most inconsiderate with thoughtfulness; but if the spectacle alone has excited the regret of the Committee, their sorrow has been much enhanced by the conviction, that to the defective system of discipline, which exists in the prisons of London, the evil of Juvenile Delinquency owes in a great measure its aggravation. In these establishments, the youth committed for his first offence has been placed indiscriminately with hardened criminals. . . .

Dreadful, therefore, is the situation of the young offender: he becomes the victim of circumstances over which he has no control. The laws of his country operate not to restrain, but to punish, him. The tendency of the police is to accelerate his career in crime. If, when apprehended, he has not attained the full measure of guilt, the nature of his confinement is almost sure to complete it; and discharged, as he frequently is, pennyless, without friends, character, or employment, he is driven, for a subsistence, to the renewal of depredations.

Of the many boys, whose cases have been investigated by the Committee, they have met with very few, of whose amendment they should despair by the application of proper means. Small indeed is the number of those, in whom the sense of virtue is wholly extinct—who do not retain some portion of valuable feeling—some latent seed, which, if judiciously cherished, would flourish and expand. The Society have, in fact, been instrumental in assisting and restoring to credit and usefulness, many who had widely wandered from the paths of honesty; and, from the success which has hitherto attended the exertions of the Committee, they feel a decided and growing conviction, that, if in the treatment of juvenile delinquents the degree of punishment were proportioned to the nature of the offence—if the operation of that punishment were uniform and certain—if, during confinement, they were not exposed to the temptations of idle hours and corrupt society—if the infliction of bodily punishment were to give way to mildness of persuasion and gentleness of reproof—if appeals were oftener made to the moral sensibility of these youths; and exertions used to raise, rather than degrade, them in their own estimation—the number of juvenile depredators would materially diminish, and the conductors of public prisons would frequently enjoy the unspeakable felicity of turning the culprit from the "error of his ways." . . .

The following brief Outline of a few Cases is given, in order to convey a general Idea of the Characters that have come under the Notice of the Society.

A. B. aged 13 years. His parents are living. He was but for a short time at school. His father was frequently intoxicated; and, on these occasions, the son generally left home, and associated with bad characters, who introduced him to houses of ill fame, where they gambled until they had spent or lost all their money. This boy has been five years in the commission of crime, and been imprisoned for three separate offences. Sentence of death has twice been passed on him.

C. D. aged 10 years. He was committed to prison in the month of April, 1815, having been sentenced to seven years imprisonment for picking pockets. His mother only is living, but he does not know where she resides. He has a very good capacity, but cannot read. When first visited, he discovered much anxiety about his situation; but every favourable impression was effaced shortly after his confinement in prison. . . .

Further Description of Juvenile Delinquency in London, 1818

[First] *Report of the Committee of the Society for the Improvement of Prison Discipline, and for the Reformation of Juvenile Offenders* (London, 1818), pp. 8, 13, 15, 17, 20, 32 (Brit. Mus.)

Patron, His Royal Highness the Duke of Gloucester
Treasurer, Thomas Furly Forster, Esq.
Chairman of the Committee, Samuel Hoare, Jun. Esq.
Secretaries, Peter Bedford, William Crawford

[During their visits to prisons to interview young offenders, members of the Committee for Investigating the Causes of the Alarming Increase of Juvenile Delinquency in the Metropolis, first organized in 1815, were so impressed "with the conviction that the neglect of prison discipline was one great cause of crime and misery" that they decided to enlarge their sphere of action, and "to make the consideration of prison discipline a primary object of their association." Consequently, the name of the committee was changed to that of the Society for the Improvement of Prison Discipline and for the Reformation of Juvenile Offenders. Quakers were the leading spirits of the Society, which was made up of fifty or more "benevolent and intelligent gentlemen of various religious denominations." The first annual report of the Society in 1818 was followed by other reports in 1820, 1821, 1822, 1823, 1824, 1827, and 1832. Perhaps because of their scarcity these important reports have been largely overlooked by the present generation of penologists.

The Society gradually became more interested in general prison reform than in reclaiming juvenile delinquents. Prisons throughout the Kingdom were visited, their individual condition described in a manner reminiscent of Howard and Neild, local reforms were noted and further improvements recommended in the Society's reports. Even foreign prisons were visited. "In the years 1818 and 1819, Mr. William Allen, a member of this Committee, accompanied by Mr. Stephen Grellet of New York, made an extensive tour of the Continent. These gentlemen devoted much time and attention to ascertain the state of the prisons in the different countries they visited." The Committee also maintained frequent correspondence with leaders in prison reform in Philadelphia and in New York, and exchanged prison documents and reports.

The warm, humanitarian spirit of the Society, so evident in its early efforts to save juvenile delinquents, was slowly replaced somehow by a reactionary, "hard-boiled" attitude, typical of prison administrators. The Society strongly believed in employment for all prisoners, both tried and untried. In 1821 it noted with great satisfaction that the tread-mill system of prison labor invented by Mr. Cubitt of Ipswich had a very repressive effect on prisoners subjected to it, in that few prisoners returned, and the Society urged the wide-spread adoption of the tread-mill. The philosophy of the Society as expressed in 1822 was "that severe punishment must form the basis of an effective system of prison discipline. The personal suffering of the offender must be the first consideration, as well for his own interest, as for the sake of example; he must be made to feel that this suffering attends the infringement of the laws." It favored hard labor, regular employment, spare diet, occasional solitary confinement, habits of order and silence, seclusion from vicious associates, constant control, religious instruction, and moral restraint. Tread-mill and hand-crank labor, described in great detail in the annual reports were ideally adapted to carrying out these views. One notes with disappointment, too, that in the midst of the nation-wide debate on reform of the criminal law the Society refused to offer an opinion "on the efficacy of capital punishment, or of transportation."

The Society did perform a real service, however, in calling attention to the worst prison abuses: use of underground dungeons, as at Yarmouth Town Gaol; immorality in the prisons (Fleet Prison was described as the greatest brothel in the city); whippings and chainings of prisoners; long-term gaol confinement of the insane; and mixing of adult prisoners and children. A case is cited of a nine-year-old boy who had been in prison eighteen times.

In addition to investigating and reporting on prison conditions and problems of prison administration and labor, the Society as early as 1818 established in connection with the Refuge for the Destitute, a Temporary Refuge for Discharged Prisoners, some of whom were young children recently released from gaols.[1] This Temporary Refuge was maintained as long as the Society was in existence and was a constant drain on its finances. In 1827 and again in 1832 the Society reported an increasingly heavy debt, which, with dwindling voluntary contributions to the Society, probably accounts for its closing in 1832. It was not until 1866 that a general prison reform agency was again set up in England, when Lord Brougham organized the Howard Association, which, under the name Howard League for Penal Reform, continues its valuable work to the present time.]

London, 16th May 1818.

[ATTENTION IS CALLED TO THE ALARMING INCREASE OF CRIME, MORE ESPECIALLY AMONGST CHILDREN AND YOUTH OF BOTH SEXES]

The lamentable depravity which, for the last few years, has shown itself so conspicuously amongst the youth of both sexes, in the Metropolis and its environs, occasioned the formation of a Society for investigating the causes of the increase of Juvenile Delinquency. It required no depth of penetration to foresee, that persons, early inured to crime, would, if no means of correction or prevention were employed, sink deeper in the abyss of vice. . . .

The Society in 1815 commenced its labours; and, sensible that an accurate knowledge was first indispensably requisite, spared no pains to procure the best information. For this purpose, the Committee arranged their members into subdivisions, who visited the various prisons in London and its neighborhood; examined the boys apart, pursued their inquiries amongst their parents, friends, or associates; kept a journal of many hundred cases, in which all particulars deserving of consideration were carefully recorded and preserved; and, in short, adopted every possible measure to acquire an

1. See pp. 97-98.

accurate knowledge of the extent of juvenile delinquency, and the principal causes that occasioned its extraordinary and still advancing increase. Experience has shown that the information thus obtained was generally correct, though of course, incorrect statements and erroneous accounts were at times received. The Committee however are satisfied, that they have prosecuted the investigation successfully; the general results of their labours have already been submitted to the public, in a short Report.

. . . The records of all the police offices; the commitments, trials, and convictions at Newgate and other gaols; all the information, howsoever acquired, unites in demonstrating the lamentable fact, that juvenile delinquency has of late years increased to an unprecedented extent, and is still rapidly and progressively increasing; that the crimes committed by the youthful offenders are often of the worst description; and that an organized system for instruction in vice, and the encouragement of depravity is regularly maintained.[2]

The first and principal cause of youthful aberration from the path of virtue, is the neglect of moral and religious Education. . . . Subsidiary to this cause, and most powerfully operative, is the bad example of parents, who, by their own conduct, initiate their children in vice, and by participating in the gains of plunder, encourage them in the commencement of their wicked and dishonest career.

The second cause is the want of suitable Employment for children in early life; whence arise habits of idleness and dissipation, permanently injurious to their future welfare.

The third cause is one which every humane mind must contemplate with deep regret and compassion; the strong temptation to dishonesty, which has too frequently of late years prevailed, from a want of the necessaries to support life. The Committee have great pain in stating, that many such instances have come to their knowledge: it not unfrequently happens, that boys, committed to gaols for petty offences, are discharged upon the wide world, without any alternative, but plunder or starvation. It is in vain to exclaim, that by the laws of England, no such extremity is permitted, that the parishes or workhouses afford a retreat; it may be so in theory, the truth is otherwise in practice. Much has been done by the Refuge for the Destitute, and other institutions; but there is the strongest call for more extensive remedies, or the evil will still continue to prevail. . . .

There exist in this Metropolis and its vicinity, houses of public

2. Figures are cited showing that in 1813 there were 123 boys of 17 years and under in Newgate; in 1816, 247; in 1817, 359.

resort, technically termed Flash-houses: some of these, boys and girls frequent, in company with the most notorious thieves; others seem more exclusively appropriated to youth of both sexes. The Report of the Police Committee, and the Evidence upon which that Report is founded, will furnish more detailed information to those who may wish to acquire it; here it is enough to say, that no terms can characterize the diabolical depravity, the gross profligacy, the detestable practices, which are there suffered to range at will, uncontrolled, and unrestrained. In these retreats of infamy, children live in habits of promiscuous prostitution; dram drinking prevails in all its horrors; rapine and theft are planned, arranged, and matured. Woe be to the child who once enters these sinks of iniquity; at once assailed by example, temptation, and deliberate seduction. If still untainted by crime, hence he dates his first transgression; if conversant with petty offences only, hence he plunges into all the depths of vice and misery. Here he finds a ready associate in guilt, an instructor in the arts of depredation, a sale for the fruits of his dishonesty. Ingenuity could not invent more powerful means to corrupt and destroy the seeds of virtue; to debase and pollute a rising generation. And yet these scenes of abomination continue to exist, and, though exposed to the indignation of the public, still hold their unhallowed reign, under the eye of the police, in the very heart of that metropolis, where is placed the seat of government. Nay, strange to say, some have even expressed a doubt as to the propriety of their suppression, on the supposition, that occasionally they have been the means of securing the apprehension of notorious offenders, by making known their haunts to the officers of justice. But surely this flimsy pretence will not bear the test of the slightest examination; where one criminal has been secured for punishment, hundreds have been seduced to the commission of crime, or encouraged in habits of dishonesty. All facilities to conceal and foster guilt are iniquitous, and it is high time we should awake from our day dreams, and utterly extirpate all these nurseries for depravity, and retreats of vice.

Whilst these houses are uniformly and daily adding to the catalogue of criminals, the Fairs in the Neighborhood of the Metropolis afford, occasionally, a superabundant supply. In the immediate vicinity of London, there are no less than eighty-two fair days in the space of seven months. Every species of debauchery and profligacy is here encouraged and promoted; gambling, drunkenness, seduction, and all the train of vices necessarily concomitant with unrestrained licentiousness. These fairs are a general rendezvous for all the most infamous characters, and furnish a plentiful harvest for swindlers, pickpockets, and all who prey upon the community. It is difficult to conceive what beneficial end can be answered by their continuance.

. . . The public has repeatedly heard that the Criminal Code is not carried into execution against adults, from the forbearance of prosecutors, and the humanity of juries, and that the consequence is impunity. No one doubts, that where offences pass entirely unpunished, vice is promoted and encouraged; but all do not perceive, that where the offender is of tender years, the chance of impunity is still greater, its effect still more mischievous. Mankind are naturally more compassionate to youthful errors; much is attributed to the power of temptation, to the want of thought and reflection; there is scarcely any one of common humanity who would not shudder at taking away the life of a child under sixteen or seventeen; resentment at the loss of property quickly subsides, where the agent is so much in our power, so incapable of resistance. Hence it is, that reluctance to prosecute, where the punishment is very severe, prevails more when the offender is in childhood, than when of more advanced age; the law draws no distinction, but the humanity of individuals, the fear of inflicting punishment disproportionate to the crime, deters them from recourse to justice, and the consequence is impunity. On the same principle, juries are more inclined to acquit, and acquittals therefore are more frequent. Inpunity to early offenders is productive of infinite injury; crime and punishment should be inseparably connected in their view; certainty alone can deter from the commission or repetition of the offence; hope of escape operates as a direct encouragement; for young minds are naturally sanguine, and though they would shudder at a small, but certain, suffering, would readily hazard the risk of a precarious, though a greater, punishment. What then should be done? To execute against children the severe code of criminal jurisprudence, at present prevailing in this country, is impossible: the legislature is incapable of enforcing it, religion, humanity, public feeling, revolt at the idea. Surely it is high time that some modification should take place; that a system should be organized, more consonant to public opinion, a scale of punishment more proportionate to the offence, should be adopted. . . .

A cause still remains, more fruitful of crime, more baneful in its effects, and more disgraceful to a moral and religious nation, than any or all of the causes before enumerated. This cause is the present state of our Prison Discipline. It is certainly not too much to say, that amongst children of a very early age, absolute impunity would have produced less vice than confinement in almost any of the gaols in the Metropolis and its neighbourhood. It is painful to reflect, that the remedy provided by the law should be one great cause of the evil. . . .

Deeply do the Committee lament that their exertions have been so disproportionate to the great extent of evil, which investigation proved to prevail . . . a careful examination into the cases of the individuals, enabled them to furnish useful information to those who had the power and authority to mitigate or enforce the sentence of the law. On one or two occasions they have ventured to submit strong facts, discovered by their inquiries, to the Secretary of State for the Home Department, and from the mercy which has been extended by his wisdom, they hope thay have been instrumental in preserving the lives of youthful offenders. In cases of a less flagrant nature, they have secured to many, an asylum in the Refuge for the Destitute; in others, they have provided the means of gaining an honest livelihood, on discharge from prison; and in very many instances they have offered relief and assistance, as the circumstances of the particular case required. The Committee are convinced, by experience, that great and permanent good has been effected by the measures thus pursued: they have the satisfaction of stating, that a considerable proportion of the youths to whom assistance has thus been rendered, have since conducted themselves meritoriously. . . .

[The Committee also "arranged a proposition for a Reformatory for Boys" to accommodate 600 boys properly classified and laid the plan before Lord Sidmouth. Desirability of similar Societies in Manchester, Bristol, Leeds, etc. is suggested. The remainder of pamphlet taken up with description of the Society's plans for promoting prison discipline, and acting as a clearing house of information on prisons—Drawing up plans for superior prisons, collecting books on the subject, circulating questionnaires on prisons, etc. —Also makes an appeal to public for funds.]

All who reverence the sacred memory of the illustrious Howard, will look with a favourable eye on the humble efforts of those who, taking his bright example for their guide, seek to follow in the same path.

Summary of Parliamentary Action Regarding the Trial and Treatment of Delinquent Children, 1828-1850

During the second quarter of the nineteenth century numerous bills were introduced in Parliament attempting to bring about a reform in court procedures in handling juvenile delinquents. Under the existing system children charged with minor offenses frequently had to wait weeks and often times months for their trial at the Quarter Sessions, during which time they were in almost constant association with the adult criminals in the gaols. Even though many of these children were found not guilty at their trials, their forced association with criminals while awaiting trial developed delinquent interests, attitudes, and habits and started them on the highway to crime. The main problem therefore, was to provide for an immediate hearing of children's cases. If this could be done it would save from gaol contamination those who were found not guilty, but for those found guilty in summary proceedings, it offered no remedy, for after sentence such children were committed to the gaols and houses of correction to mingle with the vicious and criminal adults. To protect this latter group of children it gradually dawned upon Parliament that special institutions should be established for delinquent juveniles. This end was achieved through the establishment of Parkhurst Prison, on the Isle of Wight, in 1838, for juvenile offenders. The repressive discipline at Parkhurst proved unsatisfactory, however, and the movement was soon started to set up reformatory schools, not prisons, for the juvenile delinquents. This led to the passage of the Reformatory Schools Act of 1854 and the Industiral Schools Act of 1857.

In view of the fact that many of the bills of this period relating to changes in court procedure in handling delinquents in England contained provisions closely approximating those of progressive juvenile court laws today, it may be worth while to examine some of them in detail, as they are described by friend and foe in the Parliamentary debates.

In May, 1828, shortly after the petition was presented from the Magistrates of Warwickshire for more adequate laws to deal with juvenile delinquents, Mr. E. D. Davenport, member of Commons from Shaftesbury, introduced a bill relating to summary convictions for petty felonies. Under this bill magistrates were to be given power of committing boys under sixteen years of age to solitary confinement for a limited period, if it was their first offense, and thus would be avoided the usual evils of gaol association. For a second offense, whipping in private might be employed, but only when there was no chance of reforming the offender by other means.[1] This bill evidently did not get out of committee.

During the following session of Parliament, in March, 1829, Mr. Davenport introduced another bill on juvenile offenders. He pro-

1. *Hansard's Parliamentary Debates*, New Series, Vol. 19 (1828), 716-18.

posed that in lieu of trials of juvenile offenders at Quarter Sessions, two or more magistrates in petty sessions, should be empowered to try and dispose of cases of persons under sixteen years of age charged with petty larcenies. He would dispense with the intervention of juries in children's cases whenever possible, but when a jury was necessary, he would make it possible for the offender to give bail for his appearance, instead of commitment to a house of correction to await trial. He thought the magistrates should have a limited power to punish, but he doubted if the lash should be used with children, especially first offenders. The punishment should be graduated according to the tender years of the offender.[2] This bill, like many, made no progress in Commons after its introduction.

Sir Eardley Wilmot, who had been elected to Parliament from Warwickshire in 1832, brought in a bill[3] in April, 1833, embodying the principles set forth earlier in his pamphlet. He would have boys under seventeen years of age charged with petty larcenies brought at once to the petty sessions, there to be tried by the magistrates and summarily punished or discharged. He had no objection to juries assisting at petty sessions, if necessary. Furthermore he would have many offenses that were classed as felonies under the existing code reclassed as misdemeanors if committed by youths. In the discussion of this bill many members objected to taking away jury trial, others thought the plan might work with country trials but would not work in the cities, while still others pointed out the difficulties of fixing an arbitrary age limit for juvenile offenders (should it be at ten years of age, at fourteen, or at sixteen?), etc.

A Parliamentary Committee of Inquiry into County Expenditures in 1834 earnestly recommended establishing some tribunal for the speedy trial of young offenders charged with comparatively light offenses—a tribunal to which immediate appeal could be made and which could award the species of punishment most suitable to the nature of the offense, and the character and habits of the offender, etc.[4] The report of the Criminal Law Commissioners in 1837 also recommended giving this discretionary power to magistrates for summary trial of young offenders.[5]

In 1838 the Duke of Richmond presented a petition in the House of Lords signed by a great number of the acting magistrates of the county of Sussex, expressing the opinion that it would be better for juvenile delinquents to be handled summarily by magis-

2. *Ibid.*, Vol. 20 (1829), 995-98.
3. *Ibid.*, 3rd Series, Vol. 17 (1833), 146-56.
4. *Ibid.*, Vol. 90 (1847), 430-40.
5. *Ibid.*

114

It was stated in Commons that the object of this bill was to transfer from the hands of parents to the care of a private benevolent society those children who should have been convicted of crime. The principle established here of State guardianship of delinquent children under twenty-one years might have had far-reaching possibilities under two conditions: first, if the Government had been really interested in exercising such jurisdiction; and, second, if the proper machinery had been set up for carrying out the administrative details. Both conditions were lacking here. The Court of Chancery was a judicial, not an administrative agency. If the responsibility for carrying out the provisions of this act had been placed upon the Secretary of the Home Department it might have proved effective. As it was, it remained a perfectly dead letter on the statute book, and Sir George Grey, nine years after its passage, expressed the belief that no case had occurred in which that Act had been made available.[11]

In 1842 Mr. G. Bankes of Dorsetshire made an unsuccessful attempt to secure the approval of the House of Commons of a bill that would give to magistrates in petty sessions summary power to inflict punishment on all offenders who were disposed to plead guilty to the offense charged against them.[12]

Five years later, in 1847, Sir John Pakington, who stated that he had received applications from every county in England desiring him to urge forward as speedily as possible a measure for summary proceedings in juvenile cases, brought in a bill proposing that two magistrates, sitting in private, might hear cases of delinquent children under sixteen years of age, where the larceny did not exceed forty shillings in value. It further provided that magistrates might punish by imprisonment for not over six months, or they might impose a fine in place of imprisonment. The bill was much debated. Great objection was raised to the "secret proceedings" clause, especially when "these extraordinary powers were to be given, not to a learned Judge, but it might be to a fox-hunting justice." It was admitted that there were many anomalies under the existing law which needed reform. For instance, it was simply a trespass for boys to steal apples from a tree, but a felony for them to pick up apples from the ground under the tree. Opponents of the measure also asked what advantages were to be gained by summary proceedings, if the child afterwards was to be committed to prison for six months.

Owing to the force of public opinion, this bill was finally passed

11. *Hansard's Parliamentary Debates*, 3rd Series, Vol. 107 (1849), 105.
12. *Ibid.*, Vol. 63 (1842), 94-96.

in amended form. It provided that children not exceeding fourteen years of age found guilty of simple larceny might be summarily convicted by two justices of the peace in petty sessions assembled. The justices were empowered to commit such children to the common jail or house of correction, with or without hard labor, for a term not exceeding three months; or they could impose a fine not exceeding three pounds. If the delinquent were a male, he might be privately whipped by a constable designated for that purpose. Apparently, the punishment of juvenile delinquents in the opinion of Parliament was paramount to their reformation. Surely the passage of this act must have proved bitterly disappointing to those members who for two decades had labored so valiantly in behalf of delinquent children. But the fight was not yet over.

On July 4, 1848, the Duke of Richmond presented in the House of Lords a petition for sending juvenile delinquents to reformatory institutions instead of to prisons. This petition had been adopted at a meeting called in London and had been signed by many magistrates of the metropolitan county, merchants, bankers, gentlemen connected with the Philanthropic Society, and the Society of Refuge for the Destitute, who felt that the success of these private reformatory institutions would justify government aid in setting up such institutions throughout England. Parents of delinquents committed to these reformatory schools would be required to pay a portion of the expense of maintaining them, while the remainder of the costs could be met by a rate and by private contributions. Lord Kinnaird supported the petition and called attention to the successful operation of such a school which had been recently established at Aberdeen.[13]

A bill was introduced in the House of Commons in 1849 to raise the age of juvenile offenders who might be handled by the justices in a summary manner from fourteen as authorized by the act of 1847 to sixteen. The apparent object of this bill was to extend the powers of justices to flog offenders up to sixteen years of age. In the debates on the bill Mr. Charles Pearson objected to a return to "the body tormenting system of former times." Although juveniles up to fourteen were often flogged as many as six times a year it had not reduced delinquency. A Middlesex justice was quoted as saying that within the past year in Middlesex alone the number of juvenile delinquents had increased from 898 to 1,240, and there had been the same proportional increase throughout England and Wales. Children needed food rather than flogging and corrective treatment instead of punishment. The following year (1850) after a long and

13. *Ibid.*, Vol. 100 (1848), 82-84.

spirited debate on the question of flogging the bill to increase the jurisdiction of justices to delinquents of sixteen was finally passed, although it was expressly provided that flogging could not be used on delinquents beyond the age of fourteen.[14]

Another bill relating to juvenile offenders received considerable attention in Parliament in 1850.[15] Mr. M. Milnes who was connected with the Philanthropic Society called attention to the uncertainty regarding the legal status of the juvenile delinquent. "In England the law had never laid down a distinct rule as to the age under which a child could be convicted, except, as he had been informed, that no legal conviction could be had of an offender under seven or eight years. But how little that rule, if it existed, had been adhered to in practice, might be inferred from the fact that Lieutenant Tracy, the governor of Westminster Bridewell, had had under his charge one boy not much over five years old, and ten more under eight years. Cases had even occurred in which mere children had been put to death under circumstances of great cruelty." Although the bill emphasized the need for establishing country industrial schools, the most important clauses were those relating to the responsibility of parents for the delinquencies of their children. One clause enabled magistrates "to summon the parents of any child who, by neglect, ill-treatment, evil example, or direct instigation, had led such child into the commission of any offence. Such parent was to be deemed guilty of a misdemeanor, a fine of not less than 5s. nor more than 5£. inflicted, and sureties might be required for the better behavior of the child for the next twelve months. This, he was aware, might be considered an innovation upon the existing law, but it had been suggested by high legal authority who had well considered the subject. Mr. M. D. Hill, the Recorder of Birmingham, had given conclusive evidence in its favor. Mr. Bullock, Judge of the Sheriff's Court; Mr. Russell, Prison Inspector; Mr. Rushton, the Liverpool Magistrate, in their evidence before the Lord's Committee; and Lieutenant Tracy, governor of one of the largest houses of correction . . . expressed their opinion that the proposed alteration would have the most salutary operation."[16] Other adults, contributing to the delinquency of a child, likewise were to be liable to the summary jurisdiction of two magistrates. Considerable objection was raised to the bill, largely because it was regarded as impractical. It was pointed out

14. Statutes at Large. Vol. 90, 13 & 14 Vict. C. 37. "An Act for the further Extension of Summary Jurisdiction in Cases of Larceny."
15. *Hansard's Parliamentary Debates*, 3rd Series, Vol. 110 (1850), Juvenile Offenders Bill, 767-83.
16. *Ibid.*, p. 769.

also that another Parliamentary Committee on prison discipline was considering the same subject, and it would be wise to wait for that Committee's report before proceeding to legislate on the question.

The Warwick County Asylum for Juvenile Delinquents, 1818-1854

[H. Townsend Powell,[1]] *A Memoir of the Warwick County Asylum, instituted in the Year 1818, and supported by Voluntary Contributions, Shewing that it has answered the Purposes of Reformation, and Diminished the County Expenditure* . . . (London, 1827), pp. 7-8, 23-26 (editor's lib.)

The Warwick County Asylum was instituted, in the year 1818, by the united endeavours and liberal contributions of the benevolent in the County. Its professed object was to afford a place of refuge to the criminal boy, who, having been initiated in the ways of vice, and having forfeited his character for honesty, had no other prospect, but that of infamy and misery, for the remainder of his days. . . .

Nine years have now elapsed, and the charm of novelty is worn away. Those feelings, which were once excited at the prospect of rescuing the youthful culprit from his miserable situation, do not any longer answer to the touch; and it is a truth, which must not be concealed, that unless the funds of the County Asylum receive an early and a large increase, it must rapidly decline.

The friends of the Institution must again come forward to solicit the support of the County. . . . They can shew that a large proportion of the boys sent to the Asylum have been placed out from thence in respectable situations, and have become permanently reformed characters. They can prove that the Asylum has actually been the means of reducing the County expenditure. . . .

There have been 81 boys discharged from the Asylum since its establishment. If it can be shewn that the average expense, which 81 criminal boys bring upon the County, is greater than that which those 81 Asylum boys have brought, it is clear that the County has been benefitted to that amount, whatever it may be.

The boys at the Asylum have, with very few exceptions, been guilty of crime; consequently, the saving contemplated, must have arisen from preventing their return to crime, or, more properly, to Warwick gaol.

1. Rev. Powell was curate of Stretton-upon-Dunsmore and chaplain of the Asylum. The institution closed after his death in 1854.

The question therefore is—1st. On the average, how many return to gaol out of 81 criminal boys? And 2ndly. How many have returned to gaol out of those 81 discharged from the Asylum?

It is presumed however that 81 is a sufficiently large number to form an average in itself; and therefore that, if we ascertain the number that return to crime out of 81 boys taken indiscriminately from any of the gaol returns, the result will be nearly correct.

The two tables, marked No. 3 and 4, in the Appendix, have been drawn up for this purpose. The first, to shew how many of the Asylum boys have returned to gaol; and the consequent expenses which have been incurred by the County. The second, to shew how many out of the same number taken from the gaol calendars have returned to gaol, and the consequent expenses incurred upon them. The names, which appear, are those which first occur in the assize calendars, beginning from Lent, 1820 i.e. all between 13 and 18 years of age inclusive, with the exception of such as were condemned, or sentenced to transportation; it being evident, that, in the event of either sentence having been executed, it was impossible their names should again appear.

From these tables it appears that, of the 81 Asylum boys 21 have returned to gaol; and that the consequent expenses incurred by the County have amounted to £381. 16s. 9d.

Of the 81 criminal boys, who, being of a like age, and under similar circumstances, were not sent to the Asylum, 38 have returned to gaol, and the consequent expenses incurred by the County have amounted to £716. 2s. 6d.

The inference is, that the Asylum has benefitted the County to the amount of the difference between those two sums, namely, £334. 5s. 9d.

Now, though it may thus be shewn that the Asylum has benefitted the County to that amount, yet it would be very fallacious to conclude that the advantage amounts to so much, and no more.

When a criminal is transported, the County is freed from the risk of his returning to gaol: in like manner, when it is clearly ascertained that he is a reformed character, the county is freed from the same risk. What may be the exact value of that risk is another question; it is clearly worth something, and that well deserving of being taken into account.

Of the Asylum boys, 39 are clearly ascertained to be reformed characters; 14 have been transported from Warwick: there is, therefore, no further risk upon them. The remainder, on whom there is a risk, are 28.

In like manner, of the 81 not sent to the Asylum, 22 have been transported; none are clearly ascertained to be reformed characters. The remainder therefore on whom there is a risk, are 59.

Now, since the number on whom there is this risk is less in the former case than in the latter, by 31, it is clear that, in addition to the former sum of £334. 5s. 9d. the Asylum has benefitted the County by 31 times the value of that risk, whatever that value may be.

. . . The County Asylum must be considered merely as an experiment; and the result of that experiment, with regard to the expenses attending prosecutions, is, that they may be reduced by one half of their amount.

[In the *Appendix*, Table No. 1 gives a short history of every boy that had been admitted to the Asylum from the date of its establishment to March 1, 1827. Table No. 2 shows how many of the 81 boys discharged from the Asylum had since been tried at Warwick and the consequent expenses to the county.]

An Intermediate Tribunal for Hearing Cases of Delinquent Children Proposed by Sir John Eardley-Wilmot, 1820-1828

[A] John Eardley Eardley-Wilmot, *A Letter to the Magistrates of Warwickshire, on the Increase of Crime in General, But More Particularly in the County of Warwick; with a Few Observations On the Causes and Remedies of the Increasing Evil* (London, 1820), pp. 9, 11-12 (Harvard Law Lib.)

[A justice of the peace for the county of Warwick calls the attention of his fellow magistrates to "the rapid and extraordinary increase of crime in this county, but especially in the town of Birmingham." The ruthless severity of the criminal code and the uncertainty of punishment are cited as the principal causes of this increase in crime.]

. . . Crimes are now brought before the public, which formerly were passed over, if not without observation, at least without comment; the thoughtlessness of childhood does not now save a first offence from being treated with all the rigour of repeated transgression: and the little wretch, who might by timely and judicious correction have become a valuable member of society, is hurried to associate with those, who will soon perfect him in those depredations on the public, for which he has so early suffered, not so much for his guilt, as for his unskilfulness.

. . . I most readily admit, that the seeds of wickedness are seldom sown in the hearts of those juvenile offenders, with whom our prisons abound, by their being placed in those receptacles of vice and depravity. But are there not many cases, and I beg to call your attention to the calendars of this county in particular, where, was it not for the indiscriminate severity, which considers only the violation of a law, those seeds by timely attention might either have been eradicated, or might have withered away from their own weakness? Whereas must it not strike every thinking mind, that, by a mistaken zeal to repress a growing evil, human aid contributes largely to the perfecting of those fruits, which are nourished by the intercourse with hardened villains, are swelled by the want of separation of prisoners, and are finally ripened to maturity by every aid, which bad example, and total ignorance of the laws of their Creator cannot fail to administer. Nor is this all;— in his dismissal from the walls of his prison, (to him often, in his forlorn state, his most comfortable home,) the juvenile delinquent has lost that feeling of shame which the name of prison must at first invariably excite; without character, without friends, and without the means of gaining an honest livelihood, he plunges at once into those vicious courses of profligacy and crime, which increase in magnitude as they increase in number, till an ignominious death closes his career, at an age when his mind has not yet reached the first dawnings of sober reflection. Can we wonder, therefore, at our gaols being crowded with juvenile criminals, many of whom have repeatedly visited the same dungeons, and almost consider them as the friendly protectors of their wretchedness, rather than the frowning instruments of their punishment? Can we be surprised, that in every calendar, one-third at least of the culprits are of an age hardly beyond the impotence of childhood? And is it not a subject of deep reflection that, while the age of infancy is incapacitated by the civil law from doing almost any act that can injure itself or others, such is the weakness and wickedness of man, that no years, however tender, no circumstances of distress, however uncontroulable, no neglect of parents, however culpable, can secure it from being amenable to the criminal jurisprudence of the country?

[B] John Eardley Eardley-Wilmot, *A Second Letter to the Magistrates of Warwickshire, etc.* (London, 1820), pp. 11-13 (Harvard Law Lib.)

[The *Second Letter* was written in response to numerous appeals "to offer some practical alteration in our penal statutes." The author claimed that an inquiry into the whole criminal code was too wide a field for one man to cover, so he promised to limit his remarks on criminal jurisprudence to juvenile delinquency. Crimes are committed, he said, at a much earlier age than formerly was the case. The primary causes of crime are ignorance and early imprisonment.]

It is exactly this point of my inquiry which has led me to the true remedy for the second overwhelming cause of early depravity, and it is in consequence of the inadequacy of parental and magisterial authority, that I would delegate both to the Magistracy of the County as an intermediate resource between private exertion and the heavy arm of the law. It is to prevent the contamination and stigma of a gaol, and the publicity of trial, those great sources of confirmed villainy that I would delegate to the impartial administrators of justice, that paternal vigilance and magisterial power, which in their hands would yield a surer prospect of success. I would give to them the power of correction and reform, before the bad inclinations of the young offender are more deeply rooted by the bad habits of a gaol, and I would invest them with the power of immediate conviction, without making the yet unhardened culprit a public spectacle or a public example.

For this purpose, I propose that the law of felony should no longer affect adults of both sexes under [blank] years of age, who are charged with stealing to the value of [blank] shillings; but that the offence should be cognizable by two magistrates; who, on confession of the party accused, or on the oath of two witnesses, should have the power of convicting the offender, and of sentencing him to imprisonment in that part of the House of Correction set apart for the especial purpose, and there kept to hard labour for any time not exceeding [blank] months. The expenses of such conviction to be paid by the county, on an order made by the convicting magistrates.

[He admits that his proposal was open to the objection that it would prevent trial by jury.] . . . But the offence which is to bring the delinquent under the power of the magistrate, ceases, by this new enactment, to be a felony, and assumes the character of a minor transgression. The *corpus delicti* is wholly altered, and is expunged from the penal table of the law, to take its place among those misdemeanours which are already cognizable by the magistracy of the country. It becomes in its character and its consequences on a level with the robbery of gardens, with the destruction of game, and with all other offences already punishable by summary process.

Gentlemen, it is with the utmost diffidence that I offer to the consideration of the legislature this proposed alteration of our penal code, as respects Juvenile Delinquents. If I am not mistaken, the advantages to the public will be immense; and by the adoption of this new enactment, those deserted objects who have so early fallen the victims of Ignorance and Depravity, will be guided through this world, and prepared for a better.

[C] Sir Eardley Eardley-Wilmot, *A Letter to the Magistrates of England on the Increase of Crime; and an Efficient Remedy Suggested for their Consideration* (London: John Hatchard and Son, 1827), pp. 2, 14-16, 19, 23 (editor's lib.)

[In this pamphlet Wilmot addresses the magistrates of England not just those of Warwickshire as in 1820. He first treats the secondary causes of the increase of crime, such as increased population, the abuse of the poor laws, poaching, uncertainty of punishment, and the payment of expenses to those who bring offenders to justice. Then he emphasizes the chief cause, *early imprisonment*, and discusses in considerable detail his proposed remedy, an *intermediate tribunal*. In the last three pages of the pamphlet Wilmot presents a "Scetch of an Act of Parliament, for altering the law of simple larceny as affecting juvenile offenders."]

The Middlesex jury having lately noticed the great increase of juvenile delinquency, and having expressed an opinion, "that the law of Petty Larceny should be revised, and that the magistrates should be enabled to proceed in a summary way against such offenders." has induced me once again to trespass upon the public attention. . . .

In searching for a remedy by which this increasing evil may be effectually checked, the only true foundation of success must rest upon the just and accurate view of the cause which produces it. It is not to save the youthful delinquent from punishment, but in order to prevent that very punishment from being the instrument of increasing the evil, that I would apply the remedy; and if, long *before* he has become a public spectacle at the bar of a criminal court, I could save him from so great and fatal a degradation; if *before* his heart is hardened in villainy, or rendered desperate by a verdict of *guilty*, I could inflict a punishment which should produce better effects; then, I confidently assert, that a step would be gained in the prevention of crime, which would soon be felt in every part of this extensive empire.

The remedy therefore that I would propose, is not a restoration of those tribunals which formerly existed in every hundred, and every village, in the time of our ancestors; but I would recommend the adoption of the *principle* in which they originated, viz. the *immediate* and *summary* cognizance of offences committed by the youthful depredator; to be heard before an intermediate tribunal, where petty offences may be instantly proceeded against and punished, without sending the offender to undergo the stigma and contamination of a public prison, the publicity of trial, and all those evils which infallibly result from early imprisonment. I would change the law of larceny as affecting offenders of a certain age, and convert the offence into one of a minor character, cognizable by two magistrates, in the same way as offences now are under the Malicious Trespass Act, and many others; and by thus arming the magistracy with the power of immediate conviction; on sufficient evidence, or on confession of the parties, I would empower them to punish the young culprit by whipping, confining him in an asylum set apart for this purpose, or by discharging him without punishment at all. . . .

It is therefore to give him a chance of regaining the character he is on the point of losing for ever, that I would delegate to the magistracy of the county that power, as an intermediate tribunal, which our ancestors formerly exercised with so much wisdom and success; and long before the bad propensities of the youthful delinquent are too deeply rooted, and long before he is stigmatised with the name of *felon*, I would try the effect of immediate and summary punishment.

Instead, therefore, of the law now affecting young culprits for simple larceny, (by which I mean those minor offences which subject them now to trial at the sessions,) I would change the *corpus delicti* into an offence of a lesser character, cognizable by two magistrates; who should be empowered on sufficient evidence to convict the offender, and sentence him to such imprisonment in an asylum set apart for such convictions, and supported by the county rate, as they should think the nature of the offence, and the benefit to the boy himself should require: such imprisonment not to exceed a limited time, to be appointed by the act, and to be shortened afterwards according to circumstances. If a discharge with whipping, or a discharge only, shall appear sufficient, then this to be at the option of the magistrates.

The advantages resulting from this alteration in the law, are too manifest to need repetition—immediate punishment, the avoiding the contamination of a gaol, of the disgrace of a public trial, and of the stigma of a verdict. The effects likely to be produced on the offender's mind, and that of his neighbours, by the offence and the punishment being immediately connected together, must have a decided effect in checking a repetition of the crime. The magistrates themselves under this new enactment, will have the power of inflicting a minor punishment, and one from its nature infinitely more likely to deter others from committing similar offences. A boy, hardly above the age of childhood, is detected in an offence, which, if at school, would have subjected him, and has subjected his superiors in rank and fortune, to a flogging or a task. It is his first offence; his master gives him an excellent character, and will continue him in his employment, the theft is an ounce of cheese, four oranges; a bun, or the removal of some article two or three inches from its place, but without taking it away. The magistrate feels disposed to discharge the culprit; and is of opinion, that neither public justice, nor the welfare of the boy, demand his committal. But the felony is clear, and he has no option: and a boy of ten years of age is sent to gaol for two or three months, till the next gaol delivery releases him. No bill is found, or if found, the culprit is acquitted; and if convicted, his previous imprisonment, his youth, and his master present in court to take him back to his employment, operate upon the mind of the court to give him a nominal punishment; and the boy is dismissed with confirmed vicious inclinations, and with a depravity of mind previously unknown and unfelt. . . .

When therefore by the loss or neglect of his *natural* guardian, the youthful delinquent is thrown upon the world without any guide to direct or befriend him, instead of being subject to the utmost severity of the law, he will experience only its protection; and he will find already appointed as the *legal* guardians of his infancy, those who by judicious restraint, and by well-timed instruction, will supply the place of his own relatives. It will be an "act for appointing guardians for the deserted and friendless," rather than an addition to our Criminal Code: and instead of being a law of punishment, will be the dispenser of blessings.

Scetch of an Act of Parliament
For altering the Law of simple Larceny as affecting Juvenile Offenders

Whereas it has been found by experience, that great evils have arisen from the commitment for trial of offenders of tender age accused of simple larceny; whereby such early imprisonment has tended to harden them in vice, and to render any attempt at reform more difficult and unavailing; and whereas it is expedient to provide a summary mode of proceeding against such offenders instead of that now in force; Be it therefore enacted, &c, &c, That where any person shall be accused of simple larceny before two or more justices of the peace, it shall and may be lawful for such justices to inquire into the age, or reputed age, of such offender; and if it shall appear to them, that he or she shall be under the age of twenty-one years, every such offender, being convicted of the offence so charged by one or more credible witnesses, or on their own confession, shall, at the discretion of such justices, be committed to an asylum or house of correction set apart exclusively for the reception of such offenders, there to be imprisoned only, or imprisoned and kept to hard labour for any time not exceeding twelve calendar months; or the said justices may order the said offenders to be whipped and discharged, or discharged only, at the discretion of such justices; and if any person so convicted shall be afterwards accused of simple larceny before one or more justices of the peace, then such person shall be proceeded against in the manner pointed out by the various statutes now in force respecting simple larceny.

II. And be it further enacted, that the two justices of the peace, before whom such offenders shall be brought, shall have authority to summon all persons, who know or declare any thing touching the offence of which the party stands accused, to appear before them at such time and place as they shall appoint, then and there to give evidence against the party accused, or on his or her behalf; and in case such person so summoned shall neglect or refuse to appear, it shall and may be lawful for the said justices to issue their warrant to compel such persons to attend.

III. And be it further enacted, That the two justices, before whom such offender shall be convicted, are hereby authorized and empowered, at the request of the prosecutor or any other person who shall appear voluntarily or on summons to give evidence against any person so accused, or on his behalf, such sums of money as to them shall appear reasonable and sufficient for the expenses they have incurred in such attendance; and also to compensate them for their trouble and loss of time herein. And although no conviction shall take place, it shall still be lawful for the said justices, where any person shall have attended voluntarily or on summons, to order unto such person such sums of money as shall appear to them reasonable and sufficient to reimburse them for the expenses which they have incurred by reason of such attendance; and also to compensate them for their trouble and loss of time. And the amount of the expenses of attendance before the said justices, and the compensation for trouble and loss of time, as well as the expense of conveying the offender to the house of correction or asylum, shall be ascertained by the certificate of such justices, delivered to the treasurer of county, where such conviction or proceedings shall take place, and he is hereby authorized to pay the same.

IV. And be it further enacted, that the two justices of the peace, before whom such offender shall be brought shall take the information on oath of those who give evidence of the facts and circumstances of the case, and shall put the same in writing; and such justices shall subscribe such information and examinations; and shall deliver the same, together with the conviction, to the clerk of the peace or other proper officer of the court of the next gaol delivery in the county where such conviction shall have taken place.

V. And be it further enacted, That the justices of the peace, at their next quarter-sessions of the peace after the passing of this act, shall appropriate some convenient and sufficient part of the house of correction for the exclusive reception of offenders committed under this act, entirely distinct from all other prisoners, or they shall erect, purchase, or rent some building or buildings with or without land, in any part of the county, which to them may seem most fit and convenient, for the exclusive reception of such offenders; and shall provide whatever appears to them to be necessary for the maintenance, labour, and instruction of the said offenders; the expenses incurred thereby to be defrayed out of the produce of the county-rate, in the same manner as the other expenses of the county are defrayed.

[D] Sir Eardley Eardley-Wilmot, A *Letter To the Magistrates of England on the Increase of Crime, etc.* (2nd Ed.: London, 1828), pp. 26-27.

[As a result of Wilmot's *Letter* of 1827, the General Quarter Sessions of the Peace for the county of Warwick on January 14, 1828, passed a resolution for petitioning Parliament for a revisal of the criminal law as affecting juvenile delinquents. This action induced the author to publish a second edition of this *Letter*, with certain changes. In the *Scetch of an Act of Parliament*, etc., appended to this edition, Wilmot limits the jurisdiction of the Act to persons "of or under the age of seventeen years" instead of "under the age of twenty-one years," as in the edition of 1827. He replies also to two objections to his proposal, namely, that it was an encroachment on the constitutional safeguard of English liberty, Trial by Jury, and that it gave an unwarranted increase of power to the magistrates.

To the first of these objections Wilmot replies that "it is not the Trial by Jury which is to be abrogated, but *the felony itself.*" But admitting, he says, that it was an encroachment on the Trial by Jury, he asks which is of the greatest moment, "to have numbers of our fellow creatures ruined by a strict adherence to ancient rules of trial; or numbers saved by a salutary departure from them?" As to the other objection he states that "the power of the magistrate is in fact the delegated authority of the parent, and he is empowered to do by the laws of the state, what every father can do by the laws of nature. No one can doubt, but that a parent can correct his child; or can delegate his authority to a master; who, standing *loco parentis,* may use every reasonable and moderate coercion to train the child committed to his care in the principles of virtue and religion. By the proposed enactment, the same authority is vested in the magistracy, who thus standing also *loco parentis,* is empowered to exercise a similar authority, and *not a greater one,* for the education of children, who either having no parents at all, or what is worse, depraved and wicked ones, are rescued from the path of wickedness by the mercy of the law."

In this connection it may be of interest to note the comments on Wilmot's *Letter* in the *Quarterly Review.*[2] This reviewer says that Wilmot's bill, which applies to simple larceny, would not take care of young pickpockets, who constituted the most numerous class of juvenile depredators. The reviewer continues, as follows:

"The act, to be really operative and beneficial, should be made to extend to all stealing from the person without violence, with perhaps some greater limitation of the powers delegated to the justices: their jurisdiction might be limited to offenders whose age does not exceed sixteen years; and as a safeguard to innocence and a prevention of any mischief that might arise from a proceeding conducted too much 'a la chaude,' it might be provided that the justices shall not award their sentence until after a certain lapse of time, or that the offender shall be remanded to the next petty sessions which usually in the country, we believe, take place every week or fortnight. . . ."

In accordance with the resolution of the magistrates of Warwickshire, mentioned above, Mr. D. S. Dugdale presented a petition to Parliament, calling attention to the great increase of crime, especially among juvenile offenders, and praying that the House of Commons

2. *Quarterly Review,* Vol. 37 (1828), pp. 489-504.

would take the subject into their most serious consideration in order to apply such a remedy as its importance demanded. The matter was referred to the Committee on the Increase of Crime.[3]]

[E] Rev. T. Coker Adams, *A Letter Addressed to Sir Eardley Eardley-Wilmot, Bart in Answer to His Letter to the Magistrates of England, on the Increase of Crime, &c.* (London and Coventry, 1828), pp. 15-22 (editor's lib.)

[Rev. Adams, like Wilmot, one of the justices of the peace for the county of Warwick, was for several years a visitor of the Gaol and House of Correction at Warwick and was also one of the original promoters and staunch supporters of the Warwick County Asylum. He takes issue with Wilmot as to the principal causes of crime and is strongly opposed to Wilmot's remedy. According to Rev. Adams the principal causes of crime are the *increase of the inhabitants* ("crime increases not only in its numerical proportion with population but in a ratio far beyond it"), *fluctuation in the affairs of the commercial world, the mode in which the criminal law is administered, half-pay apprenticeships, and an overweaning tenderness for first and juvenile offences.*]

We have now arrived at that part of your Pamphlet which projects a measure for diminishing the cause of Crime. In itself the most important part, in its propositions the most objectionable.

Let us first turn our observations to those inestimable privileges, of which your alteration of the law so sweepingly deprives us.

It abrogates that merciful provision of the Law, which enacts that the Person charged with felony shall be taken before a Magistrate, in order that it may be clearly ascertained by him, whether there be a reasonable *suspicion* of guilt, before he be committed for trial.

It removes that important Ordeal of the Grand Inquest, whose duty it is, to inquire whether there be at least sufficient prosecuting Evidence for putting him on his Defence.

It takes away that glory of our Constitution, his Trial by Jury, which we are told, by the highest authority, "is an admirable criterion of Truth, and a most important guardian both of public and private Liberty."

It robs him of that safe means of Defence, which, a technical, a watchful and a skilful advocate is the most competent to suggest.

And lastly it deprives him of That intricate knowledge of law, of evidence, and of the mode of giving evidence, and that learned and

3. *Hansard's Parliamentary Debates*, New Series, Vol. 18 (1828), pp. 985-87.

unbiassed judgment which the Judges of the Land and the Magistrates collectively are presumed to possess.

And from whom are these dear-bought privileges to be withdrawn? Not from the old and hardened offender; not from him, whose previous conviction might substantially justify a further suspicion of guilt: But from one whose tender years render him incapable of defending himself, expose him to the artful designs of the deceitful and the wicked, and ought therefore to obtain for him additional safeguards to protect his innocence and secure him justice.

What do you give the *supposed* offender (for such he must be deemed to be till he be found guilty) in return for all these deprivations? Without any previous enquiry you place him at once before his *Judges*. He is put upon his trial, while the irritation of recent injury pervades the Prosecutor's mind. His Judges must hear all the loose evidence that can be raked up against him; for they have no means, if they have the knowledge, of distinguishing what ought to be heard and what ought not, till the whole has been related. From the want of that respect and awe, and that fear of detection which our Courts of Justice so invariably inspire, some of the witnesses may allow their prejudices to obscure the truth;—the triumph of a conviction may lead others to do the same; and I am fearful the angry and bitter feelings which usually prevail against an apprehended felon will operate too powerfully on the prosecuting party. And yet the youthful prisoner will be deprived, by his inexperience and want of preparation, of the means of defeating such a dangerous combination.

What likewise shall we say of those who are to be his exclusive Judges? I mean not to speak personally nor disrespectfully; but in a matter of this urgent nature I must speak plainly. Are they *all* (for under the new law all ought to be) sufficiently acquainted with the laws of the lands;—with the practice of Courts of Justice,—with the practice of what is, and what is not evidence? Are they all skilled in the knowledge of human nature? Are they all men of undoubted mental acquirements and enlightened understandings? Are they all free from those prejudices which local knowledge must necessarily engender? Are they all divested of that interest, which the friendship or enmity of the Parties brought before them, naturally incites?

If they have not all these substantial requisites of Justice,—if they are tinged with a shade only of these derogatory propensities, they cannot be fitting to be intrusted with an increase of power, much less with that judicial power, which is to decide *without appeal*, upon the moral character of an accused but perhaps innocent individual. I know that it may be said that this power is to be placed in the hands of a Magistracy bearing the character of high independence and of tried honour; and I believe as a collective body they are an ornament to their Country. But, as in all other large societies of men there must be some tinctured with the frailties, if not with the vices, of human nature, so ought especial care to be taken, that such men be divested of the opportunities of individually tampering with justice, and destroying the fair-fame of those who may be placed within their jurisdiction. Few men it must be allowed, are entirely free from undue bias; and the only way to controul this erring propensity in cases where power is to be exercised, is to make them pass their judgments *publicly,* and in the presence of those, who, if not possessed with equal authority, are possessed with equal knowledge of how that authority should be exercised. It is true that in many cases Magistrates do already possess a similar power to that, with which you would invest them; but *that* is no reasonable argument for an extension of that power, especially when it is recollected that in most instances where this authority is given, and in *all* instances it ought to be, the parties aggrieved have an appeal to a higher tribunal and may thus set themselves right again in the eye of the world. But it would be but a poor recompence to the youthful misdemeanant, after he has been well whipped or set in the stocks, to be allowed an appeal at the Court of Quarter Sessions. If it should be said that the same failings may be inherent in the Judges of the land, as well as in the Justices, so let it be allowed; but let it also be remembered that if we may have again one Judge Jeffreys, so may we also have many Justice Shallows.

I know that Justice, substantial Justice, is coupled with the object which you have in view, though I must confess that your measures appear to be founded on the supposition that every youthful prisoner is *guilty,* who perchance is apprehended for a felony; and that therefore it is only a waste of time and ceremony to go through those slow and lingering forms which the law has hitherto prescribed. And this perhaps has made you overlook, or dismiss, for you could not overlook, those highly treasured safeguards of innocence and honesty with which our Ancestors have fenced the liberty of the subject.

I know also that the intended change of the law is founded by you on the purest principle of humanity towards the implicated felon; but, as an innocent man, I should prefer a commitment to prison, with a reasonable prospect of acquittal by my Peers; rather than put my moral character into the hands of men who may be impatient, uninformed, and perhaps prejudiced against me. Ay! or into the hands of any two men in their own justice-room, let them be as enlightened as the very best of us.

But even supposing that *impartial* Justice could be obtained by this new mode of administering it, I do not believe that the scheme is *practicable*.

Where can we find the Magistrates, who can or will dedicate such a lengthened portion of their time to the patient and diligent enquiry demanded in a judgment and sentence upon felonious offences. If, from the present irksome business at Petty Sessions, it is difficult to get two together for discharging the laws relating to parochial concerns, how is it to be expected that, with the prospect of such an increase of labour, this difficulty can be removed; especially in large and populous Towns, where criminal cases must be daily occurring, and where the Magistrates are already much harassed with important concerns.

The consequence must be the appointment of stipendiary Magistrates, and I ask, if the Public would then be better satisfied with the administration of the criminal law. For many years I have weekly attended a Petty Sessions, in a populous part of the County and after witnessing the false swearing, the irritated evidence, and the round-about mode of giving it, usual on such occasions, I candidly confess, I do not think there are many Magistrates, who have time and patience enough, to decide *judicially* in Petty Sessions on the moral character of a person, charged, and perhaps *maliciously* charged, with an act of felony.

There are also minor difficulties to be provided for in carrying into effect the plan proposed. It frequently occurs for many days together (I have known it for many weeks), that *two* Magistrates do not meet. What then is to be done with the Prisoner? Places of security must be erected in every district, and proper officers and guards appointed to secure and maintain those in custody. The Magistrates themselves must also be protected in the discharge of their duty; and where there is to be no appeal and perhaps corporal punishment is to be inflicted, it may be thought only commonly prudent to place the Judges in such a situation, as to be perfectly free from all chance of intimidation. The judicial proceedings of the Court and the evidence taken there, must also be recorded, and some official person must be appointed to fill that situation.

These may, perhaps, be considered trifles in the general calculation; but still they are trifles which cannot be dispensed with, and if a saving of expence be contemplated, these are items which must quickly turn the balance.

Transportation for Life Recommended for the Delinquent and the Destitute Children of England, 1829

[John Wade], *A Treatise on the Police and Crimes of the Metropolis; especially Juvenile Delinquency, Female Prostitution, Mendicity, Gaming* . . . (London, 1829), pp. 159-64 (Brit. Mus.)

There are, probably, 70,000 persons in the Metropolis [London] who regularly live by theft and fraud; most of these have women, with whom they cohabit, and their offspring, as a matter of course, follow the example of their parents, and recruit the general mass of mendicancy, prostitution, and delinquency. This is the chief source of juvenile delinquents, who are also augmented by children, abandoned by the profligate among the working classes, by those of poor debtors confined, of paupers without settlement, and by a few wayward spirits from reputable families, who leave their homes without cause, either from the neglect or misfortune of their natural protectors. Children of this description are found in every part of the metropolis, especially in the vicinity of the theatres, the market-places, the parks, fields, and outskirts of the town. Many of them belong to organized gangs of depredators, and are in the regular employ and training of older thieves; others obtain a precarious subsistence by begging, running errands, selling playbills, picking pockets, and pilfering from shops and stalls. Some of them never knew what it is to be in a bed, taking refuge in sheds, under stalls, piazzas, and about brick-kilns; they have no homes; others have homes, either with their parents, or in obscure lodging-houses, but to which they cannot return unless the day's industry or crime has produced a stipulated sum.

It is from the thousands of children so situated that the chief mass of criminals is derived, who fill our prisons, the hulks, and convict-settlements. It is a most extraordinary fact, that half the number of persons convicted of crime have not attained the age of discretion. During the last seven years, out of 16,427 commitments in the county of Surrey, 7292 were under twenty years of age, and 370 under twelve years of age, and several of these not more than eight or ten years of age.

. . . In the present state of the law, the magistrates have little power, and the punishments that are inflicted mostly tend to harden the offenders and return them upon society with additional aptitude for mischief. . . .

In the *Morning Chronicle*, September 27, 1828, it is stated, that

135

120 miserable creatures were brought up at one of the public offices; they had been found sleeping in a brick-field, and twenty-eight were sent to the *House of Correction*. In the same journal, September 17, is the following occurrence:—

"*Middlesex Sessions.*—John Murray, a little hungry looking boy, about twelve years of age, was indicted for stealing two buns and eight biscuits. The Chairman, in passing sentence, said, 'That it was a melancholy thing to see the crowd of children then in the dock. Here are nearly twenty children, all of them, I fear, belonging to organized gangs, in which every member has a peculiar department. The only effectual mode of putting down this system is, to send every one of them out of the country for life. Whipping used to make some impression upon them, but now they quite disregard it. However, I'll give these boys another chance—let them be confined for *three months, and be twice well whipped.*'"

Now, this mode of proceeding is both cruel and absurd. It is certain these poor creatures, at the expiration of their punishment, will and must return to their old courses; they have no other means of living, and perhaps have never been taught any other; the punishment awarded is a gratuitous aggravation of the hardships of their lot, and neither reforms them nor benefits society. Even boys sentenced for a short period to transportation, or to confinement on board the hulks, mostly return to their old courses. . . .

Out of 4000 Convicts on board the hulks, 300 boys under sixteen years of age were taken and placed on board the Euryalus, at Chatham. Of these boys,

199 had fathers living
66 had only mothers living
35 had neither fathers nor mothers
133 had been in custody more than once
66 could read and write on their arrival
64 could read only
170 could neither read nor write
2 were eight years of age
5 were nine years of age
13 ten years of age
23 eleven years of age
59 twelve years of age
69 thirteen years of age
82 fourteen years of age
42 fifteen years of age
5 sixteen years of age

All the suggestions of modern philanthropy for the reform of these offenders have been adopted on board the hulks; they are separated from older criminals, the ignorant are instructed, useful trades are taught them, and they have nothing before them but examples of industry, sobriety, and religion. Yet such is the force of early impressions, that they no sooner return to their native element, as it may be termed, in the purlieus of Covent-garden, Tothill-fields, Bethnal-green, or Saffron-hill, than, like ducks at the sight of water, or a wild Indian who has been temporarily clothed in the habiliments of civilization, they rush into their former scenes of iniquity and crime.

The methods now employed to dispose of delinquent children failing either to reform them or relieve society from their presence, it is certainly expedient a new experiment should be tried. . . .

Under an act of Anne, a magistrate is authorized, with the consent of the church wardens of the parish, where the delinquent is found, who either begs or his parents beg, who cannot give a proper account of himself, to bind that boy to the sea service. This, in time of war, afforded a convenient outlet for profligate youths, but now it is with great difficulty persons can be found to take them, as is proved by the experience of the Marine Society. On shore, as at sea, the market is overstocked, and boys, if willing, cannot always find employment, as errand-boys, pot boys, stable-boys, etc.

But the difficulty of dealing with the destitute children of the Metropolis consists not so much in providing a suitable punishment for the actually delinquent as in disposing of the multitudes against whom no offence can be proved. However much their wayward-ness and wretchedness may be deplored, and however strongly their incipient guilt be suspected, still having committed no offence known to the law, they are not within cognizance of the civil power. Now it appears to us that it would be real humanity towards these unfortunate creatures to subject them to compulsory and perpetual exile from England. . . . Abroad, in New South Wales, they often become prosperous and useful citizens; but, at home, they seem incapable of resisting the temptations presented by a luxurious and refined community. . . .

The Society for the Suppression of Juvenile Vagrancy, 1830-1832

[A] *Statement of the Views and Reports of the Society for the Suppression of Juvenile Vagrancy, upon the Plan that has*

Proved so Successful in Holland, by Providing Agricultural and Horticultural Employment for the Destitute Children of the Metropolis (London, 1830), pp. 8-10, 21, 24, 27 (Goldsmiths' Lib.)

At a Meeting of the Society for the Suppression of Juvenile Vagrancy held at the Mendicity Society's Office in Red-Lion-Square, July 6th, 1830 . . . the following Paper was read and unanimously adopted.

SOCIETY FOR THE SUPPRESSION OF JUVENILE VAGRANCY, &C, &C.

The object of this Society, is to rescue from early depravity children who are actually running wild about the streets, daily progressing in crime, and ultimately becoming the tools of the most hardened offenders in committing every species of depredation upon the Public.

With a view of accomplishing this desirable object, the society proposes the establishment of "Agricultural Workhouses," on a tract of waste or poor land, at such a convenient distance from the Metropolis as will admit of a constant inspection by the public, and the members of the Institution.

The Society proposes to raise the Funds in support of the Establishment by an annual subscription of Five Shillings from each subscriber.

This is the plan that was adopted in Holland. . . .

Every degree of publicity will be given to the proceedings of the Society, and a Periodical Report will be published, giving such details of their operations, as may be deemed interesting to the Public.

Should it be found impracticable to provide employment for the Youth so trained at home, facilities will then be given to them to proceed to our Colonies, where there is a great demand for their labour. . . .

BRIEF EXPLANATORY OBSERVATIONS

In the first instance, it is intended to take such boys chiefly as are recommended to the Institution by the Magistrates before whom they are so frequently brought for acts of Vagrancy.

It is also proposed to take those who are rejected by the Marine Society, and such as apply to the Mendicity Society between the ages of 8 and 16, who amount upon an average to three per day, throughout the Year.

138

It is also presumed that Parishes may be disposed to send to the Institution refractory boys, a great many of whom are alternately the inmates of Gaols and Workhouses. . . .

It is calculated by those who have the best means of forming a correct estimate, that there are at the present moment about 15,000 boys in the Metropolis, children of the poor, who have no visible means of subsistence, and who in fact are many of them trained to every variety of vice. They are to be found sleeping in groups under the stalls of the public markets, in empty and ruined houses (See Appendix A) and other similar situations; the state of vice, misery and degradation, succeeded frequently by punishment, to which these unhappy beings are reduced, must be admitted to be as disgraceful to the institutions of the country as it is revolting to humanity itself. The Committee feel . . . that the unchecked continuance of such a state of things threatens to sap the foundations of civilized society, by extensively contaminating the morals of the lower orders, and that it is consequently the duty of the public to attempt to abate the evil. . . .

Signed EDWARD P. BRENTON, CAPT. R.N.
Honorary Secretary

APPENDIX A

[Mr. H. Wilson in a letter to the Rt. Hon'ble R. Wilmot Horton, dated 9th August, 1830, describes his visit to Cold Bath Fields Prison, London.]

On entering the first yard, we were shewn 49 reputed thieves, under 16 years of age.

. . . casting my eye from countenance to countenance, as they turned themselves round to examine their visitors from their elevated situation on the Treadmill, I could not select one from amongst them who had the appearance of being a novice. . . .

They were all upon the Treadmill, the power of which is applied to no useful purpose. . . .

Just as I was leaving the yard, a boy was brought to the gate, six years of age. He was dressed from head to foot in a new prison suit, and as he was endeavouring fruitlessly to roll up his trousers, which were much too long for him, he joined in the mirth which his appearance occasioned. . . .

[B] Edward P. Brenton, [Report of the] Society for the Suppression of Juvenile Vagrancy (c. 1832) pp. 1-3, 10-11 (editor's lib.)

It is nearly two years since this Society first commenced its labours. The objects of its solicitude during that period have not decreased. Our streets, our jails, our workhouses and penitentiaries, are crowded with unhappy children of both sexes, whose crimes have been occasioned by destitution and neglect in early youth. To provide an asylum for the Boys, to give them, at least, temporary relief, food and raiment,—to instruct them in the most useful employment, spade husbandry,—and to give them moral and religious instruction, have been the objects of this Society. An experimental establishment was several months since formed at West Ham Abbey, near Bow, Essex. . . . Twenty boys, whose forelorn and neglected condition gave them a just claim upon the compassion and benevolence of a Christian public, have been selected and placed under the care of Mr. Henry Wilson, at the expense of seven shillings per week, and £3 for equipments for each boy. . . .

Should the Society, by a continuation of this public bounty, be enabled to prosecute its plans, it is the intention of the Committee to send a large portion of the boys to the Cape of Good Hope,—the Government having consented to be at half the expense,—and to establish a protectorship for them on their arrival. . . .

It has been proved that it costs the country about £17 a year to maintain each juvenile offender in prison. It certainly costs about £7 to prosecute them, whether they are convicted or not: and it is evident that, for a much smaller sum, they might be educated, rescued from crime and punishment, and rendered useful members of society. . . .

[Case descriptions of nine boys admitted into the Society's Model School of Industry during the period Oct. 20, 1831, to Jan. 4, 1832, are presented, pages 5-11 inclusive. The ninth case presented below may be taken as representative.]

Joseph Wood, twelve years of age, belongs to the parish of Limehouse. His mother died seven years ago. Never been taught any trade. After his mother's death he was neglected by his father; and a poor woman who got her livelihood by shaving took compassion on him, and kept him for three years; not being able to keep him any longer, he went to his father, who turned him out of doors, and said he did not care for the parish officers, or anybody else. His father got his living by carrying out coals, and is much addicted to drinking. The boy was in Limehouse workhouse about four years, and ran away from it (as he says, for ill usage,) about a year ago. Slept in a privy, the first night, and was taken up by a police-officer, and carried to Lambeth street office, where he was sentenced for a month to the tread-mill at Brixton.

There were several boys in the yard with him, and some of them younger than himself.

The first night he came out of prison, he again sought shelter in a privy, and was again disturbed by a police-officer, but he escaped from him. Since then, he has sheltered himself in yards and out-houses in the neighbourhood of Limehouse; and recently slept for three weeks in a baker's barrow.

Wakefield Describes Nurseries of Crime in London and Shows How Capital Sentences Imposed upon Children Are Generally Commuted, 1831

Edward Gibbon Wakefield, *Facts Relating to the Punishment of Death in the Metropolis* (London, 1831), pp. v, viii, 16, 80-81, 88, 138, 140-41, 176 (Brit. Mus.)

INTRODUCTION

The object of the following pages is to lay before the public some information illustrative of the effects of Capital Punishment, as administered in London and Middlesex.

Part of the facts stated are derived from a Return made to the House of Commons early in the present year; but the greater number of those facts came under the observation of the writer himself, during his confinement for three years in the county jail of London and Middlesex. . . .

Some of the descriptions of scenes occurring within the walls of Newgate will be hardly believed, by persons who see the outside of the building every day of their lives. The great Metropolitan prison is a *terra incognita* even to those by whose habitations it is surrounded. The writer expects, therefore, to be charged with exaggeration, as if he had described a far distant and unknown country. He expects this the more, because he has related facts, of which he must have doubted if he had not actually witnessed them. But here is his principal motive,—as he trusts it may prove a justifi-cation,—for publishing what he has seen. Incredible scenes of horror occur in Newgate. Is it to be desired that such evil should remain unknown? By the answer to this question the writer must be blamed or excused for doing what, to those who do not ask them-

141

selves the question, may seem like ministering to a vulgar appetite for horrors.

Whatever justifies telling the truth on this occasion, imposes an obligation to tell the whole truth. The whole truth is told, therefore, precisely, and fully, without any regard to the reader's supposed credulity or scepticism, and with but one purpose in view throughout—that of leaving nothing material untold on those points with which the public is least acquainted. . . .

A. NURSERIES OF CRIME

Newgate itself, as I shall have occasion to show hereafter, is the greatest *Nursery* of capital crime. London abounds with smaller nurseries of petty offences by persons of every age, from infancy to manhood. I had the opportunity of strictly examining more than a hundred thieves, between eight and fourteen years, as to the immediate cause of their becoming thieves; and in nineteen cases out of twenty it appeared, that the boy had not committed his first crime spontaneously, but had been persuaded to commence the career of thieving by persons whose business it is to practise this kind of seduction.

The most numerous class of such seducers consists of experienced thieves, both men and boys, who look out for boys not criminal, to whom they represent the life of a thief as abounding in pleasure. The object of these representations is to obtain instruments, with which experienced thieves may commit robberies with less danger to themselves—participators, whose ignorance of the trade subjects them to be put forward into the most dangerous situations, and to be cheated in the division of the spoil. But words are not the only means of seduction employed in such cases: food is given to the hungry, and all kinds of stimulating enjoyments are presented to others, who do not want the means of subsistence. I state what I know to be a fact, in saying, that a practiced thief often spends as much as £10 in the course of a few days for the purpose of corrupting a youth, by taking him to playhouses and other shows, and allowing him to eat and drink extravagantly at pastry-cooks, fruit-shops, and public-houses. The inevitable consequence of such indulgences is the victim's discontent with his previous mode of life; and when this feeling predominates, he is considered ripe for receiving without alarm the suggestions of his seducer. Very often a still more effectual means of seduction is applied, viz. the precocious excitement and gratification of the sexual passion, by the aid of women in league with the thieves, and to

whom is commonly entrusted the task of suggesting to the intoxicated youth, that robbery is the only means, and a safe means, of
continuing to enjoy a life of riotous debauchery. This method of
seduction succeeds, I believe, *invariably*. For the information of
those who may think the statement overcharged, I add, that a large
proportion of the boys above twelve years of age, and some even
younger, committed to Newgate, have been connected with women;
a fact of which there is constant proof, since these boys are every
day visited by their mistresses, under the name of "sisters;" and the
greater part of their conversation in the prison, which is sometimes,
and might be always, overheard, turns upon their amours. In very
many cases women are wholly maintained by young thieves, whom
they will dress in a frill and a pinafore to appear at the bar of the
Old Bailey. But such boys as these, however young, are of the class
of seducers, being already practised thieves. Where women are
employed as seducers, they are but the instruments of practised
thieves—of those whom the law designates as "notorious thieves,"
and with whom, nothwithstanding, the Police seldom interfere, unless they be taken in the act of robbery. From this statement it will
be seen, that one of the most effectual means of *preventing* robberies would be an active, watchful, and constant interference with
the measures pursued by thieves for increasing the number of their
own body.

Another class of seducers consists of both men and women, but
principally of old women, the keepers of fruit-stalls and small cake-
shops, which stalls and shops they keep but as a cloak to their real
trade,—that of persuading children to become thieves, and receiving
goods stolen by children. The methods of seduction pursued by
these people are for the most part similar to those adopted by the
class mentioned above; but they are distinguished from the thieves
by some peculiarities. Residing always in the same spot, and apparently engaged in an honest calling, they have superior opportunities of practising on children, who, until known to them were
perfectly well disposed. Several instances came to my knowledge
of boys, the sons of decent trades-people, carefully educated, apprenticed to some trade, and with every prospect of leading an
industrious and honest life, who were seduced by persons of the
class in question. The course of seduction is about as follows.

The child buys fruit and cakes at the stall or shop, of which the
keeper takes pains to form a familiar acquaintance with him, by
conversation, artful it must be called in this case, but such as is
used by all good teachers in order to gain a pupil's confidence. He

passes the shop one day without money, and is invited to help himself upon trust. If he yield to the first temptation, it is all over with him. Considering his previous acquaintance with the tempter, it is almost a matter of course that he yields. Once in debt, he continues to indulge himself without restraint, and is soon involved far beyond his means of repayment. Where is the Police to save him? No act of robbery has been committed, and the Police therefore is absent. Probably his parents or master have impressed on him that it is wrong to run in debt. He is already criminal in his own eyes. Instead of confessing his difficulty to his friends, he thinks of them with fear. All his sensations are watched by the wretch, who now begins to talk slightingly of harsh parents and task-masters, and insinuates her own superior affection. By degrees, more or less slow according to the degree of her art and the excitability of the boy's temperament, she gets a complete mastery of his mind. At length she guides him to the first step in crime, by complaining of want of money, perhaps threatening to apply to his parents, and suggesting that he may easily repay her by taking some trifling article from his master's shop. The first robbery committed, the chances are a thousand to one that the thief will sooner or later be transported or hanged. He goes on robbing his master or perhaps his parents: the woman disposes of the stolen property, giving him only a moderate share of the money obtained: she introduces him to other boys, who are following the same career: he soon learns to prefer idleness and luxuries to labour and plain food; and, after a while, becoming an expert thief, deserts his original seducer, with whom he is no longer willing to share the fruits of his plunder, connects himself with a gang, probably takes a mistress, and is a confirmed robber on the high road to Botany Bay or the gallows. . . .

B. CAPITAL SENTENCES AFFECTING CHILDREN

When sentence of death is passed on a murderer, he is executed forthwith. The cases of all other persons under sentence of death are referred to the King in Council; and those sentences which the King in Council confirms, are again referred to the King out of Council, which means to the Secretary of State for the Home Department. . . . The sentence of death in London is, in truth, a conditional sentence. The Judge virtually says to the convict, "I condemn you to death; and your life will be taken, unless you can satisfy another tribunal that it ought to be spared. That other tribunal will not decide on your case for six weeks to come. I condemn you, meanwhile, to the most horrible suspense." I shall

144

endeavour to show presently that this is the real meaning of the sentence, as passed in London. It is passed indiscriminately on almost every capital convict, from the hardened burglar, whose crime was attended with violence to the person, to the child ten years old, who has pushed his hand through a pane of glass and stolen a cake *after dark.* . . .

Boys under fourteen years of age, who are sentenced to death, generally remain in the school, and are treated like all other prisoners of their own age. These form an exception to the ordinary practice as to convicts under sentence of death. They and the officers of the prison know, that they will not be executed; and the sentence passed on them, being a mere formal lie, they are not placed, as one may say, betwixt life and death, and do not require any unusual precautions for their safe custody. . . .

The Recorder of London informs the officers of Newgate of the decisions of the Council; and it is the duty of the Ordinary to tell each convict under sentence of death what the Council has decided for him. . . .

The Recorder's Report having reached Newgate, the Ordinary visits every convict under sentence of death, and informs him of his fate. The scenes of passionate joy, wild despair, jealousy, envy, hatred, malice, and brutal rage, which follow this proceeding of the Ordinary, should be witnessed in order to be thoroughly conceived. . . .

Generally, the Recorder's Report reaches the prison late at night. If there be any convicts in the School under sentence of death, all the boys in that ward are made to sit up during the night when the Report is expected. About midnight the Ordinary, attended by some officers of the Sheriff, enters the School, dressed in his canonicals, and calls over the names of those under sentence of death. They step forth from the crowd, three of them, let us suppose, of the respective ages of fourteen, twelve, and ten. The Ordinary, in his most solemn tone, says—"I am happy to inform you, A. B., and you, C. D., and you, E. F., that your cases have been taken into consideration by the King in Council, and that his Majesty has been mercifully pleased to spare your lives." Instantly, the boys fall on their knees, and recite a thanksgiving to God and the King for the mercy graciously vouchsafed to them.

To an uninstructed observer this sight might be very edifying; but to those engaged in the scene it is, in truth, only a mockery. The whole scene is got up betwixt the Ordinary, the Schoolmaster, and the boys,—the Ordinary instructing the Schoolmaster, and the

Schoolmaster instructing the boys, as to the part which these last are to play in the farce. The boys, amongst themselves, will recite the whole scene before hand; sometimes giving it a different turn, by causing one of themselves, who plays the Ordinary, to say, that the King has ordered the law to take its course; when those who play the convicts will act the most violent distress. Of course, the idea of what they are always made to profess, viz. gratitude to God and the King, never enters their heads; since every one is convinced that, as to these children, there never has been a question of danger. It is curious, however, to observe the satisfaction of the boys who are distinguished by taking a part in this ceremony. . . .

C. EFFECT ON BOYS OF WITNESSING PUBLIC EXECUTIONS

From inquiries made of the boys confined in the School Yard of Newgate, or rather, I ought to say, from having overheard the conversation of the boys amongst themselves, I am satisfied that every public execution *creates* some criminals. Every execution in front of Newgate is attended by some boys not yet criminal, apprentices, errandboys, and children on their way to or from school; and though, unfortunately, I neglected to keep an account of the number of cases ascertained by myself, I am confident, that few Old Bailey Sessions pass without the trial of a boy, whose first thought of crime occurred whilst he was witnessing an execution. Not less, I venture to say, than a dozen boys have assured me, that they were led to become thieves by attending executions. To some of them, the idea occurred simply through witnessing the struggles of a dying thief; to others, it was suggested by thieves, with whom they were led to form acquaintance by the excitement of the occasion, and who took advantage of that excitement to speak, with success, of the enjoyments of a thief and his many chances of impunity. . . .

Delinquent Children in the Eighteen-Thirties in London

Anon., *Old Bailey Experience: Criminal Jurisprudence and the Actual Working of Our Penal Code of Laws. Also, An Essay on Prison Discipline, to which is Added a History of the Crimes Committed by Offenders in the Present Day* (London, [1833]), pp. 38, 72, 300, 302, 297-98, 312-13, 361, 363, 393-99, 290 (editor's lib.)

[This work was published anonymously, but on the title page

appears the statement that it was written by the author of *The Schoolmaster's Experience in Newgate*. Some of the material in this volume appeared in the latter part of 1832 in *Fraser's Magazine*.

With regard to his qualifications for writing on this subject, the author says:

"Nearly three years experience in Newgate, and at the court where they are tried, have enabled me to arrive at certain conclusions. The circumstances under which I obtained these opportunities for observation is not necessary for me to state; suffice it to say, I was brought immediately into contact with the inmates of the prison, and that I had opportunities of seeing the prisoners in their unguarded moments—freed from all caution, and without their having had any motive for practising deception. During the period of my attendance I was employed in giving them advice, and was confidentially intrusted with their secrets for the purpose of defending them when in danger of punishment. I was, moreover, engaged as their amanuensis, both before and after their convictions, by which means I have become possessed of their true feelings, together with their standing and grade as professed thieves."]

A. Boy, Five and One-Half Years Old, Tried at the Old Bailey on a charge of Stealing a Watch

. . . I will add one more [case], that of a child committed to Newgate, as illustrative of magisterial carelessness. A baker, residing at Ealing, missed his watch, and was unable in any way to account for the loss of it. Two or three days subsequently a little boy, only five and a half years old, was seen in the road with it in his hand, showing it to every one he met, saying, "Look what I have got; I shall give it to my mother." An officer hearing of the circumstance took the child and watch before the magistrate, who questioned him regarding his possession of it. The little fellow told him he had just given another boy, whom he met on the common while at play, three marbles and two apples for it. The officer was sent with the child to the common to seek the other boy, but he was not to be found, and the child did not know his name, for which he was committed to Newgate, to be placed at the bar of the Old Bailey. Nothing could be more ludicrous than the appearance of this child in court. There was the clerk reading over the indictment to this little urchin, whose chin did not reach the bar, concluding with, "Are you guilty, or not guilty?" the judge, essaying an air of extraordinary gravity upon the occasion, shaking his head most portentously at the little boy, because he would call out, "Not guilty, my lord."

There was the minister of the parish, who had come up to town on the occasion, besides his mother, and other friends, together with the governor, all engaged in persuading this little fellow to plead guilty. In vain did they promise his mother would take him home, and that he should have a tart, if he would pronounce the word "guilty," without the addition of "not." But "not guilty, my lord," was all they could get from him. The fact is, they were ashamed of the farce of trying such an infant, and had arranged for him to pronounce the word guilty, then to respite the judgment, and immediately send him home with his mother. But the boys with whom he had been during his stay in prison, had so drilled him in what he was to say when he came before the judge, telling him, if he said "guilty," he would be hanged, that no power could induce him to say otherwise. The acting this farce concluded by a jury pronouncing him not guilty, after all the gravest heads in the court had concerted a record of guilty. . . .

B. Children Sentenced to Transportation for Minor Offenses

. . . The Old Bailey court, however, in proportion to the numbers, as often sentence boys as men to transportation for fourteen years and life. For one prisoner I felt very much, who was sent for the latter term; he was under thirteen years of age, and not a known offender; his crime was stealing his companion's hat, while they were looking at a puppet-show. The unfortunate boy says, "he knocked it off in fun," and that some other person must have found it. He was not taken up until the following day, and the hat was never produced. The policeman who took him into custody resided next door to the prisoner's mother, and was heard to say, "the boy had thrown stones at him, and that he would give him a *lift*." I know not what he said on the trial, but such was his heavy sentence. The mother was a widow, and he was her only son. I shall never forget her distress and agony of feeling when she heard his fate. Nothing can be more absurd than the practice of passing sentence of death on boys under fourteen years of age for petty offences. I have known five in one session in this awful situation; one for stealing a comb almost valueless, two for a child's sixpenny story-book, another for a man's stock, and the fifth for pawning his mother's shawl. In four of these cases the boys put their hands through a broken pane of glass in a shop-window, and stole the articles for which they were sentenced to death, and subsequently

148

transported for life. This act, in legal technicality, is house-breaking. The law presumes they break the glass, and it is probable in most instances they do so. In two of the cases here named, however, the prosecutrix's daughter told me there was only a piece of brown paper to supply the place of that which once had been glass. In the latter case, the unfortunate mother caused her son to be apprehended, in the hopes of persuading the magistrate to recommend him to the Refuge for the Destitute, or some other charitable institution. She, however, in the course of her examination, said she was from home, and that the house was locked up at the time of the shawl being taken, which was afterwards found at a pawnbroker's. This made it housebreaking; and, in spite of all the mother's efforts, he was condemned to death. He is now in the Penitentiary. The judges who award the punishments at the Old Bailey appear to me as if they were under the influence of sudden impulses of severity, there being at no time any regular system to be recognized in their proceedings. This the prisoners know, and speculate on, particularly the boys. . . .

May 15th, 1833, a boy of twelve years of age was sentenced to seven years transportation for stealing two penny rolls; it was said he was a bad character, but if we are to transport all the bad characters at twelve years of age, that is, all who are the sons of low, vulgar, and uneducated parents in this metropolis, there will soon be a great demand for tonnage amongst our shipping interest. And if we are not to transport all for like offences, being the same characters, why one? . . .

C. Theatres, Low Publications, and Dance Halls as Causes of Delinquency.

. . . The seducers of youth find an able auxiliary in the minor theatres, where they are generally sought. The men know, if a boy has a passion for these low exhibitions, that he is a sure prize. This the boys acknowledge; and full one half have confessed to me, that the low theatres have been the cause of their entering into crime, and in very many instances the offences for which they stood committed were occasioned by their want of money to gratify this passion. When they know they are about to be discharged, the first pleasure they anticipate is going to the theatre the same evening. Although turned out without hat or shoes, and in rags, they make sure of getting the money for this purpose; and I have no doubt many go from the prison-door to stealing for no other object,—such is their infatuation for these places. . . .

Although an advocate for the fullest liberty of the press, I regret to add, that if means could be taken to suppress the low publications, of which there are now so many sold, many boys would be saved from destruction who are now lost entirely by the influence these works have on their vitiated tastes, viz. the fictitious lives of robbers, pirates, and loose women. There is scarcely one in print that these boys have not by rote; their infatuation for them is unbounded, and the consequent perversion of their minds very fatal, in every instance when this passion seizes them. Although naturally restless in their habits, they will sit for six or eight hours together, relating and hearing tales of criminal heroes. A boy expert at telling these stories will exact and obtain half the allowance of food from the others, to gratify them in this passion.

. . . There is, however, one regulation which I think might be adopted without meeting with objection or opposition from any man, namely, that the proprietors of all theatres, other places of amusement, and public-houses, tea gardens, &c. &c. (i.e. of every place of entertainment,) should be prohibited, under pain of fine, &c. from admitting any boy or girl, under the apparent ages of fifteen years, unless in company with, and under the protection of, an adult. Although this measure would not entirely meet the evil, yet, it would throw so many obstacles in the way of young persons catering for themselves in matters of amusement, as to lessen the number of instances of corruption, and constrain youth to seek their pleasures through the concurrence only of their parents and guardians. Many licensed victuallers too pander to the appetites of youth, and betray them into crime; those who have back rooms in private parts of the town allow mere children to meet and dance the night through, providing them with music, lights, &c. for the sake of their custom, and other advantages they contrive to pick out of them, not unfrequently buying their stolen property; but cheating them in every way. I have myself known of thirty of these placed at one time, where females, but mere children to view, from twenty to fifty in number, might every night be seen, tawdrily decked out with baldrick and tiara, dancing with all the airs of a *Bona Roba*, with their fancy men. Sometimes, too, they mask it, by exchanging the whole, or part of each others dresses, or casmisating themselves—an amusement always reserved for gala nights. These assemblies are flashly designated cock and hen, chicken hops, or the freaks of the swell kids; uncoruncated Gynecocrasy is the prevailing form of government among them, and the female's every vanity is gratified, through the males, at the public expense. Libidinous desires are early excited, and crime becomes (if not before known) contemporaneous with them. If heavy fines, and other penalties, were visited on those, whether licensed victuallers or any other persons, who harboured boys and girls, the progress of this growing evil might be arrested; but a mere law being placed in the statute books will not affect it: a board of morals, having the command of their own officers, especially informed on all these subjects, can only effectually put down these, and other nuisances to the public, which affect the morals of the people.

D. BOY PICKPOCKETS

. . . When the sneak comes into the hands of the pickpocket, he is instructed and practised every hour of the day, until made tolerably perfect; he is then taken into the streets, to make his first essay in the presence of those who have taught: and it has been given in evidence, that they dress up a *lay* figure, hanging bells all over it, on which they practise. When the tyro can empty all the pockets of the figure, without occasioning a bell to sound, he is considered fit for the street. He generally begins with a pocket-handkerchief, whilst another takes "ding," that is, receives it from him. In almost all cases of robbery, one commits the act and another receives the article from the thief, which is called taking "ding." If they find a boy dull, they forthwith turn him out of their party.—

. . . The qualifications for a pickpocket are a light tread, a delicate sense of touch, combined with firm nerves. These boys may be known by their shoes in the street; they generally wear pumps, or shoes of a very light make, having long quarters. There is about their countenances an affected determination of purpose, and they walk forward, as if bent on some object of business: it is a rule with them never to stop in the street. When they want to confer for a moment they drop into some by-court or alley, where they will fix on an object of attack, as the people pass down a main street; when they start off in the same manner, the boy going first, to do what they call "stunning," that is, to pick the pocket. The first-rate hands never, on any occasion, loiter in the streets, unless at a procession, or any exhibition, when there is an excuse for so doing. Many have a notion that instruments are used in disencumbering the pockets: this is a false idea; the only instrument they use is a good pair of small scissors, and which will always be found on the person of a pickpocket when searched: these they use to cut the pocket and all off, when they cannot abstract its contents.

To these qualifications they unite a quick sight, and a tact of observing when the attention is engaged, or of devising some means to engage it themselves, until the act is done. They are most busy in foggy weather. When in prison, they will be heard to say on such days, "What a shame to lose such a fine day as this!" On great public days, when the streets are expected to be crowded, and much business is anticipated, several parties of them will unite for the day, under special contract, either to divide all gains between them, or for each one to retain what he gets, agreeing, under every circumstance, to mutually assist each other in the bustle of the crowd. . . .

E. NEED OF PUBLIC INSTITUTIONS FOR JUVENILE DELINQUENTS.

[The author severely criticises the majority of the private societies for reforming juvenile delinquents on the ground that such societies handle too few cases, that they select those least in need of attention and refuse to take the worst delinquents, and that they hold that "their own interests are paramount to that of the public." He urges the government to make the experiment of reclaiming juvenile delinquents, both boys and girls, through institutional care.]

. . . For [boys brought up in crime] there should be an establishment on an extensive scale in the country, where they should be brought up to useful labour for terms not less than from five to seven years. . . . For . . . (incidental juvenile offenders,) there should be a town penitentiary, where rigid discipline for one year might be usefully applied, their parents being called on to enter into security for their future good conduct.

Parents Should Be Held Responsible for the Delinquencies of Small Children, 1834

[Thomas Jevons], *Remarks on Criminal Law; with a Plan for an Improved System, and Observations on the Prevention of Crime* (London, 1834), pp. 92, 94-95, 98-99, 101 (Boston Pub. Lib.)

JUVENILE DELINQUENCY

Of all the sources of crime, juvenile delinquency is beyond all doubt the most prolific. It appears in evidence before a committee of the House of Commons, that three-fourths of the offences committed in London are by children. . . .

[The principal causes of delinquency are given as, beggary; want of education and instruction; habits of gambling, particularly on Sundays; the neglect of the poor, as to any care of their children; and fairs.]

On consideration, it will be found that all sources of crime just enumerated, together with those that spring from mendicity, may be traced to one original cause, namely, *the neglect of parents as to a proper care of their children;* which, without further argument, may be admitted to be the true one, and to this point we ought therefore to direct our principal attention, before we can hope to effect much good in the prevention of crime.

What, then, is the course we must pursue, to bring about a reform of this state of things? Not, certainly, the punishment of the children, for that is the course now pursued, and it notoriously fails in producing the desired result. Indeed the effect produced is the very opposite to that which is intended; and it has been said, that "a child once punished in a court of justice, or a jail, is lost for ever." Boys are found to be re-committed oftener than grown-up persons; and it is on record that one boy, who had not completed his twelfth year, had been confined within the walls of every prison in the Metropolis.

The answer to the question we have proposed is plain and simple. If the neglect of a parent occasions his child to commit a crime, such parent is in fact the author of that crime, and ought to be made accountable to the state. It must be understood that we speak of the delinquencies of small children. The particular age to which it may be proper to confine this accountability, must be open for future discussion; the principle alone is what is now wished to be established. . . .

In some particulars, the law of our land has already sanctioned the principle here contended for; for the parent is always liable for the reasonable debts of his child, until he becomes of lawful age to act for himself. And until this period arrives, no action for debt can lie against any individual in our courts of law, nor any one under twenty-one years of age hold some species of property in his own name.

There is some analogy between the principle of the law proposed, and that of the law which makes every man liable to prosecution for any damage or depredations committed by cattle belonging to him, caused by his want of proper care in guarding them. And until a child arrives at an age when it is enabled to provide for itself, and is free entirely from the control of its parents, why should they be released from all responsibility as regards any depredations which it may commit in consequence of their dereliction of duty?

But, on a more extended view, it will be perceived that the question involves in it the education of the people. There has always been some repugnance to treating the youngest class of delinquents in the same way as older criminals; and the practice has become very general to substitute schools and instruction for cells and the whip. But to commence a school education of the poor after the character has been formed to vice, is little more efficacious than closing the stable after the steed has been stolen, and, under all the circumstances, is indeed labour in vain. . . .

The subject at length resolves itself into this question. Is it possible for a government to take upon itself, and fulfil, the duties that naturally belong to the father of a family? It is to be presumed that the answer must be in the negative. It is the tendency that the criminal law has to usurp the parental authority that has chiefly occasioned its inefficacy; and to this cause we are most likely indebted for the original idea of punishment for crime, which we have contended against as being in every point of view improper. Punishment by law is severe, unmitigated, indiscriminating, unrelenting, ignorant, and blind, and acts upon a mind and disposition of which it knows nothing, and cares nothing beyond the infliction of its due measure of pain; in fact, it is not punishment, but REVENGE. Punishment, as administered by a father, is the reverse of all this; and it is so because it operates upon a mind of its own creation, and which is, or ought to be, the picture of its own purest ideas of virtue.

Delinquent Children, Seven to Fourteen Years of Age, Committed to the House of Correction, Cold Bath Fields, London, 1835-1837

Report from Select Committee on Metropolis Police Offices; with the Minutes of Evidence, Appendix, and Index ([London], 1838) (Brit. Mus.)

Return of Children, from the Ages of 7 to 14, Committed to the House of Correction, Cold Bath Fields, in the Years 1835, 1836, 1837

Ages	By Summary Convictions of Magistrates	By the Central Criminal Court and the Sessions
7	7	—
8	29	1
9	72	4
10	121	8
11	186	17
12	314	21
13	429	43
14	667	77
	1,825	171

Children in the Gaol at Warwick, 1836

Esther Tatnall,[1] *A Narrative of Twenty-three Years Superintendence of the Women and Boys' Wards in the Gaol at Warwick* (London, 1836), pp. 11, 17-23 (editor's lib.)

A NARRATIVE, &c.

At the particular request of my children, I have endeavoured to recall to my remembrance some of the most impressive and striking occurrences which fell under my observation during that most momentous period of my life, the twenty-three years I passed in Warwick gaol, as the wife of the Governor.

. . . even girls as young as from ten to twelve years of age were often committed for trifling offences. These were objects of particular attention; and I selected one of the women to teach them to work, read, and say the catechism, and prayers, for which I made her a trifling compensation.

These unfortunate children were generally the offspring of prostitutes, or of those whose crimes had brought on them the punishment of banishment or death, and had left these children to struggle through life how and where they could. They were generally much smaller than children of the same age usually are;

1. The reforms carried out by Mrs. Tatnall in the Women's Ward were very similar to those of Mrs. Fry at Newgate Prison in London. She tells of an appreciative visit by Mrs. Fry in 1823.

155

but their features and countenance bore no marks of the simplicity of childhood. On the contrary, they were strongly marked by the cunning and depravity but too visible in old offenders. I found that they had been employed by them to pass their days in purloining all that came in their way. If the means equalled the rapacious views of these wretches, they were regaled at night with a hot supper and a few pence, never more than twopence. Those to whom the day had been unsuccessful were dismissed to a wretched apartment with a severe reprimand, and a piece of dry bread, to rest on a little straw, and a rag to cover them; and, as may be imagined, they were often wet through, and destitute of shoes and other clothing. Such were their daily habits, till the hand of justice overtook them: a prison had no terrors for them; they seemed as much at home as the most hardened. It was long before I could fix their attention to the instructions I wished them to receive; but in time I had the satisfaction to perceive an alteration in their manner and appearance. They became anxious to obtain my approbation for what they had done or learnt; and as these favourable symptoms increased, I felt the more grieved to think that a short time would in all probability throw them again on the world, destitute of a home or advice, but such as the *most degraded* of the human species had to offer. This latter class of female prisoners were those I most dreaded to see enter the gates. Many instances could I bring forward, to shew that the counsel and example of these wretches had led the young in age and crime to commit the most aggravated offences; and led me often to wish that an asylum was established for girls, as had been provided for boys by the benevolence of the county.

Nor was my attention wholly confined to the unfortunate of my own sex, for many of the boys were even younger than the youngest of the girls. When I first went to the prison, in 1803, if there was a child under sixteen it was a rare occurrence: but, in the course of six or seven years, the number increased to more than twenty.* For these very young depredators I was anxious to do something, to amend their characters and condition; and, as a first step towards this desirable end, I consulted the governor as to the possibility of separating them from the older prisoners. He was so well pleased with what I had effected in the women's side of the prison, that he allowed the boys to be removed to an unoccupied room under the chapel, which had formerly been used as a workshop for

* At the spring assizes, in 1821, the calendar contained 226 prisoners, 110 of whom were between the ages of 13 and 20.

the male convicts; but the work at which they had been employed not answering, it had been discontinued.

I collected all the boys under 16 years of age (some were under 10 years of age), and arranged a school as well as my limited means would allow. The governor fixed on one of the prisoners, whose conduct and character were least exceptionable, to take the management of them, teach them to read, and say their prayers and catechism. The master took great pains with them; and in time some began to read tolerably, and repeated the prayers night and morning. The want of books was a great drawback to my progress. The moral and religious condition of these poor children was truly deplorable. They were entirely ignorant of the existence of a Supreme Being, never having heard the name of God but in conjunction with oaths and blasphemies. If they had ever been in a church, it was to steal whatever they could lay their hands on. It was the practice with the old offenders to send these boys out in gangs by day to purloin what they could; much in the same way as the little girls were sent out; but with this difference—that the boys were not allowed the same portion of rest, as it was customary, on their return in the evening, if well loaded with spoil, to regale them with unwholesome food and ardent spirits, to stimulate them to fresh acts of dishonesty, to which they were accompanied by the old offenders, who sallied forth at night to commit burglaries, in which these children, from their diminutive size, were convenient assistants.

These remarks, however, do not apply to all, or even to the majority of the boys who were committed for petty thefts to the walls of a prison. Many of them were far from being depraved characters; but, either from destitution, bad example, and other causes, which so frequently tempt children to act dishonestly when left without parents or friends, had been induced to commit offences, of the nature of which they did not appear to be aware. Among others, two little boys, one thirteen, the other fourteen years of age, were brought to the prison for some trifling depredation, committed more through necessity than wickedness. Both were in the last stage of consumption; emaciated, and destitute of clothing: much fitter objects of commiseration than punishment. Neither had any rememberance of their parents: they had been left destitute at too early an age to know who or what the beings were to whom they owed their birth, and had been in the habit of wandering about during the day, subsisting on precarious charity and theft. Their nights had been passed near a brick kiln; and thus day after day had been spent, till they were providentially sent to a prison, as their only place of refuge, where they terminated their earthly career within a few days of each other, enjoying comforts and attentions before unknown to them. I watched, I may say, with a mother's care, the progress of the disease, and administered all the little comforts in my power to bestow, in conjunction with some of the ladies who were accustomed to visit the prison, and who felt much interested for the poor sufferers. I was fortunate in being able to provide them an excellent nurse in one of the female convicts, and obtained permission from the humane surgeon to remove them from the boys' ward to the female infirmary. Such had been their extreme destitution that it was with great difficulty they were made to believe that some sheets hanging at the fire were intended for their use. After their removal to the infirmary, a few weeks terminated their lives. The night previous to the death of the first, he asked repeatedly how long it would be before the clock struck nine (the hour at which I usually went to see them). On entering the room, I perceived a marked alteration in his appearance. When I was seated by his bed, he put out his emaciated hands, wished to be raised, laid his head on my shoulder, looked at me with a smile of delight, then kissed me, and instantly expired. The other poor child departed in the same happy, composed manner, a few days later. . . .

Having thus settled a boy's and girl's school, no great alteration took place till the year 1814, when a new set of magistrates were appointed. These gentlemen inspected the prison, were much pleased with my arrangements, and with what I had done; agreed with me, that more might be done if space and accommodation were allowed: for which purpose, they gave an order to have the school-room properly fitted up, and every thing was done to further my plans. . . .

As I found my school arrangements succeed beyond my most sanguine expectations, I turned my attention to some means of securing employment, to fill up the time not devoted to learning. We inquired, among our Birmingham friends, as to what employment they could furnish the materials; and the heading of pins was at last fixed on as sufficiently easy, and well-adapted to our purpose, requiring no tools, that, by an improper use, might be the means of effecting an escape. The children in the Birmingham asylum were thus employed, which induced the Governor to visit it; and he had an interview with the manufacturers, who agreed to supply work free of expense to the county. The boys were set to work immediately, and received one third of the earnings for their immediate use; the remainder was reserved for them till they left the prison. . . .

The number of boys admitted into the [Birmingham] asylum, since its first establishment in 1817, is 203; of these, 117 are known to have been permanently reformed, and to be getting an honest livelihood in trade or service. The number now in the asylum is 18, which leaves 68 unaccounted for. Of these 68 there is satisfactory evidence that many have become better members of society.

Institutional Training to Be Followed by Compulsory Emigration Recommended for Juvenile Delinquents, 1837

William Augustus Miles, Esq., *A Letter to Lord John Russell, concerning Juvenile Delinquency, together with Suggestions Concerning a Reformatory Establishment* (Shrewsbury, 1837), pp. 2, 5, 6, 7, 9, 13, 15 (Goldsmiths' Lib.)

I have not followed the opinions of persons who have superficially examined the subject in order to obtain notoriety, but I have at various times examined many hundred boy thieves; and it is from close observations of the human mind, influenced by uncontrollable circumstances, that I have arrived at my conclusions. . . .

There is a marked tendency in many dispositions to early crime. This remark holds good among all classes of society, even from our universities to our prisons. . . . It is among these children [of the poorer classes] that the youngest in years may be found to be the most reckless and the most hardened in crime.

A boy only ten years of age was sentenced to death, together with his father, for housebreaking, and on his return from the court to his cell, preceded by the clergyman and his father, he said in an under-tone to the prisoners who were anxious to know the result of the trial, "I'm bless'd, if they haven't stuck it into our old chap at last!," pointing with his thumb to his doomed parent.

My observations upon the subject of Juvenile Crime induce me to attribute it chiefly to the following causes:

I. The congregating of the poorest classes in the low neighbourhoods.

II. The neglect of parents.

III. The facilities of selling every sort of stolen property.

A very great proportion of juvenile thieves in large towns are *thieves from necessity.* . . .

[To these wretched children] prisons are in many cases a refuge of luxury and comfort. A poor ragged Sweep about sixteen years of age, without shoes or stockings, and his red legs cracked with the cold, was brought to prison for some trifling offence. The warm bath into which he was put much delighted him, but nothing could exceed his astonishment on being told to put on shoes and stockings. "And am I to *wear* them? and this? and this too?" he said, as each article of dress was given to him. His joy was complete when they took him to his cell; he turned down the bed-clothes with great delight, and, half-doubting his good fortune, hesitatingly asked if he was really to sleep in the bed! On the following morning the governor, who had observed the lad's surprise, asked him what he thought of his situation. "Think of it, master! why I'm damn'd if ever I do another stroke of work!" The boy kept his word, and was ultimately transported. . . .

The nucleus of crime in St. Giles's consists of about six streets, riddled with courts, alleys, passages, and dark entries, all leading to rooms and smaller tenements, crowded with a population existing in all filth attendant upon improvidence, crime, and profligacy, as if the inhabitants by common consent deem themselves only "tenants at will" till the gallows or the hulks should require them.

Every room in the houses, from the cellar to the garret, is let separately to different persons at an enormous rent (say ten shillings per week.) These renters take others to lodge with them, so that frequently ten or twelve persons of both sexes may be found laying naked on the floor of the same apartment. An Irishman told me that he paid 10 s. a week for a front room, but that he contrived to live rent-free, having three men and their women domiciling with him, who each paid three-pence a night for their accommodation. . . .

The women and the girls in these districts live with their men as long as they can agree together, or until one or the other be imprisoned or transported. The very children are prostitutes living with their "fancy lads"; and it is difficult to say which are the most degraded, the men or the women, the girls or the boys.[1]

There are some parents who turn their children out every morning to provide for themselves, not caring by what means they procure a subsistence, so that the expense of feeding them does not abstract from their means of procuring gin or beer. Other

1. See also the testimony given by William A. Miles included in the *Second Report from the Select Committee of the House of Lords Appointed to Inquire into the Present State of the Several Gaols and Houses of Correction in England and Wales* . . . (1835), pp. 395-96.

parents require their children to bring home a specified sum every night, to obtain which they must beg or thieve. Others hire out their children to beggars for three-pence a day (a cripple is considered worth six pence); and many women hire children in arms about the same age, to pass them off in the public thoroughfares as twins. Groups of these young neglected vagabonds herd together, and theft becomes their study; even if a child was well disposed, it is not probable that he could escape the contagion of such bad example. There is a *community of children* who live and are separated from persons more advanced in years. Moreover, there is so rapid and so certain a communication among them all over the metropolis, that if they discover any of their slang or flash words to be known out of their circle they will substitute another, which in the course of a day or two will be adopted by the fraternity. There are lodging houses exclusively for their accommodation, public houses which are chiefly supported by their custom, and the landlords of both sorts of establishments are ever ready to purchase any plunder they may bring. . . .

My conclusion, therefore, is, that the neglect of parents in these low neighbourhoods renders them *nurseries* of crime. . . .

The receivers of stolen property abound in every district. . . . There is not a boy thief but who knows that he can immediately dispose of any property at any hour of the night or day. Many men who deal in plunder keep lodging houses, in which only boys and girls are admitted, upon condition that they board in the house and sell to the master all their booty. These houses are known under the flash term "Kid Kens". A pretended account is kept against these children, and they are duly forced to go out and thieve. Watches, bank notes, in short, every species of property, is bought for a mere nominal value—a few shillings is given to the thief, and the presumed balance is taken in liquidation of the previous debt or in earnest of future payment. These children have stated to me that they live in a complete state of thraldom. . . .

There are various grades or "castes" of these boys—a kind of aristocracy among them. There is the incipient house-breaker, or swell-mob-man; the pickpocket, a subdivided class however, for the boy who dives for purses or for watches, would scorn to take a handkerchief. Then, again, there is a class called "sneaks," who enter shops slily, or crawl upon their hands and knees to abstract a till. There is another "caste" or class called "bouncers," who enter a shop, and, while bargaining, contrive to steal property. Another class steals exposed property about shop doors or windows; others break, by means of a nail, the glass in windows in order to abstract goods; some rob from mercers by inserting a jagged wire and drawing silks through the bolt holes. There is one class who ride behind carriages to steal the leather braces, which they can sell for nine-pence each pair: but the lowest of all thieves (despised even of his fellows) is the "pudding snammer." These "pudding snammers" are young urchins whose love of pudding far exceeds all love of work; so they loiter about cook shops, and when customers are departing with plates of beef or pudding, the choice provision and the "pudding snammers" have vanished like magic! They sell the surplus, after gratifying their own hunger, to others boys or to coster-mongers, and then seek a shelter in some nest of crime, where they can be accommodated with a bed for three-pence, or a stair to sleep upon for a half-penny!

These above-mentioned grades generally herd together, and the "pudding snammer" is deemed unworthy of higher fellowship. . . .

In considering the subject of juvenile delinquency, it is requisite to take into account the various causes which compel them to be vicious. . . .

Young thieves have often confessed to me, that their first attempts at stealing commenced at apple stalls, and that having acquired confidence by a few successful adventures, they have gradually progressed in crime, allured by others, and in their turn, alluring. They find companions to cheer them and instruct them, girls to share their booty and applaud them, and every facility to sell their daily booty. There is, moreover, a kind of lottery adventure in each day's life; and as these excitements are attainable at so easy a rate, is it strange that these children are fascinated with, and abandon themselves to, crime?

Imprisonment to a young urchin who steals, and has no other means of subsistence, is no punishment, for it is indifferent to him where he exists so long as he has food and raiment. It is in prisons that boys form acquaintances more mischievous than themselves. Many lads have owned to me that they learned more in a gaol than out of one. . . .

The frequent number of re-committals in all our prisons proves the utter inefficiency of prison discipline with respect to reformation, and proves that such treatment only hardens in crime, whereby society is at considerable cost to make the bad, worse. The governors of many prisons have told me that boys are more astute, more hardened, and more difficult to conquer than adult thieves.

I have seen young children, not in their "teens," placed behind large iron bars, strong enough to restrain an elephant. And what is the effect? . . . The mind of the boy becomes impressed with an idea that he must be a very clever lad to require such barricadoes, and that society has a great dread of his talents. The elder thieves patronize a boy of this class. . . . I have observed that boys in Newgate who have been sentenced to death (although the boy, as well as the Judge and every person present, knew that he would not be hung in pursuance of that sentence,) conduct themselves as boys of a superior class to the transport lads. The boy under sentence of transportation for life is of greater consequence than the boy who is sentenced to seven years, while the lad whose sentence is a short imprisonment is not deemed worthy to associate or converse with them: in short, the daring offender is a member of the prison aristocracy or (rather *kakistocracy*), and severity of punishment is by them converted into a scale of merit. The pomp and panoply of justice only gives to these lads a feeling of self-importance: they never had any feeling of shame and disgrace; but this idea of self-importance might, if properly acted upon, be turned to the advancement of industry and honest emulation.

. . . There is a library in the boy's ward at Newgate: it contains a great number of evangelical books and lives of a great number of dissenting ministers; among the other books, however, there are a few containing history and travels, and it is with these latter books that the boys are delighted; they read them with eagerness, and the more illiterate boys will subscribe portions of food to engage the services of a boy to read to them aloud. . . . [Some who] did not know their letters when they came to prison . . . . were enabled to read before they left it.

. . . The lad is hopeless, consequently reckless in his conduct,— hardened to the present, and irreclaimable as to the future.

It is not by prison discipline that reformation can be effected: the temptations, the facilities, and the love of idleness, are too alluring. Crowds of young thieves will wait round a prison gate, to hail a companion on the morning of his liberation, and to carry him off to treat him and regale him for the day.

I have asked boys under sentence of transportation if they thought they *could* reform, if returned again upon society, and the general reply has been, "No." Their reasons for that conclusion I give in their own words: "if we were to be free to-morrow, we must go to our old haunts and our old companions, for where else *can* we go? If we try to be honest we cannot, for our 'Pals' (associates) would torment us to return; in short, we should only have to come back here at last, but we are now going to another country, where we hope to be honest men."

. . . There remarks bring me, my Lord, to the subject of a RE-FORMATORY ESTABLISHMENT, or HOME COLONY; and although my suggestions may be novel, I hope they may not be rejected as impracticable.

I therefore respectfully suggest that some district or Island be allotted for the reception of juvenile delinquents or vagrants, and that the lads should be instructed in trades, handicraft, and agriculture.

The ultimate object should be COMPULSORY EMIGRATION . . . [Estimates 11% of all criminals to be juvenile delinquents.]

. . . I should commence a treatment very different to the present system.

First, I should remove, as much as is consistent with safe custody, all idea of immediate restraint.

Secondly, I would instill habits of order, cleanliness, and punctuality.

Thirdly, the employments should be so varied, that the mind should be constantly employed.

Fourthly, the system of discipline should be rewards: all punishments should be as much as possible carefully avoided.

Fifthly, and lastly, each boy should of his own conviction find it to be his *interest* to behave well; that he is an integral part of the community in which he is placed; that the ultimate object of the establishment is more for his future benefit than a punishment for his past misconduct. When a boy is sent to this establishment, the period of his leaving it to go abroad (not to a penal colony) would depend upon his own good conduct, and the demand for juvenile labour in the colonies, (whither they should be sent as apprentices). . . .

If, however, the demand from the colonies should not be sufficient to take these youths, a free colony of them might be established near the Cape of Good Hope, or elsewhere; and as they would be instructed in various trades and agriculture, ultimate success might be reasonably anticipated.

In further continuance of my remarks concerning the suggested system of rewards, I should suggest that the executive part of the management should be entrusted, as much as possible to the youths, who among themselves should, at stated periods, elect their officers, whose duty it would be to enforce the standing orders. The Governor should supply a list of names of those, whose conduct should merit distinction, and from the list the youths should proceed to select their officers. . . .

Juvenile Prostitutes in Birmingham, 1840

> *Birmingham Society for the Protection of Young Females and*
> *Suppression of Juvenile Prostitution* (Birmingham [1840])
> (Brit. Mus.)

[This Society, which was established November 13, 1840, had for its objectives (1) the suppression of houses of ill-fame, especially those where juvenile prostitution was encouraged, (2) the punishment of procurers and procuresses to the limit of the law, and (3) co-operation with other institutions having a similar object].

REPORT OF THE PROVISIONAL COMMITTEE

In accordance with the resolutions of the Meeting by which they were appointed, the Provisional Committee have framed the Laws and Regulations of the Society. They have also inquired into the necessity which exists in Birmingham for such a Society, and they find that such necessity exists to an alarming extent.

They find, from statistics which have been laid before them, that in the town and neighborhood of Birmingham there are upwards of 700 infamous houses, in each of which from one to twelve young females are kept for licentious purposes, and in many of which juvenile and even infantine prostitution are carried on. They find also, that, in addition to these, there are numerous houses of assignation, where boys and girls, from eight to fourteen years of age, are encouraged to spend the whole nights together, the boys being thus trained to a course of immorality and crime, the girls to degradation and ruin.

They have also ascertained that there are in Birmingham procurers and procuresses, moving apparently in respectable spheres of life, who, though ostensibly living by trade, are, in reality, mainly dependent for subsistence upon the number of thoughtless and innocent girls they trepan, to feed the mortality of the bagnios, where the average of human existence, after entering upon their dark scenes of pollution, is, at the utmost, not more than seven years.

Juvenile Delinquency in Manchester, 1840

William Beaver Neale, *Juvenile Delinquency in Manchester: Its Causes and History, Its Consequences, and Some Suggestions Concerning Its Cure* (Manchester, 1840), pp. 7-8, 13-16, 46, 52-53, 40-41, 37 (editor's lib.)

[PRIMARY CAUSES OF JUVENILE DELINQUENCY]

The primary causes of juvenile delinquency, like that of crime in general, are deeply implanted in the fallen nature of man, and the vicious constitution of the present state of society. . . .

The existence of the class of juvenile delinquents, like that of adult and aged criminals, is unhappily a peculiarity of no quarter of the globe; but wherever men are associated together, there will be found both young and old ready to violate the laws, and to prey upon their species. . . .

[THE "MORAL TOPOGRAPHY" OF MANCHESTER]

While, therefore, the prevalence of juvenile delinquency is one of the characteristics of Manchester and the manufacturing districts, resulting (as we have observed) from this congregation of so many young persons, *there are certain classes of society, and certain quarters,* (especialy in great cities) *more congenial to criminals, and from whence they more especially emanate.*

Thus, in Manchester and the manufacturing districts, as everywhere else, the class of criminals spring chiefly from the most abject, ignorant, improvident, and poverty-stricken of the population; and the quarters which they occupy are the lowest, the most incommodious, and loathsome in the city; showing *that poverty is the parent of crime, and that misery is allied to guilt.*

As a general rule, in the manufacturing districts, these quarters are principally occupied by the lowest class of the Irish, who while they are not to be charged solely or beyond their fair proportion with crime, are yet at the same time in that condition of life from which criminals principally emanate: while, by reason of their poverty, they occupy those quarters which are found to be the most congenial to criminals, of whatever nation they may happen to consist.

Thus, in the moral topography of Manchester, Angel Meadow, which comprises a number of streets, New Town, Blakely-street, St. George's-road, Oldham-road, Great Ancoats-street, and Pollard-street, Deansgate, Little Ireland, Pop Gardens, Gaythorn and Knott

Mill, are the districts which may be pointed out as principally occupied by the criminal portion of society; and in describing these
quarters and the character of those who occupy and frequent them,
we shall have to exhibit, only in their more aggravated forms, that
improvidence, that poverty, and those criminal characters, occupations, and pursuits which are unhappily not confined to these
quarters alone: and it is presumed that in so doing, some light will
be thrown upon the causes of juvenile delinquency and of crime in
general.

Here, then, the narrow, ill-ventilated, and filthy streets, with
their stunted and dirty hovels, markedly contrast with the spacious
warehouse, the lofty factory, and the public buildings situated in
the more airy and commodious quarters of the town; and while
such is the uninviting character of the external appearance, it is
only exceeded by the confinement, darkness, nakedness, and filth
which characterize the thickly populated dwellings of a class, who
live by a mingled recourse to elemosynary relief and criminal pursuits, and whose honest or illicit gains are spent with equal improvidence and profligacy. Here may be found the habitual dependent
upon the public charity; here, the vagrant and sturdy mendicant;
here, the symbols are displayed of the low pawn-broker, who
exchanges for the clothing and other necessaries of the poor, money
to be spent in profligacy, or to supply the cravings of nature; here,
in some dark and remote cellar, the philosophic coiner of bad
money and the illicit distiller carry on their dark designs; here is the
den of the prostitute, infested by the lowest and most abandoned
of her sex, and their retainers: here is the low beer and spirit shop—
the resort of gamblers, thieves, and prostitutes—and where gains
which should be applied to the support of a family, or have been
fraudulently obtained, are spent in brutalizing debauchery; and
lastly, here is that focus of contagion—the low lodging house, which,
rented at a few shillings a-week, is sub-let again to a variety of
persons, and where, for the sum of twopence or threepence a night,
vagrants, thieves, prostitutes, and a nest of juvenile delinquents find
shelter. It is from such a region of physical degradation that
contagion and pestilence spread abroad, and it is out of such a community that crime has its birth, and principally emanates; and here,
at least, on account of the facilities which it affords, criminals of
all kinds and from all quarters congregate, as the soil most congenial to them. And to be born and bred in such a region, and exposed to such influences, what is it but to be predestinated to a life
of poverty, ignorance, misery, and guilt?. . .

Juvenile vagrancy is . . . the first step in juvenile delinquency, and is the high road to felony, pauperism, and prostitution.

Sent forth at an early age as beggars, and venders of matches, tape, sand, &c., they are early instructed to add theft to vagrancy; and instinctively conscious that all is not right with them, they even at this early period of life, shun the constable as the enemy of their race: and those who are best acquainted with this class can testify to the precocity of their minds, the ingenuity of their devices, and the cunningness of their shifts and evasions, when questioned by the agents of the police.

The aptness of the infant mind to receive the seeds of evil as well as good impressions, is well known; and in the class of whom we are speaking, this ingenuity of mind is called forth and quickened by chastisements and privations.

The child is sent out by its indigent parent, its hostile stepmother, or still more interested and unfeeling guardian, with strict injunctions not to return home without having obtained a certain sum of money, or quantity of provisions.

If it has been obtained, well and good, and he returns home to receive the commendation of his parent, and to share in what he has himself been instrumental in obtaining; but on the other hand, should he fail, through negligence, to procure the requisite supply, he dares not venture home—or if he does, nothing but chastisement awaits him, and he is driven forth and denied shelter and food.

Unhappily, this system is too often put in practice; and so much so, that even where it does not exist, it is a ready tale with young vagrants, who, when soliciting relief, seek to excite sympathy for their case by declaring that they dare not venture home unprovided.

It therefore becomes the interest of the child to make up by peculation what cannot be procured by solicitation; till the sale of matches, &c. is only the ostensible object of the young delinquent, and serves as a blind to cover his real purpose—which is to commit depredations in every way suitable to his age—such, for instance, as creeping behind the counter in shops, and stealing the money from the till; and prowling about with a watchful eye, they pick up every thing loose at shop windows, or gentlemen's houses, or wherever else they may hawk their commodities. At the same time, it is well known that young children are often employed by more experenced thieves, to bring them information as to where and how property is situated; and they are also employed by house-breakers, to enter through windows and small apertures, and at the proper time to open the doors for the admission of their older accomplices.

From twelve to fourteen years of age, a new and more extensive career of depredations is carried on. The juvenile vagrants now become initiated by their parents, their brothers, or companions, (who are probably themselves thieves) in the art of picking pockets, and shop-lifting; clothes-lines are now stripped by them, gardens plundered, dogs stolen, and hen-roosts and dove-cots invaded—from which latter depredations they are familiarly called *"dog and pigeon fanciers."* To these they add, robbing from drunken persons in the streets; plundering uninhabited houses, where property has been left; and cutting the lead and piping, and abstracting the panes of glass from newly-constructed buildings—a mode of depredation which is very prevalent in Manchester.

At this period of life, they are usually associated in gangs of from two to five, and generally place themselves under the guidance of the most expert among their number, or under that of some old and experienced thief; who, while he carefully screens himself from the reach of the magistrate, employs these young persons as his instruments, and directs their operations.

The number of those who set out upon any marauding excursion, of course varies according to its nature: pocket-picking is generally accomplished by four or five persons, petty larcenies by two or three, and in robbing drunken persons in the streets, generally in numbers, assisted by prostitutes.

In pocket-picking, from persons walking in the streets, or standing at shop doors or windows, it is the lesser of the gang who picks the pocket, by slily approaching the person, and is generally without shoes, that the sound of his footsteps may not be heard; an adult accomplice stands immediately behind him, in order to intercept the view of passengers, and in case of detection, to come to the rescue of the principal, by scuffling with the person whose pocket it has been attempted to pick, or if necessary, by dealing him a heavy blow, by which means the principal often effects his escape. Others, again, employ themselves as lookers-out, or hunt for fresh prey; and attempt, by sham fighting in the streets, and every other device, to collect a crowd together, and thus afford facilities to their accomplices for picking pockets.

In robbing clothes-lines, the usual practice is, for one of the party to watch the person who hangs them out into the house; one then is stationed at the door to give the alarm, while the others proceed to strip the line, and make off with their booty. This practice is carried on to a great extent in Manchester.

In robbing houses, during the absence of the inmates, the first object is to ascertain if the key is in the lock, by one of the party introducing his little finger into the key-hole; he then knocks, and receiving no answer, immediately communicates with the others, who are close in ambush awaiting the result. One then goes with the skeleton-keys, and as soon as the door is open, the signal is given and they enter. Their first object is to bolt the door after them, and open the back door, ready for escape; and while one remains down stairs, the rest ransack the house: they then retire by the back-door, taking what is most valuable with them. Should they fail in opening the front-door, the plan next adopted is, to go to the back-door, get over the yard, break a pane of glass underneath the window fastening, and to introduce their hand and unfasten the window: but should this expedient likewise fail, the smallest of the party is passed through the aperture,* who affords an entrance to the rest of the gang: but once entered, the first object is to secure the front-door.

In the early part of the morning, juvenile delinquents are to be found at home, at the homes of one another, or at some lodging-house, beer-shop, or place of common resort.

Towards noon, they may be seen hanging in groups about the corners of the streets—some eagerly engaged in playing at pitch and toss, or some other game of chance; others diverting themselves with foot-racing, and similar sports; and others again in small knots, concocting some new robbery.

In the evening, towards dusk, they sally forth to commit the various depredations that have been enumerated; and again assemble to relate their adventures and to divide the spoil, the contests respecting which often lead to their detection.

At a late hour of the night, they are to be found in cellars and low lodging-houses, where they pay from twopence to threepence a night, and sleep three or four in a bed, in a confined room, where there are from three to six, and sometimes fourteen beds, occupied by vagrants, prostitutes, thieves, and characters of all descriptions; who, with juvenile delinquents and children, are without distinction of age, or sex, or character, promiscuously mingled together. . . .

* An instance occurred in Manchester, where a little boy was passed into a shop, through the aperture or box in which the shutters are deposited during the day.

[The "Toffy-Man"]

. . . The author has often witnessed a remarkable sight in the streets occupied by the poorer classes in Manchester; it is the custom there for the toffy-man to traverse them periodically with his tray of sweetmeats, and those who have witnessed the effect produced upon the canine and feline tribes, by the appearance of the dog and cat's-meat man, may form some conception of that which is produced upon the children of the poor by the arrival of the toffy-man; immediately upon his appearance, and as he passes along the streets, the children of the poor are seen to issue from their dwellings, each with a supply of rags and old metal; and, in some instances, with their own clothing, or that of their parents, which they hasten to barter for toffy. Venial as this practice may seem, it leads to peculation which must also be resorted to when the penny showman presents himself; but in this case money must be got, and when to these sources of petty depredations we add the sum that is necessary for the support of the unfortunate passion of gambling where it has been acquired, some opinion may be formed of the amount of petty larcenies to which parents among the poor are subjected from their children. . . .

[Three-Penny Lodging Houses]

. . . In connection with the subject of juvenile delinquency, the author may be expected to offer some observations upon the low lodging-houses, and other places, more particularly frequented by this class of offenders; and this he is prepared to do, having explored upwards of a hundred of them, accompanied by the agents of the police. As was elsewhere observed, the day is usually passed by juvenile offenders, as well as by adult criminals, in the lowest class of beer and spirit shops, where they spend their time "from morn till noon, from noon till dewy eve," in fiddling, dancing, gambling, drinking, and every species of debauchery. It is from these dens of iniquity that, when night has darkened the streets, these sons of Belial wander forth, inflamed with insolence and wine, to commit the various depredations and offences which so much excite the public surprise; till at length, when satiated with debauchery, and tired with the activity of criminal enterprises, they steal home at a late hour of the night to take their rest in those sinks of infamy—the low three-penny lodging-houses, more particularly frequented by vagrants, but which are the common resort of all species of criminal characters. The impression which a visit to these places has left

171

upon the mind of the author, cannot easily be effaced; but language is inadequate to describe the extent of the moral and physical degradation in which the inmates of these places are found to exist, which, to be known, must be seen. The following picture, however, may convey some faint idea of the general characteristics of this class of houses.

Let the reader imagine himself introduced into a damp cellar, or dark and dirty garret, where he sees as many beds as it will hold, (from six to fourteen in number) ranged side by side, and closely adjoining one another; that in each of these beds he discovers from two to four persons, of either sex, and of all ages and character, who are, however, hidden from his view by the mass of clothes taken from those in bed, and now hanging in lines in various directions about the apartment, and he will form some conception of the scene which a lodging-house at first view presents. Let him imagine that the temperature of this room is at a fever heat, owing to the total absence of all means of ventilation, and in consequence of so many persons breathing and being crowded together in so small a space; let him imagine himself assailed by a disgusting, faint, and sickening effluvia, to which the pure breath of heaven is a paradise, and he then may conceive the effects produced, on entering these crowded dormitories, by the vapour and steam floating about them. Let him remember that the bed-linen is rarely changed—once in six months—and that in these beds, meanwhile, have been located an ever changeful race of diseased and sick, as well as convalescent persons; and let him imagine these beds to be likewise visibly infested with all manner of vermin, and he will form a conception, far short however, of the reality of the horrible spectacle presented, not by one, but by many hundred lodging-houses in Manchester.

While, owing to the filthy state of these lodging-houses, juvenile offenders are generally found afflicted with scabies or itch, and the tinea capitis, or scald head, with a variety of other infectious diseases, it is here that they become familiarized with scenes of infamy offensive to every principle of morality; and here it is that they become initiated into every species of criminality, by the precepts and example of adult and hardened offenders. The proprietors of these lodging-houses, and of the low beer and spirit shops, are the principal foils and receivers of stolen goods of the young delinquent; and hence these houses are always open to him, at times when his resources are low, as well as when he is flush of money. The juvenile delinquent, who is in general a gambler and a drunkard, is also a debtor, and usually behind-hand in his payment of the beer and

Marine Society Apprentices Vagrant and Delinquent Boys
to Sea Service, London, 1756

Boston Boy Thieves Running Away, 1815

House of Refuge, Philadelphia, Pennsylvania, c. 1812

Nathaniel C. Hart, Superintendent, New York House of Refuge,
New York, *c.* 1826

Rev. E. M. P. Wells, Superintendent, Boston House
of Reformation, 1826-1832

The Philanthropic Reform in St. George's Fields, London, 1814

lodging-house keeper; hence, whatever sum he may plunder from the public, it goes to pay old scores, or is spent as fast as it is obtained upon his expensive passions; hence, while the delinquent in general finds the means of subsistence, either in plunder or upon credit, he is, in a great measure, in the power of the proprietor of the lodging-house, the spirit shop, or of that in which stolen property is received—who, for indemnification of the lodging, the food and liquor, or the money given in advance, stimulate him to fresh plunder, the greater proportion of which they find means of appropriating to themselves. . . .

[REFORMATION NEEDED IN CRIMINAL CODE, AS IT AFFECTS JUVENILE OFFENDERS]

[After calling attention to the evils in the existing system of handling delinquents, Neale suggests the steps needed to effect a cure, as follows:]

1st. The refusal of all entire pardon upon the first or second offences of juvenile delinquents, unless the parents or guardians of the child can show good cause to expect that a recurrence of the offence will not take place; and when the pardon is obtained by the solicitation of the parents, they should be responsible (at least for a certain period) for the good conduct of the offender; and in all such cases, where it is proved that any adult has been the instigator of the offence on the part of the juvenile delinquent, such offender or offenders should be treated with the utmost rigour of the law. This would tend far to deter many a crafty resetter, who employs children and youths to commit criminal actions, the profits of which they reap, while they themselves escape punishment.

2dly. A better graduated scale and system of punishments, more applicable to juvenile delinquents, should be introduced which, while they did not shock the feelings of the enlightened and humane, would tend by the very certainty of their infliction to operate more powerfully in preventing crime than the most severe punishments; and while the certainty of punishment is thus ensured, it

3rdly. Should be carried into effect with the least possible delay and expense, which might be accomplished by making it lawful for any two magistrates to deal summarily, or upon the verdict of a jury of five assembled every week, in all such cases of larceny and misdemeanor, where the offender is under 16 years of age. And

4thly. These magistrates should be directed to commit him or her to some penitentiary or asylum (established for the purpose) for a certain limited period, AND AT THE SAME TIME EMPOWERING THE

173

MAGISTRATES TO COMMIT CERTAIN CASES TO THE SESSIONS, THERE TO TAKE THEIR TRIAL AND RECEIVE SENTENCE; BUT IN NO INSTANCE SHOULD THE DELINQUENTS BE COMMITTED TO A COMMON GAOL, BUT TO THE ABOVE MENTIONED PENITENTIARY, THERE TO BE DETAINED TILL THE PERIOD OF THEIR TRIAL, AND AFTERWARDS FOR SUCH TIME AS THEY MAY BE SENTENCED TO IMPRISONMENT. These observations are partly the substance of a bill introduced this session by Sir Eardley Wilmot, who, for the last twenty years or more, has laboured unweariedly in the benevolent and patriotic cause of diminishing crime by the industrial training and amelioration of the class of juvenile offenders. . . .

[THE CHILDREN'S FRIEND SOCIETIES]

In connection with the institutions for juvenile offenders[1] in this country and on the Continent, there have existed associations of a highly interesting and benevolent order, which have been justly called *The Children's Friend Societies*, and it is in imitation of these that it would become desirable that one should be formed in Manchester. The duties of this society will extend, not only to the protection and future provision in life of reformed offenders, but they will be pledged to collect every information on the subject of juvenile delinquency, in order to render themselves capable of discharging their duties, and with a view of enlightening the public upon this subject. The immediate duties of this association will be to take cognizance of all those cases of destitute or ill advised young persons who are abandoned by want, or evil companionship, to all the seductions of misery and crime, to whom they will open the gates of the asylum. The association will then have to watch over their progress while in the refuge, and will receive from the governor a succinct account of the birth, parentage, history, and character of each of the pupils, as they are about to leave it. Each member will then become the protector and guardian of one or more reformed delinquents, and will have to point out how their little capital can be laid out to the best advantage; and in short will, by their counsel and aid, guide in every way the inexperienced steps of their ward upon his first entrance into the world. The Association will likewise act as a collective body, and make arrangements in some of our

1. In an earlier section of this report, the author had recommended the establishment in Manchester of a penitentiary for juvenile delinquents, had presented probable costs of such an institution and its internal economy, and had proposed a program of trade training, secular education, and moral and religious instruction. In the *Appendix* he presents also short accounts of several institutions for delinquents including those in Glasgow, Rotterdam, and Paris.

colonies (*not penal, and where labour is in demand**) for the reception and provision of a certain number of young persons, who will be sent out as they are required. It is PROPOSED THAT THIS AS-SOCIATION SHALL CONSIST OF THE PRINCIPAL PUBLIC MEN IN MAN-CHESTER AS EX-OFFICIO MEMBERS, WITH ALL SUCH OTHERS AS MAY ENROL THEIR NAMES; AND FURTHER, THAT THE GOVERNMENT OF THE INSTITUTION SHALL BE ESPECIALLY UNDER THE CONTROL OF THE ABOVE MENTIONED PUBLIC AUTHORITIES AS EX-OFFICIO AND PERMANENT DIREC-TORS, AND LIKEWISE UNDER THAT OF TWENTY-FOUR MEMBERS, AN-NUALLY ELECTED FROM THE MEMBERS FORMING THE ASSOCIATION CALLED THE CHILDREN'S FRIEND SOCIETY.

Punishment of Children for Offences in Prison, 1840, 1846, 1849

[A] *Sixth Report of the Inspectors . . . to Visit the Different Prisons of Great Britain. I. Home District, London, 1841. Digest of Gaol Returns, Relating to the Prisons of England and Wales* (London, 1840), p. 205a (editor's lib.)

* For this purpose, while the trades taught in the Institution should be those generally in demand in all parts of this country and the world, a certain number of pupils ought to be instructed in agriculture.

Total Number of Punishments[1] for Offences within the Prison in England and Wales, in the Course of the Year (1840)

	Handcuffs and Other Irons		Whipping		Dark Cells		Solitary Cells		Stoppage of Diet		Other Punishments		Total	
	M	F	M	F	M	F	M	F	M	F	M	F	M	F
Total Adult	183	154	70		6956	1554	7702	1462	32141	8417	1945	1450	48997	13037
Total Juvenile	10	5	88		1338	100	1722	253	8560	520	483	57	12201	935
Total Adult and Juvenile	193	159	158		8294	1654	9424	1715	40701	8937	2428	1507	61198	13972
Grand Total Both Sexes	352		158		9948		11139		49638		3935		75170	

1. A preceding table shows that 491 juvenile males and 94 juvenile females were sentenced by courts of justice in England and Wales to solitary confinement during the year 1840 and that 75 boys were sentenced to be publicly whipped and 626 to be privately whipped during that year.

[B] Sir Peter Laurie, *"Killing No Murder;" or, The Effects of Separate Confinement on the Bodily and Mental Condition of Prisoners, etc.* (London, 1846), pp. 15-17 (editor's lib.)

[PUNISHMENT OF CHILDREN IN THE READING GAOL]

. . . I have extracted from the list of Prison Punishments in this Gaol (at p. 67)* the cases of eight convicted children, varying from ten to fourteen years of age, punished for what these lauded prison authorities term "offences." This is bad enough; but it sinks into insignificance before the second list, of fifteen cases of punishment, inflicted on children from *nine* (!) to fourteen years of age, all *unconvicted*. It would be a waste of words to denounce such unheard-of treatment; the common feelings of our nature denounce it as an outrage on humanity; and yet I regret to be obliged to add, that the Inspectors record this list without one syllable of reproach, or even a hint of its impropriety.

CONVICTED CHILDREN

Age

A.A.	13.	Disobedience	1 hour in dark cell.
L.B.	14.	Neglecting to clean cell	1 hour in dark cell.
W.M.	12.	*Turning round to look at another prisoner*	1 hour and 20 minutes in dark cell.
W.M.	12.	Endeavouring to converse with another prisoner	quarter hour in dark cell.
T.M.	10.	Ditto	Ditto
W.L.	11.	Cutting table	9 hours in dark cell on bread and water.
W.S.	13.	Endeavouring to look at another prisoner in chapel	Deprived of dinner.
S.L.	14.	Talking in chapel	8 hours in dark cell on bread and water.

UNCONVICTED CHILDREN

R.L.	9.!!	Improper conduct in chapel	1 hour in dark cell.
S.L.	14.	Turning up veil (girl)	1 hour in dark cell.
J.L.	12.	Disobedience of orders	Ditto

* Tenth Report of the Inspectors of Prisons for the Home District.

J.L.	12.	Repeated disobedience of order.......................	*12 hours in dark cell on bread and water*
S.Y.	14.	Disobedience of orders and insolence....................	4 hours in dark cell and deprived of supper.
S.L.	14.	Ditto........................	Ditto
S.L.	14.	Wilful damage	*1 day and 4 hours in dark cell on bread and water.*
I.N.	11.	*Endeavouring* to communicate....	2 hours in dark cell
W.L.	11.	Cutting table..................	*9 hours in dark cell on bread and water.*
S.L.	14.	Talking in chapel..............	9 hours in dark cell on bread and water.
S.L.	14.	Ditto........................	21 hours ditto!!
S.L.	14.	Ditto........................	2 days in dark cell and deprived of dinner!
I.L.	14.	Ditto........................	2 hours dark cell, and deprived of dinner.
G.N.	13.	Ditto........................	Ditto
S.L.	14.	*Endeavouring to communicate*....	Deprived of dinner.

I think it would be difficult to find a more revolting catalogue than these lists present: nor do I envy the man who can read them without feelings of the strongest indignation and disgust. What the feelings of those must be who could order or sanction such treatment of helpless and unfortunate children, I confess myself utterly unable to imagine. It is idle to talk of the legality of thus punishing and terrifying unconvicted children: the question is not, is it not illegal? but is it not inhuman? Here is an infant almost, of nine years of age, incarcerated in a dark cell for "*improper* conduct in chapel;" another child, *twelve years old,* immured in a dark cell for the heinous offence of turning round to look at some other unhappy child!

[C] Joseph Fletcher, *Statistics of the Farm School System of the Continent, and of its Applicability to the Preventive and Reformatory Education of Pauper and Criminal Children in England* (London, 1878), p. 61 (editor's lib.). Reprinted from the *Journal of the Statistical Society of London,* 16th February, 1851 (editor's lib.)

Punishments for Offences in Prison, inflicted on Juvenile Prisoners [under 17] in the Gaols of England and Wales, in the Course of the Year 1849

Punishment	Males	Females	Total
Handcuffs and other irons	18	5	23
Whipping[1]	85	——	85
Dark Cells	1627	135	1762
Solitary Cells	2418	311	2629
Stoppages of Diet	12,770	581	13,351
Other Punishments	280	38	318
TOTAL	17,198	968	18,168

Development of Unofficial Probation System in Warwick and Birmingham, 1841 (c. 1820-1854)

[A] Matthew Davenport Hill, *Draft Report on the Principles of Punishment** (London, 1847), p. 9 (editor's lib.)

By an arrangement which has been in operation at the Birmingham sessions from the beginning of the year 1841 young convicts who are not hardened in crime are, after trial, delivered to the care of their employers or parents, as the case may be.

These persons enter into an engagement to superintend the conduct of their young wards, and to furnish them with the opportunity of earning or assisting to earn their livelihood.

Both guardians and wards are visited from time to time by one of the superior officers of police, for the purpose of ascertaining the conduct of the parties.

The results of this treatment up to October last were as follows: 113 convicts had been so delivered up. Of these 44 were reformed, 40 relapsed, and of 29 the conduct was doubtful.

The majority of these 29 there was reason to fear had relapsed. But all having left their masters, and many having left the town, nothing certain was known of them.

This experiment, which at all events is inexpensive, may be called satisfactory, when it is considered that from the moment

1. According to a table on the preceding page (p. 60) the number of juvenile prisoners sentenced by the courts to be whipped was, publicly 4, and privately, 1,852; in all 1,856.

* Presented to the Committee on Criminal Law Appointed by the Law Amendment Society, in December, 1846. This draft was adopted by the Committee only in part.

the young offender leaves the bar, the Court has no legal control either over him or his guardian, who of course acts gratuitously.

[B] Matthew Davenport Hill, *Suggestions for the Repression of Crime, Contained in Charges Delivered to Grand Juries of Birmingham* (London, 1857), pp. 347, 351-52 (Brit. Mus.)

Five-and-thirty years ago I joined the Bar of the Midland Circuit, and became an attendant at the Warwickshire Sessions. At that time the whole judicial business of the county, including that which arises at Birmingham, was transacted at Warwick; with the exception only of such as belonged to Coventry and the small district forming the county of that city. . . . Sometimes [the magistrates of the Warwickshire Sessions] ventured, when the prosecutor came before them and humanely consented to receive back his dishonest young servant or apprentice, to consign the youth immediately to his care. On these occasions I have narrowly watched the countenances of the prisoner and his friends, including the prosecutor—his best friend—to enable me to form a conjecture as to whether the experiment was likely to be successful; and the conclusions which I drew from the imperfect evidence at my command were favourable to the plan. But it was tried under many disadvantages. It frequently happened that the evidence of the prosecutor not being required, he remained at home, and in such case his assent could not be obtained. Again, the magistrates had no means of forming an estimate of the prosecutor's respectability but from his appearance; and, if that were against him, they felt, and rightly felt, bound not to entrust the prisoner to his care. But the most serious defect of the plan was that they had no sure means of learning the results of their clemency; except that, in case of failure, it sometimes happened that the prisoner came again before them, but not always, as he might have chosen a field for the exercise of his calling in a district out of their jurisdiction. Being, however, much impressed with the value, or what, with all its drawbacks, I considered to be the value, of this mode of disposing of juvenile prisoners, I determined, when I was appointed Recorder of Birmingham, to try the experiment myself, under circumstances more favourable than those under which the County Magistrates acted; because at Birmingham the master or the parent was at hand, even if not in court; because inquiry could readily be made as to their character; and, above all, because by keeping a register, the failure and success of the plan, in each instance, could be recorded. Aided by the Chief Superintendent of Police, I have had inquiries made, from time to time, as to the conduct of the prisoner; and the result of these inquiries being reduced to writing, I am possessed of all the means necessary for accurately testing the value of such a measure. I hold in my hand an abstract of my register, which dates from the beginning of 1842. The abstract was made after the April Session of last year, 1854, and, consequently, extends over the space of twelve years and a quarter. The total number of prisoners during that period consigned to their friends is 417. Of these only 80 are known to have been reconvicted. Of the remainder, 94 bear a respectable character; many of them retaining this character after long years of probation. Of 143, the best we can say is that they are not known to have been in custody since they were so given up to their friends. 68 could not be found. 15 were given up to friends residing at a distance from Birmingham, and, therefore, the periodical inquiries which have been made as to the others do not apply to them. But as they were taken away from the evil associations of a large town, I consider them placed under very advantageous circumstances for redeeming their character. 17 were dead; thus making up the total number of 417 of which I have been speaking. These results, I submit, would, of themselves, prove the fact—which, to be sure, has been abundantly proved by a varied experience, both at home and abroad—that the reformation of youthful offenders is far from being so difficult and hopeless as was formerly the prevalent belief. . . .*

Institutions for Juvenile Delinquents, Aberdeen, Scotland, 1841

Alexander Thomson, *Social Evils: Their Causes and their Cure*, (London, 1852), pp. 68, 70-73, 111-12 (editor's lib.)

[THE ABERDEEN, SCOTLAND, EXPERIMENT]

The state of the criminal juvenile population in the city of Aberdeen became an object of particular attention in the year 1840. Returns were procured from the records of the various courts of justice—the police and the prisons—which shewed that, though this population was numerous, still it was not so great as to appear altogether unmanageable; and it was resolved that an attempt should

* Taken from an address made by Recorder Hill in April, 1855, at a meeting called by the Sheriff of Warwickshire to consider the establishment of a county reformatory school—as reported by the *Leamington Spa Courier*.

be made to reclaim them. Hence arose the Aberdeen Schools of Industry.

It was ascertained that, in June 1841, there were in Aberdeen 280 children, under fourteen, who maintained themselves professedly by begging, but partly by theft; of whom 77 were committed to prison, during the previous twelve months for crime of one kind or other. Most of these children went out to beg, on the alleged ground, whether true or false, that they had no other means of procuring their daily food. It was abundantly clear that, while they continued to pursue this mode of life, there was no prospect of their ever becoming useful members of society. To reclaim them —to put their feet, as it were, on the first step to the path of usefulness—it was obvious that any institution which was really to benefit them, must provide them with food—with training in some industrious employment, and instruction, especially religious; for these three things were all required to be furnished to them, in order to have a hope of reclaiming them. . . .

The principle on which the Aberdeen Industrial Schools are founded, is to combine all these three objects in one and the same institution. . . .

In October 1841 a small subscription, under £100, was collected for the purpose of making the experiment. Rooms sufficiently extensive, but of the humblest description, were hired, and a teacher engaged. Notice was given that such an institution existed, and that poor children who chose would be admitted into it, on application, up to the number of 60, beyond which it did not seem prudent to extend the institution at first—and that there they would receive food and instruction, and be employed in such work as was suited to their years.

The attendance at the school is wholly voluntary; but the child who is absent from morning hours receives no breakfast; absent from the forenoon hours, receives no dinner; and if absent from the afternoon, receives no supper. And, influenced by these attractions, the attendance on the whole is excellent—better than at an ordinary day school.

The general arrangement of the day is four hours of lessons, five hours of work, and three substantial meals.

The whole procedure of the work of the children goes towards defraying the expense of the establishment—thus effecting several important purposes; reducing the expense of the school, and teaching the children practically the value of their industry, in procuring for them food and instruction, and fostering in them, from the first, a sound principle of self-dependence; inasmuch as they know, from the moment of their entering school, that they give (or pay), in return for their food and education, all the work they are capable of performing.

The institution does not profess to clothe the children; but, by the kindness of benevolent persons who take an interest in the school, there is generally a small store of old clothes on hand, from which the most destitute are supplied.

The school was not long in operation before its results began to appear. Those who were in the habit of visiting it were struck by the improvement in the appearance of the pupils. The regular supply of wholesome food soon told on their bodily frames, and the half-starved vagrant children began to assume the aspect of healthy thriving boys. The outward moral change was not less conspicuous; the turbulent unruly urchins were, in a wonderfully short time, converted into tolerably quiet, orderly school-boys. In accomplishing this, much, of course, depended on the teacher, and the committee of management were highly fortunate in the person whom they selected for this important officer; and also, in having the effective assistance, from first to last, of the experienced superintendent of the House of Refuge.

The good effects of this school were soon visible beyond its own precincts. The removal of so many youthful beggars from the streets of the city could not fail to attract notice, and the city police authorities reported a perceptible diminution in the number of juvenile offenders. . . .

[THE CHILD'S ASYLUM]

The experience acquired in these schools, and the connexion which most of the managers had with the criminal courts of the city, led to the opening of a fourth institution—the Child's Asylum. Acting from day to day as judges, these gentlemen had occasionally cases brought before them which gave them extreme pain. Children, nay, infants, were brought up on criminal charges—the facts alleged against them were incontestably proved—and yet—in a moral sense, they could scarcely be held *guilty;* because, in truth, they did not know that they had done wrong; while it might be well questioned whether the public had any right to demand sentence against them, considering that the public had not taken pains to see to it that no child was left to grow up in utter and total ignorance of the difference between right and wrong; and that, if this duty had been neglected, the punishment ought more justly to fall on the public than on the poor neglected child—just because the public was more guilty in the matter than the child.

There were, however, great practical difficulties in the way, which could only be got over indirectly. The magistrate could adjourn the case, directing the child to be cared for in the meantime, and inquiry could be made as to his family and relations, as to his character, and the prospect of his doing better in future; and he could either be restored to his relations, or boarded in the House of Refuge, or with a family, and placed at one or other of the Industrial Schools; the charge of crime still remaining against him to be made use of at once if he deserted school and returned to evil courses.

The great advantage sought here was to avoid stamping the child for life with the character of a convicted felon before he deserved it. Once thus brand a child in this country, and it is all but impossible for him ever, by future good conduct, to efface the mark. How careful ought those who make our laws to be, and those too, who administer them, not rashly to impress this stigma on the neglected child!

Lodging-Houses and Juvenile Delinquency, 1845, 1852

[A] *The Lodging Houses of London. Extracted from the "London City Mission Magazine" of August, 1845* (London, 1846), p. 4, 6, 8-10 (Goldsmiths' Lib.)

[Quoting from "The First Report of the Commissioners appointed to inquire as to the best means of establishing an efficient Constabulary force in England and Wales . . . 1839," the author states, "The trampers lodging house is . . . the most extensively-established school for juvenile delinquency, and commonly at the same time, the most infamous brothel in the district."]

. . . We have recently been induced to make inquiries of those of our missionaries who have lodging-houses on their districts, as to their regulations and practices. They have reported to us much which is so bad that it cannot be published; and we confess that we have felt peculiar difficulty in committing to the press even the particulars which are contained in this article. . . .

OCCUPATION OF LODGERS

The class of persons who frequent these lodging-houses, are beggars, street-sweepers, hawkers, hay-makers, travellers, costermongers, dock-labourers, vendors of lucifer matches, actors in public houses, navigators, brickmakers, cab-men, and such like. With these are mingled on the one hand, large numbers of fallen females; thieves; high fliers, as they are called, or writers of begging letters; Molbursers, or boys who dive their hands into ladies' pockets; and parties who live by sin; and on the other hand, parties who have once filled somewhat respectable situations in life, but who, having become reduced, are driven to a resort to these places. . . .

LOCALITIES OF LODGING HOUSES

The lodging-houses of London are scattered throughout the poorer parts of London, especially in parts in which many Irish live. . . .

PROMISCUOUS ACCOMMODATION OF THE SEXES

Some of the lodging-houses have written up at the entrance "Lodgings for single men," and in a few of these men only are accommodated, although if women apply, and beds are vacant, the temptation to gain on the part of the landlord is frequently too strong to be overcome, and they are admitted. Other lodging-houses have a room for married persons, in which perhaps five or six married couples with their children are accommodated; another room for single men, which is called "Bachelor's Bay," and another room for single women. But it is the common practice in these houses, when the single men's or the single women's room is filled, to send single men and single women into the married-couple's room, rather than lose their custom. In a large number of cases the sexes are accommodated quite promiscuously; and in all cases a couple have only to say they are married and no questions are asked.

EXCESSIVE CROWDING TOGETHER OF LODGERS

One missionary reports on this particular:—
"On my district is a house containing eight rooms, which are all let separately to individuals, who furnish and re-let them. The parlour, commonly called the tap (as it was formerly a public-house), measures 18 feet by 10. Beds are arranged on each side of the room, and are composed of bundles of straw, shavings, rags, &c. In this one room slept, on the night previous to my inquiry, twenty-seven male and female adults, thirty-one children, and two or three dogs (for there are few roomers without dogs), making in

185

all fifty-eight human beings, breathing the contaminated atmosphere of a close room, the windows of which I have never seen opened! . . ."

EXTREME FILTH AND IMPURITY OF AIR

Many of these lodging-houses seem never to be cleansed or ventilated, and, as might be expected, the consequence is that they literally swarm with vermin. . . .

For the calls of nature there is ordinarily no other accommodation provided than an uncovered tub behind the door or in a corner of the room. And for washing there is only the same common room as for cooking and all other purposes, except sleeping, with probably simply a butt of water, the lodger paying for his own soap, and using his own wearing apparel for a towel; while in many cases even water is refused, the consequence of which is, that the lodgers lose all care about cleanliness. . . .

The annoyance of vermin is so great, that it adds greatly to the evils which attend the promiscuous accommodation of the sexes. For it obliges all who have any regard to comfort or cleanliness to sleep in a state of entire nudity, which may almost be said to be the ordinary practice in lodging houses. . . .

GAMBLING AND INTOXICATION

In the lodging-houses generally, gambling is practised to a fearful extent, and there is also much intoxication. . . .

DANCING

There are dances at some of these lodging-houses, especially on Sunday evenings, at which a fiddler ordinarily attends. One penny is charged for each dance to each person. The dancing is continued till late at night. These dances are often scenes of great evil. Boys entice girls to dance with them, and afterwards to sleep with them. One missionary knocked in the middle of the day at the door of one of the rooms of these lodging houses. A voice from within directed him to enter, when he saw two young men and two young women dancing together, all in a state of entire nudity, a fiddler playing to them in another part of the room, while they danced. . . .

LODGING-HOUSES AND LODGING-ROOMS FOR BOYS AND GIRLS

The worst of the lodging-houses are those which are let out to boys and girls. . . .

[One boy describing the lodging house-keeper said] She'll do *anything* for money. If she cannot fill the beds in our room with boys, she puts in girls. She does not put them in the same bed, but that's no odds. We often entice girls whom we meet in the streets. Two girls were put in our room a little while ago. When we thought they were asleep, we gently raised the clothes off their feet, and slipped a cord over their great toes and pulled them out of bed. There was nothing but a complete game the whole night. . . .

[Another boy testified, in part] . . . Seven sleep in a bed at ——, where I am now; but then it is in the cellar. There is neither door nor window; but being 7 feet underground, and very damp, the vermin are not half so bad. Boys and girls sleep in the same cellar. The cellars are very warm in winter, but very bad in summer. . . . You saw all those little fellows (alluding to a number of children I saw about the door), none of them are more than 7 years old; they are all in training; most are counter sneaks, that is, they crawl into bakers' and other shops and frisk the till or whatever they can lay their hands on. . . .

[B] *Report from the Select Committee [H.C.] on Criminal and Destitute Juveniles* . . . (London, 1852), p. 468 (UNC Lib.). Letter addressed to the Chairman of the Committee by the Rev. *John Clay,* B.D., Chaplain of the House of Correction at Preston.

I have not spoken in my evidence of the incentives to juvenile crime existing in the low lodging-houses scattered throughout the country; and now I only beg to be the medium of testimony confirmatory of that which, no doubt, other witnesses will give more directly, as to the unspeakable and dangerous corruption festering in those places. The following are extracts from papers drawn up by a convict whose experience and practice in criminal life, combined with an unusual share of intelligence and observation, render him a useful witness on any matter relating to criminal life, in which, as in this, he is willing to speak without reserve: "From infancy up to 13 or 14 years of age and older, they lie together promiscuously—father, mother, or oftener stepfather or stepmother —with lads and girls of all ages, from the infant to the adolescent. This is done to save lodging-money; for a bed is only 6d., no matter how many sleep in it, except in some houses where a penny a head is charged for children who sleep with their parents, and are above the age of 10. . . . It may easily be guessed that such places are the very hot beds of disease, as they are of vice and crime of every shape and complexion. . . . Any number of beds that can be forced into an apartment are tolerated; and I have seen them covering the floor betwixt others that are on bedsteads, so as to render it almost impossible to move without treading on a man, woman, or child. Age, sex, relationship, all crowd together, and the conversation is brutal, obscene, and unrestricted; and various practices are carried on irrespective of time, place, or witnesses; cursing, fighting, smoking, &c. &c., and men and women dress and undress without the slightest attempt at privacy. . . .

Juvenile Delinquency in London, 1846

> [A] Walter Buchanan,[1] *Remarks on the Causes and State of Juvenile Crime in the Metropolis; with Hints for Preventing Its Increase* (London: Printed by Richard and John E. Taylor, Red Lion Court, Fleet Street, 1846), pp. 3-10, 14-16, 18-19, 22, 24-25 (Crerar Lib.)

To My Brother Magistrates.

Every magistrate of this great County who has sat on the Bench at Clerkenwell and Westminster, or visited the Prisons and Houses of Correction, has had his feelings aroused and his sympathies deeply excited by the sight of so many juvenile offenders, during their trial or after their conviction. Many a wish has been expressed to jurors and courts, that means could be found to prevent the constantly increasing numbers. . . .

Public meetings have been held at the Mansion House and Westend of the town, at which a great deal *has been said* on the subject of Crime; still *no remedial plan has been adopted;* and, although *we* know the contrary to be the fact, there are many amongst the public who believe that conviction for offenses, and not prevention and reformation of juvenile delinquency, has been our main object. . . .

Some persons cry out for summary conviction and a good flogging; but, as will be seen by and by, these will not be found to be cures; because the smart will not be long felt and not long remembered, and the stomach will soon crave again for vituals.

Another set of persons, of humane character but speculative and Utopian notions, have complained that we have not effected so many conversions to honesty and morality as we might have been expected to do; but *we*, who have had a deeper and constant insight into the characters, habits, and pursuits of young thieves, are fully

1. One of the Justices of the Peace for the County of Middlesex.

aware how unreasonable and fallacious such expectations are. The number of reformed convict children discharged from our Houses of Correction, notwithstanding every solicitude on our part and the vigilant supervision and careful instruction of the officers, we must admit with sorrow and regret, have not been numerous; but *we* well know, from long experience and long trial, that all moral sense has been so long extinct in them, if it ever existed at all, and there is such a total absence of all religious sentiment, as to defy the most persevering attempts to effect durable amendment amongst this unfortunate and miserable set of human beings.

The class of juvenile criminals to which my Hints will principally be applicable is that of *Thieves,*—such as steal from the person, from shops, houses, areas, laundresses' drying-grounds, yards, carts, vehicles, etc.; the far greater proportion of which is composed of boys of from eight to fifteen years of age. Of this description of wretched boys, from thirty to forty are put upon their trials every Session (the Sessions being fourteen days only apart), and there are not less than *three hundred and twenty* of them undergoing their sentences in the two Houses of Correction at this period. Some few girls are engaged in thefts of the like kind; but the younger female criminals are more frequently child-strippers, shoplifters and workhouse window-smashers: but girls I will not now take into consideration, because they do not come within the scope of my plan. I also confine my views to such boys only as are sent to our own Houses of Correction for Felony, etc. . . . Offenses of a deeper dye, committed throughout the County, and all offenses committed in the City of London, are, as is well known, tried at the Old Bailey, and the convicted prisoners distributed in various directions.

Of this class, and who in case of conviction are imprisoned in either Cold Bath Fields or the Westminster Houses of Correction, it is lamentable to reflect that *two thousand and thirty-two young Boys* have been in custody for trial or re-examination in our County Prisons between the 29th of September, 1843, and the 20th of April, 1846; about thirty-one months, the average number being sixty-six per month; and their sentences have varied from seven days to six months, but the greater proportion were for two and three months. And though every care is used both in their religious and moral instruction, and every precept of good conduct and honest practice inculcated, whilst they remain in these prisons, such is the depravity of the greater number of them, and so early have they been initiated into and inured to vice, that no sooner do they escape from durance within the walls, than they return to their former bad associates and their former evil courses, and, often within a few hours, (no home to shelter them, and no creditable or legitimate pursuit to employ their hands or thoughts,) are again detected, and again sent to the prison which they had so recently quitted. Time after time they are thus discharged and re-committed. I have known several instances of boys under twelve years of age who have undergone sentences in one or both of the Houses of Correction, six or seven, or even more times, within a few years; and some who, after previous convictions, have been transported beyond seas for terms of seven and ten years; whilst a few have been received at Parkhurst, and a very few restored to their families or former employers. Many are orphans, and know not where to go. A few, after being discharged from prison, would willingly work if they knew where to find work with a blemished character.

Amongst so large a mass of delinquents, it is certain that very few have been reclaimed, which fact has led me the more to consider whether any means of prevention can be devised. . . .

There are many hundreds—perhaps I may safely say thousands— of such children in this Metropolis who have been thieves from their infancy, and who have no other pursuit, on whom the light daily dawns, without their knowing when or where to gain a scanty meal during day or shelter from the elements, by any other means than robbery.

The great recesses of juvenile crime in the Metropolitan Districts to the north of the Thames, are Spitalfields, Bethnal Green, Shoreditch, Hoxton, Wapping, Ratcliffe, White Chapel, Saffron Hill, Field Lane, Gray's Inn Lane, St. Giles's, Seven Dials, Drury Lane, The Almonry, Tothill Fields (Westminster) and Lisson Grove; and although in some parts of Marylebone, St. Pancras, Chelsea, Islington, Clerkenwell, Limehouse, Paddington, Kensington, and elsewhere in and about the Metropolis, young thieves resort, they are not to be compared in number to those who are to be found issuing from the above-named places. In the densely crowded lanes and alleys of these localities wretched tenements are found, containing in every cellar and on every floor, men and women, children both male and female, all huddled together, sometimes with strangers, and too frequently standing in very doubtful consanguinity to each other. In these abodes decency and shame have fled; depravity reigns in all its horrors.

The inmates of these dens are not often, indeed very seldom, Artisans and Workmen . . . but they consist usually of bricklayers' labourers, scavengers, sweeps, carmen, cabmen, coalheavers, helpers in stables, coal, fish, and fruit porters, costermongers, ballad-singers, nightmen, and often of old thieves, dog-stealers, and of many persons of a loathsome anomalous description amongst the men; whilst the females are chiefly charwomen, garden-porters, washerwomen, bone-collectors, match-sellers, rag-sorters, cat-skin-ners, prostitutes, beggars, and such like. Almost all are of the lowest and vilest grade and character. Such then are the progeni-tors of our young thieves and mendicants, and in such dark holes and noxious corners are they brought into life. All—of both sexes—sally forth, often into distant localities, at from five to seven o'clock in the morning throughout the year,—a few constantly employed, but the bulk of them getting a scanty and precarious meal, when, where, and how they can; this meal is consumed at stalls in the streets, or in public houses near the places of their resort and calling. They leave their rooms closed during their absence, having previously turned adrift all their children, or taken the youngest along with them, and do not return to their abodes until perhaps six or eight o'clock in the evening. During these ten, twelve or fifteen hours their unfortunate offspring are not only suffered to roam at large, but are often let to beggars by the day or hour, or in many instances compelled to beg and plunder in order to satisfy the cravings of hunger; moreover forced to bring to their parents or as-sociates some fruits of their purloining and begging (for they often combine the practices of stealing and begging), and are cruelly beaten and maltreated for failing or neglecting to do so. These abandoned children have never offered up a prayer; have never been inside a place of Worship, nor at school; they swear most profane and disgusting oaths; they indulge in the worst passions; they are abominably wicked. The want of a regular supply of food; the dissolute conduct of parents (if any they know); the total dis-regard of those wretches to supply or make any attempt whatever to meet the wants, either physical, moral, or religious of their chil-dren; their frequent desertion of them altogether; the cruel step-fathers, or as unfeeling step-mothers;—all combine to brutalize them. In fact these persons care no more for their offspring than hyaenas for their whelps after they are suckled. Their object is *to get rid of them as soon as they can*, in order to have all their gains to squander in gin and debauch. Having thrust them out at dawn of day, they never see them again until night, and probably not then, nor for many days afterwards, and ofttimes never again.

Such then are the fruitful *first causes of juvenile crime*. Then follow idleness; corrupt association with other boys, and with prostitutes as young as themselves, who often aid them to rob; the joining of gangs for the sole purpose of thieving; the facility of finding purchasers for their illicit gains; the resorting to low public-houses and gin-shops and penny theatres; the gaming for pence, or shillings, or drink, and divers other causes of corruption;—all conspire to form adept thieves at a precocious age. Amongst the many such who become inmates of our prisons, and are repeatedly found therein, scarcely one can be discovered to possess any redeeming quality in his character.

These children thus set at liberty prowl about all day, and,—mendicancy being much interfered with by the Police and the Mendicity Society,—the majority thieve. Their early attempts are directed to the areas of houses, where they beg or steal as opportunity presents, and generally alone. As the day advances they form parties of three or four, and extend the sphere of operation to most parts of the town and the outskirts. We rarely hear of any depredations by night being made by boys so young. Occasionally a boy of better parentage is vicious, but very seldom so depraved as one of this sort.

They often escape detection for months, notwithstanding the vigilance of the Police; and although occasionally some of that efficient body are in plain clothes for the purpose of easier apprehending them than if they were in uniform, these young thieves have so much acuteness, or an intuitive perception of character, that they are enabled to elude the snare. Their skill and adroitness in their vocation are astonishing. They speculate deeply on the chances of evasion, act now with caution, now with daring, and are not easily dismayed. They have a nomenclature of their own, and a sort of conventional law too.

When apprehended they go to the Police-office readily and silently, and exhibit neither shame nor compunction when placed before the Magistrate. When the evidence against them is strong, their committal follows of course to the prison, where they await the forthcoming Session. When placed in the dock for trial, we find diminutive boys, the heads of some of whom do not reach the top of the panel, and whose countenances can scarcely be discerned from the Bench. In this situation, notwithstanding the array of a full Court, Jurors, Officers, and Witnesses, they evince not the least sign of fear, but gaze at the face of the Assistant-Judge with perfect composure, listen to all that is adduced against them attentively, and await their sentence with the utmost indifference. The evidence against them is often very curious: the details of creeping on all-fours into a shop round the counter to the till, or making a bold dash at the shillings and pence lying on it,—the near chance of escape—the jingling of the halfpence arousing the poor chandler from his back room just in time to reach the culprit; of a poor laundress's drying-ground being stripped of all the dangling shirts and stockings; of a covering party at the extraction of a pocket handkerchief from a country squire just arrived in town "to see the lions"; of a long and arduous chase by a policeman after the offender, who, after various doublings, is caught in a blind alley; and now and then of the inveigling of a little boy into a piece of unoccupied lonely ground, set apart for being built upon, and leaving him in the state of an unfledged sparrow;—such-like, and various other strange evidence we hear; whilst sometimes an offender, well-known by the Bench, will raise a quibble, or argue a point with the learned Sergeant, in order to mislead the jury, with all the confidence and modest assurance of a well-trained counsel. He can produce no witness to good character; the jury pronounce a verdict of "guilty" against him; he never sues for mercy; and forthwith he is re-consigned to the prison which in many instances he quitted only forty-eight hours before; but, weeks or even years absent, he is instantly recognized on arriving there by the lynx-eyed Warders to be the same boy who has been in their custody before, let him meanwhile have used a dozen *aliases* to his name, and changed the scene of his operations as many times. There can be no doubt that some of these lads hail a sentence of imprisonment for a period not exceeding six months as a boon, especially at the approach of winter; and that a few commit offenses in order to get into a prison, (and amongst older vagrants and thieves this is not at all an uncommon practice) for the sake of food and covering.

Most of these boys are familiar with the discipline and usages of the prison, and ordinarily are obedient; but some are most audacious fellows, and, next to the workhouse window-smashing girls and the most depraved of women, cause the greatest trouble to the authorities. Their tricks are almost incorrigible and indefinable, and sometimes put the acuteness and vigilance of a *Chesterton* and a *Tracey* almost at a nonplus. I have heard one of these experienced Governors declare, amongst other singular facts, that these young thieves can telegraph each other, and know each other's meaning full well by the manner in which their caps are put upon the head, without a finger or a wink being used for the purpose. . . .

The number of juvenile offenders has been constantly on the increase, notwithstanding all the charity of the clergy and laity, the provisions of the Poor Law, and the assiduity of Visiting Societies. . . .

I find there were on the 31st March 1846, in both Houses of Correction, 313 *convicted boys;* viz. in the House of Correction at Westminster:

Boys under 15 years of age............................. 93
Boys between 15 and 17 years of age.................... 74
                                                      ———
                                                       167

In the House of Correction, Cold Bath Fields:

Boys under 15 years of age............................ 46
Boys between 15 and 17 years of age...................100
                                                      ———
                                                       146
                                                      ———
                                    Total............313

Of these 139 convicted boys under 15 years of age:

60 had not been in either House of Correction before;
35 had been in once before;
14 had been in twice before;
19 had been in thrice before;
11 had been in repeatedly before.

The Boys constitute rather more than one-third of the male prisoners of all ages, there being at that same date 1125 of them in both Houses of Correction.

A Committee, consisting of twenty-two Magistrates . . . was nominated on the last County day (9th April), "to report upon the Letter from the Philanthropic Society, and to offer their Suggestions for Checking the Growth of Crime, and Promoting the Reformation of Juvenile Offenders."

Destitution, Want, Ignorance and Idleness we find prevail to a fearful extent in certain localities, and are the main sources of crime. They are the bane; the remedy I think is, *Food, Useful Employment,*—employment both of hands and thoughts,—*Removal from bad associates, and good Training.*

This metropolis boasts, and boasts justly, of its noble charities. We have Christ's Hospital, and many others less known for the nurture and education of the young. We have hospitals for the cure of every disease, bodily and mental; asylums for the aged and infirm, in which they may eke out their appointed time in peace and comfort; all these, more or less, sprung from charitable bequests. Then again are to be found the Philanthropic Society, for children of felons; the Refuge for the Destitute, to receive juvenile malefactors discharged from prison; Manor Hall Asylum, Chelsea . . . for the reception of young female convicts discharged; and the Ladies' Patronage Society: all four highly to be commended, supported by voluntary contributions; but there is not one which meets our exigency. Their object is *to reform*: mine is *to prevent*. . . . Let us therefore try Prevention, and in one or more of the populous Localities named,—for instance, Shoreditch, Whitechapel or Drury Lane,—as early as possible, let us establish *Day Refuges for Unemployed Boys Under Twelve Years of Age* for the purpose; and if one or two answer our expectations, extend the Institutions into other districts of the metropolis. They at first should be for *boys only;* those for girls might be afterwards formed on a much smaller scale, but on regulations only varying from the Boys' Refuge as the difference of sex points out. I would make the trial with 100 or 150 in the first year, or with 200 at most.

Means of Formation and Support. . . . The *Government* has so many momentous measures to dispose of, that no support can be expected from the Home Office at this time . . . therefore to the *County of Middlesex* we must first direct our views; and I am sanguine in my belief that our Court of Magistracy, if it has the power, will promptly and willingly grant a sum of £3000 or £4000 out of the County Rates, which will be as much as will be requisite, for the trial to be made, and that the Rate-payers will cordially sanction an expenditure for such humane purposes. On the score of policy alone, such an outlay would in the end prove to be an enormous saving; for *prevention of crime* will cost infinitely less than *prosecution for offense and confinement in prison*. . . . It should be made a County or Municipal measure. Failing, however, to be supported by the County, an application must be made to generous individuals and the public at large; and we may be quite sure that the appeal to their sympathy in such a cause will not be made in vain. Large subscriptions are raised to convert cannibal New Zealanders and predatory Caffres, thousands of miles off; to restore losses caused by conflagrations in Germany and floods in Switzerland: I do not wish to depreciate acts of duty and benevolence towards our suffering fellow-creatures anywhere; but I say, let us look at home, and put our heads out of our own doors, and perambulate our streets, first, and see what a heap of misery and corruption has to be swept away; and let contributions be made to purge our moral and social diseases. . . .

Building.—Our first endeavour should be made to find out a large dry house, warehouse, or tenement, in the center of one of those populous quarters of the metropolis before mentioned. It should, if possible, be surrounded by a wide yard, and be of easy access and egress. . . . This Building should be *rented . . . not purchased.* . . . A good sized kitchen will of course be requisite, and the usual appurtenances; also books, tools, benches, forms, tables, &c. for the School and Workrooms.

Convenient lavatories, unless there be a Wash House for the Poor in the neighborhood, and water-closets must immediately be formed in befitting parts of the building. . . . Special precaution must be taken to have the building well-ventilated and warmed, and that no noxious smells present themselves in it.

The work-rooms and School-room should be assimilated in construction, in arrangement, &c., to those of our Houses of Correction; and the boys be all seated, when at work, with their faces towards the Superintendent. In the early stage of the plan it is not intended to have sleeping-rooms, except for two or three of the officials, although they are extremely desirable, and I trust they will be added before twelve months have passed away. . . .

Administration and Direction—The direction and administration of the establishment should rest entirely in the hands of Visiting Justices of the County, a Committee of whom should be chosen in the same manner as the Committees of the two Houses of Correction now are. . . . The Superintendent and all the officers should be appointed by them; all regulations be formed by them. . . .

I would suggest to the Committee so constituted, that they select from amongst the most intelligent and discreet of the Warders in our Houses of Correction . . . a Superintendent, (to be recommended by one of the Prison Committees,) and the Staff under him, from the school-rooms and wards. . . .

I would have the practice in the Refuge conform as nearly as possible to that of our Houses of Correction, though of course in many respects it may be less cogent.

Admission.—The admission into the Refuge must be *free and unrestricted, not compulsory:* all boys, natives of the United Kingdom, *between the ages of eight and twelve years,* and whether they have been tried, convicted and imprisoned, or have not been so degraded, who came, *should be admitted.* The doors of the Refuge should be open to them from seven o'clock in the morning in summer until seven at night; and from October to March from eight o'clock in the morning until six o'clock in the evening, allowing an hour for recreation daily, and a half-holiday every Saturday afternoon. Close inquiry should be made on their first entry of their age, their parents, their late and present residence, their birthplace, their recent pursuits, their religious belief; whether they can read; how many brothers and sisters they have, &c.; and the answer be recorded in a book to be kept for the purpose. . . .

No boy should be admitted beyond the age of twelve years; nor any boy under ordinary circumstances be suffered to continue at the Refuge beyond fourteen, because at the latter age, having been two years subject to its discipline and partaken of its benefits, it is to be hoped he will have gained a knowledge of some useful trade by which he may be enabled to earn a livelihood for himself. . . .

The Refuge is intended for such boys as can not find shelter, employment or instruction elsewhere. . . .

Probably few will neglect regular attendance, for, to the majority of such boys as these, according to an old adage "the way to the heart lies through the belly," and they will apply, I expect, every day to have their hunger appeased. . . .

Instruction and Observances.—The first observance after the arrival within the Refuge by the boys must be of course to wash their hands and faces, comb their hair, and make themselves as neat and tidy as circumstances will admit. . . . *Complete silence must reign,* and decency of demeanour be rigidly enforced: plain religious truths must be strongly urged, and moral duties assiduously inculcated from the moment they enter. . . .

Boys of every religious denomination (or of none when they enter) must be made to attend the Service [prayers, scripture reading, etc.]. Then Instruction in reading should follow, but I would confine instruction to the knowledge of the Holy Scriptures and of the Church Catechism; not taught parrot-like, *but to be thoroughly understood;* and I would not attempt to teach geography, chronology, or any other *graphy* or *logy.* . . . I would make *good conduct* and *useful labour* the primary object in a Refuge, and combine instruction with them. . . . Breakfast . . . should then be given to the boys.

The next undertaking should be Work at some useful trade, under competent task-masters, until dinner-time, and again on their return into the Refuge after it, and recreation. The trades chosen should be such as contribute to the covering of the body, viz. tailoring, shoe-making, shirt making, stocking-weaving, cap-making, if there be opportunity in the Refuge to carry them on; but if not, net-making, mat-making or oakum picking may be advantageously substituted.

The first proceeds of the labour should be applied to the supply of covering to them; the surplus produce should next be sold, and the sum it produces go into the fund for supplying food to, and defraying the expenses of, the establishment; and to an industrious boy, on his *finally quitting it with a good character,* a gratuity either in money or outfit should be granted. . . .

Dinner . . . should be served to the boys at one o'clock. After dinner they should be allowed recreation for an hour, and then resume work, and continue at it uninterruptedly until three-quarters of an hour before the time appointed for their departure; then their supper should be ready, and when that is finished a short Prayer to the Almighty be read, as in the morning, and afterwards they should be suffered to depart until the next day.

On Sundays three meals should also be given to them at stated hours. More extended liberty of breathing the air than on the week days must be allowed; but attendance in a place of public worship, and *twice* during the Sabbath, must be enforced if possible by the Visiting Justices. . . . Victuals, of course, must not be supplied unless they attend the Services. Discussion on points of faith must be avoided at all times.

The silent system must strictly prevail within the Walls of the Refuge; not only in the school and work-room, but in the yard or airing ground.

Emulation must be excited, and encouragement to become honest and good be afforded, by rewards; such for example as being made monitors and messengers. Incentives to moral demeanour must be liberally held out, as well as restraints be put to evil communications and bad practices. And in like manner as rewards are bestowed on the deserving, so should punishment be inflicted, either by being mulct of meals, or by having stripes on the person with the birch rod, on the offending boys. Expulsion and future exclusion should be the consequence of gross misconduct.

Food and Drink.—The want of a regular supply and distribution of sustenance being one great cause of juvenile crime, the matter requires attention. In respect to food and drink, I would act upon the principle, "You shall not be fed unless you earn by labour your 'daily bread'". . . .

The Diet should be assimilated to that of our Prisons, both at breakfast, dinner, and supper. No better Dietary Table than the

"'Third Class" one can be used: it has stood the test of experi-ence. . . .

The *drink* should be pure *spring water,* if it can be obtained readily; if not, a Water-Works Company must supply it. Perhaps beer may be issued on Sundays at dinner-time as a reward for good conduct.

Appropriation.—I am sanguine in my expectations that most of these boys will have conducted themselves so well up to the time of departure, and have become so expert in their several trades, as to be worthy of recommendation as apprentices to tradesmen, or into ships, or lighters, or boats on the river. They might become errand-boys, carters, porters, etc., with advantage to their em-ployers.

They might to a certain extent also be made substitutes for agricultural laborers,—who can now be ill-spared,—by voluntary Emigration to the Cape of Good Hope, or Canada, or to our West India colonies . . . they might be allowed to enter into Queen's ships, to become sailors or mariners; or enlist into colonial corps, or regiments on foreign stations. . . .

> [B] Benjamin Rotch,[2] *Suggestions for the Prevention of Juvenile Depravity* (London: Printed by H. Court, 26, Brooke Street, Holborn, 1846), pp. 7-10, 13 (Crerar Lib.)

. . . It must be an obvious and admitted fact that old offenders for the most part rise from the ranks of Juvenile Depredators, and to cut off the supply to the former from the latter class would un-doubtedly be striking at the root of the evil, and which might be done at home, where we can get at it conveniently instead of deal-ing with the branches many thousands of miles off, and at every possible disadvantage in Van Diemen's Land and Norfolk Island. Surely, then, common sense points out that all our efforts should be directed to stay the plague of Juvenile depravity at home. . . . [Points out that "the Ministry of the Gospel," "education as now conducted," and "an improved Prison Discipline," have all proved ineffectual in staying the plague of Juvenile depravity.]

Mr. Buchanan does not contemplate any legislative Interference —I contend that nothing effectual can be done without it—Mr. Buchanan looks to the County Rate for the means which however, unfortunately is not available for the purpose—I look to the Trea-sury—Mr. Buchanan proposes a withdrawal from contaminating As-sociation only during the day—I propose an entire separation day

2. A Justice of the Peace for the County of Middlesex.

and night from all bad Companions—and lastly Mr. Buchanan's is a voluntary System—mine a compulsory one. . . .

I propose that a bill should be passed by the Legislature, the Preamble of which should in effect state, that the fearful extent of Juvenile Depravity and Crime in the Metropolitan Districts and in large and populous Towns requires generally immediate Interference on the part of the Legislature.—That the great causes of the said Juvenile Depravity and Crime appear to be the absence of proper Parental or Friendly care, and the absence of a comfortable home, and that all Children above the age of 7 and under the age of 15 years suffering from either of these causes require protection to prevent their getting into bad company, learning idle and dissolute habits, growing up in ignorance and becoming an expense and burthen on the Country as Criminals, and that such protection should be afforded by the state.

I propose that the various clauses of the Act should enact as follows—

I. That an Asylum for unprotected and destitute Children be founded by the Government to be called the *Child's Home.*

II. That Commissioners be appointed to manage such Asylum.

III. That provision be made in such Asylum for instructing Children in all useful arts, trades and occupations suitable to the working classes.

IV. That unprotected and destitute children shall be deemed to include all children above 7 and under 15 years of age under the following circumstances,—Children driven from their homes by the bad conduct of Parents—Children neglected by their Parents—Children who are Orphans and neglected by their friends—Children who are Bastards, and Children who are Orphans and have no one to protect them or provide for them, or for whom no one does provide—Children who from their own misconduct have no protection or provision found them—Children who are idle or dissolute, and whose Parents or Friends cannot controul their bad conduct—Children who are destitute of proper food, clothing or education owing to the poverty of their parents or friends, but whose parents or friends do not apply for, or receive parish relief—Children who are destitute for want of employment, and children of the class which become Juvenile Offenders generally.

V. That any such Child as aforesaid may be brought before any Two Justices of the Peace by any Constable or other Peace Officer or by any Overseer of the Poor or other Parish Officer and evidence on oath being given to the satisfaction of such Justices that the

Child is one of either of the classes enumerated in the foregoing clause, such Justices may sign an order for the admission of the Child into the Asylum.

VI. That when in the Asylum if not claimed or redeemed as hereinafter provided, the Children shall be subject to be dealt with as the state thinks proper, to serve as Sailors or Soldiers or Workmen in public works, or as Artificers or Tradesmen, or as Household Servants, or as and wherever the state may require.

VII. That on a Child being admitted into the Asylum, enquiry shall be made by the Commissioners as to the circumstances of the Parents or other persons now by law bound to support the said Child, and if found able to support, or to contribute to the support of the said Child, the Justices sending the said Child to the Asylum may make orders from time to time for any amount of contribution to be paid, for or towards the support of the said Child in the said Asylum.

VIII. That such sums be collected for the use of the Asylum by the Overseer or Rate Collectors of the Parish where the persons on whom the order is made reside, and that power be given to attach the property of such persons, or wages in the hands of Masters, or due from Masters of such persons, in cases of working people or servants, to satisfy the amount named in such order.

IX. That all Children sent to the said Asylum be taught several useful Trades, Arts or Occupations, besides the usual education of Reading, Writing and Arithmetic.

X. That if at any time any Parent or Friend should be able and willing to afford proper Protection and Employment for any Child in the said Asylum, subject to the approbation of two Justices the Child may be permitted to leave the Asylum on such Parent or Friend's paying a sum to be settled by the Commissioners of the Asylum for such Permission. . . .

The Experiment has never been tried of a STATE PROVISION *for innocent, but destitute and unprotected Children*, nor of a compulsory payment from the parent for *the proper maintenance and education of his Child.* I must not be told therefore of Refuges and Magdalens and Schools of Industry and Philanthropic Societies and Provisions for Poor Criminals on their release from prison, or of any results which have followed on their adoption, as reasons why my plan should not be tried, they are no examples for this purpose. I am satisfied from a long experience in such matters, that no difficulty would be found in placing out boys well taught, well brought up, under rules of strict discipline, and who have not yet become criminals. The expense of maintaining them as innocent children will be far less than that of maintaining them as felons while we shall be destroying the root of this Upas Tree which stands in the midst of every densely populated Neighbourhood, spreading its branches so far in every direction that the good and virtuous even can at length reach them, and think they are destroying the tree by endeavouring to keep its unwieldly limbs within bounds by the pruning knife. A most fatal error!

. . . It must be remembered that the Children with whom I propose to deal are the very same beings who are now dealt with by the state under the far more expensive character of criminals, and the simple question in the case as a matter of finance will be whether it would be more expensive to maintain any given number of innocent Children, and educate them as I propose they should be educated, than to capture, try, and maintain an equal number of Adult Felons at home and abroad at the enormous cost at which they are now dealt with . . . how far more desirable must it be to prevent than to punish crime? . . . In a word to dry up the springs of Juvenile depravity at their source, instead of endeavouring to deal with the raging flood of Crime, which experience has long taught us when once abroad sweeps away with resistless force every barrier which finite wisdom has ever yet suggested for arresting its awful progress.

"Ragged Schools" for Neglected and Destitute Children, 1846

[A] [Antony Ashley-Cooper, Seventh Earl of Shaftesbury], "The Ragged Schools,"[1] *Quarterly Review,* Vol. 79 (Dec., 1846-March, 1847), pp. 127-33, 135-39, 141.

It is a curious race of human beings that these philanthropists have taken in hand. Every one who walks the streets of the metropolis [London] must daily observe several members of the tribe—bold, and pert, and dirty as London sparrows, but pale, feeble, and

1. Edwin Hodder, *The Life and Work of the Seventh Early of Shaftesbury* (1892), p. 355: "In the *Quarterly Review* for December, there appeared a startlingly graphic article from his pen on 'Ragged Schools,' in which he gave the results of his own observations of the habits of the clientele of those schools, founded upon his recent visitations.

"This admirable article was the means of giving a great impetus to Ragged School Work. It was the talk of the town; people ran wild about it; extracts were inserted in all the papers; and innumerable people made applications to be taken to see the Ragged Schools."

sadly inferior to them in plumpness of outline. Their business, or pretended business, seems to vary with the locality. At the West End they deal in lucifer-matches, audaciously beg, or tell a touching tale of woe. Pass on to the central parts of the town—to Holborn or the Strand, and the regions adjacent to them—and you will there find the numbers very greatly increased: a few are pursuing the avocations above mentioned of their more Corinthian fellows; many are spanning the gutters with their legs and dabbling with earnestness in the latest accumulation of nastiness; while others, in squalid and half-naked groups, squat at the entrances of the narrow, foetid courts and alleys that lie concealed behind the deceptive frontages of our larger thoroughfares. Whitechapel and Spitalfields teem with them like an ant's nest; but it is in Lambeth and in Westminster that we find the most flagrant traces of their swarming activity. There the foul and dismal passages are thronged with children of both sexes, and of every age from three to thirteen. Though wan and haggard, they are singularly vivacious, and engaged in every sort of occupation but that which would be beneficial to themselves and creditable to the neighbourhood. Their appearance is wild; the matted hair, the disgusting filth that renders necessary a closer inspection, before the flesh can be discerned between the rags which hang about it; and the barbarian freedom from all superintendence and restraint, fill the mind of a novice in these things with perplexity and dismay. Visit these regions in the summer, and you are overwhelmed by the exhalations; visit them in the winter, and you are shocked by the spectacle of hundreds shivering in apparel that would be scanty in the tropics; many are all but naked; those that are clothed are grotesque; the trowsers, where they have them, seldom pass the knee; the tailed coats very frequently trail below the heels. In this guise they run about the streets, and line the banks of the river at low water, seeking coals, sticks, corks, for nothing comes amiss as treasurer-trove; screams of delight burst occasionally from the crowds, and leave the passer-by, if he be in a contemplative mood, to wonder and to rejoice that moral and physical degradations have not yet broken every spring of their youthful energies.

Eccentric doubts flit through our minds; and we are tempted to ask whether these nondescripts ever had a parent, or whether there be parents to be found in the district. 'They look not like the inhabitants o' the earth, and yet are on't.' A feeling of curiosity arises, and the next step is to investigate their natural history, their haunts, their habits, their idiosyncrasy, their points of resemblance to the rest of mankind, and the part they sustain in the great purpose of creation. The stranger dives into the recesses from which they seem to issue—and there he sees, before and behind, on the right hand and on the left, every form and character of evil that can offend the sense and deaden the morals. Let those who desire a minute description of these horrid retreats, in which thousands of our country-people cower by day and by night, consult the admirable Reports of the Sanitary Commissioners, and the Health of Towns' Association, which have told us as much as language can convey. But language is powerless to exhibit the truth: personal experience alone can give the reality; and then many a weary and pestilential search, and many a sick headache, will prove to the disgusted inquirer that a large proportion of those who dwell in the capital of the British empire are crammed into regions of filth and darkness, the ancient but not solitary reign of the newts and toads.

Here are the receptacles of the species we investigate; here they are spawned, and here they perish! Can their state be a matter of wonder? We have penetrated alleys terminating in a *cul-de-sac*, long and narrow like a tobacco-pipe, where air and sunshine were never known. On one side rose walls several feet in height, blackened with damp and slime; on the other side stood the dwellings, still more revolting, while the breadth of the wet and bestrewed passage would by no means allow us the full expansion of our arms. We have waited at the entrance of another of similar character and dimensions, but forbidden, by the force and pungency of the odours, to examine its recesses. The novelty of a visit from persons clad like gentlemen gave the hope that we were officials; and several women, haggard, rough, and exasperated, surrounded us at once, imploring us to order the removal of the filth which had poisoned their tenements, and to grant them a supply of water, from which they had been debarred during many days. Pass to another district; you may think it less confined—but there you will see flowing before each hovel, and within a few feet of it, a broad, black, uncovered drain, exhaling at every point the most unwholesome vapours. If there be not a drain, there is a stagnant pool: touch either with your stick; and the mephitic mass will yield up its poisonous gas like the coruscations of soda-water.

The children sit along these depositories of death, or roam through the retired courts in which the abomination of years has been suffered to accumulate. Here reigns a melancholy silence, seldom broken but by an irritated scold or a pugnacious drunkard. The pale discoloured faces of the inhabitants, their shrivelled forms, their abandoned exterior, recall the living skeletons of the Pontine Marshes, and sufficiently attest the presence of a secret agency, hostile to every physical and moral improvement of the human race.

The interior of the dwellings is in strict keeping: the smaller space of the apartments increasing, of course, the evils that prevail without—damp, darkness, dirt, and foul air. Many are wholly destitute of furniture; many contain nothing except a table and a chair; some few have a common bed for *all ages and both sexes;* but a large proportion of the denizens of those regions lie on a heap of rags more nasty than the floor itself. Happy is the family that can boast of a single room to itself, and in that room a dry corner.

But these creatures have pursuits of their own, certain occupations whereby they obtain a scanty subsistence; for, though there are, perhaps, many persons who may not admit the necessity, they themselves have a conviction that they must live. The children, that survive the noxious influences and awful neglect, are thrown, as soon as they can crawl, to scramble in the gutter, and leave their parents to amusement or business: as they advance in years they discover that they must, in general, find their own food or go without it. The 'duris urgens in rebus egestas' stimulates these independent urchins; and, at an age when the children of the wealthy would still be in leading-strings, they are off, singly or in parties, to beg, borrow, steal, and exercise all the cunning that want and a love of evil can stir up in a reckless race. They are driven to these courses, in many instances, by their parents; in more by their step-mothers; in most by necessity and general example. The passion for shows and the lowest drama is nearly universal; 'Panem et Circenses'—food and the penny theatres—these are their paradise, and their chief temptation to crime. They receive no education religious or secular; they are subjected to no restraint of any sort; never do they hear the word of advice, or the accent of kindness; the notions that exist in the minds of ordinary persons have no place in theirs; having nothing exclusively of their own, they seem to think such in fact, the true position of society; and, helping themselves without scruple to the goods of others, they can never recognise, when convicted before a magistrate, the justice of a sentence which punishes them for having done little more than was indispensable to their existence. . . .

The *Ragged Schools* owe their origin to some excellent persons in humble life who went forth into the streets and alleys, not many years ago, and invited these miserable outcasts to listen to the language of sympathy and care. We are not able to say when exactly the first beginning was made, nor to apportion the merit of the earlier efforts; but praise and fame are the last things such men thought or think of. Much, no doubt, must be ascribed to the zealous humanity of the City-missionaries. It is certain that those who undertook the task were of various denominations—church people and dissenters—animated, all of them, by a common sentiment of compassion and piety, which they proved by the ready and liberal contributions for this good purpose from their precarious and scanty earnings. Rooms were hired in the worst localities, and at the cheapest rate; lights provided; and, Sunday after Sunday, as the evening closed in, a band of voluntary teachers, both male and female, continued to struggle, in patience and faith, against the repulsive difficulties of their obscure occupation. It would be curious to see a minute record in print of the events that attended the opening of any one school; of the noise, confusion, and violence, that have, as we believe, signalized the commencement of nearly all of them. We have just seen a gentleman who came, in breathless dismay, to announce the misconduct of the boys in a school recently opened; 'The neighbours,' said he, 'are alarmed—the landlord will close the doors—the teachers will flee.' 'Well,' we replied, 'you have only added another instance to the many we had already heard of; you cannot have a *ragged school* without its preliminaries; but persevere as others have done, and you will soon overcome the tumult; those who came for a *lark* will be wearied out and stay away; those who have the least hankering after better things, will remain and obey you.' Such is the general course of events in all the most degraded localities; we have heard the various teachers narrate most graphically the drumming at the doors, the rattling at the windows, by those who demanded admittance; the uproar of their entry; the immediate extinction of the lamps; the dirt and the stones that flew in all directions, rendering this service of love in no slight degree a service of danger. Oftentimes these lads got possession of the apartments; and, refusing either to learn or to retire, continued lords paramount until the arrival of the police. But patience and principle have conquered them all; and now we may see, on each evening of the week, hundreds of these young maniacs engaged in diligent study, clothed, and in their right mind.

Ladies and gentlemen who walk in purple and fine linen, and fare sumptuously every day, can form no adequate idea of the pain and the toil which the founders and conductors of these schools have joyfully sustained in their simple and fervent piety. Surrendering nearly the whole of the sabbath, their only day of rest, and often, after many hours of toil, giving, besides, an evening in the week, they have plunged into the foulest localities, fetid apartments, and harassing duties. We have heard of school-rooms so closely packed, that three lads have sat in the fire-place, one on each hob, and the third in the grate with his head up the chimney; and frequent are the occasions on which the female teachers have returned to their homes covered with the vermin of their tattered pupils. All this they have done, and still do, in the genuine spirit of Christian charity, without the hope of recompense, of money, or of fame—it staggers, at first, our belief, but nevertheless it is true: and many a Sunday-school teacher, thus poor and zealous, will rise up in judgment with lazy ecclesiastics, boisterous sectarians, and self-seeking statesmen.

. . . The very title [Ragged School] denotes their purpose: they are open to receive all those who are excluded from superior schools by the rules and regulations indispensable to their discipline. The decent apparel, the washed face, the orderly behaviour, the attendance by day, the penny a week, amount to an interdict on their admission, were they even so disposed, to the National and British Schools; and, over and above the regulations, the dignity of the parents of the 'respectable' pupils—such is the term—would prompt them to withdraw their children from schools where an inter-mixture like this was allowed. We entertain no fanatical passion for the name, though we could quote many instances in which some of the most degraded of the race have been invited by the belief that the place and the service were not too grand for their misery. The name, too, reminds us all of the single purpose of these schools; of the peculiar sphere in which we are to labour; that our business is not in transparent lakes and flowing rivers, but in the gutter and in the mire. Finally, the permanence of the title does not condemn the pupils to the permanence of their condition; the children, if improved, are drafted off to better places of education; but the Ragged School remains for those who are still ragged. . . .

The last Report [of the Ragged School Union] shows a return of 26 schools, with an average attendance of about 2600 children, and 250 teachers. Since that period 4 more have been added, making an amount of 30 schools (still much below what is required), with an average attendance of at least 3000 children. Some are opened on Sunday evenings only, and in that case are managed entirely by voluntary teachers;[2] some are open two eve-

2. Footnote omitted.

nings in the week—others five—and, in these last cases, the education is conducted by a paid master; not more than two or three are open during the day. In the schools which are open on the Sunday only, nothing is taught but religion; in those which receive pupils on week-days, though the whole begins and closes with religious exercise, there are super-added reading, writing, and arithmetic. We may describe one lately established, as a sample of the extension and improvement which may be generally anticipated by and bye: —its system is that recommended by the British and Foreign Society; the studies begin with Scripture lessons, are carried through all the manipulations of the Primer, slate-pencil, and Cocker, aided by a variety of attractive illustrations; and end with a hymn. This is the course for the four first days of the week; on the fifth (and here is the new feature), the children, having commenced as usual, are disposed in industrial classes—the girls to every kind of needlework, the boys to the crafts of tailoring and shoemaking. Admission to the industrial class is treated as a reward, none being allowed to join it who do not present a ticket as an evidence of their regular attendance during the former days of the week. The numbers present on the last evening of which we have a return, were 63 girls and 42 boys, all of them brought from the most miserable localities; they were diligent, and well pleased with the notion of mending their own clothes; and a bargain was soon struck between the two classes of the lads—that the tailors should mend coats for the shoe-makers, and the shoemakers return the compliment to the tailors. Though the numbers which have been received into the school amount to 283, the average attendance, such is their spirit of rambling, goes no higher than 53 boys and 71 girls; the school being open from half-past six to nine. The expenses of the establishment are very moderate: the entire cost, inclusive of wages to the master-shoemaker, master-tailor, and mistress-needlewoman, being only about 3d. a-week for each child on the average attendance of 124, and not much more than 1d. a-week on the full complement of those admitted.

It is worth our while to devote a few moments to the details that exhibit the social condition of a large part of these children. We have been unable, through want of time, to obtain minute returns from every school; the statements, however, with which we are furnished, may we believe, be relied on as supplying a just notion of the whole mass. We have examined fifteen schools, and have arrived at an amount of 2345 children and young persons between the ages of five and seventeen, with some few even older, who are occasional hearers. The number of average attendants will be less by at least one-third, or about 1600. Now of these we find that 162 confess that they have been in prison; 116 have run away from their homes; 170 sleep in lodging-houses (the chief sinks of iniquity in the metropolis); 253 live by begging; 216 have no shoes or stockings; 280 have no hat, cap, or bonnet; 101 have no body-linen; 249 never sleep in beds; 68 are the children of convicts; 125 have step-mothers; and 306 have lost one or both parents, a large proportion having lost both.

Here is subject-matter enough for the sentimental, for spare tears and wandering sympathies! Those who, amidst the enjoyments of existence, seek the luxury of woe in a poem or a romance, may learn that the realities of life are more touching than fiction; and the practical alleviation of sorrow quite as delightful as the happy conclusion of a novel. . . .

It is indeed matter of astonishment to all those who are conversant with this class of our population, that so much success has attended these humble missionaries. They seek to reclaim a wild and lawless race, unaccustomed from their earliest years to the slightest moral influence, or even restraint, and bring them back to notions of civilization and domestic life. Their first difficulty lies in the roving habits of many of these infants of nature, who oftentimes quit their residences, if residences they have, and migrate in flocks to other districts of the great city. Those, again, who, while in town, are more stationary in their nightly resorts, indulge, nevertheless, in long absences from London, and roam for weeks together over the neighbouring counties. The fine months of summer are fatal to learning; the chills and rains of winter drive them to the schools for warmth and shelter. But such broken studies and imperfect discipline leave, on such vagrants, few traces of progress in which the teacher can find his consolation. Authority he cannot exercise; the children may be coaxed, but they cannot be coerced; fines it is absurd to think of; beating would not be efficacious, nor indeed safe; expulsion is no punishment. They must come when they like, or they will not come at all, for we offer neither food, nor clothing, nor immediate temporal advantage of any kind; their hopes and their fears are alike unawakened, and wanton tastes find nothing to counteract them. A procession or a new show throws confusion into every 'gymnasium,' and shears the master in the twinkling of an eye of half his listeners. It was our lot, a few weeks ago, to visit one of these Ragged-schools at 8 o'clock in the evening. we found it comparatively deserted; but the mystery was soon solved by the announcement that, it being Lord Mayor's Day, many had determined to avail themselves of so glorious an opportunity for pleasure or for profit.

The habits, too, of their daily life, the associations they necessarily form, are all alike in the way of the teacher: the lessons of the evening are reversed by the practice of the following day—passed, too probably, amidst the lowest scenes of vice and revelry. If kept at home, they are witnesses of all that is most vile in language and conduct; if sent abroad, it is to beg on prepared falsehoods—or cheat methodically in their small trades—or steal for immediate consumption or for sale at the receiving-shop. Hence the difficulty of infusing into these wanderers a sense of shame, and delicate notions of 'meum and tuum'. Having nothing of their own, they are under no terrors of the law of retaliation; being destitute of common necessaries, they cannot recognize the exclusive possession of superfluities; and so, less with a desire to infringe another man's rights than to assert what they consider to be their own, they help themselves to everything that comes in their way. They make little or no secret of their successful operations, cloaking them only with euphonous terms: they 'find' everything—they 'take' nothing; no matter the bulk or quality of the article, it was 'found,'—sometimes nearly a side of bacon, just at the convenient time and place; and many are the loud and bitter complaints that the 'dealer in marine stores' is utterly dishonest, and has given for the thing but half the price that could be got in the market. . . .

Indeed, it not unfrequently happens that the boys, on quitting the prisons, will march straight to the schools, and resume their accustomed places, with an apology to the teacher—'Sorry I could not come before; had ten days of Bridewell.' . . .

We are often met with the interrogatory—'What will you do with these children when you have educated them?' A reply may partly be found in the statements already given; but question for question—'What will you do with them, if you neglect to educate them?' They are not soap-bubbles, or peach-blossoms,—things that can be puffed away by the breath of a suckling: they are the seeds of future generations; and the wheat or tares will predominate, as Christian principle or ignorant selfishness shall, hereafter, govern our conduct. We must cease, if we would be safe, to trust in measures of coercion and chastisement for our juvenile vagrants; they are not too many to be educated as infants; they are far too many to be punished as adults. We must entertain higher thoughts for them and for England—and, with a just appreciation of their rights, and our own duties, not only help them, by God's blessing, from these depths of degradation; but raise them to a level on which they may run the course that is set before them, as citizens of the British Empire, and heirs of a glorious immortality.

[B] [Mary Carpenter], *Ragged Schools: Their Principles and Modes of Operation.* By a worker (London, 1850), pp. 11, 16 (editor's lib.)

Ragged Schools, when first commenced under that name, were simply Sunday Schools for those whose miserable condition precluded them from any religious instruction on the Lord's day. They now include Day Schools, where such instruction is given as the children are prepared to receive; and schools where, in addition, food is provided, and where they remain the whole day, some portion of their time being occupied in industrial work. . . .

Believing, as we do, that it is the religious element alone which can regenerate mankind, aided as it must always be, to effect any high object, by the exercise of all the noble powers with which man is endowed by his Creator, it is not surprising that this movement was commenced by some Sunday-school teachers in our great metropolis. The first organized attempt to concentrate their efforts was made in April, 1844, by a meeting held at the St. Giles's Ragged School. "These teachers," says the Report, "having often observed with regret the many children that are excluded from the regular Sunday or Day-school, in consequence of their *ragged and filthy condition,* and also the great numbers who constantly infest our streets and alleys, to idle, to steal, or to do mischief,—resolved to establish schools expressly for that destitute and depraved class, in the very localities, courts, and alleys where they abound." The result of their determination was that from time to time schools had been opened; the rent and other expenses being generally paid by the teachers themselves—sometimes by one or more benevolent individuals in the locality of the schools. There was no lack of pupils; numbers very often could not be admitted for want of room, or want of teachers, and a policeman, in some cases, was kept at the door to drive away those who wished to force themselves in. Thus, then, in faith and love, was the mustard-seed sown, which has now become, with the Divine blessing, a large and flourishing tree. . . .

. . . we shall present another picture of the first commencement of a similar school situated in Old Pye-street, Westminster, which is extracted from the *Ragged School Union Magazine,* January, 1849.

"One fine Sabbath afternoon, in the month of April, when the streets were unusually crowded, after having provided a large room, we went forth in the company of a poor tinker (the only person in the neighbourhood who would render us any assistance), to gather these poor and outcast children of the streets. After no small effort, forty were taken to the room, all of whom looked as wild as deer taken from the mountains, and penned up within the hurdle, when approached by man; the matted hair, the mud-covered face, hands, and feet, the ragged and tattered clothes, that served as an apology to cover their nakedness, gave the group a very grotesque appearance, and would have been a fine subject for the painter's pencil. Little was done that afternoon besides taking their names, and even in this we had to encounter difficulties. Beginning with the first bench, a boy was asked, 'What is your name?' He answered, 'They calls me Billy.' 'Where do you live?' 'I lives in that yer street down the way, at mother M———'s rag shop; I have a tother brother, but I am older than he.' The next boy was ten years of age; he said his name was Dick. 'Any other name besides Dick?' 'No, they calls me Dick; I sells matches in the streets, and live in that tother room next to Jimmy that sells oranges.' Such is a specimen of the answers given to questions respecting names, age, and residence!"

The character of the children here described will prevent its being any subject for surprise when we read of the tumultuous conduct which has distinguished the opening of most Ragged Schools in our large towns. The floors sprinkled with blood, benches broken down, lesson-boards torn asunder, the scholars tumbling over each other in wild confusion, the master with his clothes torn, teachers obliged to escape for their lives out of the windows, and over the roofs of houses,—all these things have but afforded a type of the moral chaos which was to be reduced to order by the power of love and faith.

[C] C. J. Montague, *Sixty Years in Waifdom; or, The Ragged School Movement in English History* (London, 1904), pp. 47-48 (editor's lib.)

The founders of the R. S. U. [Ragged School Union] had to consider, when framing the constitution, the schools that were already affiliated, the schools that might become so, and new ones that would be subsequently formed. They felt that the basis must be broad and deep but the aim must be specific. Accordingly, they drew up very early a list of the children who should be the special subjects of ragged school labour. They were—

1. Children of convicts who have been transported.
2. Children of convicts in our prisons at home.
3. Children of thieves not in custody.
4. Children of the lowest mendicants and tramps.
5. Children of worthless drunken parents.
6. Children of stepfathers or stepmothers; often driven by neglect or cruelty to shift for themselves.
7. Children of those suitable for the workhouse but living a vagrant semi-criminal life.
8. Children of honest parents too poor to pay for schooling or to clothe the children so as to enable them to attend an ordinary school.
9. Orphans, deserted children, and runaways, who live by begging and stealing.
10. Workhouse lads who have left it and become vagrants.
11. Lads of the street-trading classes, ostlers' boys, and labourers' assistants, who otherwise would get no schooling.
12. Girl-hawkers working for cruel and worthless parents.
13. The children of poor Roman Catholics who do not object to their children reading the Bible.

Children Committed to Prison in Edinburgh, 1847-1872

David Harris, *A Plea for Industrial Brigades, as Adjuncts to Ragged Schools* (Glasgow, 1873), p. 9 (Brit. Mus.)

JUVENILE CRIME IN EDINBURGH.

Return of the number of juveniles committed to the prison of Edinburgh in the twenty-six years ended 30th November, 1872

Dates		No. under 14 years of age	No. 14 and under 16 yrs of age
Year ending 30th Nov.	1847	260	—
	1848	193	552*
	1849	149	440
	1850	61	361

*Before the establishment of Ragged Schools in the City.

	1851	56	227
	1852	57	270
	1853	117	295
	1854	103	253
	1855	81	142
	1856	137	134
Year ending 31st Dec.	1857	92	130
	1858	71	138
	1859	56	130
	1860	84	78
11 Mon. ending 30th Nov.	1861	81	76
	1862	52	89
	1863	50	70
	1864	56	73
	1865	57	91
	1866	64	97
	1867	76	84
	1868	52	76
	1869	47	76
	1870	57	104
	1871	51	102
	1872	46	80

Crime Is Hereditary and Should be Controlled by Rescuing Juvenile Delinquents, 1848

[Hugh Barclay],[1] *Juvenile Delinquency: Its Causes and Cure* Edinburgh and London, 1848), pp. 6-7 (London Sch. Econ.)

[The author maintains that morbid philanthropy that shows only sympathy for the criminal without weighing the injury done to society and Draconian severity alike are wrong approaches to dealing with juvenile delinquency. Most criminals are young and are lacking in education. He emphasizes the contaminating influence of gaol confinement and states that a majority of juvenile offenders committed to prison become recidivists. Very effectively he traces the short and sad career of the typical juvenile delinquent.]

. . . We have it established that crime is hereditary, and that for generations the same names are familiar as household words in our district criminal courts. In some towns, where there exists a considerable aggregate of crime and convictions, on investigation it is found that these are apportioned amongst a circle of families, some of whom give half-a-dozen of its members to swell the records of

1. Sheriff Substitute of Perth, Scotland.

crime. In the Seventh Report of the Inspector of Prisons, a case is mentioned under the head of Hoddington, where seven children out of a family of nine had been in prison, some of them several times. This fact proves the expediency of cutting at the root of the evil, and rescuing the young before being indurated in habits of criminal indulgence, and so prevent them in their turn becoming the youthful parents of households of vice, and generations of neglected and hopeless, helpless criminals.

Juvenile Delinquency in Glasgow, 1848

William Logan, *The Moral Statistics of Glasgow* (Glasgow and London, 1859), pp. 49-51 (Brit. Mus.)

[The author, a city missionary and Commissioner of the Scottish Temperance League, shows the relationship among intemperance, disease, mental derangement, pauperism, crime, female prostitution, juvenile delinquency, industrial schools, etc. The book consists largely of quoted replies of authorities and officials in Glasgow to questions submitted by the author and official statistics specially collected for this study.]

THE GLASGOW FEMALES' HOUSE OF REFUGE

The Magdalene Asylum was established about 35 years ago, for the reception of penitent *unfortunate females.* . . . The institution is now designated the Glasgow Females' House of Refuge. . . .

We addressed a note, with a number of queries, to the matron, per Mr. Davie, town-clerk, on the 3rd November, 1848; in reply to which we received the following communication:

Query 1. Number of inmates in } children 62 } Total 126
           the House of Refuge   } women   64 }

Query 2. Number from
         8 to 10 years of age......................17
         10 to 15.................................45
         15 to 20.................................40
         Above 20...............................24

Miss Sliman, the respected matron, adds the following note:— "The matron of the House of Refuge is decidedly of opinion, that intemperance is a most fruitful source of juvenile delinquency, and also crime and profligacy in those of riper years. Perhaps nineteen cases out of twenty are traceable, in one form or another, to this terrible evil. Along with making, selling, and drinking intoxicating liquors should be placed pawnshops, shows, dancing saloons, the Glasgow Fair, etc., as the principal parts of the machinery which are so fearfully spreading desolation, crime, and ruin in the community."

[CHILDREN IN THE GLASGOW JAIL]

The following return, furnished by Mr. Mullen, the governor, will show the number of prisoners at different ages in Glasgow jail during the year ending 30th June, 1848:

	Males	Females	Total
Total number of prisoners committed during the year	2221	1327	3548
Average daily number in confinement	353	221	574
Under 16 years of age	372	126	498
16 years and under 18	227	177	404
18 years and under 21	384	301	685
21 years and under 50	1159	665	1824
50 years and upwards	79	58	137

Prize Essay Contest to Prove That Intemperance Is the Major Cause of Crime and Juvenile Depravity, 1849

[A] Rev. Henry Worsley, *Juvenile Depravity.* £100 *Prize Essay*[1] (London, 1849), pp. v-vi, 217-19, 226-28, 235 (editor's lib.)

The following Advertisement, by which the subject of the Prize Essay was first introduced to Public notice, appeared in Ten London Papers:—

£100 PRIZE ESSAY

The fearful and growing prevalence of Juvenile Depravity, and the inadequacy of the various means hitherto employed to meet

1. Rev. Worsley was from Easton Rectory, Suffolk. The adjudicators were Dr. John Harris of Cheshunt, the Rev. James Sherman Surrey Chapel, and Dr. Charles John Vaughan of Harrow. The prize was offered by Mr. John Eaton of Bristol.

the evil, have long challenged inquiry, both as respects its causes, and the nature of the most probable and efficient remedies. No one conversant with the evidence furnished by our judicial tribunals, and with that accumulation of facts which is now accessible to every inquirer, can fail to corroborate the testimony of the highest authorities in the land, that the monster evil of our country, and the source, directly or indirectly, of the greater portion of Juvenile Depravity and Crime, is Intemperance. It is this tremendous agency which perverts, where it does not prevent, the benefits of Education, and is continually training up a succession of victims for the jail and the scaffold. It is a vast national evil, which, in whatever light it is viewed, has long demanded a searching investigation. With a view, therefore, to engage an amount of labour and talent commensurate with the importance of the inquiry, a premium for the best Essay on the subject is offered, of *One Hundred Pounds.*

[Fifty-two essays were submitted in competition for this one Hundred Pound Prize. Some of the treatises were found to be elaborate and valuable, but Rev. Worsley's essay was adjudged as "that which best satisfied the conditions stated in the Prospectus." A second prize was awarded to a Miss Meteyard (Silverpen), whose essay was not published apparently (p. 65), but Rev. Worsley is indebted to her for numerous facts, figures, and illustrations. He quotes freely from official reports describing social and economic conditions of the laboring classes, the extent of crime, prostitution and drunkenness, but preserves throughout his essay a strongly religious tone. The following extracts present the conclusion reached, and the remedy proposed]:—

We have examined minutely the facts of country life, and we have found drunkenness always associated with other crime, and either originating or fostering it. To quote a high authority . . . "The insane fondness for drink is not confined to the criminal population of the country. The infatuation prevails among the whole working part of the people." In scrutinizing the natural tendencies to evil in manufacturing life, we have observed the manifest temptations to intemperance. We have reviewed the parliamentary enactments, regulating the sale of strong liquors, and remarked that these have afforded easy indulgence to a taste stimulated by factory labour, and kept under little control. In short, the breaking up of old checks and restraints on vice, has been found coincident with enlarged means and opportunities of sinning. Juvenile crime must be mainly attributed, either to *parental neglect* or *parental example,* or the *absence of all necessary parental government through or-*

phanage. The connexion is indisputable. The origin of the wide-spread mis-conduct in parents has been sought; and it is demonstrated to be *intemperance;* to use the words of the excellent authority above quoted—"mingling with all other causes, *yet pre-dominating above them*—drunkenness." Wherever we have turned our view, whatever agency we have examined, we have met the monster cause, either as prime mover to mischief, or in association with immediate incitement. The conclusion is irresistible; and the conviction must fasten itself on every candid mind, that ignorance and depravity, thieving and prostitution, pauperism and want, the vice of parents, the crime of their children, to an extent beyond what has ever been appreciated, or even surmised by the community at large, are produced, proximately or remotely, but really—really produced by *intemperance*. The case is of the clearest conceivable character. The enormous mass of juvenile delinquency in our own times, is traceable to parental neglect and bad example, which are mainly chargeable on the prevalence, almost universal, of drinking habits. . . .

It was under the deep conviction of the misery produced by drunkenness that the Temperance Society was first formed in 1830. It received powerful support: the Queen herself became its patroness; and the Vice-patron and President, the Bishop of London, joined with her Majesty in taking the pledge. The operations of the *Old* Temperance Society were extensive, and energetic; yet it failed to realize the expectations built upon it. The causes of *failure* may perhaps be reduced to the following:

1. It attempted to define between different kinds of strong drink; it prohibited the use of ardent spirits only. It is, however, an ascertained fact that *malt liquor* is among the *principal* agents in producing drunkenness in England.

2. It taught *moderation* in the use of all intoxicating liquors except ardent spirits, which were prohibited altogether. But the very notion of a habit involves the influence of association; and, therefore, to be connecting the chain by the commencing act, is to bring against the recent resolution of amendment, all the force of reminiscences and excited sensations. To tantalize the drunkard with a little, to grant a sip, is not the way to rid him of his vice. The doctrine of degrees supposed that the *habitual* drunkard *could be* moderate in the use of liquor,—a plain contradiction in terms.

Drunkards themselves raised their voice against it; they stated that they could not thus be reclaimed, that *inveterate habit excluded* the very notion of *moderation,* that the alternative in their case must be either intoxication or not a single drop.

Thus the finding part of a truth and acting experimentally upon it, led at length to the discovery of the whole truth: *and under the conviction of necessity, total abstinence from all that could intoxicate* was boldly proclaimed in 1834, by seven working-men of Preston:—*not as a theory or speculation, but as the only remaining resource.*

There were numerous dogmatic predictions of its failure, on the assumption that strong drink is necessary to the labouring man: but the result of the experiment proved successful.

The idea soon spread: a society was formed, the perfect adaptation of the means to the end being palpable. It has been proved, that not only is entire abstinence from intoxicating liquors safe, as regards the physical constitution, but that wherever it has been tested on a large scale, perfect success has been the result: it has been evidenced by facts to be a perfect cure and preventive. . . .

The following declaration has received the signatures of more than 1500 medical men, including many of the most eminent of the profession, in the metropolis and other parts of the nation:—

"We, the undersigned, are of opinion—

"1. That a very large portion of human misery, including poverty, disease, and crime, is induced by the use of alcoholic or fermented liquors, as beverages.

"2. That the most perfect health is compatible with total abstinence from all such intoxicating beverages, whether in the form of ardent spirits, or as wine, beer, ale, porter, cider, etc., etc.

"3. That persons accustomed to such drinks may with perfect safety discontinue them entirely, either at once, or gradually after a short time.

"4. That total and universal abstinence from alcoholic liquors and intoxicating beverages of all sorts, would greatly contribute to the health, the prosperity, the morality, and the happiness of the human race."

> [B] Thomas Beggs, *An Inquiry into the Extent and Causes of Juvenile Depravity* (London, 1849), pp. 74-75, 84, 118, 121-22, 124, 149 (editor's lib.)

[The title page describes the author as "Late Secretary of the Health of Town's Association, and Author of 'Lectures on the Moral Elevation of the People.'" This essay was adjudged worthy of a second prize in the contest won by Rev. Worsley. Though written "in the intervals occurring during the discharge of heavy official duties," it is a scholarly work showing the author's wide range and thorough mastery of the subject, enforced by facts and statistics. The chapter titles indicate the scope and arrangement of the material, as follows: I. Introductory—The Subject stated; II. The Dangerous Classes—Numbers of the Criminal, Pauper, and Vagrant Classes; III. The Dangerous Classes—State of Education; IV. The Dangerous Classes—Domestic and Social Conditions; V. Juvenile Depravity—An Inquiry into its Causes—The Mining Population; VI. Juvenile Depravity—An Inquiry into its Causes—The Factory and Agricultural Population; VII. General Condition of the Poorer Classes—Means spent in Drink—Prison and Police Statistics; VIII. Prostitution. Its Extent and Causes; IX. Vice and Profligacy among the more educated Classes—the Drinking Habits a Cause of Individual Degradation—Sabbath Schools; X. Consideration of Remedies; Appendix.

From such a wealth of material it is difficult to make a selection. The two extracts presented here cover subject matter (narcotics) and views not included in the works of preceding writers in this series.]

[MOTHERS GIVE THEIR CHILDREN NARCOTIC DRUGS]

. . . One half of the children dying before the age of five years, is a sufficient indication of the unfavourable physical circumstances to which they are subject. But the moral evils are far more appalling. As an instance we may name the practice of administering narcotic drugs to children, and which prevails so extensively in many of the manufacturing towns. The custom is thus described by Dr. Lyon Playfair, who made it a subject of special investigation when engaged in similar inquiries among the Lancashire population. The mother has to go to a mill to her employment, and leaves her child at home under the care of some little girl, another very imperfect superintendence. In order that the child may be as little troublesome as possible, a dose of "quietness" (a preparation of opium) is given to it, and it dozes away its hours until the return of the mother at mid-day: another dose is then given to it, to carry it safely through until the evening. The evening brings its duties and fatigue for the parent, and as she must sleep through the night to enable her to follow her labour next day, the child has again given to it a portion of this horrible mixture. Thus the poor babe is supplied two or three times a day with a deadly drug. The vital energies are repressed, the growth checked, and disease induced.

Vast numbers are relieved from the suffering by early death. Many continue to linger out a wretched existence. . . . The use of these stupifying drugs induces a morbid condition of body and a depraved appetite that food will not satisfy; and thus we have the children of these districts rushing with the greatest avidity to intoxicating drinks at the tenderest age. . . . In certain districts of the country, mothers are known to dose their children with narcotic drugs, inflicting a lingering death, in order to procure a few pounds from a burial club in which the child has been insured. . . .

[SUNDAY-SCHOOLS UNABLE TO CURB DRINKING HABITS WHICH ARE APPROVED BY ALL CLASSES OF SOCIETY]

But there is a large amount of vice and profligacy which does not belong to the uneducated classes, and which never appears in the statistics of crime. Much of this is associated with drinking habits. . . .

. . . The Committee of the Rochdale Temperance Society commenced, a short time back, a most important inquiry in relation to Sabbath-school children. "A few months ago a member of the Committee visited one of the singing saloons in Rochdale, and on a Saturday evening, about eleven o'clock, he observed sixteen boys and girls seated at a table in front of the stage; several of the lads had long pipes each, with a glass or jug containing intoxicating liquor, and no less than fourteen of the number were members of the Bible classes in different Sunday-schools. There they sat, listening to the most obscene songs, witnessing scenes of the most immoral kind, and swallowing liquid fire. . . . These sinks of iniquity are thronged with old Sunday scholars, especially on Sunday evenings, and not infrequently until twelve o'clock" . . . "many a promising teacher has fallen a victim."

. . . Venerable ministers have sometimes asked with amazement, what becomes of all the children educated in our Sunday-schools? It is clear, a very small portion of them become united with the churches in whose bosom they have been cherished. Mr. Michael Young, in a valuable essay on the subject of Sabbath-schools, has calculated that more than one-third of these who receive instruction fall into habits of drunkenness. . . .

Is it not, then, a matter of grave moment to ascertain what influences are at work to thwart the labours of so admirable an institution [as Sunday-schools], and cast so much of its promise upon the winds? We look abroad, and we find, among other evil agencies, a popular delusion with regard to one article. The English people have always been a drinking people; stimulating drinks have been regarded by them at all times with great respect. It has been considered an indispensable medicine in almost all cases of disease, a representative of hospitality, the inseparable and essential symbol of friendship and conviviality, and, in addition to all this, it has been established as an article of diet, as necessary to the Englishman as his beef or bread. . . .

. . . If it were only the idle, the worthless, and the profligate, who countenanced the drink, the youth would be safe, for he would not think of following an example set by such. But he finds the pious, the intellectual, the benevolent and the wise, take it and give it freely to others. Early impressions are the most lasting, and the youth, surrounded by such associations, feels it right, (how should he do otherwise?) to use the drink. How many a fond father, while dandling a beloved boy, has taught him to drink mamma's health, while he could barely lisp her name. That is one step in the child's education, and it may be the first in a drunkard's career. This subject must be well considered by all interested in the education of youth. Gin-shops and public-houses, fruitful as they are, are not productive of so much evil as our system of home drinking. . . .

Intemperance may not be the parent of all our social ills, but it originates many, and aggravates the malignancy of those it does not actually produce. We find it associated with a low order of intelligence and debased morals—and undermining the social and domestic character of the people. Judges have repeatedly given expression to their feelings, that if it were not for intemperance their office would be a sinecure. Magistrates have borne testimony to the same thing. Those who have gone carefully over this work will not doubt that a great portion of our juvenile delinquency may be ascribed to intemperance. . . .

Rookeries as Nurseries of Felons, 1850

Thomas Beames, *The Rookeries of London: Past, Present, and Prospective* (London, 1850), pp. 95-96, 119, 122-24, 132 (Brit. Mus.)

[This work was written by a clergyman who had labored for ten years in densely populated districts of London and who speaks, therefore, from first-hand experience. Considerable attention is devoted to the historical development of rookeries, outgrowths of a faulty social and economic system, which had become the festering plague-spots of the metropolis. The author quotes freely from current periodicals, particularly some able articles that first appeared in *The Morning Chronicle* and later were printed in pamphlet form. A short extract from this pamphlet, quoted by Beames, gives some idea of the nature of the material presented.]

"We then," says the author of the pamphlet, "journeyed down London street (that London street we have spoken of before, the best specimen of Rookeries, two hundred years old, and upwards). In No. 1 of this street the cholera first appeared seventeen years ago, and spread up it with fearful virulence; but this year it appeared at the opposite end, and ran down it with like severity. As we passed along the reeking banks of the sewer, the sun shone upon a narrow slip of water. In the bright light it appeared the colour of strong green tea, and positively looked as solid as black marble in the shadow; indeed, it was more like watery mud than muddy water: and yet *we were assured this was the only water these wretched inhabitants had to drink.* . . . As we stood, we saw a little child, from one of the galleries opposite, lower a tin can with a rope, to fill a large bucket that stood beside her. In each of the balconies that hang over the stream the self-same tub was to be seen, in which the inhabitants put the mucky liquid to stand, so that they may, after it has rested for a day or two, skim the fluid. We asked if the inhabitants did really drink the water? The answer was, they were obliged to drink the ditch, without they could beg a pailfull or thieve, a pailfull of water.[1] 'But have you spoken to your landlord about having it laid on for you?' 'Yes, sir, and he says he'll do it, and he'll do it, but we know him better than to believe him.' . . ."

Yet hitherto we have considered Rookeries as means of demoralising the present generation. We fear them for what they are, —beds of pestilence, where the fever is generated which shall be propagated to distant parts of the town,—rendezvous of vice, whose effects we feel in street robberies and deeds of crime,—blots resting upon our national repute for religion and charity. Still they are dangerous, not on account so much of what they are, as what they

1. A writer in the *Edinburgh Review* ("Supply of Water to the Metropolis"), April, 1850, p. 201, makes the following pertinent comments: "We fill our gaols with felons, and we have City Missions, and put our trust in education; but the influences of filth are stronger than the policeman, the schoolmaster, and the preacher; and we ought by this time to have learned that the very foundation of moral training in a London tenement is a pipe of wholesome water from the top to the bottom of the house."

may be;—they are not only the haunts where pauperism recruits its strength—not only the lurking-places, but the *nurseries* of felons. A future generation of thieves are there hatched from the viper's egg, who shall one day astonish London by their monstrous birth. . . .

It was reserved, perhaps, for the Rookeries of our day not to rear a few anomalous instances, but whole gangs of juvenile delinquents; to send forth children trained adepts in wickedness, these poetic innocents calculating chances of discovery, watching times and seasons for theft,—conversant with the habits, scrutinising the weak and unguarded points, of those by robbing whom they must thrive, —taught noiselessly to do their deeds of darkness, not singly, but in gangs, where concert aided the theft, where numbers made it difficut to trace the delinquent; so that hours, days must have been spent to make them adepts in their calling,—oaths of fearful import administered to bind them to silence,—laws enacted to regulate these bodies corporate,—the wires carefully adjusted along which the electric fluid passes, if we may be allowed the figure,—schools, in a word, formed, whose task-book is the Newgate calendar. No one who knows Rookeries will doubt this. . . .

It is no uncommon thing for boys to stay out all night, and when they return, not to be able to give a satisfactory account of themselves. Though their parents are honest, there is little doubt that they themselves have been entrapped by designing criminals, and made the instruments of nefarious practices. Thus the poor are often disgraced by their own offspring, who have fallen under the evil influence of some professor of wickedness. Boys are easily tempted by some bait suited to their years,—are initiated into the unhallowed mysteries of the craft,—are taught to deceive by plausible excuses the vigilance of their parents. A poor man is bereaved of his wife by disease,—is left with young children, his trade being one which takes him much from home; he leaves his children under the guardianship of a neighbour who has children of her own, and can feel no particular interest in the welfare of another's offspring. In the very Rookery which he inhabits are people of questionable occupation,—old and juvenile victimizers. What a tempting speculation, to make these poor motherless children—such at least as are old enough—the means of carrying out their iniquities! These harpies know the occupation of the father,—daily experience teaches them to calculate the moment of his return,—his habits are no secret, the dispositions of his family easily ascertained,—they are tempted, in their ignorance, by a bait they cannot resist, and enter gradually on the course of crime. The writer has known more than one such instance, and has had reason to be thankful that Refuges for the destitute afforded an asylum for those thus early betrayed. But too often—hard as it may seem to write such things—female children, in haunts like these, have fallen victims to the gross passions of abandoned men, when their tender age would have seemed to have put such dangers out of the way, and when their very ignorance was the cause of their fall. And recollect, the arrangements of Rookeries foster such things. When distinction of sex is practically ignored, can you expect decency to survive?

. . . Are you aware that several sweetmeat shops exist in the neighbourhood of Rookeries, where children are enticed to gamble for the tempting articles exposed on the counter?—that one mode of carrying on such practices, is this: —A doll is fixed to a board, the body of which is hollow; through the head of this figure a marble is passed, which, after circulating through it, falls into one of the many holes made for it in the board beneath; these holes are numbered, and accordingly as he exceeds or falls below a given figure, the youthful gambler wins or loses? At first sight such a practice seems comparatively innocent; but too often, from the thirst for gaming in this small way, children rob their parents.

Thomas Plint Stresses the Need for Inductive Research into the Causes of Crime and Delinquency, 1851

Thomas Plint, *Crime in England, its Relation, Character, and Extent, as Developed from 1801 to 1848* (London, 1851), pp. 156-57, 170 (editor's lib.)

. . . Every section of society has its intractables and incorrigibles,—those on whom moral appliances have failed, who are either cast out by society itself, or isolate themselves because they are in all parts of their nature antagonistic to it; and such of the humble operative classes as fall below that moral standard of their grade in society, which is the basis of admission to its privileges and friendships, are necessarily thrown off, and, as they can fall no lower, constitute a class apart,—"their hand against every man, and every man's hand against them."

. . . The existence and the numbers of the criminal class is a great evil, and, it may be, a great and grave error on the part of society at large. How it is engendered—what are its elements—must be of permanent importance to be known. The first step to the effectual correction, or the greatest possible mitigation of this great evil,—and no less calamity,—will be the recording with more accuracy and minuteness whatever information can be elicited respecting the criminals who pass through our courts of justice. More would be known, after five years of careful scrutiny into the previous history of our criminals, than will be got by fifty years of the superficial and desultory observation which is at present practised. The inquiry should extend to the place of birth, occupation, place of residence, and to education, and other moral influences; in one word, all that is comprehended in the phrase—the "Natural History" of the class. The philosophy or theory of a criminal class, will assume a tangible shape when that is accomplished, but not before: and as, until the true theory be known, so neither can the true remedy be known, the nation may lay its account in the expenditure of a vast amount of money, on schemes of prison discipline, and penal infliction, and industrial schools, and national education—only to arrive at the conclusion at last, that it has applied remedies without an accurate knowledge of the disease, and has therefore acted the part of the empiric or the quack, to the disgrace of its philosophy and its statesmanship. . . .

[Plint is quite critical of Worsley's *Juvenile Depravity*, which is based on the thesis that juvenile delinquency was greatly on the increase. Actually, says Plint, juvenile crime in all England except Middlesex decreased by 20 per cent between 1842 and 1847.] It is painful to see a vast amount of talent and labour expended in bringing together the incidental notices of social conditions and social evils, which by their very isolation acquire an apparent magnitude and importance which they would instantly lose, if relieved by the filling up of the entire picture of society. Any person accustomed to refer to the authorities quoted by public writers on the subject of crime, cannot but be aware what a thoroughly one-sided view of things is presented, partly because one set of phenomena only is selected, and partly because what is selected is made to clench a foregone conclusion, or becomes the ridiculously narrow basis of an entire theory. Mr. Worsley's book is again reluctantly referred to in proof of this.

Miss Mary Carpenter Leads Movement to Set up Industrial and Reformatory Schools, 1851-1853

[A] Mary Carpenter, *Reformatory Schools, for the Children of the Perishing and Dangerous Classes, and for Juvenile Offenders* (London, 1851) (editor's lib.)

[In this book Miss Carpenter attempts to rouse public interest in the condition of thousands of destitute and delinquent children in England, especially in the large cities, and to convince the public that special institutions should be established for giving them industrial, moral, and religious training over an extensive period of time, as a substitute for the pernicious system of gaol confinement of children. The author quotes widely from official reports of prisons and private institutions for delinquents, and she points out the characteristic features of the leading reformatory institutions in France and Germany. A deeply religious tone permeates this work, as in all of Miss Carpenter's writings. Her chapter headings are as follows: Introductory Chapter; I. First Principles; II. Evening Ragged Schools; III. Free Day Schools; IV. Industrial Feeding Schools; V. The Gaol; VI. Penal Reformatory Schools.]

[B] Mary Carpenter, *Juvenile Delinquents, their Condition and Treatment* (London, 1853), pp. 376-80 (editor's lib.)

[In many respects this work is an enlarged and revised edition of *Reformatory Schools*. It presents more descriptive material of delinquents, their parental and home conditions, lays more emphasis on female delinquents, enlarges on the experience of Continental countries in handling delinquents, and adds a chapter on American houses of refuge. Many extracts from case histories of delinquents are presented. The chapter headings are as follows: Introduction; I. Characteristics and Classes; II. A Single Captive; III. The Girls; IV. The Parents; V. Present Treatment; VI. American Experience; VII. Continental Experience; VIII. Individual Experience; IX. Principles of Treatment; X. Application of Principles.]

[APPLICATION OF PRINCIPLES]

Surely, we require to return to first principles, and to learn from our Saxon ancestors, as well as from our French neighbours, that a child acts without discernment of the true nature of his crime, and *"shall be pardoned, of course, because he is a child."*

The following principles, then, appear to have been already acknowledged in the laws and social economy of our country, and only require a fuller development than now exists, to meet the condition and treatment of the children of the "perishing and dangerous" classes of our community and juvenile delinquents.

Firstly, That all parents are responsible for the maintenance and education of their children, and amenable to punishment when they neglect it through their own misconduct.

Secondly, That where a child has no parents, or where, having them, such parents prove themselves incapable of discharging the duty devolving on them, this duty rests upon society,—the child being, by nature, in a condition in which he is irresponsible. Society cannot neglect this duty without incurring a heavy penalty.

Thirdly, That where a parent, through his culpable neglect, or actual criminalty, proves that he cannot retain the guardianship of his child without injury to society, and therefore is deprived of it, he is not thereby freed from the duty imposed by nature of maintaining his child, and must be compelled to do so, while losing his legal right over him.

Fourthly, That when society, embodied in the State, assumes the guardianship of a child . . . it is bound to discharge this duty, so as best to fulfil the end for which God sent him into the world,— namely, that he may become a useful member of society, and prepare for another state of existence. This principle equally applies to orphans, to morally destitute children, and to those who have been legally convicted of breach of the law.

Fifthly, That the State in thus assuming, so to speak, a parental relation towards the child, may consign the care of him, as is done by natural parents, to those who can discharge the duty satisfactorily,—a strict inspection being exercised by the State, to ascertain that this duty is well discharged.

Sixthly, That though it may be necessary, in default of better provision, to employ large government institutions for the maintenance and education of such children, it is important to enlist in these as much individual and voluntary effort as possible, as the best means of supplying to the child the parental relation; but that every inducement should be held out to lead individuals, or individual bodies, themselves to establish such institutions, where the child may be, in a measure, restored to the natural condition of a family, and brought under individual influence. The State should, however, always exercise a close inspection of such institutions.

. . . But our present inquiry more particularly regards convicted children; any legislative measure especially intended for *them* should not only be founded on the foregoing principles, but distinctly recognize the following, which arise from them:

That the child, when by conviction of crime he becomes a child of the State, must still be treated as a child, and be dealt with by corrective training, not by mere punishment, as at present.

That he should for this end be placed in a Reformatory School, where he shall be submitted to such training and discipline as may best prepare him to become a useful member of society.

And that, wherever practicable, such schools should be conducted by individual bodies, with inspection from the State.

Such a measure will have as its object—

1. To give power to magistrates and judges to sentence any young person convicted of offence against the laws, to detention in a Reformatory School for a period not less than a year, or exceeding the term of his minority, the period to be dependent on his reformation, and decided by the managers of the school and the government inspector. A discretionary power to rest with the magistrates and judges to restore the child to his (or her) parents or guardians on the first offence, provided they give satisfactory security for his future good conduct.

2. To give power to magistrates and judges in all cases as aforesaid, to charge the parents of such offender with a weekly contribution in aid of his (or her) maintenance in the Reformatory School, such amount to be paid by the parish, and in all cases to be recoverable by the parish officers from the parents.

3. To enable the Secretary of State to pay an annual sum from the public funds towards the expense of such Reformatory School, and a sum towards the erection of the same; provided always such School be duly certified by Her Majesty's inspectors, as to be so conducted as to carry out a reformatory discipline calculated to train up useful members of society.

4. To enable magistrates in all districts where such Schools have not been established within a certain specified time, or do not exist in proportion to the wants of the districts, to erect and establish such schools by aid of a local rate.

5. To give sufficient power to the managers or directors of such Schools for the necessary correctional discipline of offenders committed to them, for the detention of the same, and for the recovering them is case of absconding; such managers or directors being responsible for their safe custody.

6. To appoint inspectors who shall frequently examine the working and management of the School and its reformatory effect on the children, the care of the religious instruction being left entirely to the managers of the School.

Birmingham Conferences on Juvenile Delinquency, 1851, 1853

Report of the Proceedings of a Conference on the Subject of Preventive and Reformatory Schools, held at Birmingham, on the 9th and 10th December, 1851 (London, 1851) (editor's lib.)

[There were two Birmingham Conferences on the subject of industrial and reformatory schools: the *First*, held in December, 1851, and called at the request of Miss Mary Carpenter, of Bristol, after consultation with Matthew Davenport Hill, Recorder of Birmingham, and other leaders in the field; and the *Second*, called by Mr. C. B. Adderley, M. P. for December, 1853. The *First* Conference advocated the setting up of industrial feeding schools for vagrant children, supported by public funds, and urged legislative enactments for establishing correctional and reformatory schools for the seriously delinquent children. These steps had been recommended by Miss Carpenter in her book on *Reformatory Schools*, which had been published earlier in the year. In May, 1852, on motion of Mr. Adderley, a Committee (of the House of Commons) on Criminal and Destitute Juveniles was appointed, and collected evidence through public hearings until Parliament adjourned in the summer of 1852, dissolving the Committee. This body of evidence was published, without report or recommendations from the Committee itself. The proceedings were renewed under a new Committee of nearly the same composition after Parliament opened in November, 1852. This Committee on Criminal and Destitute Children issued a voluminous report with minutes of evidence in the summer of 1853. This report supplemented by the resolutions and the publicity of the *Second* Birmingham Conference in December resulted after some delays in the passage of the Youthful Offenders Act of 1854, setting up reformatory schools, and the passage of the Industrial Schools Act of 1856.]

The following *Resolutions* were unanimously adopted at the Conference:—

1st.—That the present condition and treatment of the "perishing and dangerous classes" of Children and Juvenile Offenders deserve the consideration of every Member of a Christian community.

2nd.—That the means at present available for the Reformation of these Children have proved totally inadequate to check the spread of Juvenile Delinquency; partly owing to the want of proper Industrial, Correctional, and Reformatory Schools; and *partly* to the want of Authority in Magistrates to compel attendance at such Schools.

3rd.—That the adoption of a somewhat altered and extended course of proceeding, on the part of the Committee of Privy Council, is earnestly to be desired for those children who have not yet made themselves amenable to the law, but who, by reason of the vice, neglect, or extreme poverty of their parents, are not admitted into the existing Day Schools.

4th.—That for those Children who are not attending any School, and have subjected themselves to police interference, by vagrancy, mendicancy, or petty infringements of the law, legislative enactments are urgently required, in order to aid or establish Industrial Feeding Schools, at which the attendance of such Children shall be enforced by Magistrates, and payment made for their maintenance, in the first instance from some public fund, power being given to the public authorities to recover the outlay from the Parents of the Children.

5th.—That legislative enactments are also required in order to establish Correctional and Reformatory Schools for those Children who have been convicted of felony, or such misdemeanours as involve dishonesty; and to confer on magistrates power to commit Juvenile Offenders to such Schools instead of to Prison.

6th.—That the following Gentlemen form a Committee, with power to add to their number, to adopt such measures as they may think desirable, in order to obtain the requisite Parliamentary enactments, as well as to prepare a Memorial to the Committee of Council, and for the attainment of the specific object laid down in the foregoing Resolutions:—

J. Adshead, Esq., Manchester
C. H. Bracebridge, Esq., Warwick
Dr. G. Bell, Edinburgh
W. Campbell, Esq., Glasgow
Rev. J. Clay, Preston
J. Corder, Esq., Birmingham
G. Edmonds, Esq., Birmingham
Rev. J. Field, Reading
W. Grant, Esq., Bristol
W. Gladstone, Esq., London
M. D. Hill, Esq., Q. C. Birmingham
J. Hubback, Esq., Liverpool
Chas. Jenner, Esq., Edinburgh
Wm. Lucy, Esq., Birmingham
W. Locke, Esq., London
A. M'Neel Caird, Esq., Wigton
J. M'Gregor, Esq., Temple, London
J. W. Nutt, Esq., York
Rev. W. C. Osborne, Bath
J. Platt, Esq., Regents Park, London
D. Power, Esq., Recorder of Ipswich
J. F. Ranson, Esq., Ipswich
Rev. Sydney Turner, London
A. Thomson Esq., Banchory, Aberdeen
W. Watson, Esq., Sheriff-Sub Aberdeen

R. W. Winfield, Esq.,
Birmingham

Jos. Hubback, Honorary Secretary.

Lady Noel Byron's Prize Essay Contest on Juvenile Delinquency, 1851-1853

(Rev.) Micaiah Hill, and Miss C. F. Cornwallis, *Two Prize Essays on Juvenile Delinquency* (London, 1853), pp. iii-v (UNC Lib.)

NOTICE

In December 1851, a First Conference was held at Birmingham, for the purpose of consulting on the means of establishing preventive and reformatory schools for those classes of children which have come, with an appalling sort of propriety, to be distinguished as the "perishing and dangerous." On that occasion the chairman, M. D. Hill, Esq., announced to the meeting that he was authorized, anonymously, to offer a prize of £200. for the best Essay on the subject then under consideration.

That offer is now acknowledged to have originated with Lady Noel Byron, who will have the satisfaction of presenting some of the fruits of it at the Second Conference, to be held at the same place, the 20th December 1853.

The objects specifically to be kept in view were set forth with the utmost precision in the following advertisement:—

"PRIZE ESSAY

"Objects:—I. To prove that it is the duty of society—1. To save the young, as far as possible, from the commission of sin. 2. To save them, as far as possible, from becoming worse after its commission.

"II. To show that public opinion requires to be elevated and enlightened, until it shall be considered utterly unworthy of a civilized and Christian people to view these questions merely, or even principally, in an economical light; and until it shall be generally recognized as a barbarism and disgrace that any child should be allowed to form habits of begging and stealing, or be left exposed to the danger of corruption in the haunts of vice and schools of crime.

"III. To state in detail the means whereby the objects above-named (I) may be obtained; and to consider the consequences likely to follow from the adoption of those means to -1. The children intended to be benefited- 2. Their parents and families- 3. Their parishes, neighbourhood, the Government, and the Christian community.

"*Conditions:*—The prize to be £200.; to be paid as soon after Christmas 1852, as the award can be made.

"The essays to be sent by the 1st of November, 1852, addressed to the care of Alfred Hill, Esq., 44, Chancery-lane, London, post or carriage free.

Adjudicators.

The Very Rev. the Dean of Salisbury.

John Shaw Lefevre, M.A.

Matthew Davenport Hill, Recorder of Birmingham

The Author of 'Reformatory Schools.' "

. . . Twenty-eight writers competed for the prize, with essays which were, many of them, in different respects, of considerable value; but four were plainly distinguishable from the rest. . . . Of the four thus selected from the others for further consideration, the merits of the two best appeared to the adjudicators to be too nearly balanced to justify their awarding the prize exclusively to either, and in consequence of this difficulty of decision, the donor augmented the amount of the prize, and assigned £150. to each of the successful competitors [Rev. M. Hill and Miss C. F. Cornwallis].

[Both essays, in accordance with the conditions of the prize contest, have a strongly religious tone, which detracts somewhat from their use as secular documents. Neither author makes use of first-hand material. Rev. Hill draws his descriptive material largely from Mayhew's *London Labour and London Poor* and a limited number of official reports and popular works on education. His chapter titles are, I. An Inquiry into the Present State of Juvenile Depravity. II. The Sources of Juvenile Depravity Considered. III. Children—Their Moral Claims Upon the Community. IV. Preventive Measures. V. The Gaol—Abortive and Ruinous. VI. Reformatory Institutions. VII. Statement of Objectives, Obstacles, and Indispensable Qualifications.

Miss Cornwallis presents quite effectively the enormous cost to society of caring for some 150,000 juvenile delinquents under existing conditions of gaol confinement. As a *practical* remedy she suggests setting up four national establishments of the nature of those at Red Hill and Stretton-on-Dunsmore, each with a capacity of caring for five or six hundred children. She would also extend the process of summary conviction *to all first offences of children under thirteen years of age.*]

Parliamentary Hearings on Methods for Reclaiming Delinquent and Destitute Children, 1852-1853

[A] *Report from the Select Committee on Criminal and Destitute Juveniles; together with the Proceedings of the Committee, Minutes of Evidence, Appendix and Index* ([London], 1852), 59, 118-19, 140, 190-91, 216, 294-95 (UNC Lib.)

[These Parliamentary Blue Books are excellent illustrations of a particular type of investigation by legislative bodies, namely, the calling of expert witnesses to testify, on matters of fact as well as of opinion, before a selected committee of that body. The procedure consists of hearings before the committee, in which the Chairman or some member of the Committee, asks the witness a question bearing on the subject of the investigation and the witness gives an oral reply, supplemented occasionally by prepared tables, statements, or reports, which are submitted and filed with the Committee. Sometimes the questions follow an orderly sequence, but usually they are more or less random questions as they occur to members of the committee. The published form of the report usually consists of a great mass of minutes of evidence in the form of questions and answers transcribed at the hearing from all the witnesses appearing consecutively before the Committee; an appendix embracing the papers filed by witnesses in support of their evidence; an index arranged topically to bring into some order the mass of disorganized and frequently contradictory evidence; and the report or conclusions reached by the Committee on the basis of the hearings and the evidence submitted. These two reports of House of Commons Committees, covering over a thousand pages, represent probably the greatest accumulation of data on juvenile delinquency ever assembled at one time. Because of their scarcity these reports are practically unknown to the present generation of writers in this field.

Among the witnesses testifying before the Committee on Criminal and Destitute Juveniles were prison inspectors; chaplains of gaols, houses of correction, and private institutions for delinquents; police magistrates; recorders (Birmingham and Ipswich); governors of prisons, and of houses of correction; lawyers; teachers of "ragged schools"; a member of a prison board; a poor law commissioner; an author (Miss Carpenter); an interested citizen; a former delinquent, etc. From such an overwhelming mass and variety of data it is quite difficult to make a representative selection. The extracts presented below are chosen chiefly for their general applicability and for their significance later on in the determination of a national policy for the treatment of juvenile offenders.]

[The Legal Status of the Delinquent Child in England and in Scotland]

1. [Testimony of Miss Mary Carpenter in replying to question #935.]

... In the English law, as far as I understand it, children are considered incapable of guiding themselves, they are therefore entirely submitted to the guidance of their parents; they are not permitted to perform so good an act as apprenticing themselves to a trade; that cannot be done without the permission of their parents, and I have known cases in which children have been prevented from apprenticing themselves, by the father's withholding his permission. I know one case in which a boy has fallen into vice from this very cause. A child, likewise, has not the power of disposing of his own earnings. The parent has a right to demand from him his earnings if he is not apprenticed, till 21. He has also not the power of willing his property; he is very properly considered as incapable of guiding himself. The father is therefore considered as responsible for his maintenance; if he neglects to provide him with proper food, the child can appeal to the parish, who will punish the father for so neglecting him. But the moment the child shows he is really incapable of guiding himself by committing a crime, from that moment he is treated as a man. The expence to the country is exactly the same as if he were a man. He is tried in public, and all the pomp and circumstance of law is exercised towards him as to a man, while his father is from that moment, according to the present law of the land, released from obligation to maintain him. The City solicitor, Mr. Pearson, stated before the Lords' Committee in 1847, "that the law of England is not fairly dealt by in its administration as regards children. By the common law of England a child under years of discretion is not taken to be *capax doli*. By the theory of our law it is necessary that you should prove against a child charged with crime a precocious capacity for evil, or as Lord Hale describes it, a mischievous discretion; whereas every person above the years of discretion is by law presumed to be cognizant of the law, and unless the con-

235

trary be proved, he is held answerable for his acts. A child under years of discretion has applied to him by the law the converse of that proposition; he is not held to be capable of crime unless from intrinsic and extrinsic evidence his capacity is proved." We want you to restore the law of England to its original state. We hold that children should not be dealt with as men, but as children.

936. [Mr. Fitzroy.] At what age?—The law of England says until they are 21. I am not wishing to give such latitude as that; I should, from my own judgment point out 16 as a more correct line. . . .

2. [Testimony of A. Thomson, Deputy-lieutenant and Justice of the Peace of the Counties of Aberdeen and Kincardine in Scotland.]

3084. What are the defects in the law as it now stands, to remedy which you think it would be advisable to apply for legislative aid?— The great difficulty arises from this: When is a child a proper object of punishment? You are aware of the distinction made by the penal law of France upon the subject, where, up to a certain age, children are presumed to have acted without discernment, and are therefore, instead of being sent to prison, sent to school. We would wish . . . to have a similar power given to our magistrates. At this moment, if a child is brought before myself, for example, as a magistrate, I have no power not to award punishment; I am bound to do it; I should be glad to have the power of sending the child to school, instead of sending it to prison. The sending a child to prison is a very serious matter. When you come to reflect upon it; you destroy his or her character probably for life; if you once give them the taint of a prison mark, it is very difficult for them to shake it off; and it is a very great hardship upon a poor infant that he should have this stigma upon him. I have known instances of children of six and seven years of age sent to prison for petty theft, and once a justice of the peace actually convicted and sentenced a child of 18 months along with its mother, and of course they have been registered in the prison books, and they have thus been registered as convicted thieves for life.

3085. Can a child of that age by the law of Scotland be punished for theft?—I believe so.

3086. Then your law of Scotland differs from ours in England in that respect?—I believe so.

3087. There is no limitation as to age with you?—There is no limitation as to age with us.

3088. Then a child of any age is liable to the criminal law of

236

Scotland?—Decidedly; there is no distinction; it is left to the discretion of the judge. . . .

[FOR IMPRISONMENT]

1. [Testimony of Rev. John Clay, Chaplain of the Gaol and House of Correction at Preston, in Lancashire.]

1623. Would you propose at once to commit children to reformatory institutions . . . in lieu of committing them to prison at all?—No; I would rather they would go to a prison for three or four or five or six months, and then afterwards go to a place like Red-hill [Philanthropic School]. I know that a child is in many instances ignorant of the nature of crime. I know that in many instances a child does not know that he has committed an act which is in itself criminal; he knows that he has done something which will get him into a scrape if the policeman finds him, but he certainly does not know that he has committed a wrongful act; and therefore we have in prison to make him know that he has committed an offense, and we have to fix in his mind that criminal act that he has been guilty of, and which must be explained to him as a criminal act. He must be made to feel the punishment for such act, and then he must be made to see that his welfare, morally and physically, is generally desired by those who are above him. . . .

1632. [Mr. Fitzroy.] Then what time have you contemplated as necessary to produce reformation within the walls of a prison?—If I had my own way I should prefer that a boy on his first conviction should never be without imprisonment for less than six months. . . .

2. [Testimony of Mr. Serjeant Adams, Assistant Judge of the Middlesex Quarter Sessions.]

1877. I think you suggested, that in the case of a child up to a certain age, you would have no imprisonment at all, but that you would send him in the first instance to a reformatory school?—No, on the contrary, I say that I woud send him to a prison at first, but I would not educate him in that prison. I would make the prison painful to him, as painful as a prison could be, and after that, I would send him to a reformatory school, and there I would show him the difference between what he had got for his bad conduct, and what he might now get for his good conduct.

1878. What sort of discipline would you recommend?—During the time he was in prison occasional solitary confinement, and as hard labour as a boy could have. I do not mean to say, that I would bear him down by hard labour.

[AGAINST IMPRISONMENT]

3. [Testimony of Matthew D. Hill, Recorder of Birmingham.]

528. Then in your opinion the discipline of a prison prevents the effect of any reformatory punishment?—I think it does. For instance, I should think a boy would have a greater chance of being effectually wrought upon by reformatory discipline, who could be sent to that reformatory discipline at the shortest possible interval after his apprehension, and that even the imprisonment preparatory to trial is very likely to turn his mind into a course adverse to reformation; and I am of opinion, that all punishment which has for its object the infliction of pain, and thereby example to others and to the criminal, (apart from its being a portion of the discipline of reformation), is injurious, and an impediment to his cure. . . .

4. [Testimony of David Power, Recorder of Ipswich.]

1114. Will you be so good as to point out to the Committee in what respects it [the present system of treatment of juvenile crime] seems to you defective?—I cannot illustrate it better than by mentioning what I felt compelled to do in Ipswich. So strongly do I feel the evil of committals for short terms of imprisonment, that one of the first steps I took was to call some of the principal inhabitants of the borough together, with a view of establishing, if possible, an institution, in which we might get together the children after they came out of gaol, in order that they might be reformed. The very fact of the recorder of a town, whose duty it is to commit young prisoners to gaol, feeling it also part of his duty to get an institution established by which he could do away with the ill effects arising from the sentence he is compelled by law to pronounce, argues very strongly against the expediency or justice of the present system.

1115. One defect, as I understand you, in your opinion, is the custom of awarding short sentences of imprisonment?—Yes. Another objection that I have is this, that reformatory treatment in a gaol is perfectly impossible, for this reason, that the genius, if I may say so, of gaol discipline is the restraint of the individual; and what a convicted child wants is not to be restrained, but to be given a character in himself, by which he may be able to resist the temptations to which he will be exposed when he leaves the gaol. . . .

[B] *Report from the Select Committee on Criminal and Destitute Children; together with the Proceedings of the Committee, Minutes of Evidence, and Appendix* ([London], 1853), pp. iii, iv (editor's lib.)

[RESOLUTIONS OF THE SELECT COMMITTEE ON CRIMINAL AND DESTITUTE CHILDREN, 1853.][1]

Resolved.

1. That it is the opinion of this Committee that a great amount of juvenile destitution, ignorance, vagrancy, and crime, has long existed in this country, for which no adequate remedy has yet been provided.

2. That the existence of similar evils in France, Germany, Switzerland, Belgium, and the United States, has been met by vigorous efforts in those countries; and in the opinion of this Committee, sound policy requires that this country should promptly adopt measures for the same purpose.

3. That it appears to this Committee to be established by the evidence, that a large proportion of the present aggregate of crime might be prevented, and thousands of miserable human beings, who have before them under our present system nothing but a hopeless career of wickedness and vice, might be converted into virtuous, honest and industrious citizens, if due care were taken to rescue destitute, neglected, and criminal children from the dangers and temptations incident to their position.

4. That a great proportion of the criminal children of this country, especially those convicted of first offences, appear rather to require systematic education, care, and industrial occupation, than mere punishment.

5. That the common gaols and houses of correction do not generally provide suitable means for the educational or corrective treatment of young children, who ought, when guilty of crime, to be treated in a manner different from the ordinary punishments of adult criminals.

6. That various private reformatory establishments for young criminals have proved successful, but are not sure of permanent support; and are deficient in legal control over the inmates.

7. That Penal Reformatory Establishments ought to be instituted

1. The method of procedure of this Committee was essentially the same as that of the Committee on Criminal and Destitute Juveniles which preceded it and which has already been described.

for the detention and correction of criminal children convicted before magistrates or courts of justice of serious offences.

8. That such penal reformatory establishments ought to be founded and supported entirely at the public cost and to be under the care and inspection of the Government.

9. That Reformatory Schools should be established for the education and correction of children convicted of minor offences.

10. That such reformatory schools should be founded and supported partially by local rates and partially by contributions from the State, and that power should be given for raising the necessary amount of local rates.

11. That power should be given to the Government to contract with the managers of reformatory schools, founded and supported by voluntary contributions, for the care and maintenance of criminal children within such institutions.

12. That the delinquency of children, in consequence of which they may become subjects of penal or reformatory discipline, ought not to relieve parents from their liability to maintain them.

13. That in any legislation upon this subject, it is essential that power should be given, under such restrictions as may be necessary to prevent hardship or injustice, to recover from parents the whole or a portion of the cost of the maintenance of their children while detained in reformatory institutions.

14. That it is also essential that power should be given to detain children placed in such institutions so long as may be necessary for their reformation; provided always that no child be so detained after the age of 16.

[Resolutions 15-25 inclusive have been omitted]

A Newcastle Committee Studies Its Delinquency Problem, 1852

Report of A Committee Appointed to Examine into the State of Juvenile Crime in Newcastle and Gateshead, December, 1852 (Newcastle, 1852), pp. 3, 5, 7-8, 15 (Columbia Univ. Lib.)

On the 27th of October, 1852, a meeting was held at the house of Michael Longridge, Esq., of gentlemen taking interest in the subject of Juvenile Delinquency. It appeared to them that it would be highly desirable to establish Reformatory Schools for the moral, intellectual, and industrial training of Juvenile Criminals; and, as a preparatory step, that a Committee should be formed, to collect information on this subject. A Committee was then appointed [consisting of the mayors of Newcastle and Gateshead, the recorder, town clerk, and sheriff of Newcastle, and fifteen other gentlemen]. On the 17th of December, 1852, they presented their Report. . . .

REPORT OF THE COMMITTEE

The first point to which we directed our attention was the state of Juvenile Delinquency in this district. In prosecuting this enquiry, we thought it desirable to confine ourselves . . . to the town of Newcastle. . . .

The following Table has been compiled from the police books:—

Juveniles* Apprehended by the Police of Newcastle in the Year Ending 10th November, 1852

Age	Males	Females	Total
8	4	–	4
9	8	2	10
10	17	2	19
11	26	4	30
12	28	6	34
13	56	6	62
14	81	11	92
15	107	16	123
16	95	26	121
17	134	34	168
	556	107	663

*Throughout this Report the designation Juvenile means a person not more than seventeen years of age.

A similar return, prepared for the year 1838, shows that the number of Juveniles arrested in that year were—Males, 236; females, 78; total, 314.

. . . Although the periods for which these various comparisons are made are not strictly the same, they are sufficiently exact for all practical purposes, and the results are brought together in the following comparative Table:—

Comparative Table, Showing the Progress of Crime and Population

	Period	Period	Increase Percent	Percent Decrease
	Years	Years		
England and Wales.	1840, '41, '42	1849, '50, '51		
Commitments for trial] or bailed]	86,526	82,589		5
County of Northumberland.				
Commitments for trial] or bailed]	667	783	12	
Newcastle Upon Tyne	Year 1841	Year 1851		
Population of Borough	70,337	87,784	24.7	
Juveniles arrested by] the Police]	Year 1838	Year 1851		
	314	663	100	
Commitments, viz:—				
Male juveniles.	95	191	100	
Female do	35	73	100	
Total	130	264	100	
Committed as known or] reputed thieves]	57	125	120	
Committed under 12] years of age]	17	26	53	
Recommitments	29	85		

We wish to draw attention to the fact disclosed in this table, that in Newcastle Juvenile Crime is increasing four times as fast as the population, and in thirteen years has doubled its amount. . . .

Publications have lately appeared describing the frightful state of some of the pauperised districts of London, and it is a prevalent idea that these scenes of vice and misery are to be found in London alone.

We have ascertained, however, that all these evils exist in Newcastle, the same in degree though not to the same extent, and we doubt not they will continue and increase until remedial measures are adopted. We think it right to state a few cases to show the actual circumstances under which many children become criminal, and to enable persons to form their own judgment on the propriety of punishing such children by whipping or imprisonment, and on the possibility of reformation under our present system.

"In M——'s entry there are 45 families; of these 45 mothers, 40 are more or less addicted to drink; in some houses, six or eight persons may be found sleeping in one room without any separation or distinction of sex or age; the language is most obscene—the place is the picture of misery."

"In D——'s Court, there is a woman with her two sons, one 19 years of age, a miserable, sickly boy; the other 10 years of age. They live in a room 10 feet by 5; it is nearly dark, and contains no furniture. The mother is a habitual drunkard, the children without food, and nearly naked, are driven out upon the streets, where they exist by begging."

"In D—— Street is a man who is a drunkard, and a professed infidel; he has two little boys, who are compelled to beg to supply their father's wants.

"A. B. lost her mother when she was fourteen; her father, a drunken profligate, sold every article of furniture, and turned her on the streets. At seventeen, she was found in a dark, damp cellar in G—— Street, where she had lain down to die—and in fact she died shortly after."

It appears from [a table presented]—that these fifteen boys have been committed to the *same prison* 247 times, or more than 16 times each; and that so far from being deterred from crime (the presumed intention of the law), they have proceeded from bad to worse, until they have been almost all transported. . . .

We would suggest, therefore, that the subject of Juvenile Delinquency be brought under the special notice of the Magistrates at the ensuing Quarter Sessions. If they concur in the views which we have expressed, we trust they will address memorials to the Secretary of State for the Home Department, recording their opinion that the provisions of the Criminal Law, as applicable to very young persons, are not found to work well, and admit of great improvement,—and that a child, even when criminal, should be treated as a child, and sent to a Reformatory School and not to a gaol.

Cruel Treatment of Boys in the Birmingham Gaol, 1852-1853

Joseph Allday (ed.), *True Account of the Proceedings Leading to, and a Full and Authentic Report of, the Searching Inquiry, by her Majesty's Commissioners, into the Horrible System of Discipline Practised at the Borough Gaol of Birmingham* (Birmingham and London, [c. 1853]), pp. 2, 7-8, 12-14, 97-99, 105, 118-21 (editor's lib.)

The object of the present publication is to place on record a faithful and authentic account of the important investigation which recently took place before the Commissioners appointed by the Crown to inquire into the discipline pursued and the cruelties practised in the Gaol of the Borough of Birmingham, and also the preliminary proceedings which led to that inquiry.

An investigation so important in its character and so extraordinary in its results—disclosing, as it has done, scenes far surpassing anything that has ever appeared in the pages of fiction or romance—will long live, not only in the minds of the public of Birmingham, but of the people of this great and enlightened country—the public press of which has teemed with expressions of those feelings of indignation which the disclosures revealed as having taken place in, alas! our "Gaol of Horrors" have excited throughout the length and breadth of the land.

It is fervently to be hoped that the exposures which have taken place of the unheard-of barbarities which have been allowed to be perpetrated in the Borough Gaol of Birmingham—barbarities long screened from the public eye, and which were at length brought to light by dint of great labour and perseverance—will not merely be the means of preventing a repetition of such cruelties, but will lead to the modification generally of prison punishments and prison discipline, and be the means of placing the management and control of such important institutions under better qualified and more responsible authority.

"Another Suicide at The Borough Gaol
"Extraordinary Revelation

"On Friday night the Borough Coroner and a highly respectable jury were engaged for six hours in the investigation of the circumstances attending the death of a youth named Edward Andrews, an inmate of the borough gaol, who had committed suicide on the previous Wednesday night. The inquest was held at the sign of the Golden Eagle, Winson-green. From the evidence of Lieutenant Austin, the Governor of the Prison, it seemed that deceased, who was fifteen years of age, had been about the middle of March summarily convicted under the Juvenile Offenders Act, for stealing four pounds of beef, and sentenced to two months' hard labour; this was his third committal, having had previously fourteen days' imprisonment, for throwing stones in the streets, and a month for stealing garden fruit. In the present instance, the hard-labour punishment commenced two days after his admission to the prison. In lieu of the old-fashioned tread-mill, the prisoners have to turn what is called a crank, the movement being somewhat similar to that employed in turning a common grindstone. This crank labour is connected, we believe, with the water supply of the gaol; but, as a direct means of punishment, it is capable of being regulated according to the strength of each prisoner, and while the pressure representing only five pounds was put upon it in the case of the deceased prisoner, in consequence of the weak state of his health, he had to turn this crank ten thousand times every day, two thousand revolutions before breakfast, four thousand between breakfast and dinner, and four thousand betwixt dinner and supper. If this task was not performed, he was dieted upon bread and water until he had made up the deficiency, each day's short-comings being carried forward as a balance against him. On many occasions the deceased had failed to turn the crank the required number of times, and twice or thrice he broke the glass covering of a dial which indicates the number of revolutions, in order that he might push forward the index finger to the proper figure, and so avoid punishment; for these breaches of prison discipline he was punished, by being restricted to bread and water diet on Sundays. On another occasion, having been noisy in his cell, he was put into a strait jacket, by which his arms and head were rendered immovable, and in this condition he was strapped to the wall of his cell, thus to remain 'until he behaved himself.' On Sunday week he committed another breach of prison discipline, and having been brought before the governor, that gentleman said he should not punish him any more, but would report his case to the visiting justices, and leave them to deal with him. He was still on bread and water diet, and he continued at the crank labour until Wednesday night. About half-past six he was seen in his cell by Cotterill, one of the warders. Another punishment to which he had been subjected for having his cell in a dirty condition was, the withholding of his bed for an hour and a half after the time at which the prisoners retire to rest. Accordingly it was not till ten o'clock that Jones, another of the warders, entered his cell, for the purpose of spreading his mattress, and he then found deceased hanging to the iron bars of his window, quite dead, though still warm. Having broken two squares of glass, he had fastened his hammock-straps to the bars, and, tying his neckerchief round his neck, had flung himself off the stool by which he was enabled to reach the window. Lieutenant Austin produced the 'crank-labour book,' in corroboration of his statement of the facts bearing on the punishment awarded deceased. The Rev. A. Sherwin, the prison chaplain, voluntarily offered to put the coroner and jury in possession of the circumstances within his knowledge, as to the state of deceased's mind. Deceased had told him that the pangs of hunger which he suffered from the bread and water diet, together with the 'crank' punishment, were greater than he could bear. He appeared to be a willing lad, but seemed very weak. Upon passing his cell one day, witness heard some groans of a very peculiar character, and on going in he found him with a strait jacket on, and strapped up to the wall in the manner above described. Witness had remonstrated with the governor on several occasions with regard to the Sunday punishments, but without effect. Deceased had lately seemed to be in a very low and melancholy state of mind. Two other prisoners who attempted to commit suicide had also told witness that the pangs of hunger, resulting from the bread-and-water diet, had driven them to think of self-murder. One of them was now in the gaol, the other was undergoing sentence of fifteen years' transportation. This being the whole of the evidence, the Coroner briefly commented on the system of discipline carried on in the gaol, and left it to the jury to say whether they might not reasonably conclude the deceased was of unsound mind at the time he hung himself. With the causes of his mental aberration they had nothing to do, unless they considered some one culpably blameable. After half an hour's deliberation, they returned a verdict of 'Suicide in a state of Insanity,' unaccompanied by any remark. The case, however, is the subject of much comment throughout the town. This is the third suicide which has taken place in the gaol, the last one only three weeks ago. The circumstances have attracted the attention of the visiting justices, and they have had a meeting on the subject.

"From the above report, your lordship will find that the suicide there referred to is the third which has taken place in the gaol within a short period, besides many attempts of a like nature, which have been made; and your memorialists cannot reflect upon such facts without feelings of utter abhorrence and detestation of a system, the harshness and inhumanity of which can drive even criminals to the commission of the dreadful crime of self-destruction." [Copied from the *Birmingham Journal*, May 7, 1853.]

INSPECTOR PERRY'S REPORT. "WESTBOURNE STREET, MAY 24, 1853.

". . . In the course of this inquiry, facts have been brought to my knowledge which warrant me in stating that the Governor is in the habit of inflicting on the prisoners, especially those of the juvenile class, punishments not sanctioned by law, which, while they are not even effectual in repressing disorder, are in their nature repugnant to the feelings of humanity, and likely to drive the prisoners to desperation.

"By the Act of the 4th George IV., cap. 64, section 41, the Governor of the prison is empowered to punish certain offences therein enumerated, by ordering any offender to close confinement in the refractory or solitary cells, and by keeping such offender upon bread and water only for any term not exceeding three days; and by section 42, it is further enacted, 'that in case any criminal prisoner shall be guilty of any repeated offence against the rules of the prison, or shall be guilty of any greater offence than the gaoler or keeper is by this act empowered to punish, the said gaoler or keeper shall forthwith report the same to the Visiting Justices, or one of them, who, after inquiry on oath, may order the offender to be punished by close confinement for any period not exceeding one month, or by personal correction in the case of felons or others sentenced to hard labour. It is generally held that a Governor possesses no power to punish any prisoner a second time for any offense of a similar character to that for which he has once awarded punishment, and that neither the Governor nor the Visiting Justices possess any right of devising punishments of a nature different from those defined by the act above cited.

"Upon this assumption, I proceed to describe the various punishments which I have ascertained to be inflicted upon the prisoners for neglect of crank labour, whistling, or talking in their cells, and other offences of a more or less serious character, including attempts (especially by boys) to converse with others in neighbouring cells, a breach of the prison rules to which the defective construction of the prison offers peculiar facilities and temptations.

"The first to which I feel it necessary to call attention is the strait jacket, which is not only put upon prisoners who are thought to require restraint to prevent them doing injury to themselves or others, or from damaging the prison property, but also as a punishment for ordinary prison offences or short-comings. It is not, however, to be understood that the strait jacket here employed is merely (as in lunatic asylums) a jacket with long sleeves, to be tied around the waist, so as to confine the arms without causing pain; there are adjuncts contrived by which this comparatively harmless instrument is converted into a means of considerable suffering. A stiff leathern stock is buckled round the neck of the prisoner, his arms are pinioned behind him by means of a tighter leathern strap, which exerts an antagonistic power to the sleeves that hold the arms forward over the chest, and in this cramped position the sufferer is held by another strap, standing against the wall of his cell, for varying periods, amounting in some cases before me to twelve hours. I find, as might be anticipated, that this proceeding has often been attended with serious consequences, by causing ecchymosis of the arms, and pains and numbness of the arms and hands—that it has caused faintness—and in some cases actual syncope, and that it has not unfrequently occurred that when prisoners, after punishment, have refused to work, or declared their inability to do so, buckets of water have been thrown over them by order of the Governor. In one case, proved before me, three buckets of water were thus thrown by the Governor's authority, and in his presence, and he has acknowledged that it has been done even with his own hand.

"Another punishment, which is very common in this prison, consists in sentencing a prisoner to be deprived of his bed for two hours beyond the usual bed-time, for terms varying from one to fourteen nights, with or without the privation of gas-light in his cell; when it is considered that this is used as an exaggeration of the punishment last described, and in the cases of the prisoners who are also suffering under bread and water diet, it will readily be seen that it must add greatly to the harassing nature of the other punishments, more especially in winter, when it has often happened that prisoners have been kept with famished stomachs for four or five hours in the dark before they were allowed to forget their sufferings in sleep; frequently being also strapped to the wall in the strait jacket during the whole of this period; for it is the custom to accumulate all these punishments at once upon a single offender.

"Another mode of punishment resorted to is the deprivation of exercise, sometimes for a week together, by confining the prisoner to his cell, in which I conceive that the Governor exceeds the power given him by law, and risks the health of the prisoners. On such occasions it is not usual to call upon the surgeon to see the prisoner daily, as provided by the rules in all cases of punishment attended with close confinement, so that the security to the prisoner's health provided by law is neglected.

"The imposition of bread and water diet as a punishment for three days, and its reimposition after a day's interval, by which the prisoner is deprived of the ordinary food of his class for six days out of seven, is generally considered unlawful, even when inflicted for different offences, and is obviously so when inflicted for a repetition of the same, and is stated to be of common occurrence. It has been proved also that the Governor is in the habit of ordering, as an aggravation of this privation, that it shall be inflicted on the three following Sundays, instead of three consecutive days, which is contrary to all usage elsewhere, and I believe quite illegal.

"In some cases the Governor has desired the steward to reduce the quantity of oatmeal in the gruel in the case of prisoners sentenced by the magistrates to protracted confinement for prison offences, under the 42nd section of the Gaol Act, below the amount sanctioned by the Secretary of State—a mode of aggravating the punishment for which there is no legal sanction. The frequent repetition, by the Governor, of punishment for the same offences in the same individuals, is plainly at variance with the 42nd section of the Gaol Act.

"It is very difficult, after much time has elapsed, to prove that punishment of which there is no record has been inflicted, but many such instances have come to my knowledge. It is needless to remark that this want of accuracy in the misconduct book must lead to falsification of the return made to the Home Office: for example, in the return of punishments ending at Michaelmas last, after stating the number by whipping, confinement, and refractory cells, and stoppages of diet, the 'other punishments' are set down at thirty-eight, whereas my inquiries would lead me to believe that number would not represent a tenth part of the instances in which the miscellaneous punishments referred to have been inflicted.

"Another deviation of very serious importance from the rules of the prison is, that the surgeon does not always visit and examine prisoners under punishment, a precaution instituted to prevent the infliction of severity beyond the strength of the offender. I have found great difficulty in properly assigning the blame of this neglect; but I have met with unquestionable proofs that prisoners have undergone the severe punishment of the jacket, combined with bread and water diet, for days together, without having been once seen by the surgeon. Had this humane precaution been adopted, it would have been impossible for many of the severities which I have ascertained to have been exercised upon mere children for several days together, to have been permitted for a single day. It would also have been impossible, had prisoners been properly inspected by the surgeon, for a whole week's bread to have been allowed to accumulate in a prisoner's cell before the discovery was made that he was too ill to eat it, which occurred in the case of one man, who, it is lamentable to add, expired a day after the discovery. With a knowledge of the facts briefly alluded to in the report, I find it impossible to disconnect the large number of suicides, and attempts at suicide, that have occurred in this prison, including that of the individual who last formed the subject of the Coroner's inquiry, from the extreme severity and irritating nature of the discipline pursued in it. The number of such cases recorded since the opening of the prison in July, 1850, has been no less than fourteen, twelve of which have occurred in the last sixteen months, including three fatal instances. After making every due allowance for those cases which might have been feigned, there will still remain a fearful number, far exceeding, according to my experience, anything recorded elsewhere.

"I am, &c.,

"John G. Perry, Inspector of Prisons."

Alfred Webb's Case

Alfred Webb was the next witness. This boy is between fifteen and sixteen years old; but he is so small that he does not look more than twelve or thirteen. He has a very mild and intelligent countenance; he gave his evidence in a clear, unhesitating, artless manner, never hesitating or contradicting in the slightest particular throughout. In fact, throughout the inquiry there has not been a witness examined whose evidence bore more of the stamp of truth.

Mr. Welsby: Webb, do you recollect being sent to gaol?—Yes, sir.

What was it for?—I got on a shed to get a cap which some boys had thrown there. There was some lead moved, but I didn't see it moved, nor yet touch it.

For how long did they send you to gaol?—Two months.

Had you ever been in prison before?—No, sir.

Where had you worked?—At Mr. Bacchus's glass-house.

Where does your father work?—At Mr. Bacchus's.

Where does your father live?—In New Town Row.

Had you ever been charged with any offence before?—No, sir.

Who was the gentleman that tried you?—I don't know, sir.

Had he a wig on?—No, sir.

Mr. Welsby: Oh! he wasn't tried at the Sessions. Well, now, has anybody been talking to you about coming here?—No, sir; only a gentleman told me to speak the "righteous."

What gentleman?—[The boy pointed to Inspector Edmonds]

When did you know you were to come here?—Last night.

Well, what did they do to you in gaol?—They punished me very severely.

How did they punish you?—They put me on bread and water, and put the strait jacket on me.

What for?—I called out to a boy, "Good bye;" it was Abner Wilkes.

When was that?—On the third day.

Did you rap at the wall?—No, sir.

Did they read the prison rules over to you?—Yes, sir.

So you knew it was wrong to call out?—Yes, sir.

How did they punish you besides the jacket and bread and water?—Strapped me to the wall.

When was that?—It was after chapel, before dinner, till supper.

How was it, tell us, little boy?—I had a leather collar all round my neck; my legs were strapped together, and my arms strapped, and I was fastened to the wall.

Had you any dinner that day?—No, sir.

Had you any supper?—"Eight ounces of bread."

Did the jacket hurt you?—The jacket hurt me very bad across the arms, round my chest, and my neck was bad with the collar. I am sixteen the 21st of this month. After I had done the three days bread and water, and the jacket, I was put ten days to the crank for the same thing. I had 10,000 turns a day. Sometimes I went down to the crank at seven in the morning, and was at it till ten at night. I may have done that four times. I was in the dark at night.

Why were you kept there?—Because I could not do the work sooner. I was not able.

What food had you while you were on the crank and did not do your work?—I got bread and water.

In the morning? What food did you get during the day?—I got nothing but bread and water at night. Cotterill, jun., said that he would keep me on the crank till I could not crawl. At night I sometimes got eight ounces of bread and sometimes six ounces.

And nothing else during the whole day long?—No.

Was the jacket ever left on you all night?—Yes; Cotterill, jun., put it on, and another man, whose name I don't know, stood by. I did not have the collar on then, and I was not strapped to the wall. The jacket was pretty tight. My arms were strapped, but not with the leather.

Did you go to bed in the jacket?—I went to my bed on the floor in it. I was put in the jacket all night, they told me, because I was not able to do my work.

Did you sleep?—Not much to speak of.

Why?—Because I was in such agonies of pain.

From what?—From having nothing to eat all day, and from having the jacket on.

Did they give you nothing to eat?—They gave me six ounces of bread that night, after the jacket was put on.

How did you eat it?—they put the bread in my mouth, and I bit and eat the best way I could.

You could not use your hands?—No.

Had you any water?—I had not a drop to drink, and I could not drink if I had.

Mr. Welsby: It is the most diabolical thing I ever heard of in my life, if it is true.

Captain Williams: It is a monstrous thing. He then examined the punishment book, from which it appeared that for being deficient in the number of his revolutions on the crank, he had been for several consecutive days on bread and water; and on one occasion it appeared that although 6,500 turns deficient, he had all his meals. Upon this entry Captain Williams remarked that it must be inaccurate, as they were not in the habit of doing these things. [Laughter.]

The witness went on to say that he did not recollect of such a circumstance, and spoke to having bread and water on three Sundays. After I had the jacket on all night I was sent to the crank at six o'clock the following morning. I was not able to do all the work, and I had bread and water again.

How many days during the ten you were at the crank did you get your regular food?—I don't remember any.

How came you to be taken off the crank?—The governor said that if I did my work he would take me off; but I could not do it, and Cotterill came and took me off. The doctor used to come every morning to the cell.

Captain Williams: Did he try the crank himself. [Laughter.] —He used to do it.

How long did he keep at it?—Only one or two turns. He said I was able to do the work every time he came round. He only came into the cell, did that, and went out again.

Dr. Baly: Did you tell him you were not able to do the work?— Yes, every morning. I said, "Please, sir, take me off; I am not able to do it." He said, "if you are able to do your work out of prison you are able to do that." I never had the jacket on after I was taken off the crank. I was treated better after that, and got my regular meals. I found the labour get hard about eleven o'clock; it pained me round the chest. I told the doctor that, and he said there was nothing the matter with me, it was only my gammon.

Are you quite sure the doctor said that word?—Yes. The witness went on to say that he had talked to nobody on the subject; and that he did not know that he was to be called until that morning. Further, he stated that before being imprisoned, he had been earning 10s. a week at Mr. Bacchus's glass establishment; that Mr. Bacchus (from whose employment he had run away in consequence of a workman beating him,) had given him a good character; and that he had got another place at 6s. a week. He now lived with his father and mother. He saw Mr. Sherwin before he left the prison; told him how he had been punished; and that gentleman took him before the governor. Cotterill was called up, and he owned that he had put him in the jacket and that he had said he would put him on the crank till he could not crawl. . . .

The Crank Question

Mr. George Heaton, Engineer, Shadwell Street, was then examined as to the construction of the cranks in use at the prison. He entered into a minute explanation of them. In his opinion the machines were calculated to extract a great amount of labour from the prisoners, and he believed much greater than was expected by the persons who had set them to work. He thought the leather facing was an advantage to the person at the crank. He explained that although the cranks were weighted at 5 lbs. it required a force equal to 14½ or 15 lbs. to work them. Four boys would thus be doing the work of one horse. The cranks could be so weighted that his (Mr. Heaton's) whole weight could not pull the handle down.

Dr. Baly: Then a boy working this machine at 5 lbs. ostensibly, would really be doing the work of a quarter of a horse?—Yes. Ordinarily a boy's work would be one-tenth. When I said that it would be equal to 14 lbs. I meant at a certain speed. I quite agree with the day's task, the number of revolutions, and the speed they have to turn; the only thing I disagree with is the miscalculation of the power put on the machinery.

If the weight had been correct, 10,000 revolutions would not have been too much?—No; they frequently do more. This sort of work used to be common in Birmingham when I was a youth. It was done by blind men and silly persons.

Do you expect that at 5 lbs. pressure with the machine, as at present, a boy could make 2,000 turns easily?—I don't think an able-bodied labourer could turn it 500 times without being greatly fatigued.

THE CASE OF BARTLEY CARNEY

In reference to the evidence given on Friday, Bartley Carney, aged sixteen years, said: I have been seven times in prison before this. It is three years since I first came in. I was in the jacket in April, and it took several persons to put me in it. Freer put the jacket on me. He said I had spat on him, and he struck me on the face. Before that they had kept my food from me. Freer kneeled on my stomach. This was on the 18th of April. Two or three days before they wanted to put the jacket on me, but I would not let them. Freer put his knees on my stomach, and trampled on me with his feet. He said he "could lick all these here bullies in Birmingham." This was after putting the jacket on me and putting his knees on my stomach. Afterwards I pulled up my cell floor because they wanted to put the jacket on me, and I put the bricks behind the door to prevent them. I threw some bricks at them, and they put a pole through my trap door. I am now under the doctor's hands. My peculiar illness made me unable to do the crank work. I have been in the jacket from seven in the morning till ten at night. I complained to the warder of the pain I was suffering from the bowel complaint and in my bones. They poured several buckets of water on me. I had a note to go to the Reformatory School, but my father would not let me, but made me work for him in Edwards's brick yard, Wheeler Street.

INSPECTION OF THE GAOL

During the afternoon, the Commissioners, accompanied by the other gentlemen present, paid a lengthened visit to the juvenile ward, and inspected more cursorily the adult department, the kitchens, crank cells, &c. The juveniles, who ranged from nine or ten to sixteen years of age, had mostly the precociously "knowing" appearance so characteristic of children whose lives have been spent in the streets; and while some had a frank ingenuous expression of countenance that seemed in no way connected with innate roguery, many, on the other hand, had the deep-sunk and half-averted eye so characteristic of natural dishonesty and cunning. The scene was one full of painful interest. All the cell doors being thrown open, the lads stood each in his own door-way, with his back to the corridor, and seemingly paying no attention to the movements of those around him, although he must have wondered what was the cause of so unusual a visit. As her Majesty's Commissioners went from cell to cell—Dr. Baly making them bare their arms to show in what condition they were, while Captain Williams and Mr. Welsby questioned them as to their history— it was melancholy to hear the tales they told. Some had run away from their homes owing to the ill-treatment of their parents; others had been led astray by bad companions. The majority of those "in for pocket-picking" confessed that the Market Hall was the first scene of their practice. All were ready enough to confess that they had been very bad boys, and assurances of reformation were plentiful. Most of them had been in prison twice or thrice, and one of them had been as many as seven times. Captain Williams promised to interest himself in removing some of the younger lads to scenes where at least the temptations of old associates would not influence their behaviour.

We had an opportunity of personally testing the merits of the cranks, of which so much has been said in the course of the inquiry. The cells in which they are placed are situated on the basement storey, although not "underground," as some of the witnesses have described them. The crank is enclosed in the brick-work of the cell, and its iron case has the appearance of a small pump set in a party wall. Projecting from it is a handle, such as is attached to the large coffee mills used by grocers; and on the crank a glass-covered dial plate is visible, capable of registering thirty or forty thousand turns. We tried a dozen or fourteen cranks until we found the one which had the heaviest pressure upon it. As vigorous, probably, as four out of every five of our predecessors, and with none of the disadvantages of ninth-class diet, to work we went, determined to keep at it as long as we could. We cannot say whether the want of a little incitement, be it the vision of stiffish-collared waistcoat or of postponed breakfast had anything to do with the results; but in five minutes, sundry spasmodic tendencies of our arms to jerk the crank handle out of its ordinary orbit, told us that our self-imposed punishment was nearly over. Three minutes more, and we were dead beat. We found that in eight minutes we had made about seventy turns, while the number usually required in that period from a prisoner was stated to be about 130.

Children Committed to Prisons in England and Wales, 1856-1871

Sixteenth Annual Report of the Reformatory and Refuge Union (London, 1872), p. 20 (Brit. Mus.)

Unhappily, some Magistrates still send children to prison; the following return shows the number committed each year since 1856; when examining it, the rapid increase of population that has taken place in these years must be borne in mind:—

England and Wales—Juvenile Offenders (under 16 years of age)

Years	Boys	Girls	Total
1856	11,808	2,173	13,981
1857	10,822	1,679	12,501
1858	8,837	1,492	10,329
1859	7,582	1,331	8,913
1860	6,765	1,264	8,029
1861	7,373	1,428	8,801
1862	7,080	1,269	8,349
1863	7,208	1,251	8,459
1864	7,536	1,321	8,857
1865	8,350	1,290	9,640
1866	8,099	1,257	9,356
1867	8,285	1,346	9,631
1868	8,702	1,377	10,079
1869	8,956	1,358	10,314
1870	8,619	1,379	9,998
1871	7,821	1,156	8,977

Liverpool Pastimes and Juvenile Delinquency, 1856

[Hugh Shimmin], *Publicity the True Cure of Social Evils. Liverpool Life: Its Pleasures, Practices and Pastimes* (Liverpool: Egerton Smith & Co., 1857), Second series, pp. 55-56 (Yale Univ. Lib.) Reprinted from the *Liverpool Mercury.*

[These papers purporting to be a true revelation of the darker side of Liverpool life appeared from week to week during 1856 in the *Liverpool Mercury.* The reporter declares, "In the course of these papers we have written nothing but what we have witnessed. Every case given, every family alluded to, has been personally seen by us, and every statement made is true, can be abundantly proved, and we challenge any man to prove the contrary. . . . We have no object to serve but one— to state facts without fear or favour. . . ." Replying to his critics in regard to the frankness of his revelations, the author says, "The informed and awakened opinion of Liverpool is the only power that can purify and regenerate Liverpool life, as the aroused feeling of the nation is the only power that can redress national abuses." The papers were issued in two series. The first series included mainly descriptions of amusements, the theatre, public dancing rooms, gambling stalls, sparring matches, dog fights, betting houses and betting men, etc. The second series discussed the principal sources of juvenile crime, minor theatres, carnivals, the Aintree horse races, lodging houses, penny ale cellars, church bazaars, the homes of the people, etc.]

If the magistrates be anxious to do what in their power lies to check the growth of juvenile delinquency, and at the same time purify the pastimes provided for the people, let them turn their attention to other licensed establishments. At one of these, which occupies a prominent position in the town, may nightly be witnessed a scene that for grossness, immorality, or obscenity stands almost unparalleled. Even what are called the decorations of the room pander to the worst passions of humanity, and vulgarity and lasciviousness are unblushingly proclaimed. Here are youths—many from the upper classes of society, mixed up with others in more humble positions. Smoking cigars, sipping ale, wine, or brandy, chatting with degraded girls, and examining "the points" of the living tableaux constitute some of the features of the evening's entertainment, and those which would appear to excite most attention. There is singing, and much of that class which cannot be described. Between forty and fifty boys . . . were the other evening in this place, and seemed delighted to hear a filthy song called "the lively flea." Now, the obscenity in this consisted more in the action and grimace of the vocalist than in the expressions used, although the latter were bad enough; but a more abominable song, as this was here given, one containing viler suggestions, could not be conceived. The girls laughed, the lads roared with delight, and one of them said "*he would do anything rather than miss such a treat.*"
. . . The proprietors of such resorts look at them in a business point of view, and supply what they think will pay. But the great moral responsibility rests upon the heads of those who year after year license the iniquity.

. . . "Minor theatres," "twopenny hops," casinos, and singing saloons are all spoken of as having a tendency to promote the growth and foster the evils attendant on juvenile delinquency and public immorality. Without doubt such is the influence of these places, but all combined sink into absolute nothingness when compared with this licensed promenade for prostitutes. Here are children from twelve to sixteen years of age who are being trained, and have already learned much of the sin and trickery of the abandoned harlot. It is in vain you look in any of our provincial towns for a festering source of moral corruption such as we see here. In London there is nothing so vile. In Paris the scene would not be permitted an hour, *if it were known*. And we are assured, by persons who have been in most of the continental cities and towns, that the iniquity here is without a parallel. . . .

Again, look at the abominable and disgusting practices at the Salle de Danse, or the degrading pastimes at the Supper Rooms. We have heard a magistrate from the bench describe the scenes nightly enacted in the street as a scandal and disgrace to the town; but what would he have said were he to behold the "chamber of horrors" within? . . . And yet, well as these places and practices are now known, we scarcely find one minister of religion in the town who has the moral courage to stand forth and declare his open hostility to such soul-destroying vanities. . . .

Minor Theatres, Dancing Saloons, and Demoralizing Publications as Causes of Delinquency, 1858

> Samuel Phillips Day, *Juvenile Crime: Its Causes, Character, and Cure* (London, 1858), pp. 54-55, 168-69, 171, 176, 180, 185, 203, 208, 211 (UNC Lib.)

[The author of this work asserts that he is a journalist and a theatrical critic. His chief aim in compiling this volume from blue books and other authoritative documents not easily available to the general public "was to throw an additional glimmer of light upon a very dark spot in our social system; believing with Dr. Arnold, that 'while history looks generally at the political state of a nation, its *social* state, which is infinitely more important, and in which lie the seeds of the greatest revolutions, is too commonly neglected or unknown.'" The writer notes also that the middle and upper classes in England were becoming deeply interested in social questions.

The eleven chapters of this book treat of the following topics: 1. Pauperism; 2. Compulsion, Evil Example, Temptation, and Hereditary Predisposition; 3. Incommodious Dwellings and Low Lodging-Houses; 4. Ignorance; 5. Intemperance; 6. Minor Theatres, Penny Gaffs, Dancing and Singing Saloons, Gaming and Betting Practices, and Demoralizing Publications, 7. Workhouses and Prisons; 8. Increase and Extent of Crime; 9. Nature and Cost of Crime; 10. Chief Preventive Checks to Crime; 11. Repressive Checks to Crime. The Appendix contains a three-page list of works on crime and delinquency.

Two selections are presented from this book; the first, showing the gradually developing concept that crime and delinquency are hereditary; and the second, showing the effect of commercial amusements on the morals of city children.]

A. HEREDITARY PREDISPOSITION TO CRIME.

In attributing to crime an *hereditary* character, I feel that I am but expressing the opinion of those physiologists who are best qualified to speak on the subject. Our prison statistics furnish indubitable evidence of this phenomenon, had other testimony been wanting. The criminal population are a *genus* in themselves, with habits, customs, feelings, and ideas differing from the rest of mankind. Whole families, nay, entire generations, have been tainted with this moral malady, which appears equally as tenacious of place as of race. The hereditary character of crime is admitted, for the physical diagnosis silences doubt; but, as to the why and the wherefore, doctors differ, and so the matter remains an open question.

From the able statistical tables furnished by Mr. Clay, of Preston Gaol (than whom few have laboured more unremittingly to obtain full information and arrive at a correct analysis), it appears that 75 per cent. of the cases of juvenile crime which he investigated partook of an hereditary character; and this he conceives to be the proportion in all prisons. At Manchester, however, it seems higher; for, from inquiries made in that city, out of 100 children who had committed offences, 90 per cent. were the offspring of criminal parents.

B. PENNY-GAFFS AND DIME NOVELS.

Equally, if not more vicious, dissolute, and demoralizing are the low play-houses known by the unfashionable epithet of "Penny Gaffs," of which there are several in various districts of the metropolis. Lately, one Saturday evening, I visited a few of those places situated in the neighbourhood of Blackfriars'-bridge and the New Cut, Lambeth. The exterior of the buildings presented rather a decent appearance, having an array of showy lamps in front, but the interior was filthy, fusty, and odious in every sense of the word.

Strange to say, the lowest and worst of these "gaffs" is situated in the most respectable locality, and the *habitues* of the one would consider it derogatory to frequent the other. Having paid the small charge of one penny, I was suffered to make my way through a long, circuitous passage, off which abutted several unfurnished rooms, one of which was appropriated to the sale of refreshments of no more deleterious character than ginger beer, or "pop," judging from the shape and description of the bottles which were scattered around. Having reached the pit, I found it literally crammed with boys, to the number of several hundred, all dirty and untidy, multitudes of whom had the appearance of having just left off work. Amongst the group were a few men and girls of the lowest class, seemingly delighted with the scenes that were being enacted before them. The yelling, hideous screams, and other horrible noises that arose from this part of the house, were truly deafening, which, combined with the close atmosphere, made still more intolerable by the smoke from tobacco-pipes, rendered the place anything but agreeable, or indeed supportable.

The evening's entertainment commenced with a series of low tumbling tricks, which a few clumsy ragamuffins, who volunteered for the purpose, endeavoured to imitate successively on the stage, to the infinite delight of the rabble audience; for each ridiculous failure on the part of the former provoked turbulent applause and uproarious laughter from the latter, until the scene became nearly as horrible and intolerable as that described by an African traveller, who, during his explorations, had his peaceful slumbers one night suddenly disturbed and dissipated by the unearthly, weird-like bellowings of a whole army of predatious wild dogs! Next followed a comic vocalist, who illustrated, in character, *Jack Rag*, the crossing-sweeper, by a variety of *pose plastique* antics, some of which were harmless enough, but others had a decided tendency not only to bring sacred historical personages, but even the Holy Book itself, into ridicule. For example, the positions in which Samson was presumed to stand during his conflict with the lion, and when he had the gates of the city of Gaza upon his back, were rudely and impiously travestied, thus making solemn subjects administer to ribald mirth. After very lusty plaudits and a shower of ovations in the shape of pence and halfpence, which the triumphant actor groped up with avidity, seemingly unmindful of the danger to his head or eyes from those friendly missiles, the curtain fell.

During the interval, and finding the air painfully oppressive, I returned to the street, and, after a little, upon payment of another penny, got a cheque for the boxes. . . .

The curtain having now arisen, a pantomimic play was produced, which, from my very slight acquaintance with the history of that notorious robber and highwayman, *Jack Sheppard*, I knew to be elucidatory of his life and acts. I never witnessed such unrestrained enthusiasm as repeatedly greeted the hero of this piece, who, when called before the curtain, received the same tangible, though more abundant manifestation of satisfaction on the part of the audience as the silly comic actor to whom previous allusion was made. When all was over, the rush from the lower part of the house was tremendous. Several boys, in their eagerness to get out, threw themselves over the closely-packed groups of people, struggling for the door, and in this manner were literally carried on the heads of their indignant supporters, whose language, as may be conceived, was neither temperate nor discreet. Having got clear outside, I noticed another assemblage of boys awaiting admission, when I was informed, upon inquiry, that there were generally two, and sometimes as many as three, performances during the evening. . . .

That the minor theatres and penny gaffs are frequented by gangs of young thieves, and other criminally-disposed children, is notorious; and it would appear from the nature of the performances introduced nightly on the boards of such corrupt and corrupting places, that their respective managers are well acquainted with the base character no less than the depraved tastes (to which they disreputably pander) of their patrons. According to the evidence of one criminal (imprisoned at Newgate, and since apprehended), before the Select Committee of the House, bands of juvenile delinquents make it a practice to prearrange their plans of depredation, so as to enable them to pass their evenings at the theatre. . . .*

Dancing and singing saloons are another source of mischief, and not only predispose, but in many instances directly lead to juvenile delinquency. In some instances houses are appropriated to only one, but frequently both entertainments are combined. It is difficult to determine which is the most fraught with evil results, the *salle de danse* or the concert-room; but they are both highly demoralizing and injurious. An exceptional example may occasionally be found where some propriety and decorum are observed, and where caution seems to be exercised in the choice of the songs introduced; but while this small improvement is to be commended, there can be no doubt that the generality of those places are vile

*Minutes of Evidence, p. 243.

beyond description; and what is worse, that those apparently of a more respectable and select character are in reality the lowest and most depraving. . . .

Highly prejudicial and pernicious as are the metropolitan casinos and singing-rooms, those of the provinces far surpass them in open, unblushing effrontery and profligacy. In the locality of Williamson-square, Liverpool, there are no less than twenty of these places, some of which are extremely vile; in fact, hot-beds of licentiousness and seduction. . . .

A further cause of juvenile delinquency arises from demoralizing publications, the number of which, from the immense circulation they obtain, it is difficult to compute. One thing is certain, that they are fraught with great evil to the community.

Under this head may particularly be mentioned the lives of notorious robbers and highwaymen, such as *Jack Sheppard, Dick Turpin,* etc., who have been apotheosized by their injudicious biographers, and ridiculously elevated to the rank of heroes! Such productions are read with avidity, even by those who peruse nothing else, and consequently cannot fail to prove highly prejudicial to morals. The young and ardent mind is naturally prone to take pleasure in works of an exciting character; and the daring exploits, rash adventures, and "hair-breadth 'scapes" recorded of these malefactors, not only gratify the fancies and excite the imagination of youth, but create a sympathy with them, if not a desire to imitate their actions.* Hence we find that many of our juvenile criminals possess little or no education beyond that of being able to read, or being otherwise familiar with those disreputable and demoralizing memoirs. . . .

But there are a class of publishers and vendors who pander to the grossest and most corrupt tastes, by issuing alleged biographies of notorious women of disrepute, spurious physiological treatises, penny numbers of letter-press obscenely illustrated,† immodest and highly-coloured prints and photographs, numbers of which are imported from France. Although establishments for the sale of such disgusting merchandize are scattered over the metropolis, they are

*Repeated cases have occurred of late years, in which young housebreakers have avowed that they were led to adopt their course of crime by the perusal of *Jack Sheppard,* written by a talented but injudicious modern author.—*Social Evils,* &c., by Alexander Thomson of Banchory, p. 35.

†A few publications of this kind, such as the *Women of London,* etc., issuing fifteen thousand copies a week, and which were made the vehicle of licentious anecdotes, tales, trials involving scandalous details, and other matters of the most obscene and offensive nature, have been very properly suppressed. It is to be regretted that *Paul Pry* did not sooner share a similar fate.

chiefly confined to Holywell and Wych Streets. At one time, as many as fifty-seven of these shops were open simultaneously; but I am happy to find, that through the efforts of the Society for the Suppression of Vice, and it is to be hoped other moral, though less coercive agencies, the number has been reduced to eighteen or twenty.‡

. . . The number of prosecutions instituted by the Society for the Suppression of Vice during the past fifty-five years of its existence, has been 159, averaging nearly 3 a year. The following list comprises the amount of seizures and the destruction of stock legally effected thereby for the past eighteen years:—126,230 obscene prints and pictures; 16,073 books, mostly filled with obscene engravings, and upwards of 5 tons of letter-press, in sheets, or ready to be made up into volumes; large quantities of blasphemous publications; 4,644 sheets of obscene songs; 5,399 cards, snuff-boxes, and other articles; 844 copper-plates; 424 lithographic stones; 95 wood blocks, engraved; 11 printing presses, with all the apparatus for printing; and above 28 cwt. of type, including the stereotype of several entire works, of the grossness and impurity of which it would be impossible to convey any adequate idea.*

Work of London City Missionaries with Fallen Girls, 1859-1867

[A] *Female Mission in Connexion With the Reformatory and Refuge Union. Report of the Sub-Committee* (London, 1859) pp. 3, 7 (Brit. Mus.)

The subject of Fallen Females having been brought prominently forward a year ago in some of the Public Journals, a Sub-Committee of the Reformatory and Refuge Union was formed to enquire into the question, with a view to devise some scheme of practical good in the least expensive and most effectual manner.

After various conferences with the Clergy of the several Parishes in the Metropolis, and the managers of some of the existing Institutions, it was resolved that a centre of action should be provided through which Institutions might be assisted, and where Contributions could be received from those who are desirous of aiding in the rescue of this unhappy class.

For this object a Handbook was compiled and published, con-

‡The trade is increasing in the provinces, although decreasing in the metropolis.
*From the unpublished Report of the Society for 1856.

taining a short account of 50 Penitentiaries and Homes for Females in London and the Provinces, with particulars as to the amount of accommodation, ages received, terms of admission, &c.

The services of two Female Missionaries were then employed [April, 1858] for the purpose of seeking out those who were desirous of leaving their evil ways, and directing them to places of shelter and protection. . . .

About 16,000 Tracts and Handbills have been distributed in the Parks and Streets, as well as in houses of bad character, into which the Missionaries have gained admission at considerable personal risk and self sacrifice.

[B] *Ninth Report of the Female Mission to the Fallen* (1867), pp. 8, 10, 11, 13, 14-15, 19, 33, 35 (Brit. Mus.)

Two Missionaries were at first employed, and these have been gradually added to until the number now is eight. . . .

The primary work of the Mission is the night visitation. The Missionaries generally spend from 8 P.M. to 12 P.M., when the weather is seasonable, in distributing special tracts amongst the crowds of women who frequent the streets at that time, and in speaking earnestly to them as opportunity offers. The tracts have been very carefully drawn up. . . . Each tract has on it the address of the Missionary by whom it is given. Many very interesting facts might be cited shewing the influence which these tracts often exert. . . .

Each of the Missionaries is provided with one or more rooms to which she may bring those whom she is endeavouring to reclaim, and keep them for a time under her own eye, before placing them in Homes or in service. . . .

Whilst the evenings of the Missionaries are employed in street visitation, the days are spent in investigating the cases; writing to friends and relatives, receiving visits from old cases, visiting houses of ill-fame, hospitals and workhouses. The Missionaries, whenever possible, place themselves in communication with the parents of the poor girls, and although a distressing amount of unrelenting feeling is often manifested, especially by the mothers, yet in many instances patient efforts have been rewarded by a happy re-union. These investigations require both tact and patience, for fake names and addresses are often given. . . .

One of the most cheering things connected with the work, is the visits of the old cases. The Missionaries who have been longest in the work have often several cases calling in one day, and when the women who have been placed in service have a holiday, they are almost sure to come and spend it with their dear friend the Missionary. . . .

VERY YOUNG CASES

And very early—almost incredibly so—does this evil sometimes develop itself. The Missionaries have had more than one case fallen at eight years of age, and many are thoroughly hardened to the life before they are twelve. These very young cases often owe their ruin to the herding together of the sexes in the lodging-houses and dwellings of the poor, and often to cruel treatment at home, which drives them to seek refuge in the streets. The following extracts from the journals of the Missionaries will illustrate these:—

E. C., an interesting little girl, only 14 years of age came, brought by her mother who implored my sympathy and help on her behalf. This poor child had been seduced six months previously—by an old man, a relative, who had a wife and six children living—and was expecting to become a mother. I placed her in a Home, where she now is, with her infant, and I trust the good seed sown may spring up into everlasting life.

E. T., 15, a very pretty attractive looking girl of superior address and manners who had only left her parents (highly respectable people) five weeks. She was taken by a young woman (unknown to her father and mother) to a place of amusement, who kept her out so late she was afraid to return home. Alas, alas, she took her to her lodgings, where she was introduced to a gentleman, who ruined her. He then persuaded her to accompany him to London, promising to obtain her a situation. She came, but only to live with him three weeks, and was then deserted, and left without even the means of procuring bread. The poor child remained in this condition for two days, then made her trouble known to a young woman residing in the same house, who gave her one of our little tracts with my address. I sheltered her for three weeks, and then had the pleasure of restoring her to her sorrowing and heart-broken mother.

One little thing at the age of 13 was driven into the streets by her drunken parents, to get her living as best she could. She was decoyed into a bad house by a female, and there ruined. . . .

E. S., 16, parents dead; lived some time with her aunt in S—— Hill, who is very poor, and told the child that "she must do the best she can," for she could not afford to keep her. The poor girl then went to the City Road, to a person who knew her parents; but she was only there a few days when that person was taken ill, and obliged to go to the Hospital. She then went back again to her aunt, who told her, "You must do as others do." The poor girl has been two months on the streets. She is now at Highgate. . . .

DOMESTIC SERVANTS

Statistics prove that fully 70 per cent of the fallen women of London come from the class of domestic servants; and those places are peculiarly dangerous where many servants are kept. Is it not surely a fearful thought, that our homes, of which we speak so proudly, the homes of England, should thus be the nurseries of crime? Nor can it be said in extenuation that the danger always comes from without—fellow servants, master's sons, nay, even masters themselves are often the causes of the mischief. . . .

CAUSES OF FALL

The Committee have felt the importance of endeavouring as far as possible to trace the causes of fall, but they are very difficult to define. Some, nay most, attribute thir ruin to an imperfect moral education and the want of religious teaching. Many are ruined by their lovers under promise of marriage; others have yielded to violence, or have been drugged, or decoyed into houses of ill-fame. Many have been ruined by the menservants employed in the same families, or by lodgers in their employers' houses; others attribute their fall to their mistresses refusing their characters which is often done for most trivial offences with little thought of the fearful consequences. Some date their ruin to going to a theatre; others to attending fairs. In several instances drink was alleged as the cause. Many pleaded friendlessness, homelessness, destitution, as the immediate reason. The language of one such, aged 17, and an orphan, was, "I was forced to it." Drunken parents are a fruitful source of the evil—but worse than this is the case not uncommon of parents deliberately training up their children to this course of life. One of the Missionaries took up the case of a young girl of 10, who was fallen and had been on the streets, and found her mother had trained her to it, and was then in prison for keeping a bad house.

Special Officer Employed for Social Investigation of Children's Cases in Liverpool, 1859

Rev. Thomas Carter "On the Effects of the Youthful Offenders' Acts as enforced in Liverpool," *Transactions of the National*

Association for the Promotion of Social Science, 1859, p. 523
(UNC Lib.)

I may be permitted here briefly to explain the method of working the Reformatory Acts in use in Liverpool. When a child under 16 years of age is charged with any offence punishable by fourteen days' imprisonment, the rule of the magistrates is to commit to prison on a general remand of a week, during which time a superior officer of the jail, who has voluntarily taken this task upon himself, directs inquiries to be made personally through the agency of an officer specially assigned to the duty, into the domestic condition and circumstances of the child, its own character, and the character of its parents. Great care is taken to obtain the most accurate information, and at the termination of the remand the result is made known to the magistrate, who, with all the facts before him in a reliable form, then decides on the desirableness of the child's commitment to a Reformatory. If committed, it becomes the duty of the officer above alluded to, on receipt of instruction to that effect from the Home Office, through the Inspector of Reformatories, to apply for an order against the parents for such a contribution towards the child's maintenance as the circumstances of the parties, of which he had previously informed himself, will justify; that order obtained, his duty then requires him to receive the amount as directed by the magistrate, and, in event of arrears or default, to adopt the measures prescribed by the Acts for enforcing payment. By this simple agency, no danger can arise either of suitable cases escaping or of improper ones being sent to reformatory treatment; nor—the circumstances of the parents being thoroughly known—can any undue severity be visited upon them, or any immunity from their proper liability be obtained. In small communities these duties may be performed through the agency of the police; but that instrumentality when tried in Liverpool utterly failed, and satisfactory results, such as have been obtained there, will be most likely to arise where similar means are adopted.

Ten Thousand Children Annually Committed to Prison Even after Passage of Reformatory Schools Act of 1854

Rev. W. C. Osborn,[1] *The Cry of 10,000 Children; or, Cruelty towards the Young: Being an Appeal to the Legislature and*

1. Chaplain of the Bath Gaol, England, and author of *The Preservation of Youth from Crime: A Nation's Duty* (1860); *Not Guilty; Prevention of Crime; The Non-Imprisonment of Children;* etc.

During the past ten years much has been done to enlighten us as to the condition of our wretched and destitute children, and their position with regard to the laws of the land. While the establishment of ragged, industrial, and reformatory schools has, in some measure, ameliorated their condition and lessened their number, still there are many thousands of young children whom these blessings have never reached. Our past efforts appear to have satisfied our consciences, and the Divine blessing, which has attended our past exertions, seems to have checked us in giving to these outcast children of our streets that measure of mercy and assistance which their condition imperatively demands.

In the three years ending September, 1856, the juvenile delinquent population of England and Wales under sixteen years of age were represented by an annual average of about 15,000 committals to our common prisons, and during the subsequent triennial period, our gaol returns give 31,753 (one-sixth females), being an annual average of more than 10,000 committals of such offenders. About one-half of these children were orphans, or deserted by their parents, 43 per cent. could neither read nor write, about 45 per cent. could read and write but imperfectly, and therefore only about 15 per cent. had the ability even to read and write. None of them had attained the age of sixteen years, and one-sixth of the whole were only twelve years old or under.

In 1854 the Legislature passed the Reformatory School Act for the purpose of encouraging the establishment of institutions for the instruction and training of criminal children, but this measure made it imperative on the provincial magistrates of the kingdom to commit the children, whom they considered fit subjects for reformatory schools, to prison for at least fourteen days, prior to removal to such institutions.

Thus an enlightened measure was damaged by a penal qualification being required for admission to its benefits. This course, adopted from prudential considerations, has not only deprived the Act of half its value to the country and the children for whose welfare it was designed, but perpetuated the very evil which we sought to remove; and as the number disgraced by incarceration has not been lessened by this Act, we are led to seek the deliverance of these helpless, destitute, and erring children from such degradation, and to insist that they be first taught what is right before they are punished as criminals for doing wrong. This, combined with the minimum, but still long period of two years' detention, for which children must be sentenced to such schools, has so hindered the operation of the Act, that, of the aggregate number (31,753) committed to prison during the last three years, only 2890 have been transferred after imprisonment to Reformatory Schools. Thus more than nine-tenths of our juvenile offenders are left unaffected by this Act of Parliament.[2]

William King Appointed First Boys' Beadle in London by the Reformatory and Refuge Union, October, 1866

[A] *Eleventh Annual Report of the Reformatory and Refuge Union* (London, 1867), p. 11 (Brit. Mus.)

BOYS' BEADLE

Public attention has often been called to the number of vagrant children to be found in most parts of the metropolis. The Council of the Union having well considered the subject, determined to try if anything could be done to clear the streets of these neglected ones. An agent has been appointed whose special duty it is to "look after" these waifs and strays who are to be found almost everywhere, wandering or begging, or, as the short days draw to a close, huddled up asleep on a doorstep, or under a dark arch. He approaches them as a friend, sifts their cases thoroughly, and deals with them as their various circumstances require. He has already been instrumental in rescuing several of these wanderers and placing them in Industrial Schools and Refuges. He has also taken many children found begging under pretence of offering articles for sale home to their parents, and cautioned the latter as to the consequences of a repetition of such illegal practices. Though known as the "Boys' Beadle," from his having most to do with boys, he helps girls also when necessary. He has now been working since last November [1866], and has patrolled those districts assigned him by the sub-committee who direct his movements. The following summary of his work will best exemplify what he has been able to accomplish.

2. It was not until 1899 that the preliminary imprisonment of a child before sending him to a Reformatory School was finally abolished.

Children taken home and parents cautioned 24
Arranged for attendance at Ragged Schools 4
Admitted to Homes, Refuges, and Industial Schools 32
Committed to Certified Industrial Schools 15
Ditto to Reformatory 1
Discharged by Magistrates 5
Refused to enter Homes 2
Sent to Discharged Prisoners Relief Committee 1
Restored to parents 5
Cases in hand, not settled 5

TOTAL   94

[B] Rob Roy, [John Macgregor], *The Boys' Beadle*[1] (2nd Ed.; London: Reformatory and Refuge Union, 1871), pp. 6-10, 13-15 (Columbia Univ. Lib.)

II. "The Industrial Schools Act, 1866," is an excellent measure, but it has one grand and simple defect—that its chief power is left to be set in action by anybody or everybody; that is to say, by nobody. This is plain enough from section 14, which begins, "Any person may bring before two justices or a magistrate any child" found begging, etc.

The power thus given to all people was employed now and then by a few active men, sometimes by an enthusiastic philanthropist, and for a brief season by the police. If, however, any busy man, such as the master of a school, brings a homeless lad before the magistrate under this Act, he has to brave the question, "Why does this man capture a strange child?" He has to spend days in inquiries, attendance, and correspondence, has to get the consent of some Institution to receive the child, and, after all, the case may be dismissed, and then the "any person" has all the cost to pay.

The Act had, indeed, built homes, provided teachers, and conferred authority on Courts and there were thousands of hapless ones in the streets who ought to be in the schools, but there was nobody enjoined to put them in. It was as if children were seen struggling in deep water, and a Receiving-house was on the shore, and a boat, but no sailor was told off to work it.

III. During a visit to schools in Sweden the idea occurred to me of supplying this want in the practical opertion of the Act. I found

1. See also Charles R. Ford, "The Boys' Beadle," abstracted in the *Transactions of the National Association for the Promotion of Social Science, 1867*, p. 296.

that the compulsory system in that country (where school plans and machinery are the best in the world) is made operative, without being oppressive, by an agent in each district called a "Persuader", whose business is precisely what we needed here in England, namely, to take up the case of the neglected child, to lead with gentleness those who will not go unasked to school, and to bring under quiet authority those who must be compelled. This was the very thing wanted to make the "Industrial Schools Act" workable. It was the *thumb* for a hand which before had only fingers, which hand could indeed push or strike, but could not well catch hold so long as it was thumbless.

The Council of the Reformatory and Refuge Union readily acceded to the suggestion for the trial of an agency like the "Persuader" in London, and, after nine unsuccessful efforts to find the proper man, Mr. William King was appointed the "Boys' Beadle" four years ago, with the following instructions:—

MEMORANDUM FOR THE AGENT OF THE REFORMATORY AND REFUGE UNION.

He is appointed—

To befriend and help the neglected children in the streets, and to discover the persons who fail in their duty to take care of them.

He is to do this—

By careful investigation of selected cases, and, according to the particular circumstances, either to restore them to their parents or guardians; to direct and introduce them to Ragged Schools; to procure them admission to Refuges; to aid in applying the laws by which they may be remitted as vagrants to Industiral Schools, or as offenders to Reformatories; to assist the authorities where payment is to be enforced from the parents.

His special duties are, confining his effort to an assigned district—

To visit each Ragged School, Refuge, and other similar institution, so as to confer with the masters and matrons, and to secure their cooperation.

To begin with the cases of children, under twelve years of age, found by himself in the streets at night, or brought under his notice by Ragged-school teachers, missionaries, subscribers to the Union, and other persons.

To provide, if necessary, immediate shelter and food while inquiries are being made.

To enter in his journal full particulars of his work, visits, and inquiries, and to receive and carry out in each case the directions of the Committee.

In order to perform these duties satisfactorily and without confusion, he is to restrict his attention only to so many cases at once as he can personally investigate thoroughly, so that he may complete a few cases rather than engage superficially in a number. . . .

The direction of this Agent's work was entrusted to three members of the Council, and the six volumes of his Journal contain a mass of valuable detailed but condensed information as to the neglected children in London which cannot be found elsewhere.

It is not desired in this paper to appeal to the sentiments of those who care for the neglected, but merely to give them the plain facts and figures deduced from many cases systematically worked. Still, it may be allowed to one who is deeply interested in this work to remind all who are about to undertake a like effort that their hearts will be stirred by three strong emotions which deepen rather than weaken as they are longer engaged. They will feel sad and poignant sympathy for the hapless little ones whose miserable woe is uncovered before us. They will feel burning shame that England can let any of her poor children lie grovelling so low for one single hour. But they will feel also, thank God! most cheerful joy at the happy rescues from such wretchedness—the beaming faces of grateful boys and girls now settled and contented in useful employment at home and abroad, to which state of comfort they have been lifted by this agency from the pit of despair.

The Beadle began in a northern district of London, bounded on the east by Edgware Road and on the south by Hyde Park, containing about 100,000 inhabitants, and not many of the squalid poor. We introduced him first to twelve Ragged Schools of the neighbourhood, and to four Refuges for children, also to the magistrates and to the police.

It is to be remembered that the Beadle has no authority whatever, more than that of "any person," to deal with the neglected children. He is not a constable nor a parish officer, he wears no uniform; but is simply a man acting on behalf of a self-constituted Society, which employs him to do what any other person is at liberty to do, but what no other person feels it to be his *duty* and *business* to do.

At first there was a little natural doubt or suspicion on the part of some authorities as to the position and work of this new officer, who was seen walking along streets and alleys, taking children to their homes or their schools, warning others, and communicating with parents and consulting with the police.

But all this coolness soon disappeared as the purpose of his visits became known; and it is very satisfactory to state that during the whole period of Mr. King's engagement, although many cases of difficulty were treated, and many bad characters and bad neighbourhoods had to be dealt with, not one single instance has occurred of disturbance, and not one complaint of misconduct.

This success may be partly owing to the careful guidance of his work by the committee, but it is certainly more due to the good sense and kind firmness of the Agent himself.

In a few days the effect of his visits became evident far beyond the streets where his presence had been observed. News of this sort travels speedily, and it was soon evident that the *deterrent* effect of an agency known to be on the look-out for cases of parental neglect or juvenile misconduct was immediate and widespread.

In three weeks he was to be moved to another district; but the schoolmasters and others of the first entreated that he might remain there, for "their streets had never been so orderly before, nor their schools so full!" Moving eastwards to the more difficult and more densely populated district, which is bounded on the east by Regent Street and on the south by Oxford Street, the Beadle's work had equal success, and again, in like manner moving east and south, he visited each district of London.

Gradually—in some cases *very* gradually—the Police Magistrates appreciated the value of our Agent's services; until now he is welcomed and constantly applied to by all of them in turn. He has numerous letters from the country and abroad, but especially, of course, from good people in London, while a succession of visitors call at his house to claim his help.

Every institution for the poor in the metropolis soon perceived the advantage of having such an Agent to give advice, to make inquiries, and to investigate thoroughly what the Governors or Matrons of Homes and Refuges and Schools could never attend to in this way without absenting themselves too long from their own proper duties.

At length it was proposed by one in authority that the Home Office should arrange for an agent of this kind in each of the twenty-one police Divisions. But just at that time the "Elementary Education Bill" was in preparation, and so it was that the section of the Act was introduced which we shall notice further on.

Mr. King's journal is kept methodically, so that each case, recurring as it does at intervals (sometimes indeed for years) can be traced by reference through 1,300 pages. A *summary* is made each month, and another every quarter, and the principal features of each case are tabulated in one general book. From this the following information is compiled as to work done up to the last day of 1870:—

(1) Number of Days Employed 1,252
    Total Number of Cases Inquired into 720
                              Boys 637
                              Girls 83
(2) Cases—How Disposed of—
    1. Restored to parents or friends 34
    2. Placed in situations 6
    3. Sent to sea 26
    4. Helped by other Agents 14
    5. Emigrated 1
    6. Temporary shelter 4
    7. Industrial Homes 289
    8. Certified Industrial Schools 85
    9. Reformatories 13
    10. Sent to Workhouse 1
    11. Refused advice 27
    12. Discharged by Magistrate 33
    13. Absconded during inquiry 23
    14. Nothing done after inquiry 123
    15. Visited parents 30
    16. Arranged for school 6
    17. Cases not settled 5
                                                        ────
                                                        720

[Next follows data on institutions for homeless and destitute and for certified industrial schools for boys and for girls.]

[EXTRACTS AT RANDOM FROM MR. KING'S JOURNAL]

[Mr. King suggests that the limit of age should be thirteen instead of twelve in section 15.]

Taking one case with another, the average time employed about each was less than two days, and the cost of a thorough inquiry 7s.6d. Frequent visits were paid to cases already well disposed of in situations or in Institutions, and a large proportion of them were reported to be "going on well." . . .

274

The Journal also classifies the difficulties met with, from 1. Children. 2. Parents. 3. Employees. 4. Public. 5. Police. 6. Magistrates. 7. Institutions. And then *suggestions* are noted under various distinct heads.

The police constables have almost always aided Mr. King judiciously. In most cases he hands over the child to a policeman at once, who then becomes the "Any person may bring", etc. in section 14. . . .

On January 1, 1868, a similar Agent was appointed by "The Birmingham Neglected Children's Aid Society", for the same purpose as the Boys' Beadle in London, and, after spending a fortnight with Mr. King to learn his duties, he began a work in Birmingham which is now most useful and satisfactory. . . .

[Boys' beadles, or children's agents, were the forerunners of the present day probation officers. Charles R. Ford, Secretary of the Reformatory and Refuge Union, in an article, "The Boys' Beadle," *Reformatory and Refuge Journal* (Oct., 1867), pp. 69-75, describes in general the work of this new expriment to put life into the laws relating to children. About 1869 he read a paper on "The Industrial Schools Act and Children's Agents" at the Manchester Conference of the National Education Union, issued subsequently in pamphlet form. Miss Mary Carpenter also read a paper on "Children's Agents" before the meeting of the National Association for the Promotion of Social Science in 1869 (abstracted in its published transactions, 1869, p. 270).

The reports of the Reformatory and Refuge Union from 1866 to 1909 contain statistical summaries of the work of the boys' beadles in London and extracts from their journals. By 1900 the boys' beadles had handled a total of 15,625 cases. The last report of their work is found in the 53rd annual report of the Union in 1909.]

Demoralized Condition of Children Employed in Agricultural Gangs, 1867

"Agricultural Gangs," *Quarterly Review*, Vol. 123 (July and October, 1867), pp. 174-75, 177-84 (UNC Lib.)

This Report* is one of the most painful which it has ever been our duty to peruse, for it proves to demonstration that the social

*Sixth Report of the Commissioners of the Children's Employment Commission, 1867.

evils which were long supposed to be peculiar to manufactures exist even in a more aggravated form in connection with the cultivation of the soil. Great numbers of children, young persons, and women, are, it appears, employed in companies or 'gangs' in certain counties which have acquired an odious notoriety for one of the most flagrant abuses which has ever disgraced a civilised land. Multitudes of the young of both sexes have been reduced to a state of the lowest moral degradation by association with each other, without any effectual supervision or control, for the purpose of field labour carried on at a considerable distance from their homes.

The system to which we refer is that peculiar organisation of rural industry known as the Agricultural Gang, and which prevails extensively in Lincolnshire, Huntingdonshire, Cambridgeshire, Norfolk, Suffolk, Nottinghamshire, and in a more limited degree in the Counties of Bedford, Rutland, and Northampton; and nothing more shocking has ever been brought to light by a public inquiry than the sufferings incidental to the employment of young children in certain kinds of agricultural labour. . . .

The extensive employment of women and children in rural labour had its rise in two causes: first in the extensive reclamation of waste lands; and secondly in the destruction of cottages and the consequent removal of the people which inhabited them, rendering labour difficult to procure, and imposing upon the farmer the necessity of obtaining it through the instrumentality of a middle man, who made it his business to supply it at a cheap rate, gaining his living by organising bands of women, young persons, and children, of whom he became the temporary master. And the 'gangs' so constituted have in some districts displaced the labour of men, and the system is favoured by the farmers for its economy no less than for its convenience. . . .

The faculty of making little children work is the peculiar art of the gangmaster, and he obtains his living by pressing his gang to the very utmost of their strenth, his object being to extort the greatest possible quantity of labour for the smallest possible remuneration. He is thus by the very condition of his occupation a hard task-master, for he must realise a profit upon every woman, young person, and child whom he employs. The gang-master is frequently stigmatised as a slave-driver, and the system has been denounced as little better than negro bondage. If the whip is not employed,[1] other modes of compulsion are resorted to, and one of the most painful facts elicited by the Commissioners' inquiries is,

1. Footnote omitted.

that children are occasionally compelled to work in the gangs for two or three hours longer than adults.

Gangmasters, as a rule, belong to a class termed catch-work labourers. They are generally men of indolent and drinking habits, and not unfrequently of notorious depravity. Their example is represented as very pernicious to the morality of the children and young persons of both sexes under their command. They are described as having almost the entire control of the children in every district where the system prevails, for they alone are able to provide them with regular employment. In some places a farmer cannot get even a boy of twelve or thirteen to do a week's work except by hiring him of the gangmaster. These men collect their gangs very early in the morning, and the scene, when 500 or 600 women, boys, and girls assemble at early dawn, to be marshalled by their respective gangsmen, and led off in different directions to their work, is described as most revolting. There are to be seen youths who have never known either the restraints of parental discipline or the humanising influences of a respectable home; girls depraved by constant association with some of the worst characters of their sex; married women who prefer the rude independence of the fields to the restraints of domestic life; little children who should be receiving their first lessons in the village school instead of imbibing those of premature and certain vice; and, above all, the gangmaster, often hoary with years, too certainly profligate in character, 'corruptus simul et corruptor,' and therefore more disposed to encourage obscene language than to check it.[2] As it is important to the gangmaster that the whole of his flock should arrive at the scene of their labour quickly and simultaneously, the pace at which the gang travels is trying to the strongest. When driving is found ineffectual, the younger children are tempted to over-exert themselves by the promise of sweetmeats. The ages at which young children commence work, and the distances they have to walk, or rather to run, before they begin the labours of the day, are astounding. Eight appears to be the ordinary age at which children of both sexes join the common gang, although seven is not unusual, and instances are mentioned in which children only six years of age were found regularly at work. One little girl only four years old was carried by her father to the fields, and put to work under a gangmaster, and it seems to be a common practice with parents to stipulate that if the elder children are hired the younger ones shall be so too. When the gangs are working at a considerable distance from home, the chil-

2. Footnote omitted.

dren leave as early as five in the morning and do not return before eight at night, and the few who attend the Sunday-schools after the labours of the week are described as in a state of exhaustion which it is distressing to witness. A little boy only six years of age is stated to have regularly walked more than six miles out to work, and often to come home so tired that he could scarcely stand. Walking, the gangmasters themselves admit, is more trying to the children than working. When the gang has a long distance to go the children become so exhausted, that the elder ones are seen dragging the younger ones home, sometimes carrying them on their backs. In winter, the children often return from the fields crying from the cold. 'Last night,' said the mother of a little boy seven years of age, 'when my Henry came home he lay up quite stiff and cold; he is often very tired, and will fall down and drop asleep with the food in his mouth.' In some parts of the fen districts the children are compelled to jump the dykes, and exertion causing frequent accidents, and one poor girl died from the effects of an effort beyond her strength.

It is a common practice for the gangmaster to carry a stick or a whip, but rather, it is said, to frighten the children with than for use; but the treatment depends entirely upon the disposition of the gangmaster. There is no control, or possibility of control, for the children know that remonstrance would be immediately followed by expulsion from the gang, and the parents, having a pecuniary interest in their labour, would but too certainly shut their ears to any complaints.[3] Instances are not uncommon of severe and lasting injuries having been inflicted by brutal gangmasters, and gross outrages, such as kicking, knocking down, beating with hoes, spuds, or a leather strap, 'dyking,' or pushing into the water, and 'gibbeting,' i.e. lifting a child off the ground and holding it there by the chin and back of the neck until it is black in the face, are said to be frequent. 'You see,' said the mother of two girls, one seven, the other eight years of age, belonging to a gang, 'their little spirits get so high, that they will talk while at work, and that is the aggravation.'

The constitution of a gang varies according to local circumstances. In some there is a larger proportion of women than of children; but, as a rule, children largely preponderate. In Northamptonshire, a gang of seventy-two persons was composed of thirty-five boys and twenty-six girls, all between the ages of seven and twelve, of five boys under the age of seven, and one of five

3. Footnote omitted.

years of age (who was generally carried home from his work), and of five young women.

The work done by gangs is continuous throughout the year, with the exception perhaps of the months of January and February. It consists generally of picking twitch or the roots of couch grass, spreading manure, setting, hoeing, and taking up potatoes, weeding growing crops, singling, i.e. thinning turnips, pulling flax, mangold-wurzel, and turnips, and stone gathering. Much of this labour is of a kind highly injurious to children, requiring a continued stooping posture with a considerable amount of physical effort. Pulling turnips is perhaps the most pernicious employment to which a child can be set; it strains the spine, and often lays the foundation of chronic disease. Even to strong workmen the labour is very trying and exhausting, and the children are constantly complaining of their backs and endeavouring to snatch a short interval of rest, placing their hands behind them; but the gangmaster is ever on the watch, and an oath or a blow is too often the inevitable consequence. The turnip-leaves in the early morning are often full of ice, which greatly aggravates the sufferings of those employed in the work; the backs of the hands become swollen and cracked by the wind and cold and wet, the palms blister, and the fingers bleed from frequent laceration. If strong women thus suffer, how great must be the torture of children whose frames are unknit, whose strength is undeveloped, and whose tender hands must smart and agonise at every pore under exertions so unsuited to their delicate and sensitive organisation! . . .

Stone picking is one of the worst kinds of labour in which women and children can be employed. The effect, like that of pulling turnips, is to strain the spine and the loins often to their permanent injury. Stones from the fields are collected in aprons suspended from the necks and shoulders, and as many as twenty-four bushels are not unfrequently picked up by one person in a day. It is a fearful labour for children, and yet fifty tons' weight have been collected by six, one of which was only six years of age, within a fortnight. . . .

Lamentable as are the physical results of such over exertion, which is far from being exceptional in the gang districts, the consequences of the intermixture of the sexes while going to and returning from work, as well as in the fields, are represented as most disastrous. Clergymen, magistrates, schoolmasters, policemen, even farmers, all concur in representing the corruption of morals which agricultural gangs have been the means of bringing about in the rural population as complete. The gangs are composed chiefly of young women hardened in a life of depravity, and of boys and girls early contaminated by their example. The youngest children swear habitually. The rate of illegitimacy, where the system prevails, is double that of the kingdom in general, and cases of seduction by the gangmasters of young girls in their employ are far from being uncommon. The medical officer of a Union workhouse stated that many girls of from thirteen to seventeen years of age had been brought there to be confined, whose ruin had been effected in going to or returning from gang work, and there had been six girls belonging to one small parish in the house at the same time lying-in, not with their first nor even with their second child.

Girls become quickly depraved, and boys attain a precocious independence which makes them impatient of parental or of any other control. Respectable persons, even ladies, if they are so unfortunate as to meet a gang, are certain to be assailed by foul language and ribald jests. A policeman, speaking of the gangs in his district, and especially of the gross immorality of the girls at an early age, says that although he had been employed for many years in detective duty in some of the worst parts of London, he never witnessed equal boldness and shamelessness; and that the obscenity of their conversation and of their songs was such as needed to be heard to be believed. The life of the fields seems indeed to possess a peculiar fascination for girls, for when once they have adopted it they cannot be induced to enter domestic service, nor indeed are they fit for it. 'I have no hesitation,' said a clergyman, speaking of the moral condition of his own parish, 'in saying that its corruption exceeds anything of which I have any experience. I have been to Sierra Leone, but I have seen shameless wickedness in —— such as I never witnessed in Africa; 95 per cent. of those who work in the gangs never enter a place of worship, and the system is so degrading and demoralising to those so employed that they need to be civilised before they can be christianised.' It seems almost an impossibility that a girl who has worked for a single season in a gang can become a modest and respectable woman, or that a boy who associates day after day with some of the most abandoned of the other sex can grow up otherwise than grossly sensual and profane. . . .

The temptation of adding two or three shillings to the weekly earnings of the family is generally too great for parents to withstand. Mothers are represented as forcing their children into the gangs,[4] and prefer keeping them at home to placing them in service that they may farm them out to the gangmaster; and it not unfrequently happens that the father is indulging in voluntary idleness at home while his offspring are toiling in the fields.[5]

Education is, as may be supposed, in a very neglected state in the districts where 'ganging' prevails. Children who leave school for field work at the age of seven or eight can have scarcely acquired the rudiments of knowledge, and if they return to it for a few weeks after the principal agricultural operations of the year are over, they are generally found to have become rough, demoralised, and intractable. As it is the interest of farmers that the supply of juvenile labour should always be equal to his requirements, they are represented as generally opposed in the gang districts to the education of the poor.[6]

A Distinct Criminal Class Hereditarily Disposed to Crime, 1870

J. B. Thomson, *The Hereditary Nature of Crime*[1] [1870], pp. 1-14 (Howard League Lib.)

On the border-land of Lunacy lie the criminal populations. It is a debatable region; and no more vexed problem comes before the Medical Psychologist than this—viz.: where badness ends and madness begins in criminals. The inmates of Asylums and of Prisons are so nearly allied that "thin partitions do their bounds divide." From large experience among criminals I have come to the conclusion, that the principal business of Prison Surgeons must always be with mental diseases; that the number of physical diseases are less than of the psychical; that the diseases and causes of death among prisoners are chiefly of the nervous system; and in fine that the treatment of crime is a branch of psychology. . . .

. . . Intimate and daily experience for many years among criminals has led me to the conviction that in by far the greatest proportion of offences *Crime is Hereditary.*

The proposition that crime is generally committed by criminals hereditarily disposed to it, I shall try to prove by shewing:

4. Footnote omitted.
5. Footnote omitted.
6. Footnote omitted.

---

1. The author of this pamphlet was Resident Surgeon, General Prison for Scotland, at Perth.

1. That there is a *criminal class* distinct from other civilized and criminal men.

2. That this criminal class is marked by peculiar physical and mental characteristics.

3. That the hereditary nature of crime is shown by the *family* histories of criminals.

4. That the *transformation* of other nervous disorders with crime in the criminal class, also proves the alliance of hereditary crime with other disorders of the mind—such as epilepsy, dipsomania, insanity, &c.

5. That the *incurable* nature of crime in the criminal class goes to prove its hereditary nature. . . .

The criminal class have a *locale* and a community of their own in our great cities. You never find them pursuing an honest trade or an honourable profession. They do not mingle in markets, and engage in commerce with civilized business men. The greatest number are thieves, Ishmaelites, whose hand is against every civilized man. . . . These communities of crime, we know, have no respect for the laws of marriage—are regardless of the rules of consanguinity; and, only connecting themselves with those of their own nature and habits, they must beget a depraved and criminal class hereditarily disposed to crime. Their moral disease comes *ab ovo.* They are *born into* crime, as well as reared, nurtured, and instructed in it; and habit becomes a new force—a second nature, superinduced upon their original moral depravity.

[Miners and fishermen "preserve distinct physical and mental characteristics unchanged for centuries."] Of all these varieties, we know none whose typical features and caste are so notable as those of the criminal population. They are a low class, and their physique shews it so plainly that all prison officials or detective officers could pick them out of any promiscuous assembly at church or market. . . .

The common thief, or robber, or garrotter (thieves being the chief prisoners), have all a set of coarse, angular, clumsy, stupid set of features and dirty complexion. The women are all ugly in form and face and action, without the beauty of colour, or grace, or regularity of features, and all have a sinister and repulsive expression in look and mien. These remarks apply to the *habitues* who go out and into prison now and then, who live by crime, and have been born in crime, and of whom an accomplished writer says they are as distinctly marked off from the honest industrial operative as "black-faced sheep are from the Cheviot breed." . . .

The writer has visited the great prisons of England, Ireland, and Scotland; and in all these, the authorities, governors, chaplains, surgeons, and warders, concur in stating that prisoners, as a class, are of mean and defective intellect, generally stupid, and many of them weak minded and imbecile. . . .

Before the establishment of reformatories, I used to see daily some 40 or 50 juvenile prisoners being taught together, and they seemed very dull and stupid in taking up either secular or sacred knowledge. Their experienced teacher said of this class: "I consider that more than a third of these boys are of imbecile mind. They make little progress comparatively." . . .

I shall only add to this my own testimony as a Prison Surgeon, as to the mental condition of prisoners generally. Out of a population of 5,432 no less than 673 were placed on my registers as requiring care and treatment on account of their mental condition. The forms of mental disorder were—

Weak-mindedness or Imbecility in 580
Ditto and Suicidal 36
Epileptic 57

This table showed 12 percent. mentally weak in different degrees.

[The author points out that certain physical characteristics of different breeds of dogs are hereditary.] Habits got by training are transmitted to the offspring of certain breeds of dogs as their very nature. It is so in the wolf dog and the hound. . . . It is the same in certain castes and races and communities of the human family; and is the transmission of thieving and other criminal habits to form an exception to other analogies? . . .

The family history of criminals shows their hereditary tendencies as a class. This criminal biography is not very easily got at, for they are constantly changing their names . . . [cites numerous cases of multiple criminality in families.]

One of the leading characteristics in the natural history of hereditary depravity is the singular transmutation from physical to psychical diseases; and to diversities of these diseases, interchanging often with crime. . . .

Out of a prison population for ten years, amounting to 6,273, or 627 per annum, the percentage of criminal epileptics under my charge was 0.94, or nearly one per cent. per annum, very different from the army and civil populations of England, where the death-rate of epileptics is estimated at 0.009 per cent. only. There is, therefore, a great excess of epilepsy among criminals.

Insanity shows also a great excess, one out of 140 prisoners among the criminal population becoming insane in my experience.

[Out of 904 female convicts admitted to the General Prison for Scotland from Oct., 1855, to Dec. 1866, 440 were declared to be recidivists.] Such facts press it strongly on my mind that crime (in the general) is a moral disease of a chronic and congenital nature intractable in the extreme, because transmitted from generation to generation. "The fathers have eaten sour grapes, and the teeth of the children are set on edge." So says truly the Hebrew proverb. Is it to be marvelled at, if these premises are correct, that all modes of criminal treatment, severe or mild, have failed in giving any thing like satisfactory results? Is it strange that our criminal legislation has gone from one extreme to another, and been like the web of Penelope, a system of doing and undoing? We fail to wash the blackamoor white; we cannot raise the Negro character beyond a certain stage of improvement. The criminal hereditary *caste* and character, if changeable, must be changed slowly, and how to do it must be to sociologists and philanthropists always a *questio vexata,* one of the most difficult state problems.

I offer the following conclusions from the foregoing examen:—

1. That crime being hereditary in the criminal class, measures are called for to break up the caste and community of the class.

2. That transportation and long sentences of habitual criminals are called for in order to lessen the criminal offenders.

3. That old offenders can scarcely be reclaimed, and that juveniles brought under very early training are the most hopeful; but even these are apt to lapse into their hereditary tendency.

4. That crime is so nearly allied to insanity as to be chiefly a psychological study.

A New and Distinct Tribunal Proposed for Handling Children's Cases, 1873

[Benjamin Waugh],[1] *The Gaol Cradle. Who Rocks It?*
(London, 1873), pp. 64-65, 80-85 (Brit. Mus.)

1. Rev. Benjamin Waugh was a member of the School Board of London. For other examples of his interest in child welfare see his two articles "Baby-Farming," *Cont. Rev.* (May, 1890), pp. 700-14, and "Child-Life Insurance," *Cont. Rev.* (July, 1890), pp. 40-63.

A New Tribunal.—Correction Without Ruin.

Can there be any doubt that justice towards our juvenile offenders is seriously perverted through the want of a suitable tribunal of judgment?

Some seven thousand children are brought before the magistrates of London in a single year. The stake is sufficiently serious to demand careful attention.

Our convict prisons, it is believed by persons who at once have authority to speak and lack the liberty to do so, are supplied with a large proportion of their inmates from the juvenile victims of fatally unsuitable proceedings of law. . . .

Did you ever consider that big and little offenders are passed through the same courses of law; that a child of nine hears the bolt lock him in the same station cell, is bewildered by the same "so help you God," is handled by the same gigantic officials, and stands, or surely is held up, in the same dock, and looks upon the same solemn deputy of the Crown as a murderer! . . .

A New and Distinct Tribunal! This is the best device! A tribunal of citizens—men and women—superintendents of Sunday schools, teachers of day schools, if you will,—why not? Citizens whose functions should be magisterial, whose legal qualifications should be their ability to read the living literature of English children, whose Act of Parliament should be their own moral instincts, with the discretionary powers of a domestic *Habeas corpus ad satisfaciendum,—* above all, who had committed and had not forgotten the appetitive and pugnacious follies of youth, and could "Laugh them o'er again."

Cannot some way be devised which should make clear the merits of every act of child-crime, be sensitive to fair play, be alive to the common weal, regard a child as the father of a man, see him in wider, deeper, higher, more lasting relationship than his relationship to some pitiless, petti-fogging pastrycook, recklessly indifferent to everything in heaven, earth, and under the earth, but the loss of a twopenny pie!

Is it not time to let the ridiculously big name "Juvenile Crime" drop from our language, and the consequent hideous impersonation, a Juvenile Criminal, vanish from our fancy,—time to relieve the stealing of apples of the tremendous word which law thrusts upon it,—to drop the humbug of the legislative distinctions "Felonious Intent," "Misdemeanour," "Depredation," "Assault with intent to do grievous bodily harm," and all the rest of it?—to talk and act towards a young ragamuffin sensibly, at least as sensibly as we talk and act towards the more fortunate child of our homes? Might we not by a reasonable economy in hateful and degrading names economise in robbery of juvenile chances, in soured spirits, in perverted powers, in ghastly destinies? Is it not possible that by nicer names on the tongue might be achieved ends more just to the child, more loyal to the State?

Does it not occur to you that a hard-and-fast law against children's deeds, which we have thought proper to call crimes, is horribly ridiculous? Imagine, if it be not too absurd, a collier, born and living in the grimy caverns of a coal-pit, judged by some hard-and-fast penal law of cleanliness. Where, then, is the reasonableness of judging a child born in the caverns of a moral coal-pit by a hard-and-fast penal law of virtue? Can the irrational in the physical be rational in the moral? You can never deal fairly with such a child without ungrudging and generous allowance for circumstances —circumstances which he did not make, which he could not altogether nor always resist. Even a man is to a great extent the creature of his place. What then must be a plastic child? . . .

True, Blackstone might stop his ears at the following lines, but what of that? Can Blackstone create or annul the law of the nature of things? And is not that law one for Rulers of nations and rulers of households?

> He who checks a child in terror,
> Stops its play, or stills its song,
> Not alone commits an error,
> But a grievous moral wrong.
> Then give it play, and never fear it,
> Active life is not defect;
> Never, never break its spirit,
> Curb it only to direct.
> Would you stop the flowing river?
> Think you it would cease to flow?
> Onward it must go for ever,
> Better teach it where to go.

In the 3000 children which in one year you swept from the metropolis into gaols, you grossly disobeyed this common-sense teaching,—you ruled in face of fixed, forbidding moral laws. Of what avail will it be that you have Blackstone to back you when, as surely they must, those fixed moral laws arise to judgment?—laws which are no respecters of either parchments or persons, and exact to the uttermost farthing.

Fatal Consequences of Locking Up a Young Girl in a Gaol Cell in Midwinter, 1875

"The Imprisonment of Young Children," *The Howard Association, Annual Report, September, 1875,* p. 4 (Howard League Lib.)

One of the subjects which has claimed the Committee's special attention, of late, is the evil effect of the imprisonment of children of tender years. Some peculiarly painful instances of this evil led them to organise a Deputation to the Home Secretary to plead for an alteration of the existing practice in this matter . . . the Committee stated that—

"children of seven and eight years of age, the victims of privation and parental neglect, have recently been sent to prison for petty misdemeanours. This practice, while at first greatly tending to terrify a young child, soon leads to a familiarity with prison life, and to corruptions and evil communications, and brands him, perhaps permanently, with a cruel and ruinous stigma. Your Memorialists therefore submit the desirability of making it compulsory on Magistrates to commit all such young offenders to a Reformatory or Industrial School, *without previous imprisonment."* . . .

One of the recent instances of the kind adverted to by the Deputation, was that of a child of eight years, sent to prison for fourteen days, for petty theft, at Staleybridge. Another was that of a boy of seven years, sent to prison at Chipping Norton, for injuring a sixpenny lock. In a third case a child of *seven* years was sent to gaol for three months, for stealing fourpence and some sugar plums, at Worthing. Many other similar instances have occurred.

But one of the saddest in its results was that of Harriet Gilbert, a girl of thirteen, sentenced, in February last, to a month's imprisonment in Jersey, for receiving a few ounces of stolen butter from a playfellow. She had, however, committed some petty theft previously, and some of the newspaper accounts of her treatment were partially inaccurate. But this Association, after careful inquiry, learns that, in the main, the published statements were correct. Mr. John Sullivan, Notary Public of Jersey, informs the Secretary that the child did not even know that the butter had been stolen, and that immediately on learning that it was so, she took it to the police. She was then arrested, whilst the actual thief appears to have escaped any imprisonment. The accounts state that "the child was hurried to the gaol and locked up in a stone cell, 'lighted' by a narrow slit in a thick wall, and left there. Everything was cold; the air at this inclement season was frozen, the walls and floor were frozen; the food, they called it 'food,' was bread and water. The child speedily pined away, and died in about a fortnight." A local jury, strangely enough, returned a verdict of death "from natural causes"; whereupon a journalist remarks, "as if it was 'natural' in Jersey to immure a motherless girl in a cold cell, upon a stone floor, in ghost-haunted darkness,—natural thus to bury a child that, if cared for with common humanity, might have been indeed a mother to her motherless sisters and a useful member of society."

Use of Bail and Suspended Sentence as a Form of Probation, 1879

Edward W. Cox (Serjeant at Law), "May the Practice of Admitting to Bail upon Criminal charges and taking Recognizances for future Judgment and good Behaviour in lieu of Punishment upon first Convictions be advantageously extended?" *Transactions of the National Association for the Promotion of Social Science* (1879), pp. 314-18, 323 (UNC Lib.)

There is one other form of bail which I am desirous earnestly to commend. It is, after conviction and in lieu of punishment, to admit the prisoner to bail on recognizances to come up for judgment when called upon. I have in practice found this to be excellent treatment. It is not a discharge, but a suspension of punishment. It is the strongest possible incitement to good behaviour, for it is the strongest hold that can be put upon an offender. In practice it has worked to my entire satisfaction. I cannot say in how many cases I have adopted this course with first offenders, with young persons, with persons of past good character, and in mitigating circumstances. I have preserved no record of the number, but they must now be counted by hundreds. What has been the practical result? It has been necessary afterwards to call up for judgment *three* only—this means that only three have been, to the knowledge of the police, guilty of subsequent offences.

I need not say that this is the exercise of mercy in its best form, and I cannot too earnestly commend it to judges and magistrates who administer the criminal law. . . .

The Chairman (Mr. G. W. Hastings) in discussing Serjeant Cox's paper said:—

"With regard to what was, perhaps, a still more important question, namely, how far you could extend the principle of taking the recognizances of those who have been convicted, he was glad to say that, in the Summary Jurisdiction Act, which would come into operation on January 1, 1880, there was a salutary provision, the 16th Section, which would enable justices sitting in petty sessions to exercise their own discretion, and instead of inflicting punishment for an offence, to say to the person convicted, 'We will not send you to prison, we will not even fine you; but we shall require you to enter into recognizances for your future good behaviour.' Hitherto, the want of such a power had been one of the shortcomings of our criminal law."

Court Procedure in Scotland Should be Modified for Delinquent Children, 1880

Charles Scott, "What Changes Are Desirable in the Mode of Dealing with Juvenile Delinquency?"[1] *Transactions of the National Association for the Promotion of Social Science* (1880), pp. 361-66 (UNC Lib.)

Now what is the actual state of procedure in regard to juvenile panels? The habitual criminal is defended by learned counsel who are assigned to him by the court free of cost; he is tried deliberately and impartially by fifteen citizens chosen by lot from the respectable classes of the community; his interests are watched over by a judge of the Supreme Tribunal. But what of the child? The little fellow is hurried up before some petty court, perhaps before some magistrate, who may be just as well as merciful, but who is entirely untrained in weighing evidence, and may have hurried from his shop or his office to discharge the most delicate of duties. We do not know how matters generally stand in regard to giving notice to the parents or relatives, but we know that often no notice whatever is given, and a case occurred only recently, where a father heard for the first time, in reading the evening paper, of his boy being sent for five years to a reformatory, for an alleged offence committed in a public institution where he was an inmate. A complaint is read over to the child which he cannot possibly understand or at least appreciate, and if he does not ask for time, he is at once tried then and there. He has no defender assigned to him. He cannot possibly defend himself. A boy or girl cannot appreciate the facts which

1. This paper refers particularly to court procedure in Scotland.

either tell for or against them. They neither know what to state nor how to prove it if they did. The judge may and doubtless will do what he can to act as counsel for them, but he will attempt an impossibility, as he knows nothing of the facts except what the prosecution lays before him. The prosecutor goes through his dismal duty; a policeman or two step into the box, and prove the case, or are supposed to prove it; and often in a few minutes the little panel is a thief for once and for ever, and the evidence on which the conviction was based has passed away into the air, dissipated with the breath of the witnesses who gave it. All the judges in Great Britain and all the churches to boot cannot place the hapless creature where he was half an hour before. At the time probably he only fears the gaol, and cries bitterly as he enters its iron portals. It is only as he grows older that the more terrible consequences disclose themselves. As regards these most pitiable of all cases, the Supreme Criminal Tribunal, unless by good luck an error in law has been committed, and some one has taken the trouble to unearth it, is absolutely without a function. If the child had been old enough to have some paltry debt due to him, he would have had the matter tried before a professional judge highly educated and thoroughly trained. He would have had the evidence carefully recorded by a shorthand writer. He would have had the assistance of skilful professional advisers, and he might have appealed from any judgment against him, first to the sheriff, and after that to a division, consisting of four supreme judges. If the debt had been more considerable, he might have appealed still farther to the House of Lords. Such is the different regard paid in this country to property on the one hand, and to character, liberty, and position on the other.

He would be a bold man who, after sitting for a few days in a police court, would venture to affirm that an appreciable percentage of young children are not found guilty when they are innocent; and if such is the case, there is a serious evil which it is necessary to minimise as much as possible. But there is another remark which it is requisite to make in discussing the relation of children to the criminal law. It is often forgotten that the conceptions of a young boy or girl in regard to crime must necessarily be very different from those of a tolerably intelligent adult. They cannot possibly have any correct idea of its evil effects upon the State, or upon other citizens, or even upon themselves; conceptions which are so important in defining to the mature mind the character of crime, explaining its essence, and making its evil visible. In the immense majority of cases, even where the child has not been neglected, an offence against the law can only appear to his immature mind as something prohibited for reasons which altogether escape his powers of analysis. Further, it must be extremely difficult for any child, who in this respect, as in many others, is in a mental condition very analogous to that of uncivilised races, to realise the idea of property in articles which are not in the actual natural possession of the owner. If one were trying to stretch back his memory to the obscure times of his childhood, he would probably remember that in those distant days he had formed no distinct idea of property in anything which grew in an unenclosed field, and probably regarded the farmer, or his servants who frightened him away, as tyrants who held their vantage ground merely by the superiority of physical power. On the other hand, an untrained or uneducated child has no definite conceptions of crime at all, while many are actually taught to consider some offences, such as theft, as positively praiseworthy, and the means of assisting their parents to gain their daily bread. Considerations like these are apt to strike us with overpowering force when we read of a young boy or girl being sent fourteen days to gaol for stealing a turnip; and we at once recognise the imperative necessity of the intervention of the Home Secretary in such an abuse. Of course there always recur in regard to children the same considerations that have given rise to so much difficulty in the courts in regard to persons of weak mind—namely, that it is positively necessary to put a stop to criminal practices, and that wherever the mind is capable of being restrained by the terror of punishment, there is room for its application. At the same time it cannot and ought never to be forgotten that the law is bound on every principle of reason to deal with children in an entirely different way from that in which it deals with adults, and in this department of jurisprudence there is scope for a large modification both of principle and practice. This subject, however, as yet has been much neglected, the attention of law reformers having been mostly directed either to dealing with juveniles before they have come within the grasp of the law, or to their reformation after they have been convicted. There is room, however, for very important reforms in the intermediate region, when the public prosecutor has laid hands upon them, but has not yet obtained a conviction. In a short paper it is impossible to develop satisfactorily this subject, but one or two hints may be given.

In the first place, it is absolutely essential to enact, as matter of statutory law, that in all cases where young children are charged with crime, the complaint should be served upon their parents; or when they are dead, or cannot be found, upon the persons in whose guardianship they are. The attendance of those persons at all the stages of the prosecution should be positively insisted upon, and an inquiry should uniformly take place into the share which they or others may have had in the delinquency of the child. In a large percentage of cases it will be found that they have been really the guilty parties, and it should be put within the power of the judge to include them within the sentence, or even to dismiss the juvenile, and to pass sentence upon them alone. As poor children are at this moment almost always entirely unprotected in the inferior courts, where they generally appear, agents for the poor should be appointed for these, as for the other tribunals where they already exist though less required, and their official duty should be to attend to the interests of these helpless prisoners where they have no other representatives.

In almost no instance should a trial, properly so called, ever take place of a child for a first offence. In no case do the circumstances ever warrant the terrible consequences which inevitably follow, the results of which to society are even more prejudicial than they are to the delinquents themselves. Whenever there is no danger of absconding, apprehension should, if possible, be avoided, and the initial procedure should consist in a rigorous investigation into the facts of the case, and particularly into the position of the child at home, and the share, if any, which his parents or others, by connivance or neglect, may have had in the offence with which he is charged. If the panel's advisers desire it, the investigation might take place by the inferior judge, but if not, the matter should be at once remitted to and dealt with by the sheriff. This dealing should not be in the form of a public trial, with a solemn apparatus of prosecutor and witnesses. On the contrary, it should be more in the form of an investigation by the judge as the legal guardian of the prisoner. It should not be hampered or limited by technical rules, but should embrace the whole circumstances necessary to give a correct idea of the position of the child; and it should not be reportable by the public press. No conviction should follow on such an investigation; but the judge should, at the conclusion, be entitled to call the child and his parents or guardians before him at chambers, and as the representative of the State, which is the parent of the people, deal with both, if necessary, by a solemn and kindly warning. It should be made competent at this stage, if the judge should see cause, to give decree against the parents for the expense of the investigation, and a short official *resume* of the facts should be drawn up for future reference in case of that being necessary; but in no case should the document be considered as public or as open to anyone to be examined or extracted. It should also be competent for the judge in all cases of complexity or difficulty to consult with the Lord Justice General, or other judge of the Supreme Criminal Court whom he may appoint, and this court should be constituted the general guardian, protector, and adviser of all children who come within the scope of the courts of which it is the head. These eminent judges should be entitled in all cases to deal personally and privately with the panels and with their guardians. The only example we have at present of such close and friendly dealing on the part of a judge with young persons is that of the interviews of the Lord Chancellor of England with the wards under his guardianship. There can be no doubt of the important effect which such dealing would have, and by the procedure here described the utmost possible chance would be given, not merely for the reformation of a juvenile delinquent, but for an improved course of conduct in the case of those parties on whom he may be dependent. . . .

With regard to the youthful panel himself, a second appearance before a court for offences of dishonesty, or crimes which similarly taint the character, should be held as convincing evidence that parental discipline has failed, and that severe and continuous training is imperatively demanded. In that case the child should at once be despatched for a long period to some reformatory institution. He would thus become in every sense the child of the State, and be treated as such; and it ought entirely to depend on the character of the parents whether they can henceforth be recognised in that relation, or permitted to resume any control over their trained and emancipated children. This committal to an institution ought not, however, to be accompanied by any conviction against the boy or girl who is the subject of it, otherwise more than half of the benefit to be expected from it would be lost; and the judgment ought to be founded entirely upon the narrative that the step has been found expedient. Even the very name of Reformatory had better be eliminated, and that of Training or Educational Institution be substituted. Nothing should be placed upon record which can at any time be raked up to poison the future career of the wards of the nation, or to destroy the chance of their expected reformation.

The Secretary of State Requests Opinion of Local Officials on Methods of Handling Juvenile Offenders, 1881

Juvenile Offenders. Reports to the Secretary of State for the Home Department on the State of the Law Relating to the Treatment and Punishment of Juvenile Offenders (London, 1881), (Brit. Mus.)

CIRCULAR

Sent to Chairmen of Quarter Sessions, Recorders, Stipendiary Magistrates, Magistrates of Metropolitan Police Courts, and Borough Magistrates.

Whitehall, 22 October 1880

Sir,

I am directed by Secretary Sir William Vernon Harcourt to call your attention to the present state of the law concerning the treatment and punishment of Juvenile Offenders, both under the General Criminal Statutes, and the Reformatory and Industrial Schools Acts, and to request you to be so good as to consider in what way the law ought to be amended especially with a view to the prevention of imprisonment of young children, whether on remand or after conviction.

The Secretary of State would be glad to be favoured with your views on the subject at your earliest convenience.

I am, &c
(Signed)   GODFREY LUSHINGTON.

[The Report consists of the separate replies arranged alphabetically from England; and Wales; Scotland; Ireland; and certain foreign governments. No digest or summary is given nor any expression of opinion by the Secretary of State as to the effect of these widely varying replies.]

The "Massachusetts System" of Handling Juvenile Delinquents Given Wide and Favorable Publicity in England, 1880-1881

[A] "Juvenile Offenders," *The Howard Association, Annual Report, October, 1881*, pp. 3, 5 (Howard League Lib.)

One of the first objects to which the Committee of the Howard Association devoted their attention, after the issue of their last Annual Report, was the subject of the best mode of dealing with *Juvenile Crime*, both as to its prevention and repression. This question was brought prominently before the public in the autumn of 1880, by the Circulars issued by the Home Secretary, Sir William Vernon Harcourt, for the guidance of magistrates and prison officials, with a view to discourage, as far as possible, the imprisonment of children.

As this was a subject which the Association had previously brought before the notice of the Home Office on several occasions, by Deputations, and otherwise, the Committee were desirous to utilize the increased public attention now directed to the matter, by rendering assistance towards the solution of the difficulties of the question. With this view they availed themselves of the valuable aid of their foreign correspondents and friends in collecting information as to the most practicable and efficient means of dealing with Juvenile Offenders.

On a careful survey of what had been done in this direction in other countries, the Committee arrive at the conclusion that, on the whole, the most instructive foreign experience in this department is that afforded by the recent practice and legislation of the American State of *Massachusetts*.

Comprehensive reports of this experience, and of its results, were obtained from America, and placed in the hands of the Home Secretary, who informed the Association that he found this information very useful to him. It was further summarised in a handy form for general circulation, and for the newspaper press. The Committee were thus enabled to obtain for this system a wide publicity through important journals, and otherwise. They have received gratifying assurances from competent authorities, of the utility of their endeavours in this direction. Public acknowledgments, also, of this utility, were made through the press, by Sir Charles E. Trevelyan and by Sir Walter Crofton . . . who has long devoted special attention to Juvenile Crime. . . .

[The Report describes the Massachusetts plan of providing for individual visitation, by state-appointed officers, of the parents or friends, of children who are either offenders, or in danger of becoming such—using *voluntary* effort if possible; if not *compulsory* means of persuasion. "He can bring the child at once before a court and obtain a sentence of 'Probation' for a certain period, by which the child is formally placed under the oversight and discretion of the State Agent. But even in this stage, further compulsion is deferred until it becomes absolutely necessary. For it is not found needful, in actual practice, *to remove from their homes* more than *one-fifth* of the children thus sentenced to 'Probation.'" The belief was expressed that "the general principles of State Agency for home visitation, and of 'Probation,' would be very valuable, if adopted here."]

As to the imprisonment of young children, the Committee cannot but view with satisfaction the progress made in public opinion, by the authorities generally, and by recent legislation, in the direction of substituting other modes of treatment in place of the gaol for this class of offenders. . . .

There now appears to be a general agreement on the part of the Home Office, the magistracy, and persons who have studied the question, that the imprisonment of children under the age of *twelve* years should be absolutely abolished.

[B] "Applicability of the Massachusetts Principle to Great Britain," *Juvenile Offender* ([London: Howard Association], 1881), p. 4 (Howard League Lib.)

The principle of the Massachusetts mode of dealing with Juvenile Offenders, and with their *parents,* might be adopted, in this country, without necessarily involving the use of precisely the same measures. Thus, instead of appointing a series of additional officers throughout the kingdom, as State Juvenile Agents, the services of existing officers might be effectually utilised. One *Magistrate* in each parish, or locality, might be requested by the Home Secretary to devote his sole attention to Juvenile Offenders. And in each place, this Magistrate should have one or more *Policemen,* or, better still, one or more Volunteer Helpers, placed under his orders, with the object of watching over the cases of any criminal or neglected children in the locality specially requiring *authoritative influence.* The chief purpose would be, in the first place, to give the parents or relatives of the said children such oversight or guidance as might enable them to discharge their responsibilities aright, and to *avoid* the necessity for further compulsion. But persuasions failing, fines or other compulsory influences would have to be used. If these proved insufficient, the Magistrate should be empowered to have recourse, at his discretion, and according to the circumstances of each child, to boarding out, or emigration, or an industrial school, or a reformatory, or, as a *last* resort only, to imprisonment.

Juvenile Prostitution in London, 1881

Report from the Select Committee of the House of Lords on the Law Relating to the Protection of Young Girls; Together with the Proceedings of the Committee, Minutes of Evidence, and Appendix (Session 1881 [London], Ordered to be printed 26th July 1881), pp. 62-64, 76, 92 (editor's lib.)

[TESTIMONY OF MR. C. E. HOWARD VINCENT, DIRECTOR OF CRIMINAL INVESTIGATION, LONDON, JULY 19, 1881]

567. [Chairman] Has your attention been called to the subject generally of juvenile prostitution in London?

Very much so indeed.

568. Using the term "juvenile" to apply to the prostitution of girls under 21, does it prevail largely in London?

In no city in Europe to so large an extent, in my opinion.

569. Down to what age?

Down to the statutory limit of 13; there is no protection in the present state of the law for girls over 13 years of age. . . .

579. [Chairman] To return to the subject of juvenile prostitution, where are these children of 13 years and upwards, found?

There are houses in London, in many parts of London, where there are people who will procure children for the purposes of immorality and prostitution, without any difficulty whatsoever above the age of 13, children without number at 14, 15, and 16 years of age. Superintendent Dunlap will tell you that juvenile prostitution is rampant at this moment, and that in the streets about the Haymarket, Waterloo Place, and Piccadilly, from nightfall there are children of 14, 15, and 16 years of age, going about openly soliciting prostitution. Now it constantly happens, and I believe in the generality of cases it is so, that these children live at home; this prostitution actually takes place with the knowledge and connivance of the mother and to the profit of the household. I am speaking of some facts within my own knowledge, from hearsay, of course, but I have no reason whatever to doubt them. These procureurses, or whatever you may call them, have an understanding with the mother of the girl that she shall come to that house at a certain hour, and the mother perfectly well knows for what purpose she goes there, and it is with her knowledge and connivance, and with her consent that the girl goes.

580. You speak of these children being found in great numbers in the streets; do they issue out from their own houses?

I could not say where they come from. The great majority of

them live at home, I understand, with their fathers and mothers, and the proceeds of their prostitution are devoted to the expenses of the household. They form part of the receipts of the family; at least so I am given to understand on very good authority. . . .

591. [Chairman] Do you know whether the police are able to trace these children as they get older, and to know what becomes of them?

I am afraid not. The police are absolutely powerless as regards prostitution in London.

592. With regard to children of this age, or any age, who are soliciting prostitution in the streets, have the police no power at all?

No power whatever.

593. [Lord Aberdare] Only to keep order?

Only to keep order; and the consequence is that the state of affairs which exists in this capital is such that from four o'clock, or one may say from three o'clock in the afternoon, it is impossible for any respectable woman to walk from the top of the Haymarket to Wellington-street, Strand. From three or four o'clock in the afternoon, Villiers-street and Charing Cross Station, and the Strand, are crowded with prostitutes, who are there openly soliciting prostitution in broad daylight. At half-past 12 at night, a calculation was made a short time ago that there were 500 prostitutes between Piccadilly Circus and the bottom of Waterloo-place.

594. Open solicitation in the streets is an offence against the law, is it not?

Yes, it is an offence, but the police are powerless to do anything, because it must be to the annoyance and obstruction of passengers, and no respectable person is willing to go into a police court and say they were solicited by prostitutes. . . .

[TESTIMONY OF MR. JOSEPH DUNLAP, SUPERINTENDENT OF THE C. DIVISION OF THE METROPOLITAN POLICE]

715. [Chairman] Do you agree . . . in saying that there is a great deal of juvenile prostitution in the district with which you are more particularly acquainted?

I do.

716. When you use the term "juvenile," what ages do you speak of particularly?

I should say as young as 12 years of age; I should be quite within the bounds of prudence in saying so. Some of them are quite children that are soliciting prostitution in my division. . . .

718. Generally speaking, where is the prostitution carried on?

In the brothel; there is a low description of brothel in my division [St. James's district], where the children go. I had a warrant to execute a short time ago, to arrest some brothel keepers, and I went with my chief inspector, and in each of the rooms in that house I found an elderly gentleman in bed with two of these children. I asked their ages, and got into conversation with them. They knew perfectly well that I could not touch them in the house; and they laughed and joked me, and I could not get any direct answer whatever. I questioned them, in the presence of the brothel-keeper, as to what they had paid, and so on. They were to receive 6s. each from the gentleman, two of them; and the gentlemen had paid 6s. each for the room. It was 4s. if there was only one girl, but 6s. if there were two girls for the room. The brothel-keeper was committed for trial. . . .

[TESTIMONY OF MR. WILLIAM HARDMAN CHAIRMAN OF THE QUARTER SESSIONS FOR SURREY]

915. [Chairman] Have you any knowledge whatever of any traffic in young girls between this country and the Continent?
Not the slightest. I may say that I have formed a very strong opinion that there is great demoralization amongst the lower classes which leads to the prostitution of young girls. I can see how evil influences are early brought to bear upon them; and there are assaults committed upon them in many cases by their own near relations, by brothers and even by fathers; and on the whole, the life of a great number of these children must be one of very great demoralization.
916. Which leads to their becoming prostitutes?
Yes.
917. Do you consider that that is due to overcrowding?
Yes, to a great degree.
918. [Chairman] Overcrowding in their houses?
Yes, by sleeping in the same room, and performing the offices of nature in the presence of each other.

Special Court for Hearing Juvenile Cases in Adelaide, South Australia, 1890

Reformatory and Refuge Journal, 1891, 1892, 1893 (London) p. 258 (Brit. Mus.) Bound in a single volume.

The Secretary to the Department for Neglected Children and Reformatory Schools, Victoria, Australia, gives the following account of the Special Juvenile Court held at Adelaide, and which was established there in 1890:—

"The only persons present in the court besides the adjudicating Magistrate or Justices, the clerk of the court and the children to be dealt with, were the parents, an officer of police and one of the visiting officers of the Department, by whom the court was advised of the general aspects of each case, as well as of the result of the enquiries instituted since the date of arrest or remand.

"Where these enquiries were in any case not conclusive, the children were remanded until the next court (these are held frequently, often twice a week), and were handed over in the meantime to the care of the Department and placed in a receiving depot contiguous to the Secretary's office.

"The Magistrates commended the working of the new system, as did the Minister of Education, who took great interest in the experiment. The officers of the Department spoke in strongest terms of its benefits (this after nearly a year's trial), and stated that under no circumstances would a reversion to the old method of dealing with the children's cases in the ordinary police court be entertained." . . .

English Reformatories and Industrial Schools, 1894

Gertrude M. Tuckwell, *The State and Its Children* (London, 1894), pp. 2-21 (Brit. Mus.)

CHAPTER I. REFORMATORIES AND INDUSTRIAL SCHOOLS.

Changes in the Present Day.—The proportion of children now sent to prison is much smaller than it was. Education has done much for little criminals; it has become a platitude to point out that a Board School now stands on the site of Clerkenwell gaol. Besides this, the sentences passed on children are much lighter than they were, and a check is exercised on the Magistrates by a report of their sentences being sent in to the Home Office by the Prison Boards. Here the Magistrate's sentence is sometimes overruled. As an instance, I will quote the case of a boy sentenced to a month's imprisonment for stealing fruit, whose term of imprisonment was changed from a month to seven days by a mandate from the Home Office. There is also a growing tendency, which finds its best expression in the Australian Laws regarding children, and in those of some of the American States, to make grave distinctions between the treatment of juvenile and adult criminals; and the practice of long terms of imprisonment for children is becoming unpopular. The practice of flogging nevertheless still obtains, and not long ago a policeman told me, with relish, that he had birched as many as 60 boys on a single day at one Assizes.

One outcome of the tendency I have mentioned may be found in the creation of Reformatories. When a Magistrate sends a child to prison for more than ten days, he may also order that the child shall afterwards spend a certain time in a Reformatory School. A Reformatory is a School for the better training of youthful offenders, certified by the Secretary of State, under the "Reformatory School Act." More than fifty years ago some ladies and gentlemen started a Reformatory School at Stretton on Dunsmore in Warwickshire. Their example proved infectious: Reformatory Schools were started in nearly every English County, and were placed under Government inspection. But these Schools, depending as they did on voluntary subscriptions for support, were soon hampered for want of means, and an Act was passed by Lord Palmerston's agency, giving grants to them. These grants are given to all those Reformatory Schools, which, having been inspected by H. M. Inspector of Reformatories, are certified by him as being fitted for the purpose of receiving criminal children. The certificate can be withdrawn at any time by Government if the School become inefficient, and with its withdrawal the grant ceases. The Treasury grant covers about two-thirds of the cost of maintaining the children. The other third is supplied by voluntary subscription, industrial work, charges on parents, and, in some cases, by Poor Law Guardians and prison Boards.*

Committal to a Reformatory can only follow on imprisonment. When a child, that is to say, anyone under the age of sixteen years, is convicted of an offence punishable with penal servitude or imprisonment, and is sentenced to be imprisoned for ten days or longer, the Magistrate may also sentence him to be sent at the expiration of his term of imprisonment to a Reformatory, for a period varying at the Magistrate's option from two to six years. Let me take an individual instance to show the course which is pursued with young criminals, such an instance as is typical of the stories of children in our Reformatories:—

*See *Reformatory Act,* 1866.

A little London *gamin* of thirteen years old, from the district of Wandsworth, is caught stealing a coat and a pair of shoes, and is taken by the policeman to the nearest Police Station. Attached to the Station is a large cell. The boy's relations will probably bail him out, guaranteeing that he shall appear next day at the Police Court to answer to the charge against him. If, however, they do not, he will pass the night in the cell in company with the drunken brawlers or any other offenders who have been "run in." Early next morning he will be taken with his companions in the prison van, driven and guarded by policemen, to the Court. Here he will wait till his turn comes and his case is heard. The evidence against him is then produced, and the Magistrate sentences him to twenty-one days in Wandsworth gaol, to be followed in this case by four years detention in a Reformatory. Here I must add that if our imaginary culprit had been under ten years of age, he could not have been sentenced to a Reformatory unless there were previous convictions against him.

I have given twenty-one days as the sentence which precedes the Reformatory in this case. These sentences vary usually from terms of ten to twenty-one days. As instances I will take at random:—"For stealing a coat and a pair of shoes, twenty-one days;"—"an inkstand and three books, twenty-one days;"—"stealing one shilling, ten days."

Choice of Reformatory School by Magistrate.—In the choice of a School the Magistrate must be largely guided by the child's religion. If the boy is a Catholic, he must be sent to a Catholic Reformatory; or if for any reason this is inconvenient, provision is made that a minister of the child's persuasion shall visit him in the school selected. Great attention is given to this point, and if by any chance the child be sent to a School not conducted in accordance with its religion, it can be removed on the application of its parents or guardians to another chosen by them, if the managers of such a School consent.

Seriousness of the offence also influences the decision as to choice of a Reformatory, for the Schools are to some extent graded. The admirable School at Wandsworth for example, is filled almost entirely with children who have committed but one offence; while the School at Redhill takes boys whose characters are more seriously compromised.

The situation of the School has also to be taken into account: a

School in London, for instance, does not open its doors willingly to children from its own neighbourhood, while many country Reformatories are glad to have London children.

Previous Twenty-one Days in Prison.—The child is in the first instance, as we have said, committed by the Magistrate to the prison of the district. In the case of the child which I have taken, this would be Wandsworth gaol. He is taken from the Police Court by a policeman to the gaol. Arrived at the prison, he is thoroughly washed and cleansed; his hair cut, and the prison uniform put on him. He is then placed in the cell where the greater part of his time in prison will be spent. The cells are, in many cases, much pleasanter places than their name would suggest. In this particular prison, the small, airy, well-lighted rooms open off long galleries, which lead into the main part of the prison. In the boy's little room is a narrow bed with a plank for bedstead, there is a little table at which he takes his meals, and a stool to sit on. In the corner there are three shelves on which rest his mug, his Bible, and a brush and comb; and against the wall leans a brightly polished basin, with a can beside it. His day is spent in picking rope into oakum; but meal times, chapel, school, and exercise vary this employment. Every morning the prisoners assemble in chapel, and here in the front seats the boys sit together. Talking is forbidden, but now and then a surreptitious whisper is overheard: "I say, Jim, how much longer have you got?" Exercise lasts for an hour every day, when the boys walk up and down the prison yard. For an hour, too, school lasts. The school-room, a large bare room, with long tables and benches on either side, has little in common with the Board School which our boy probably previously attended, full of pictures, apparatus, and diagrams. It is innocent of decoration, except for a very large table of the Ten Commandments, which with poetic justice for ever faces the poor little law-breaker. And the teaching differs from ordinary teaching as does the School. The boy's lessons are confined to reading and writing; blackboard illustrations, and object lessons, are conspicuous by their absence. His food, though very plain, is plentiful enough: it consists principally of bread, potatoes, oatmeal, and soup, with meat once a week at least. The term of his imprisonment over, the child's uniform is taken from him, and he again puts on the dress he wore when he came. Then he is sent off in charge of a Warder to the School which has been agreed on for his destination. Here he is delivered up by the Gaoler to the Superintendent of the School.

Life in Reformatory.—Probably in their first interview the Superintendent will talk seriously with the child, pointing out to him that his prison experience has been the punishment for his fault; that a chance is now given him to reform, and that by carefully learning a trade in the next few years, he will be able to earn an honest livelihood on leaving the Reformatory, and clear his character from stain. But the first few weeks are a trying time for the poor little criminal, his experience of discipline and routine having most likely been confined to school attendance, which he evaded as much as possible. It must be terrible to exchange the freedom of country life, or—still more exciting—the fascinations of the streets, the games in the gutter, the bustle and stir of traffic, for the machine-like regularity of the school. Cases of absconding from these Schools occur almost exclusively among new comers. After a time the monotony of the life becomes a habit, and the boy settles down to work.

He sleeps in a great dormitory with perhaps forty other children, overlooked by an officer; rises at six, and dresses silently beside his bed. At a given signal prayers are said, and the boys troop downstairs to begin their day's work. Part of his time is spent in school, and his position there will be decided by his previous attainment, for the School is classified like an ordinary Elementary School, though less teaching is attempted, as so large a proportion of time must be given to Industrial work. This latter work will at first be simple; he will be put probably to wood chopping; afterwards, as hand and eye become to some extent trained, he will choose a skilled trade: he may learn tailoring, shoe-making, mat-making, or carpentering, or, if the School has a farm attached to it, he may be able to learn farm-work; to till the fields, and tend the cows and sheep. He will do his share of housework, and will help at times in the laundry or kitchen, scrub the floor, and lay the table. If he is at all musical, there will probably be a School band which he can join. In order to give an idea of the buildings and apparatus which are used for Reformatories, I will shortly describe the capital School at Wandsworth.

The large block which contains the living rooms and dormitories houses about 170 boys. The windows of the pleasant rooms look across the Common, where the boys are allowed once a week to play, often without supervision. The long school-room contains a lending library and a collection of games with which the boys amuse themselves in their leisure time. At the back of the block of dwelling rooms is a courtyard, round which run the workshops, and woodsheds, with a balcony on the second story into which the doors of the shops open. In the shops and yard, in the woodsheds and Engine rooms, the boys are hard at work, many of the busiest without surveillance—yet everywhere there is an atmosphere of zeal and interest in the work and of general healthy tone, to which one found a key in the cordial feeling apparent between boys and Superintendent.

The Industrial School.—We now turn from the Reformatory, peopled with criminal children under sixteen years of age, who have undergone more than 10 days imprisonment, to the Industrial School, to which are sent children under twelve, "charged with an offence punishable by imprisonment, but not previously convicted of felony." No previous imprisonment is necessary in the case of children committed under the Industrial School Act, though they are sent to the Schools by a Magistrate's order.

The inhabitants of Industiral Schools are not, however, limited to the criminal children just mentioned. To them children found begging are sent, not only the children who actually run after passers-by for coppers, but those also whose ingenious relations have furnished them with a match box or a couple of leather boot laces as a pretext to cover their petition for alms. Vagrant children can be sent to an Industrial School. In a London School I saw a little fellow of three years old who had been found wandering in Hyde Park at night. He was the pet of the School, and a remarkable contrast to the coarse, dissolute-looking woman, who appeared one day to claim him.

Children whose parents are undergoing imprisonment are sent to these Schools. At one Industiral School—the Cottage Homes at Addlestone—I visited two cottages specially set apart for the youngest children. They were outside playing in the garden, but when the Cottage Mother clapped her hands, they came running to her and paraded themselves in a little row for my inspection; their ages ranged from three or four upwards, and one at least of them was only 18 months old when it first came to the School. Children, again, who frequent the company of reputed thieves or of common or reputed prostitutes, are sent to Industrial Schools, as are children found unmanageable in Workhouse or pauper Schools, and those whose parents or guardians represent that they are unable to control them. With regard to the last class, however, great discretion is exercised lest unworthy parents or guardians who wish to be saved trouble should take advantage of this clause in order to foist their duties on the shoulders of the State. The sum paid by the Treasury towards the support of this class is small, so that if parents choose to transfer responsibility they may not escape the support of their children as well. Under the Education Act one other class of children, the Truants for whom there is no available Day Industrial School, may be sent here, and a wise law, too seldom put in force, gives power to commit to an Industrial School any child who is found living in the company of prostitutes.

School Boards and Industrial Schools.—Under most circumstances the foundation of these Schools is due to private effort, but in some cases Prison Authorities or School Boards contribute money to build or maintain them. The School Boards avail themselves largely of this power—in every large town the Board has an Industrial School Committee and Industrial Schools of its own: it employs officers to assist the police in bringing delinquents before it; it investigates cases, selects schools for the children sentenced, and, as I have said above, pays towards their maintenance. In London the School Board keeps up the "Shaftesbury," a splendid training ship at the mouth of the Thames, and has established the school at Brentwood to which the poor little deformed children, among others, are sent. This class of children is avoided by most Schools, for those belonging to it are often incapable of doing their share of Industrial work, and so are a heavy expense to an Institution which cannot fall back on the Rates. Besides the payments made by the School Boards, the Industrial Schools have the same sources of income as the Reformatories, and are certified in the same manner by Her Majesty's Inspector.

The story of a candidate for an Industrial School differs little from that of the Reformatory child, except for the absence in the first case of the preliminary imprisonment. During the period which elapses before a School is decided on for the child, it will remain in the Workhouse, and thence it will be sent to the Industrial School.

Life in Industrial Schools.—Life in an Industrial School resembles in a measure the life of a Reformatory, but the children are of course younger, and as a rule more innocent, so that a less strict discipline is necessary. In a well ordered school such as the Shaftesbury the restraints imposed differ little from those of an ordinary School. The little ones will rise perhaps at 6:30, and the work of the house will then commence. About 8 will come breakfast, laid by some of the children and prepared by others in the kitchen. After breakfast half of the children will probably go to the Schoolroom for 3 hours' lessons, while the other half are busy with Industrial work. But there is no regulation as to the time at which the necessary work in school is put in, so that in some schools one day may be given to Industrial work and the next to school, though the commonest division of time is that which I gave first. After dinner the children would change: those who were in School in the morning taking their places at Industrial work in the afternoon, while those who have cleaned and swept in the morning go in to the School-rooms for three hours' educational afternoon work. Some part of the day will be set aside for play, to be spent by the children on fine days in the play-yard and on wet days probably in a covered yard or play-ground. In a boys' school cricket, football, or prisoner's base will be played, while in a girls' school the elder girls will, perhaps, tend the little gardens set apart for them in the better schools, while the little ones skip or play with their dolls or toys. In the Industrial School as in the Reformatory the girls have but a limited choice for their life's occupation as compared with that of the boys: it is confined to domestic service or laundry work, both of which from the nature of the materials to work on must be imperfectly taught. A system of rewards in money obtains both in Reformatory and Industrial Schools, and in girls' schools as in boys', so that by good conduct a child may accumulate a small sum for the time when its period of detention shall be over. The children will not necessarily be confined entirely within the School precincts; the more trustworthy are allowed by the Superintendent to go out on errands, to fetch and take back the linen, when, as in the case of many Schools, private work is taken in, and also to make little purchases for the less privileged children within the building.

Dietary in Reformatory and Industrial Schools.—The children's food will be simple enough, probably coffee or cocoa with eight or ten ounces of bread for breakfast and for supper, with butter, treacle, or dripping to make the meal appetizing. The dietary table varies within certain limits in some Schools: meat only appears three times a week on the children's dinner table, while the healthy look of the Wandsworth boys may possibly be accounted for by the fact that they have meat always five times a week, and sometimes six. Bread and vegetables form part of the mid-day meal, and on days when no meat is given, soup, cheese, or suet pudding take its place.

Rewards, Holidays, and License.—The children's incentives to well-doing take a practical form; for not only will School decorations and promotion follow good conduct, but the marks will be valued at a money rate, and in some Schools the tasks done in the shops are also valued, and money paid for them. Some of this money the children are allowed to spend when out on leave, but the greater part of it is kept for them, and only paid over when they have left the School, and are doing well in their work. In some Schools the boys can earn as much as 2/6 a week by their exertions, so that on starting in life they have a useful sum to fall back upon. The system of diminishing misbehaviour by systematic reward of merit seems efficient in Industrial Schools as in Reformatories, and as satisfactory in its results in girls' schools as in boys'. The necessity for corporal punishment is minimized by the system of rewards.

The time spent in these Schools is not necessarily unbroken by a holiday. Some Superintendents adopt the plan of allowing children, who by systematic good conduct have earned a reward, to return for regular holidays to their friends. During this period they are of course out on license, and must return to the School at the period fixed or incur a heavy penalty. In some town Schools the need for change is still further recognized, and the children spend yearly a summer fortnight in the country or at the sea. A large number of the boys from the Feltham school camp out in the beautiful country near Chertsey every year. These are the boys who have chosen the Merchant Service as their profession, and they may be seen pulling in their big boat up and down the Thames.

After children have spent eighteen months in the School the Superintendent may let them go out on license. If their homes are desirable they may be allowed to return to them, or the Superintendent may apprentice them to some trade and allow them to live with their employer, but in both cases the license may at any time be recalled, and the children must then return to School. . . .

Result of Reformatory and Industrial Training.—It may be as well to give the number of children who left our Schools of Detention in a particular year, and the manner in which they were disposed of. I will take first the Reformatories. 1495 children left these Schools in 1891, of whom 1158 found employment in trades or service, the three Reformatory Training ships sent 168 boys to sea, and 14 boys enlisted. Emigration to be carried out successfully is expensive, children must be sent out to secured situations, or through costly agencies, for if they emigrate without a situation being found for them, they nearly always return at the earliest opportunity, and so only 82 children were disposed of by Emigration. Thirty children had to be discharged from disease, five were incorrigible, and twenty-seven died. The returns show that of the boys discharged from Reformatory Schools during the years '88, '89, '90, 78% were doing well as against 2% doubtful, 14% reconvicted and

6% unknown, and that of the girls 76% were doing well, 8% doubtful, 5% reconvicted, and 11% unknown.

Meanwhile 3964 children left the Industrial Schools of England and Scotland in 1891; 129 emigrated, 450 went to sea, 99 enlisted. Besides these, 87 were discharged as diseased, 39 had to be sent to Reformatories from Industrial Schools, 105 died, and 28 absconded.

The percentage taken on those who have passed through their entire term of Industrial School life, deducting that is to say those who have been committed to Reformatories or discharged for disease, gives 86% successes in after-life. I give the official returns, but it must be remembered that the absence of any power of after-supervision on the part of the managers or School authorities renders these returns misleading. It is impossible to render accurate returns as to the future of children who are in a great number of cases altogether lost sight of.

Drawbacks to the Reformatory and Industrial School Systems.— Schemes which register so many of their children as doubtful or criminal in after-life leave something yet to be desired, and one queries whether an examination of their features will not reveal some points open to improvement. The first point which occurs to one is an initial flaw. It is recognized that a strong line divides adult and juvenile criminals, and the Reformatories were founded to dissociate children from the influence of mature delinquents. Yet the principle which is recognized in the eventual mode of their detention is ignored at the commencement. The child who is to be separated from the adult in the School is thrown into his or her company in the Police Court and the Station; and the Reformatory, which is built to deliver the child from prolonged imprisonment, can only be arrived at by three weeks in gaol. There are drawbacks also to the present lengthy residence in the School itself. The practice of keeping children for years in an institution and sending them thence into the world at the expiration of their sentence, from a state of strict discipline to perfect freedom, is open to serious objections. There is a growing feeling that confinement in these Schools is, in itself, a drastic measure to be employed in the case of extremely depraved or insubordinate children alone, and then if possible only for the probationary term required to fit them for family life. If the Industrial School has escaped the drawback of prior imprisonment, it has, nevertheless, a considerable number of faults, and not the least would seem to be its difficulties in the way of classification. It is curious to note the various classes of children which may be huddled together under the same roof. However desirable it may be to remove a child from parents who permit it to beg, it is not of necessity sufficiently depraved to be a proper companion for the child whose days have been spent in the company of women of ill-fame. The child who is too unruly to submit to the management of Workhouse authorities is not certain therfore to be an improving companion for the little one who has no fault save helplessness or destitution. It is difficult to see what many of these children have done to fit them to come under Home Office jurisdiction; they seem to be proper subjects for the Local Government Board; and one would like to see them restored to some sort of family life by being included in the Boarding-out recommendations for orphan and deserted children. . . .

We turn now to the work of the shops. The time devoted by the girls to Industrial work is, as usual, divided between domestic and laundry work, while many of the boys spend their time in occupations which must ultimately be of no service to them. If the Industrial training is to be of any use, it must fit the children for the earning of an honest livelihood; yet I question whether many of the trades taught fit them to earn any livelihood at all. Sack-making for instance is a trade in which men are not employed; basket-making and paper-bag-making are both of them occupations for women. The manufacture of match-boxes yields starvation wages, even when whole families are engaged at it. Hair-teasing and paper-box-making are neither of them paying trades, even if they were men's trades at all, which they are not. All these occupations are taught at various Schools, joined with an amount of wood-cutting, and faggot-making, which must bid fair, one fancies, to destroy all the trees in England.

In some cases the choice of the trades seems to be the result of sheer stupidity; in others, the poverty of the Schools leads them, I imagine, to eke out their finances by working at some employment which fills the school coffers, though useless afterwards to the boys. In one School where there are 75 boys, it appears from the Report that about 9 are learning a trade which will eventually be productive of a livelihood. Rope and twine-making is also practised at some Schools, and it is difficult to believe that rope-making can be practised so as to be a training of much utility, for the rope-walks in Factories are of such immense length as could hardly be compassed in Industrial or Reformatory Schools.

It is a valid reproach against many Schools and Institutions, voluntary or otherwise, that they aid in reducing wages by underselling outside workers. I found one instance of this in a Reformatory which supplied a London firm with mats at a comparatively nominal charge, because the firm provided the material on which the boys of the Reformatory were taught.

Another abuse which obtains in some Schools is the direct encouragement of the pernicious system of children's half-time work in Mills and Factories by the employment of the school boys as half-timers in a neighbouring Mill. As will be seen when I come to treat of the competition of half-timers, the system is not one which should be encouraged by the instrumentality of State-aided Schools. And lastly the powerlessness of the Managers to exercise any supervision over the children at the expiration of their sentence is a matter to be deplored. Some surveillance during the difficult years of opening manhood is most necessary for these children whose natural protectors have failed them.

Psychological Effect of Imprisonment on Young Children Described by Oscar Wilde, 1897

Oscar Wilde, "The Case of Warder Martin," *London Daily Chronicle*, May 28, 1897 (Brit. Mus.)

The Editor of the Daily Chronicle—

Sir—I learn with great regret, through the columns of your paper, that the warder Martin, of Reading Prison, has been dismissed by the Prison Commissioners for having given some sweet biscuits to a little hungry child. . . . They were quite small children, the youngest—the one to whom the warder gave the biscuits—being a tiny little chap, for whom they had evidently been unable to find clothes small enough to fit it. I had, of course, seen many children in prison during the two years during which I was myself confined. Wandsworth Prison, especially, contained always a large number of children. But the little child I saw on the afternoon of Monday, the 17th, at Reading, was tinier than any one of them. . . . The cruelty that is practiced by day and night on children in English prisons is incredible, except to those that have witnessed it and are aware of the brutality of the system. . . .

The present treatment of children is terrible, primarily from people not understanding the peculiar psychology of a child's nature. A child can understand a punishment inflicted by an individual, such as a parent or guardian, and bear it with a certain amount of acquiescence. What it cannot understand is a punishment inflicted by society. . . .

Every child is confined to its cell for twenty-three hours out of the twenty-four. This is the appalling thing. To shut up a child in a dimly-lit cell for twenty-three hours out of the twenty-four, is an example of the cruelty of stupidity. If an individual, parent or guardian, did this to a child, he would be severely punished. The Society for the Prevention of Cruelty to Children would take the matter up at once. There would be on all hands the utmost detestation of whomsoever had been guilty of such cruelty. A heavy sentence would, undoubtedly, follow conviction. But our own actual society does worse itself, and to the child to be so treated by a strange abstract force, of whose claims it has no cognisance, is much worse that it would be to receive the same treatment from its father or mother, or someone it knew. . . . Most warders are very fond of children. But the system prohibits them from rendering the child any assistance. Should they do so, as Warder Martin did, they are dismissed.

The second thing from which a child suffers in prison is hunger. The food that is given to it consists of a piece of usually badly-baked prison bread and a tin of water for breakfast at half-past seven. At twelve o'clock it gets dinner, composed of a tin of coarse Indian meal stirabout, and at half-past five it gets a piece of dry bread and a tin of water for its supper. This diet in the case of a strong man is always productive of illness of some kind, chiefly of course diarrhoea, with its attendant weakness. In fact in a big prison astringent medicines are served out regularly by the warders as a matter of course. In the case of a child, the child is, as a rule, incapable of eating the food at all. Anyone who knows anything about children knows how easily a child's digestion is upset by a fit of crying, or trouble and mental distress of any kind. A child who has been crying all day long, and perhaps half the night, in a lonely dimly-lit cell, and is preyed upon by terror, simply cannot eat food of this coarse, horrible kind. In the case of the little child to whom Warder Martin gave the biscuits, the child was crying with hunger on Tuesday morning, and utterly unable to eat the bread and water served to it for its breakfast. Martin went out after the breakfasts had been served and bought the few sweet biscuits for the child, who, utterly unconscious of the regulations of the Prison Board, told one of the senior warders how kind this junior warder had been to him. The result was, of course, a report and a dismissal.

[Wilde cites other instances of Martin's kindliness to prisoners.

He says the whole prison system contaminates the child, not the prisoners, who are kind hearted and sympathetic to them.]

The Howard Association Issues a Circular of Inquiry on the Causes and Remedies of Juvenile Offences, 1898

[A] *The Howard Association Annual Report, Oct., 1898*, pp. 4-5 (Howard League Lib.)

JUVENILE OFFENDERS AND "ROUGHS"

A marked social feature, during the past year, has been an outburst of juvenile ruffianism in certain localities and in the Metropolis. The newspapers have recorded, day after day, numbers of intolerable, and occasionally even fatal outrages upon unoffending citizens, especially on women and children, committed by gangs of young roughs, armed with belts, bludgeons, and at times with pistols.

The Committee of the Howard Association having received requests, from several influential quarters, to render assistance in regard to this matter, recently issued a *Circular of Inquiry* respecting the causes and remedies of juvenile offences, which they sent to a selected list of Chairmen of Quarter Sessions, and other Magistrates, Police Authorities and Managers of Reformatory Schools.

These replies, together with a general summary of their recommendations, were embodied in a comprehensive *Pamphlet* and widely issued by the Committee. They were also extensively noticed and reproduced by the leading organs of the Press throughout the country. In some of the newspapers they gave rise to discussions and correspondence extending over several months. . . .

[B] *Juvenile Offenders. A Report Based on an Inquiry Instituted by the Committee of the Howard Association, 1898* (London, 1898), pp. 18-20 (Howard League Lib.)

[A circular of inquiry was sent to competent practical authorities in respect to the most expedient modes of dealing with juvenile offenders. Many authorities are quoted, showing in their replies wide variation in opinion.]

SUMMARY OF RECOMMENDATIONS

I. Legislation Recommended.

The suggestions as to further legislation mostly point to the need for giving magistrates more power to order the infliction of *whipping*, and also to allow that punishment to be administered without involving the recording of a conviction. . . .

The extension of the excellent principle of the Probation of First Offenders Act, 1887, so as to provide for the appointment of Probation Officers to give better efficiency to its objects, is shown to be very desirable.

And, lastly . . . emphatically advocated the necessity for more effectual legislation for the discouragement of *Intemperance*, that great cause both of juvenile and adult crime. . . .

II. Means Already Available

. . . The abandonment of *Imprisonment* for children, except in cases of serious offences, or determined misconduct.

A much more general use of the "Probation of First Offenders Act," and of the admonition encouraged both by that measure and also by the "Summary Jurisdiction Act."

A more frequent recognition of the original object of *Reformatories* and *Training Ships*, namely, as places for the committal and prolonged training of the more dangerous class of juvenile offenders and their ring leaders; but *not* for children for whom admonition, or a whipping, or liberty under the First Offenders Act, is likely to be *adequate* for securing future good behaviour.

A more prompt and general enforcement, from parents, of some proportion of the cost of maintaining their children in Reformatories and Industrial Schools.

The disuse of *Fines* for children.

Arrangements by Magistrates boards of guardians, and other local authorities, to provide places of suitable temporary detention for children "under remand," *other* than prisons, or workhouse wards containing non-criminal inmates.

The extension and further encouragement of "Day Feeding Schools" and "Truant Schools", for destitute, neglected, and idle children.

Influence with *school board* authorities and their *teachers* to recognize more than hitherto the great importance of religious and moral principles.

The adoption, or facilitation, of any locally practicable means of helping young persons in the period which follows their leaving school.

PART II

American Colonies and the United States, 1641-1900

Punishment of Delinquent Children in Early New England Colonies, 1641-1672

> [A] *The General Laws and Liberties of the Massachusets Colony: Revised and Re-printed, By Order of the General Court Holden at Boston, May 15th, 1672* (Cambridge: Printed by Samuel Green, for John Usher of Boston, 1672), p. 152 (Brit. Mus.)

TRYALS

4. Also Children, Ideots, Distracted persons, and all that are Strangers or new comers to our Plantation, shall have such allowances, and dispensations in any case, whether Criminal or others, as Religion and Reason require [1641].[1]

> [B] *The Laws and Liberties of Massachusetts,* reprinted from the copy of the 1648 Edition in the Henry E. Huntington Library (Cambridge: Harvard University Press, 1929), pp. 5, 6, 11.

BURGLARIE AND THEFT

2. For the prevention of Pilfring and Theft, it is ordered by this Court and Authoritie therof; that if any person shal be taken or known to rob any orchard or garden, that shall hurt, or steal away any grafts or fruit trees, fruits, linnen, woollen, or any other goods left out in orchards, gardens, backsides; or any other place in house or fields: or shall steal any wood or other goods from the water-side, from mens doors, or yards; he shall forfeit treble damage to the owners therof. And if they be children, or servants that shall trespasse heerin, if their parents or masters will not pay the penaltie before expressed, they shal be openly whipped. . . .

1. F. C. Gray in his *Remarks on the Early Laws of Massachusetts Bay; with the Code adopted in 1641, and called "The Body of Liberties" now first printed,* presents A *Coppie of the Liberties of the Massachusets Collonie in New England (1641, 1647),* containing this provision regarding children but not indicating in which year the law was passed. Thanks to the 1672 revision of the Massachusetts laws it is definitely established that it was passed in 1641. As such it is the earliest known law in America relating to delinquent children. Apparently, the Court had wide discretionary power in children's cases.

13. If any child, or children, above sixteen years old, and of sufficient understanding, shall CURSE, or SMITE their natural FATHER, or MOTHER; he or they shall be put to death: unles it can be sufficiently testified that the Parents have been very unchristianly negligent in the education of such children; or so provoked them by extream, and cruel correction; that they have been forced therunto to preserve themselves from death or maiming. *Exod.* 21. 17. *Lev.* 20. 9. *Exod.* 21. 15.

14. If a man have a stubborn or REBELLIOUS SON, of sufficient years & u~derstanding (*viz*) sixteen years of age, which will not obey the voice of his Father, or the voice of his Mother, and that when they have chastened him will not harken unto them: then shal his Father & Mother being his natural parĕts, lay hold on him, & bring him to the Magistrates assembled in Court & testifie unto them, that their Son is stubborn & rebellious & will not obey their voice and chastisement, but lives in sundry notorious crimes, such a son shal be put to death. *Deut.* 21. 20. 21. . . .

CHILDREN

[The selectmen of every town are required to keep a vigilant eye on the inhabitants to the end that the fathers shall teach their children knowledge of the English tongue and of the capital laws, and knowledge of the catechism, and shall instruct them in some honest lawful calling, labor or employment. If parĕts do not do this, the children shall be taken away and placed (boys until twenty-one, girls until eighteen) with masters who will so teach and instruct them.]

> [C] *The Code of 1650, Being a Compilation of the Earliest Laws and Orders of the General Court of Connecticut* . . . (Hartford, 1822), pp. 30-32 (Brit. Mus.)

CAPITALL LAWES

[The first twelve of the capital laws under the Connecticut Code of 1650, supported by Biblical references, were idolatry; witchcraft; blasphemy; wilful murder; slaying through guile as by poisoning; bestiality; sodomy; adultery; rape; man-stealing; giving false witness to take away a man's life; and conspiracy or rebellion against the commonwealth.]

13. If any Childe or Children above sixteene years old and of

suffitient understanding, shall Curse or smite their natural father or mother, hee or they shall bee put to death; unless it can bee sufficiently testified that the parents have beene very unchristianly negligent in the education of such children, or so provoke them by extreme and cruell correction that they have beene forced thereunto to preserve themselves from death, maiming.—Exo. 21. 17.— Levit. 20.—Ex. 21. 15.

14. If any man have a stubborne and rebellious sonne of sufficient yeares and understanding, viz. Sixteene yeares of age, which will not obey the voice of his father or the voice of his mother, and that when they have chastened him will not hearken unto them; then may his father and mother, being his naturall parents, lay hold on him and bring him to the Magistrates assembled in Courte, and testifie unto them, that theire sonne is stubborne and rebellious and will not obey their voice and Chastisement, but lives in sundry notorious Crimes, such a sonne shall bee put to death. Deut. 21. 20, 21.[2]

It is allso ordered by this Courte, and authority thereof, That whatsoever Childe or servant within these Libberties, shall bee convicted of any stubborne, or rebellious carriage against their parents or governors, which is a forrunner of the aforementioned evills; the Governor or any two Magistrates have libberty, and power from this Courte, to commit such person or persons to the Housse of Correction, and there to remaine under hard labour, and severe punishmment so long as the Courte, or the major parte of the Magistrates, shall judge meete.

2. G. W. Quinby in *The Gallows, The Prison, and the Poor-House* (pp. 29-31) makes the following comment on this law:
"An English lady of much repute who visited New England not long previous to the war of '76, says in her diary of 22nd March, 1769, that a maid of nineteen years of age was put upon her trial for life, in Connecticut, by the complaint of her parents, both of whom were present and swore against her— saying that 'she was stubborn and had violated their commands.'
"The diary states that 'at first the mother testified strongly against her child; but when she had spoken a few words, the daughter cried out in great agony of grief, 'Oh! I shall be destroyed in my youth by the words of my own mother!' On which the woman did so soften her testimony, that the court being in doubt upon the matter, had a consultation with the ministers present, as to whether the accused girl had made herself justly liable to the punishment prescribed for stubborn and rebellious children in Deuteronomy, 21:20.
"When it was decided that this law applied only to a rebellious *son,* and that a daughter could not be put to death under its sanction; to which the court did assent, and the girl, after being admonished, was set at liberty. Thereupon she ran sobbing into the arms of her mother, who did rejoice over her as one raised from the dead; and moreover did mightily blame herself for putting her child in so great peril, by complaining of disobedience."

[D] *The General Laws and Liberties of the Massachusetts Colony* . . . (Cambridge, 1672), pp. 26-27 (Brit. Mus.)

CHILDREN AND YOUTH

2. *Forasmuch as it appeareth by too much experience, that diverse Children and Servants, do behave themselves disobediently and disorderly towards their Parents, Masters and Governours; to the disturbance of families, and discouragement of such Parents and Governours;*

It is Ordered by this Court and Authority thereof, That it shall be in the Power of any one Magistrate, by warrant directed to the Constable of that Town where such offender dwells, upon complaint, to call before him any such offender, and upon conviction of such misdemeanors, to sentence him to endure such Corporal punishment, by whipping or otherwise, as in his judgment the Merit of the fact shall deserve, not exceeding *ten stripes* for one offence, or bind the offender to make his appearance at the next County Court;

And further it is also Ordered, that the Commissioners of *Boston*, and the three Commissioners of each Town where no Magistrate dwells, shall have the like Power; Provided that the person or persons so sentenced, shall have liberty to make their Appeale to the next County Court, in any such cases.

A Twelve-Year-Old Pequot Indian Girl Hanged for the Murder of a Six-Year-Old White Girl, 1786

> Henry Channing, *God Admonishing his People of their Duty, as Parents and Masters. A Sermon, Preached at New-London, December 20th, 1786, Occasioned by the Execution of Hannah Ocuish, a Mulatto Girl, Aged 12 Years and 9 Months. For the Murder of Eunice Bolles, Aged 6 Years and 6 Months* (New-London, [Conn.], 1786), pp. 29-31 (Lib. Cong.)

APPENDIX

As the public may wish to be informed more particularly respecting the criminal, Hannah Ocuish, than they have yet been: we have collected the following particulars, which it may not be improper to annex as an appendix to the preceding discourse.

She was born at *Groton.*—Early in life she discovered the maliciousness and cruelty of her disposition: as appears from the following fact, which was represented in evidence before the grand jury. When about six years old, she with a brother about two years older than herself, meeting a little girl at a distance from the neighbourhood, they endeavoured to get away her clothes and a gold necklace which she had on.—After beating the child until they had almost killed her, they stripped her, and disputing about the division of the clothes the child recovered, and getting away came home, covered with blood. This affair was immediately examined into, and the select-men of the town concluded to bind them both out.

Their mother, who is one of the Pequot tribe of indians, is an abandoned creature, much addicted to the vice of drunkenness.— She, it seems, not liking to have the girl bound out; brought her away and left her at a house, about three miles from the city of *New-London*, promising to return in a few days and take her away again. But she did not return 'till after several months, when urging the family to keep her longer they at length consented.—She continued in this family until she was apprehended for the crime, for which she was executed.

Her conduct, as appeared in evidence before the honorable Superior Court was marked with almost everything bad. Theft and lying were her common vices. To these were added a maliciousness of disposition which made the children in the neighbourhood much afraid of her. She had a degree of artful cunning and sagacity beyond many of her years.—In short, her mind wanted to be properly instructed, and her disposition to be corrected.

We now come to the particulars of the horrid crime for which she suffered.

On the 21st of July, 1786, at about 10 o'clock in the morning, the body of the murdered child was found in the public road leading from *New-London* to *Norwich*, lying on its face near to a wall. Its head was covered with stones, and a number lay upon its back and arms. Upon examining the body the skull appeared to be fractured; the arms and face much bruised, and the prints of finger-nails were very deep on the throat.—The neighbourhood were immediately engaged in making search and enquiring for the murderer. The criminal made use of her usual art, to prevent suspicion. —She said that she saw four boys in her mistress's garden near where the child was found: that she called to them for being in the garden and soon after heard the wall fall down. After searching and enquiring for these boys to no effect, suspicions became strong that she was the guilty person. On the 22nd, she was closely questioned, but repeatedly denied that she was guilty. She was then carried to the house where the body lay, and, being again charged with the crime, burst into tears and confessed that she killed her; saying if she could be forgiven she would never do so again. The particulars which she then gave, and which appeared in the course of the trial were as follows.

On the morning of the 21st, she went to a brook which is near her mistress's house, to get a pail of water:—when at the brook, she saw the litle girl come into the road, going to school. She immediately hastened home with the water, and setting it down at the door, ran across the garden to overtake the child:—when near her, the criminal jumped over the wall and called to her: offering her a piece of calicoe which she then held in her hand. The child coming to her, she struck her on the head with a stone which she had taken up for the purpose, and repeating the blows the child cried out, "Oh, if you keep beating me so I shall die." She continued the blows until the child lay still. But after a few moments, seeing that she stirred; she took her by the throat and choaked her 'till she was dead. Being asked why she laid stones upon the child, she said; it was to make people think that the wall fell upon her and killed her.—Upon being asked why she killed her: she said that she had intended giving her a whipping because she had complained of her in strawberry time (about five weeks before) for taking away her strawberries.

Such an instance of deliberate revenge and cruelty in one so young has scarcely a parallel in any civilized country.

When the criminal was first committed to prison she appeared uneasy with her situation; but after a little time seemed to be quite contented and happy.—She would divert herself with the children that went to see her, and frequently would make very shrewd turns upon those persons who made severe remarks upon her.

When arraigned at the bar, she, at the direction of her council, plead "not guilty." During her trial she appeared entirely unconcerned.—After the verdict was brought in, and she was carried back to the prison; a person visited her and told her what must now be her punishment; and that she must prepare for death, and for another world: she seemed greatly affected, and continued in tears most of the day.—After this she seemed as unconcerned as before, and was very backward in conversing with the person who had thus alarmed her fears. It appeared that some persons had been there afterwards and encouraged her with telling her that she would not be hung.

When she was brought to the bar to receive sentence of death, her stupidity and unconcern astonished everyone. While that benevolent tenderness which distinguishes his honor the Chief Justice, almost prevented utterance, and the spectators could not refrain from tears; the prisoner alone appeared scarcely to attend.

About a fortnight before her execution she appeared to realize her danger, and was more concerned for herself. She continued nearly in the same state until the Monday night before her execution: when she appeared greatly affected; saying, that she was distressed for her soul. She continued in tears most of Tuesday, and Wednesday which was the day of execution. At the place of execution she said very little—appeared greatly afraid, and seemed to want somebody to help her.—After a prayer adapted to her unhappy situation, was offered to Heaven, she thanked the sheriff for his kindness to her, and then passed into that state which *never* ends.[1]

Negro Slave Boy, Fourteen, Mutilated, Branded, and Whipped with One Hundred Lashes for Aiding in the Murder of His Master, While His Older Brother Was Burned at the Stake, March, 1787.

> *Duplin County (N.C.) Records. Court Minutes 1784-1791,* Department of Archives and History, Raleigh, N.C., Part I, p. 40.

At a Special Court begun and held at the Court House in Duplin County on Thursday, the 15th day of March in the Year of our Lord 1787, for the immediate Tryal of Darby and Peter, two Negroe slaves, the Property of the late William Taylor Esq. now committed and to be tryed for the Murder of the said William Taylor, their Master, which Court being Summoned and Convened by the Sheriff of the said County and being duly Qualified according to law—were Present to wit

Thomas Routledge
Joseph Dickson } Esquires Justices
James Gillespie

1. A factual account of the murder of Eunice Bolles is given in *The Connecticut Gazette and the Universal Intelligencer* for Friday, July 28, 1786. The sentence of death as delivered by Judge Law is found in the issue for Oct. 20, 1786.

Lewis Thomas
James Middleton, Sr. } Freeholders, all being
Isaac Hunter   owners of Slaves, and
Alexander Dickson   unexceptional according to law

The said Negro man Darby being brot before the Court did Confess that he did on the thirteenth day of this Instant March felloniously, maliciously and wilfully Murder his said Master William Taylor by Strikeing him on the head with an ax into his Brains of which wound his said Master instantly Died whereupon the Court doth pass his Sentence in the words following to wit that the said Negro Man Darby be immediately committed to Gaol under a Good Guard and that on Tomorrow between the Hours of one and four o'clock in the afternoon he be taken out thence and tied to a Stake on the Court House lott and there burned to Death and to ashes and his ashes Strewed upon the Ground and that the Sheriff see this order Executed.—

The said Negro Slave Peter a boy about fourteen years of age being also brought before the Court and examined did confess that he was present when his Master the said William Taylor was Murdered and that he did aid and assist his Brother the aforesaid Darby in commiting the said Murder. The Court haveing taken into consideration the youth of the said Peter and considering him under the Influence of his said older Brother Darby, have thought proper to pass his Sentence in the following words to wit.

That the said Negro boy Peter be committed to Gaol and there to Remain under a Good Guard, till Tomorrow, and then between the Hours of one and four o'clock he be taken out thence and tied to a Post on the Court House lott and there to have one half of Each of his Ears cut off and be branded on Each Cheek with the letter M and Receive one hundred lashes well laid on his bare back and that the Sheriff See this order Executed,

To which Sentences the Court
have hereto Subscribed their Names,

Tho Routledge
Joseph Dickson
James Gillespie
Lewis Thomas
James Middleton
Isaac Hunter
Alexander Dickson
Test W. Dickson C. C.

324

Teen-Age Gangs in Philadelphia, 1791

Dunlap's American Daily Advertiser, August 5, 1791.

The custom of permitting boys to ramble about the streets by night, is productive of the most serious and alarming consequences to their morals. Assembled in corners, and concealed from every eye, they can securely indulge themselves in mischief of every kind. The older ones train up the younger, in the same path, which they themselves pursue; and here produce in miniature, that mischief, which is produced, on a larger scale, by permitting prisoners to associate together in crowds within the walls of a jail.—What avails it to spend the public money in erecting solitary cells to keep a *few* prisoners from being corrupted by evil communication, whilst we hourly expose *hundreds* of our children to corruption from the same cause; and this too, at an age, when the mind is much more susceptible of every impression, whether good or evil?—But, tell it not in New-York, neither publish it in the streets of Baltimore, that the citizens of Philadelphia thus strain at gnats, while they swallow camels,—as it were hurtle-berries!

If a *man* should wilfully set fire to his neighbour's house, he would be severely and deservedly punished. But an unlucky *boy* may, it seems, do it with impunity. At least, he may "scatter firebrands" as he pleases; and if any mischief ensues, he escapes, by saying, "Was I not in sport?"—Paper kites are every night set up, with candles to their tails; and should one of these drop on the roof of a house, Heaven only knows, what a conflagration might be the consequence. But boys do not regard consequences: and why should they, if their grey-headed fathers take no pains to admonish or correct them? It is but a few nights since a stable was set on fire by a candle from the tail of a kite; and yet boys are still permitted to go on unmolested, and hang destruction over our heads; exposing our lives and property to imminent danger, merely for their amusement!

To have seen the market-house last Wednesday night in a blaze, from one end to the other, would, no doubt, have afforded rare diversion to the crowd of idle school-boys, and apprentices broke loose, who were assembled in Market street, and whose laudable efforts were very near producing this effect by lighting a tar-barrel, or, as some say, a whole barrel of tar, so near the Market-house, as actually to set fire to a post, that stands out but a few inches from under the projection of the roof; and to singe the cobwebs hanging under the eves, and cornice.

A few nights ago, a number of boys assembled in Fifth-street, between Market and Chestnut-streets, to divert themselves with firing squibs. A gentleman on horse-back, and a servant driving a carriage, with a pair of horses, happened to pass by at the same instant; and also several persons on foot, who might have had their limbs shattered, if the horses had broken loose. The boys thought this a fine opportunity for sport and mischief, and eagerly seized the moment, to light a squib, and fling it towards the horses. Luckily, indeed, the beasts were in good hands, and, though frighted, were yet, by dextrous management, prevented from taking head. Had not this been the case, the newspapers might, before now, have given us a list of five or six persons killed or wounded. This may be sport to *boys*, but 'tis death to *us* men.

A Twelve-Year-Old Boy Acquitted by the Humanity of the Jury of a Capital Charge of Arson Is Indicted and Convicted on the Same Facts for a Misdemeanor, 1792

Commonwealth v. Dillon, 4 Dallas 116 (1792), *Pennsylvania Supreme Court Reports* (Duke Law Lib.)*

CONFESSION OF PRISONER.

The prisoner (a boy about twelve years old) was indicted for arson, in burning several stables, containing hay, &c. He was examined before the Mayor of the city of Philadelphia, on the 20th of December 1791, and then confessed the commission of the offences, with which he was charged. But as his own confession was the principal evidence (indeed, there was no other positive evidence) against him, his counsel insisted, that it was obtained under such duress, accompanied with threats and promises, as destroyed its legal credit and validity. The evidence on that point was, substantially, as follows:

On the 18th of December, the prisoner was committed to the jail of Philadelphia, and the next day was taken before the mayor; but at that time, he made no confession. On the 18th and 19th of December, he was visited and interrogated by several respectable citizens, who represented to him the enormity of the crime; urged

*The trial was held at a court of oyer and terminer in Philadelphia, on the 31st of January, 1792, before McKean, Chief Justice, and Shippen and Bradford, Justices.

a free, open and candid confession, which would so excite public compassion as probably, to be the means of obtaining a pardon; while a contrary course of conduct would leave him, in case of a conviction, without hope: and they added, that they would themselves stand his friends, if he would confess. The inspectors of the prison endeavored, likewise, to obtain from him a discovery of his offences and of his accomplices. They carried him into the dungeon; they displayed it in all its gloom and horror; they said, that he would be confined in it, dark, cold and hungry, unless he made a full disclosure; but if he did make a disclosure, he should be well accommodated with room, fire and victuals, and might expect pity and favor. The prisoner continued to deny his guilt for some time; and when his master visited him, he complained of the want of clothes, fire and nourishment. At length, however, on the 19th of December, he made successive acknowledgments of the facts contained in his confession, which was formally, and, to all appearance, voluntarily, made before the Mayor, on the succeeding morning; and which was repeated, with additional circumstances, at subsequent periods. . . .

By the Court.—The fact of arson is established; and it only remains to decide, whether it was committed by the prisoner? The proof against him depends upon his own confession, slightly corroborated by the testimony of two witnesses. The confession was freely and voluntarily made, was fairly and openly received, before the Mayor; and therefore it was regularly read in evidence. But still, it has been urged that it was thus apparently well made before the mayor, in consequence of improper measures previously pursued with the boy. The interference of the inspectors of the prison was certainly irregular; though the public anxiety, in which they participated, upon this extraordinary occasion, may be admitted as an excuse. The manner in which he was urged, though not threatened, by the citizens who visited him, may likewise be objectionable. But is it reasonable to infer, that all the prisoner's confessions were falsely made under the influence of those occurrences? Consider the nature of the offence. It cannot be openly perpetrated; for it would be instantly prevented; and if it is secretly perpetrated, how, generally speaking, can the offender be detected, but by his own declarations? If such declarations are voluntarily made, all the world will agree, that they furnish the strongest evidence of imputed guilt. The hope of mercy actuates almost every criminal who confesses his crime; and merely that he cherishes the hope, is no reason, in morality, nor in law, to disbelieve him. The true point for consideration, therefore, is whether the prisoner has falsely declared himself guilty of a capital offence? If there is ground even to suspect, that he has done so, God forbid, that his life should be the sacrifice! While, therefore, on the one hand, it is remarked, that all the stables set on fire, were in the neighborhood of his master's house; that he has, in part communicated the facts to another boy; that his conduct has excited the attention and suspicion of a girl, who knew him; and that he expressed no wish to retract the statement, which he has given: the jury will, on the other hand, remember, that if they entertain a doubt upon the subject, it is their duty to pronounce an acquittal. Though it is their province to administer justice, and not to bestow mercy; and though it is better not to err at all; yet, in a doubtful case, an error on the side of mercy is safer, is more venial, than error on the side of rigid justice.

Verdict, not guilty*

Three Boston Boys Sentenced to the Charlestown State Prison for Stealing, 1813

> The Juvenile Monitor, or Vice and Piety Contrasted. Containing Judge Dawes' Address to Three Boys Convicted of Stealing; and An Account of . . . A Remarkably Pious Boy, Who Died in New-York (3rd Ed.; Boston, 1815) pp. 3-6 (editor's lib.)

[This pamphlet designed to teach a moral lesson to youth is signed "A Parent." It went through at least four editions.]

JUVENILE VICE

[Extracted from the Palladium]

Boston Municipal Court.

On Saturday, Dec. 11, 1813, three boys, the oldest of whom was about sixteen years of age and the youngest about thirteen, were sentenced in the Municipal Court to five days' solitary imprisonment and five years hard labour in the State Prison, for breaking into a store in the night-time, and stealing a pocketbook, containing, with other articles, about nine hundred dollars in bank bills. They

*The humanity of the jury being gratified by an acquittal of the prisoner, from the capital charge, he was indicted and convicted, on the same facts, for a misdemeanor. By the reform of our penal code, arson is no longer a capital crime.

had ascended to the roof of the store, and had forced their way through the scuttle down to the counting room below, where they broke open a desk, from which they took their booty.—They afterwards divided their plunder, and made off for Providence, but were detected at Walpole, with the money upon them. It appeared on their trial, that they had used as much adroitness in committing their offence, as if they had been old offenders. The expected sentence being after school hours were over, drew together a concourse of boys from all parts of the town to hear it, and after it was read to the three prisoners by the Clerk, Judge Dawes took occasion to address them very nearly as follows:

Prisoners at the Bar!

In the course of more than thirty years acquaintance with Judicial Courts, I have seldom heard a trial more affecting than yours. I have known middle aged men scourged at the whipping post, set in pillories and upon the gallows, their faces branded with hot irons, or their ears cut off, for crimes not more aggravated than yours. In pursuance of later and milder laws *you* are sentenced to five years confinement; which the Court might have extended to fifteen. But compassion for boyhood, and a suspicion that some of the parents intrusted with your education are *themselves* too much to blame, have induced the Court to temper its judgment with lenity. Had you been convicted of a similar offence in almost any other part of the known world, you might have been "hung up between heaven and earth as unworthy of both." I do not say these things to embitter your punishment, but to excite your remorse; and, if possible, to make you better objects of future mercy. It is true, you are now going, for a considerable period of your youthful prime, to a place appointed for the wicked. But you will not be obliged to select the worst of them for your companions; and you will be there taught to gain a livelihood by working instead of stealing. Poorly as you have been educated, I hope you can read the Bible. In that book you will find forgiveness, if you repent, and at the end of your imprisonment, if you make a proper use of it, you may come out purified rather than confirmed in guilt. But if you encourage evil propensities, and learn new lessons of wickedness of your new companions, you will come out worse than you go in; and an ignominious death will soon afterwards put an end to your career. It is to be hoped that the children and young lads who have thronged this Temple of Justice upon the present melancholy occasion, perhaps from curiosity, will take warning from the fate of the poor boys at the bar. Had *they* been kept constant at school and obedient to pious instruction, they would not now be standing *there*, such dreadful sights for other boys to gaze at. The unhappy prisoners began their vicious course, first by lying and swearing, then cheating their playmates in little matters, next by pilfering small articles from older neighbours; and, on *Sundays*, either by going into water and fishing, or ripping off the lead from gates and fences, when the owners were in church at Prayers for *them*—for the rising generation.

And, still worse to relate, these boys must have been encouraged by older villains, who would not hesitate to purchase of them the lead, iron and cordage, which they had stolen from citizens who had obtained their property by the sweat of their brow. . . .

Children before the Criminal Courts in New York and in Baltimore, c. 1820

[A] *The Second Annual Report of the Managers of the Society for the Prevention of Pauperism in the City of New-York, Read and Accepted, December 29, 1819* . . . (New-York, 1820), p. 56 (UNC Lib.)

[STATEMENT OF MAYOR C. D. COLDEN OF NEW YORK CITY]

At every court of sessions, young culprits, from twelve to eighteen years of age, are presented. The court is utterly at a loss how to dispose of these children. If they are sent for a short time to the penitentiary, they are no sooner liberated, than they again appear at the bar. Since I have been on the bench, I have in many instances, sentenced the same child several times. They are seduced by old and experienced rogues, to assist in their depredations. It will not do to let them go unpunished; but it seems useless and endless, to inflict punishments which produce no reformation. . . .

[B] *Report on the Penitentiary System in the United States, Prepared under a Resolution of the Society for the Prevention of Pauperism in the City of New-York* (New-York, 1822), Appendix, p. 46 (editor's lib.)

[STATEMENT OF DANIEL RAYMOND, COUNSELLOR AT LAW, BALTIMORE, MD., JAN. 13, 1821]

I would . . . suggest the propriety of altering the law respecting children and youth, so as never to inflict either a corporal or a disgraceful punishment upon such persons. Although from seven to fourteen, a child may, according to the common law, be *doli capax*, yet if they commit crimes, it is more the fault of those who have had their training than their own, and there can be little doubt, but that with proper instruction and government, they may be reformed. When a child or youth under sixteen or eighteen, commits a crime, instead of inflicting that punishment provided for men, I would have them taken from their parents and placed under the care of some good master, who should instruct them, and teach them some mechanic art. Our temples of justice are too often profaned by arraigning children and youth, convicting and punishing them as men. . . .

[The Committee pointed out the dangers attending the indiscriminate association of youthful offenders and hardened criminals in the State Prisons and recommended (p. 60) the erection in the different states of prisons exclusively for juvenile convicts.]

The Mayor and Citizens of Philadelphia Hold Meetings to Consider the Alarming Increase of Juvenile Delinquency, 1821-1822

National Gazette and Literary Register, June 5, 1821; *Poulson's American Daily Advertiser,* June 18, 25; July 12; Sept. 1, 1821; Feb. 16; March 2, 1822.

[At the request of Mayor Robert Wharton a public meeting of citizens of Philadelphia was held on June 15, 1821, to consider what should be done to control the growing menace of juvenile delinquency. At this meeting it was decided that ward and district meetings of citizens should be held to discuss the problem, and each district meeting was requested to select three delegates to attend a general meeting to be held on July 9th. Many such district meetings were held throughout the city and delegates chosen. Before a large number of district delegates assembled on July 9, a letter from the Mayor was read calling attention to the growing number of vagrant and delinquent children and stressing certain community factors responsible for the increase, such as tippling houses where ardent spirits were sold by the cent's worth to children not more than five or six years of age, improperly regulated oyster cellars and taverns, and public gardens that were described as little better than stews. A committee of delegates was appointed to study the problem further and to draw up practical suggestions for relief to be submitted at another mass meeting to be held on August 6.

On February 19, 1822, a mass meeting of Negroes was held at the African Methodist Episcopal Bethel Church on Sixth Street, where a committee of seven was appointed to draw up a report as to what should be done to curb delinquency among the Negro youth of Philadelphia. This committee reported at a public meeting about March 1, 1822, when a resolution was adopted that a Committee of Vigilance be appointed, consisting of thirty Negro people, to co-operate with the Mayor and police in their efforts to suppress crime.]

[A] *The National Gazette and Literary Register* (Philadelphia), July 9, 1821.

[A LETTER TO THE EDITOR ON BEGGING AND JUVENILE DELINQUENCY]

To my mind it is apparent, that much of the vicious conduct of the youth of this great city, is attributable to the practice of begging, which is so universally prevalent. . . .

Closely allied in character and conduct to the race of beggars, are the little pests who dun the citizens with never ending importunity to buy their matches, balls of twine, &c. . . .

But a few years ago, a gang of about a dozen boys, from six to ten years of age, was routed from their place of rendezvous and committed to prison for theft and other crimes, nearly all of whom were beggars. They subsisted on what they could obtain from door to door in the day-time and at night prowled about to steal and to fire houses and the like, having no home but a hay loft in the southern part of the city. The same system of iniquity doubtless now exists, and it is high time that some efficient measure should be adopted to counteract its effects, or to tear it from society by the roots.

The plan which I would suggest for the relief of this very serious moral malady, is the establishment of a house of correction, in which every boy and girl found in the act of begging, together with the whole host of match and twine boys, should be confined. . . . But for children . . . a house of correction is infinitely more proper than a common prison, for this very good and substantial reason; that by confining them in the former, reformation may be effected, while thirty days residence in the latter, is equivalent to a sentence of remediless destruction. . . .

[Gives details as to how such an institution should be managed: Children should be educated for half a day, and work half a day; should be distributed into classes according to age, character, etc.;

should have no other punishment as a rule than deprivation of food for a time or an increase in quantity of work, etc.]

[Signed] —HOWARD

[B] *Report*[1] *of the Committee of the Delegates appointed by the Citizens of the several Wards and Districts, to take into Consideration the Means of Suppressing Crimes within the Same* in *Poulson's American Daily Advertiser,* August 23, 1821 (Lib. Cong.)

. . . The great objects which the committee recommend to the attention of the delegates, are to remove as far as possible the temptations to evil, to arrest the growth of vice among youth, and by a supervisory plan to prevent as far as possible, the consummation of offence. The subjects which, in this view, demand attention, are

1st. The Tippling Houses.

2nd. The Oyster Cellars.

3rd. The Shops for the purchase and sale of second-hand articles.

4th. The receivers of stolen Goods.

5th. The facilities of the concealment of offenders.

6th. The neglected education of children. . . .

2nd. *Oyster Cellars.*—These have of late been increased, not only in number, but in an extent of arrangement that calls for public interference;—under the toleration which they enjoyed while confined to their avowed business, they have been multiplied and enlarged until they have combined the tippling shop with the ordinary—they are more dangerous to a higher grade of society than the tippling houses, as they give to their customers the excuse of resorting to them for a harmless luxury, and afford a shelter for indulgences which a sense of shame would restrain from gratification at a tippling house. In truth it is here that youth from the school boy to the clerk in the counting house, attracted originally by a keen appetite for food, learn to drink, to smoke, and to connect themselves to each other by those strong sympathies in their several indulgences which too often gain the mastery over every virtue. . . .

6th. *The Neglect of the Education of Children.* This is manifest from the crowds of idle and disorderly boys who infest the streets, wharves, vacant lots, and ponds, in and near the city, and particularly on the Lord's Day, when they engage in games, sports, and mischief, to the destruction of their morals, and the annoyance of all

1. Presented at a meeting held, August 6, 1821.

well disposed people in their neighbourhoods. In such schools they learn to drink and swear, to thirst for revenge; to form parties to the redress of each other's wrongs; to assemble at oyster cellars and pleasure gardens; and to hunt after novel spectacles; allured by numerous temptations in eating and drinking, they soon get a taste for luxuries beyond their honest reach. . . . To meet these evils as far as possible, it is proposed to establish, by law, in each ward and district, two or more special assistants, to be clothed with the power of constables, so far as regards the arrest of offenders, and the preservation of the peace—that the law should define the disorderly conduct of children, which should subject them to its provisions, and give power to the magistrate to commit, for the first offence, the offenders to the custody of the assistant, to be kept in confinement, until bail be given for good behaviour, in some place separate from the common gaol, and to make it the duty of the assistant to cause notice to be given to the parent, or guardian, if known, and in the city or districts, and to increase the punishment for subsequent offences.

Your committee [suggests] the establishment of an asylum where useful merchanical arts should be taught to male children. . . .

JOHN STEELE, Chairman
JAMES M. BROWN, Secretary.

Scattered Newspaper Accounts of Juvenile Delinquency, 1821-1871

Western Carolinian (Salisbury, N.C.), September 25, 1821.

A SHOCKING INSTANCE OF INFANTILE DEPRAVITY.

About two weeks ago in Mecklenburg County, North Carolina, one of the most shocking instances of early depravity occurred that has ever come to our knowledge. While a Mr. Freeman and his wife were from home, one of their children, a boy of 9 years old, took his father's gun and shot his half brother, a child 3 years old, through the head: on the return of his father, the boy was whipped, after which he swore he would kill a younger brother, 18 months old. The father has discarded him; and he is now running at large, despised and shunned wherever he goes.

Catawba Journal (Charlotte, N.C.), February 5, 1828.

A solemn warning to Parents.—It is seldom we have to record a circumstance, which calls so loudly on parents, to bring their children up in a becoming manner, as the following. A few days past, two small boys, aged 10 and eleven years, (sons of Mrs. Rogers, a widow lady resident of Hertford County) commenced a game at cards, when a dispute arose, about a walnut, which it appears was the wager. It seems that the eldest contradicted the other, and he was told if he repeated it, he would shoot him instantly; not supposing, perhaps, that he was in earnest, the eldest boy contradicted him the second time, when the youngest, unhesitatingly, stepped in the house, which was not far distant, brought out a gun, and put his diabolical threat into execution, by shooting his brother thro' the head, when he fell and expired in a few minutes. We are told that the boy has been safely lodged in jail.—It is not unfrequent that such consequences ensue, in what some are pleased to term innocent amusements.

New England Palladium, etc., October 7, 1828.

Apprentices.—A respectable tradesman appeared before the magistrate yesterday in company with two of his apprentices, whom he accused of continually remaining out at night to a very late hour. From his statement it was shown that the offenders had been in the habit of acting as supernumeraries at one of the theaters, and by so doing had acquired habits of the most abandoned and dissolute character. They were duly admonished on the impropriety of their conduct, and after a severe lecture, informed that if ever they were discovered in a theater under similar circumstances, they would be exemplarily punished by imprisonment in Bridewell. Mr. Stephens one of the clerks, observed, that since the opening of the Grand-street Circus numerous instances had occurred of apprentices pilfering from their masters, which he had never heard of previously. At all events, he was certain that a greater number of juvenile thieves had been taken from the neighborhood of that theater than any part of the city. The very low price of admission, (we believe two shillings,) was a great temptation to youth, and many an article has been stolen merely for the purpose of procuring the means of witnessing a performance.

Tarboro' Press (Tarborough, N.C.), April 18, 1835.

Juvenile Depravity.—State of Maryland vs. Thomas Holston and others. These cases, seven in number, were of a peculiar character, and excited much interest. For a considerable time, our city and its visiters have been subjected to a series of depredations, effected in a manner that indicated the existence of a nefarious combination, which was often successful. Much had been said and published on the subject, but it remained for the trial of these juvenile offenders to prove the existence of an association of which no citizen was aware. From the evidence it appears, that for some years a gang of young desperadoes have been associated, under the denomination of "The Forty Thieves." The association was regularly organized, commanded by a captain and the necessary subalterns, and its rules were regularly enforced. One of its rules was, that each member should commit depredations to a certain amount, or be expelled from the body. The persons composing the association appeared to be on an average from 11 to 16 years of age. The captain, Holston, was a dwarfish lad about 16 years of age, and whilst standing at the bar among his colleagues, chewed his quid, and spurted his tobacco juice around him with the air of a veteran. The members of the fraternity bear on their arms decorations, impressed with India ink, gunpowder and vermillion; indicating, we presume, their proficiency in their profession, and their rank in the corps. One had on his left arm an impression, with India ink or gunpowder, of a foul anchor, a death's head; and the letter T—some few, the recently initiated, a vermillion cross—others part of a red cross. Some of these individuals had been committed on former occasions—one of them, in the course of the last five years, eight or ten times. Three of the gang were sentenced to seven years confinement in the penitentiary.—

Tarboro' Press (Tarborough, N.C.), February 13, 1836.

Extraordinary Youthful Depravity.—On the 12th inst. in the town of Hanover, Chautauque County, N. Y., as two lads—one aged 6 and the other 4, were snow-balling together, the latter became irritated, and told the other if he threw another snow-ball he would cut his head off or kill him, and another being sent, he ran up to his antagonist and stabbed him in the left side with a large pocketknife. The wound was so severe, that the boy became immediately speechless and so remained at the last moments, leaving but little hopes of his recovery. The Fredonia Censor adds: "What a theme for reflecting on the depravity of human nature does this act afford. A boy four years old thrusting a deadly weapon into the bosom of his playmate!"

Tarboro' Press (Tarborough, N.C.), August 20, 1836.

A circumstance of juvenile depravity such as is rarely seen, occurred in this city [Boston] on Saturday. Two little girls—the elder

336

apparently not more than four years old, and the other about a year younger—were playing together near the head of India wharf. In a few moments they seated themselves on a timber lying near, when the elder seized her companion by the neck, and notwithstanding her outcries forced her into the dock. Fortunately Captain Whitney of the Nantucket was passing at the time, and he succeeded in rescuing the child from the eminent danger in which she had been thrown by the deliberate act of her playmate.—The child who can do a deed like this when but four years old, bids fair to reach either the gallows or the State Prison long before she reaches the years of maturity.

The Spectator (Newbern, N.C.), September 23, 1836.

Daring outrage.—A negro boy named Jesse, was committed to the jail of this county on Sunday evening last, charged with having made an attempt to violate a white orphan girl on the morning of that day. The circumstances, as related to us, are these:—Miss Worthington, the girl assaulted, had set out from her uncle's, accompanied by her cousin, another girl, for the purpose of visiting a sister of the former at Mr. Prescott's, on Core Creek. The negro overtook them on the road, and after having made several inquiries, such as what their names, who were their fathers, etc., he seized the larger of the two, and forced her into the woods. The other fled towards her father's, for the purpose of giving the alarm. Happily for the unfortunate girl in the woods, succour came sooner than could have been expected. Judge Donnell and G. S. Attmore, Esq., were on their way to Lenoir Court, and arrived near the spot before the negro had accomplished his base design. As soon as he saw the carriage approaching, he returned to the road and pursued his way as if nothing amiss had happened. When the weeping girl had informed the gentlemen of what had taken place they immediately pursued and captured the negro, and on the evidence of the two girls, the Judge committed him, as above stated, to await his trial for the offence. The girl, it is said, is about fourteen years of age, and the negro but little older.

Southern Citizen (Ashborough, N.C.), July 15, 1837.

An interesting trial lately took place in Lowell, Mass. Two boys, one 13, and the other 10 years of age were charged with setting fire to the almshouse in Cambridge, in which were 80 inmates, one of whom was burned to death. They plead guilty, but the plea was not recorded and Counsel was assigned them. It appeared from their voluntary confessions that they were hired to do the act by one Moriarty, who left the almshouse a few days before the fire, and that they set fire to the hay in the stable, not expecting it would communicate to the house. Chief Justice Shaw charged the Jury that notwithstanding their age they must suffer the punishment of the law (death,) if it appeared that they wilfully and maliciously committed the act charged, and that it was not necessary to prove actual ill will against any one, or a design of burning the house or that they were ignorant of the extent of their crime and its punishment. If they did it for a reward, that was a wrong motive and they must abide the consequences. The Jury were out all night, and on the opening of the Court the next morning declared they could not agree and it was not probable they ever should.

The Standard (Raleigh, N.C.), December 22, 1841.

Before the Court of New Castle County, Delaware, a young girl pleaded guilty to ten different indictments for petty larceny. She was sentenced to pay two-fold the value of the stolen goods to the owners, to wear ten T's on her outer garment, and to receive twenty-one lashes on her bare back, well laid, in each case, making 210 in all.—The law that authorized this sentence is a disgrace to the country and the age. The Governor of Delaware, much to his honor, remitted the corporeal punishment.

The Patriot (Greensborough, N.C.), August 26, 1843.

Lynching.—A trifling and abandoned man named Joel Davis was tarred and feathered by a club of ten or eleven youngsters, in this place, last Monday night [August 21]. A legal investigation of the matter, on an indictment, was had before the County Court in session this week, and the perpetrators fined *sixpence.*

Davis's character and disposition were proven to be extremely bad; and it was said, as it is said in all such cases, that he could not be reached by law. But we nevertheless think that it is better to bear with *one bad man who does nothing the Law can punish him for,* than to recognize *the principle that a mob may apportion and inflict punishment at its discretion.*

Tarboro' Press (Tarborough, N.C.), February 17, 1844.

Wilmington, February 7.

Murder—On Sunday morning, a negro boy named Charles, fourteen years of age, deliberately shot his brother, named Adonis, a man twenty-seven or eight years old with a pistol loaded with two balls, causing his death in a few minutes. They had quarrelled the day before. Whilst another brother was trying to take Charles, directly after the murderous act, he shot at him likewise with a second pistol which he had concealed, but without effect. Charles is in jail. The man killed belonged to Mr. P. K. Dickinson, as does the murderer.

In investigating the affair, it was discovered that a number of small black boys about town had pistols in their possession, which they had been in the habit of sporting with, firing at marks, etc., in retired places. They were purchased, they say, and as is otherwise well ascertained, from certain men in town, who it appears have been in the practice of selling firearms to the slave population. Against these violators of the law, and disturbers of the peace, a highly excited feeling justly exists in the community. So much so indeed, that one of the largest public meetings of the citizens we ever witnessed, convened yesterday at a few hours notice, for the purpose of considering what measures should be taken to enforce the laws in their utmost vigor, and to visit justice upon the offenders.

Hillsborough Recorder (Hillsborough, N.C.), December 9, 1857.

A Warning.–The Chapel Hill Gazette states that on Wednesday morning last, William Nunn, a youth in that place, was dangerously wounded, by the accidental discharge of a pistol in his pocket, the charge entering his abdomen. The Gazette thinks "young America" ought to take warning by accidents of this kind, and mentions having noticed several boys in the streets lately popping about with pistols. The Gazette closes with the very proper inquiry, "Is there no town ordinance forbidding the dangerous practice of shooting in the streets?"

Minute Book I, Chapel Hll, N.C., May 12, 1871, p. 41.

That if any parents or guardian shall permit their children or wards to indulge upon the Sabbath day, in the streets in any game, sport or amusement which shall disturb the peace and quiet of any part of the Village, said children shall be liable to confinement in the Guard House and their parents or guardians shall pay a fine of 25 cents for the release of each.

Children in Jail in Cambridge, Massachusetts, 1822

Josiah Quincy, *Remarks on Some of the Provisions of the Laws of Massachusetts, Affecting Poverty, Vice, and Crime* (Cambridge: Printed at the University Press, 1822), pp. 10-13, 18-20 (editor's lib.)

. . . Yet, strange as it must appear to any mind, not previously formed by a knowledge of the state of things in society, while nothing is omitted to discover, to prosecute and to punish crimes, when committed, there is little, almost nothing operative, in our public institutions of the character of prevention. The children of vicious and abandoned parents are in our streets, on our wharves, in our market places, sometimes begging, sometimes pilfering, sometimes seeking a precarious and accidental employ, often spent on their vices, more often forming an apology for multiplying opportunities for stealing. In such primary schools, the children of the vicious are permitted, by society, to prepare themselves for those higher seminaries, the gaols and state prisons. . . . In that base and degraded throng . . . is there not one—must there not be many—who by a little prospective care, some additional provisions, on the part of society, might have been prevented this shame, and rescued from this ruin?

. . . It cannot be too often impressed on the consideration of the wise, the thoughtful, and the virtuous, that the existing provisions of society are shamefully deficient, in means to enable its ministers of justice to discriminate, in awarding punishment, between different classes of offenders and degrees of offence; that they are equally deficient in supplying any practical means of reformation; and that society itself does little else than plot the ruin of every juvenile offender, and every novice in crime, when it provides no other alternative for punishment, than confinement in gaol, and confinement in the state's prison. As to gaols, what condition can be better devised to effect utter destruction to body, mind, and soul, than long confinement in them; without exercise; without occupation; condemned amidst gloom, and filth, and idleness, to the society of the most worthless and depraved! . . .

There are now in that gaol three boys and three girls. The boys under an original sentence of five years' imprisonment, by the municipal court of Boston. The girls under that of three. These sentences were the least, which, under the circumstances of their offence, the court deemed itself authorized to inflict, in compliance with the law. Two of the boys are under sixteen; all the girls under fourteen years of age.

I visited these children. The room was sufficiently comfortable, for a gaol; well aired and clean. But how were they employed? Sitting opposite to one another, at a board, doing absolutely nothing. *They complained of want of employment.* The keeper had none to give them. . . .

. . . What right has society to oblige, by general provisions, its ministers of justice, to condemn children to pass the best years of life, the most important to their future prospects, immured between the four walls of a prison, in utter sloth and idleness, in a situation to incur the worst habits; and exposed to a perpetual influx and efflux of whatever is base, and vicious, and criminal?

. . . The three girls, above mentioned, were sentenced last October. They remained three months in close confinement. One of them, a girl of twelve years, was so obviously humble, interesting, and contrite, that the keeper took her out of the prison into his own house, to save her from the perdition, with which her confinement among her companions threatened her. She has been now three months at liberty; an inmate in his family. I saw her, active, industrious, happy, and respectable. Neither of these three knew their letters when imprisoned, or any thing of work. This individual could now read, and had been instructed in the usual work of the family, and had every appearance, and her uniform conduct since her release, indicated the existence of good dispositions. . . .

A House of Refuge for Juvenile Delinquents Proposed by the New York Society for the Prevention of Pauperism, 1823

New York Society for the Prevention of Pauperism, *Report of a Committee Appointed by the Society . . . on the Expediency of Erecting an Institution for the Reformation of Juvenile Delinquents*[1] (New York, 1823), pp. 7-8, 10-11, 13, 17-18, 25, 28-29, 35, 50-51 (Lib. Cong.)

At a meeting of the Society for the Prevention of Pauperism, held the 12th of June, 1823, on motion, the following Managers were appointed a Committee to prepare a Report on the subject of establishing a House of Refuge, or Prison for the Reformation of Juvenile Delinquents:—John Griscom, Isaac Collins, Cornelius Dubois, James W. Gerard, Hiram Ketchum, Daniel E. Lord. . . .

1. On page 2 of this report is written in faded ink, "Griscom is Professor of Chemistry, a Quaker, shrewd clever and intelligent. He published his travels, which were full of observation: was the person who chiefly drew up this report. . . ."

Every person that frequents the out-streets of this city must be forcibly struck with the ragged and uncleanly appearance, the vile language, and the idle and miserable habits of great numbers of children, most of whom are of an age suitable for schools, or for some useful employment. The parents of these children, are, in all probability, too poor or too degenerate, to provide them with clothing fit for them to be seen in at school; and know not where to place them in order that they may find employment, or be better cared for. Accustomed, in many instances, to witness at home, nothing in the way of example, but what is degrading; early taught to observe intemperance, and to hear obscene and profane language without disgust; obliged to beg, and even encouraged to acts of dishonesty, to satisfy the wants induced by the indolence of their parents,—what can be expected, but that such children will, in due time, become responsible to the laws for crimes, which have thus, in a manner, been forced upon them? Can it be consistent with real justice, that delinquents of this character, should be consigned to the infamy and severity of punishments, which must inevitably tend to perfect the work of degradation. . . . Is it possible that a Christian community, can lend its sanction to such a process, without any effort to rescue and to save? If the agents of our municipal government stand towards the community in the moral light of guardians of virtue . . . does not every feeling of justice urge upon them the principle, of considering these juvenile culprits as falling under their special guardianship, and claiming from them the right which every child may demand of its parent, of being well instructed in the nature of its duties, before it is punished for the breach of their observance?

. . . In order to arrive at a more correct understanding of the amount of the evils alluded to, the committee have to state, that they have been furnished by the District Attorney, H. Maxwell, Esq. with an abstract of those persons who were brought before the Police Magistrates, during the year 1822, and sentenced either to the City Bridewell, from 10 to 60 days or to the Penitentiary from 2 to 6 months. The list comprehends more than 450 persons, all under 25 years of age, and a very considerable number of both sexes between the ages of 9 and 16. None of these have been actually charged with crime, or indicted and arraigned for trial. It includes those only, who are taken up as vagrants, who can give no satisfactory account of themselves;—children, who profess to have no home, or whose parents have turned them out of doors and take no care of them,—beggars and other persons discovered in situations which imply the intention of stealing, and numbers who were found sleeping in the streets or in stables. These miserable objects are brought to the Police Office under suspicious circumstances,—and, according to the result of their examinations, they are sentenced as before mentioned. Many of these are young people on whom the charge of crime cannot be fastened, and whose only fault is, that they are incapable of providing for themselves. Hundreds, it is believed, thus circumstanced, eventually have recourse to petty thefts; or if females, they descend to practices of infamy, in order to save themselves from the pinching assaults of cold and hunger. . . .

From further information it appears, that about 60 persons are, upon an average, indicted and arraigned at each term of the Court of Sessions, for misdemeanours and felonies; and that out of this number, four or five are boys under sixteen years of age. A large proportion of them, amounting to fifty or sixty per annum, are found guilty and condemned, either to the City or State *Penitentiary,* there to associate with others more hardened in crime, and who are ever ready to impart their instructions in the acts of deception and wickedness. . . .

In the City Prison or Bridewell, it is not only impossible to separate the juvenile offenders from those that are old in crime, but the rooms are so small and very often so crowded as to produce an atmosphere both physically and morally disgusting in a high degree. . . . In rooms about eighteen feet square, there are often thirty or forty persons, confined together without any discrimination except that of sex and colour,—boys of nine years of age, and upwards, sharing the same dismal fare, and mingling in conversation with aged villainy,—and girls of ten or twelve exposed to the company and example of the most abandoned of the sex. . . .

Sleeping upon the bare floor, without covering, or at best with only a coarse and dirty blanket, they soon learn to brave the exposure, and to disregard the privation. . . .

The average number of boys sent to the penitentiary [Bellevue Penitentiary] for the last three years, has been seventy-five per year, from twelve to sixteen years old. The average at one time in the house is about thirty-five. . . . About one half are in for the second and third time. . . . They are taught the catechism and to read and write. . . . We have not put them to labour, except a part in the Pinfactory. . . .

The principal cause of Juvenile Delinquency [in the opinion of Superintendent Arthur Burtis of Bellevue Penitentiary], is, first, the bad example they have from their parents and guardians; when small, they are allowed to run at large without restraint. No child will be a vagrant, if put and kept steadily to a well-regulated school, but for a few years.—But the reason why their parents will not send them, is, the encouragement which our citizens give, (and no doubt from the best motives,) *to begging*. When a poor child calls at a gentleman's house for a little cold victuals, who can refuse, when they have it, and especially, since, if not given, it must be thrown away? But if our citizens were aware of the evil, I am sure they would make a universal stop. I cannot learn of one child that has been in the habit of begging, who has not turned out a prostitute, or vagrant; and their begging serves only to keep their parents in idleness and profligacy: for they find it so profitable, that, if they have one or two good begging children, (as they term it,) it is all they want; all they can get by other means, goes for drink. Another cause is, sending small children round the docks, under the pretence of picking chips, and whatever they can find; in peddling small articles on board of sloops, and through the streets, &c. These habits introduce them into bad company, and prove an almost certain cause of their ruin. . . .

From the exposition thus given of the subjects referred to their consideration, the Committee cannot but indulge the belief . . . that it is highly expedient that a House of Refuge for Juvenile Delinquents, should, as soon as practicable, be established in the immediate vicinity of this city.

In addition . . . the committee have no doubt that were such an institution once well established and put under good regulation, the Magistrates would very often deem it expedient to place offenders in the hands of its Managers, rather than to sentence them to the City Penitentiary. . . . But . . . it is our decided opinion,—an opinion founded not only upon the reasonableness of the proposition, but upon the result of similar institutions in Europe, that destitute females might form one department of the establishment, with the greatest benefit to themselves, and with advantage to the institution. Occupying apartments entirely distinct from those of the other sex, and separated from them by impassable barriers, the females might contribute by their labour to promote the interests of the establishment, and at the same time, derive from it their full and appropriate share of benefit. . . .

Although we are not apprized of there being any where in the United States a House of Refuge established and conducted upon the principles now proposed; yet it is known to your Committee that philanthropic individuals, in various places, have deemed such an

344

establishment a desideratum in each of our large cities. In Boston there is an institution approximating in its object, to that under consideration. It consists of a house, to which are sent those children, whose parents, through culpable and vicious neglect, leave them to roam through the streets untaught and unprotected. By the laws of Massachusetts, children thus neglected, may be taken from their parents, at the discretion of persons duly authorized, and placed at school, or at trades with suitable masters. In this asylum their time is divided between the exercises of a school and manufactory, and when they have attained to a sufficient degree of skill and learning, places are obtained for them as apprentices at some useful art or trade. . . .

APPENDIX A.

The following list affords specimens of the four hundred and fifty cases of Juvenile Offences, furnished by the District Attorney, from the Records of the Police Office, for 1822.

Henry H. aged 15, came out of Bridewell, now charged with stealing, vagrant thief; sentence 6 months to Penitentiary.

David B. aged 12, brought up by the watch, charged with stealing, vagrant thief; 6 months Penitentiary. . . .

William S. aged 11, his father turned him out of the house, was found sleeping in a boat at night; 6 months Penitentiary.

Sophia H. aged 14 years, was charged with stealing, goes about begging, has been in Bridewell six times, no means; 6 months Penitentiary.

Early Days of the New York House of Refuge, 1825-1832

[A] *First Annual Report of the Managers of the Society for the Reformation of Juvenile Delinquents, in the City of New York* (New York, 1825), pp. 7, 19 (editor's lib.)

[THE NEW YORK HOUSE OF REFUGE OPENS, JANUARY 1, 1825]

On the first day of January last [1825], the board met and opened the Institution, in presence of a considerable concourse of citizens, (among whom were several members of the Corporation) who assembled to witness the ceremony of the introduction of a number of juvenile convicts, the first in this city, if not in this country, into a place exclusively intended for their reformation and instruction. The ceremony was interesting in the highest degree. Nine of those poor outcasts from society, 3 boys and 6 girls, clothed in rags, with squalid countenances, were brought in from the Police Officer, and placed before the audience. An address appropriate to so novel an occasion was made by a member of the board, and not an individual, it may safely be affirmed, was present, whose warmest feelings did not vibrate in unison with the philanthropic views which led to the foundation of this House of Refuge. . . . The number of its delinquent inmates continued to increase until it amounted to 58. . . . Of this number, 44 were boys and 14 girls. Of the former, the oldest at the time of his admission was 18, and the youngest 9. The whole number admitted into the house, from its commencement to the present time, is 73. They have been received from the following sources, viz:—

From the Court of Sessions, for grand larceny.............. 1
———, for petit larceny..................................... 9
From the Police Magistrates, for stealing and vagrancy........47
From the Commissioners of the Alms-House, for stealing, vagrancy, and absconding..................................16

Total   73

[The boys were employed in cleaning up the premises by the removal and disposal of lumber, assisting masons and carpenters in erecting a new building, elevating a wall, making repairs, cultivating a small garden, etc. Indoor employment was shoe-making and tailoring. The girls were engaged in washing, ironing, cooking, baking, and plaiting of grass. Two hours daily were devoted to mental improvement, and the children were divided into classes for mutual instruction according to the Lancasterian method. A number of books were donated by interested citizens for starting a library for the children.]

[Testimony of Hugh Maxwell, District Attorney] "I am happy to state, that the House of Refuge has had a most benign influence in diminishing the number of juvenile delinquents. The most depraved boys have been withdrawn from the haunts of vice, and the examples which they gave, in a great degree destroyed.

"I find no difficulty now in checking the young offenders. Before the establishment of the House of Refuge, a lad of fourteen or fifteen years of age might have been arrested and tried four or five times for petty thefts, and it was hardly ever that a jury would convict. They would rather that the culprit acknowledged to be guilty should be discharged altogether, than be confined in the prisons of the state or county.

"This disposition so frequently exercised by magistrates and jurors, rendered the lad more bold in guilt; and I have known instances of lads now in the House of Refuge, being indicted half a dozen times, and as often discharged to renew their crimes, and with the conviction that they might steal with impunity.

"The consideration, however, that there is a charity which provides for objects of this character, has removed all objections to convictions in cases of guilt.

"Formerly too many citizens were reluctant in bringing to the police-office, young persons who were detected in the commission of crimes. This operated as an encouragement to depraved parents to send very young children to depredate on the community,—if detected they know no punishment would follow. This is one cause of the small number of juvenile offenders during the last year. . . .

[Short case descriptions of both boys and girls are presented.]

> [B] Nathaniel C. Hart, *Documents Relative to the House of Refuge* . . . *in the City of New-York* . . . (New York, 1832), pp. 107-8, 110-11 (editor's lib.)

[SYSTEM OF DISCIPLINE AT THE NEW YORK HOUSE OF REFUGE, 1827]

Punishments

If any child shall refuse, or wilfully neglect, to perform the work required of him or her, or to obey the orders of the Superintendent or Matron, or Assistant Keepers, or shall use profane or indecent language, or shall assault or quarrel with a fellow-delinquent, or shall make a noise, or talk after having retired to the sleeping room, he or she shall be punished at a suitable time; and if, after this, such child persist in disobedience, he or she shall be confined in solitude, for such time as the Superintendent or Matron may direct.

If any subject shall strike or resist the Keeper, or attempt to escape from the House, or shall wilfully injure any article belonging to the Society, he or she shall be punished, except the same be remitted on application to the Acting Committee.

The Superintendent shall possess a discretionary power in awarding the punishment to offenders. He may try offenders by a jury of their peers, and inflict such punishment as they shall award, subject, however to his revisions. He shall, in all cases, enter on the daily journal, and report to the Acting Committee, a brief detail of the offence, and the punishment inflicted for the same.

If it should ever be necessary to inflict corporal punishment upon *females*, it shall only be done by or in the presence of the Matron.

Kinds of Punishment that May be used in the House of Refuge

1. Privation of play and exercise.
2. Sent to bed supperless at sunset.
3. Bread and Water, for breakfast, dinner, and supper.
4. Gruel without salt for breakfast, dinner, and supper.
5. Camomile, boneset, or bitter herb tea, for breakfast, dinner, and supper.
6. Confinement in solitary cells.
7. Corporal punishment, if absolutely necessary, or if awarded by a jury of the boys, and approved.
8. Fetters and handcuffs, only in *extreme cases.*

Wardsmen or Monitors

The Superintendent may, whenever in his opinion it shall be useful, appoint for each ten or more children, one of the Delinquents as Wardsman or Monitor, who shall be selected from the most orderly, well behaved, and best qualified for the purpose.

The general duty of the Wardsmen shall be, to observe the behavior and conduct of their respective classes; to see that they daily wash their persons; that their sleeping and work rooms are regularly swept every morning, and washed or scrubbed once in each week; that the rooms and bedding be ventilated and aired, and the night utensils removed and cleansed; and that decency and good order prevail throughout the class.

The Wardsman shall be authorised to select from his class, in rotation, one of the number, to perform the duty of sweeping, scrubbing, &c., and it shall be an offence against the rules, for any of the class to disobey the reasonable commands of the Wardsman. He shall report to the Superintendent, any improper act committed by a member of his class, immediately after its occurrence, in order that it may be corrected forthwith. . . .

Classification

The Boys and Girls shall be classed according to their moral conduct, and as soon as practicable there shall be four Grades or Classes formed, viz. No. 1, 2, 3, 4.

Class, No. 1. Shall include the best behaved and most orderly Boys and Girls: those who do not swear, lie, or use profane, obscene, or indecent language or conversation, who attend to their work and studies, are not quarrelsome, and have not attempted to escape.

Class, No. 2. Those who are next best, but who are not quite free from all of the foregoing vices and practices.

Class, No. 3. Those who are more immoral in conduct than Class No. 2.

Class, No. 4. Those who are vicious, bad and wicked. Badges, bearing the number of each class, shall be worn on the arm at all times in the day.

In case of improper and bad conduct, the children in Classes No. 1, 2, or 3, shall be transferred or degraded by the Superintendent to the lower or lowest Class. And for improvement, or good conduct, in Classes 4, 3, or 2, they may be transferred or promoted to a higher class.

The children in Class No. 1, who behave well, and are orderly and correct in their conduct, shall be rewarded Monthly by the Superintendent, in the presence of all the children, and of the Acting Committee.

Those children who have behaved well for three months in succession, shall be allowed to wear a badge of distinction and approbation.

Extracts from such parts of these regulations, as relates to the several classes of delinquents, shall be printed and hung up in several parts of the House of Refuge. . . .

The influence and efficacy which the moral system of treatment pursued in the Refuge, has on the children, may be illustrated by the following facts.

Within the walls of the prison is a pretty large piece of ground, cultivated as a fruit and flower garden, as well as for raising vegetables for the use of the House. The fruits and flowers are all within reach of the children, and indeed when they are in season, are tempting them every moment. Yet there is scarcely an instance of anything having been touched without permission. It may be thought that this forbearance is produced by great severity. This is not the case. The youthful inmates of this institution are governed by appeals to their understandings, to their generous feelings, rather than by corporal punishments. It is rectitude, or the fear of disgrace, and not of pain, that has this happy influence. In this little community, each member of it is led to estimate the value of character, and is not only anxious to avoid a bad reputation, but is emulous of being distinguished among his fellows for his goodness, his proficiency, and his ability. Badges of distinction are here objects of ambition, are borne with pride, and rewarded with deference, as they are by human nature under other circumstances. With this difference, that here they are known to be always the reward of merit, and are never the adventitious appendages of birth or good fortune.

> [C] Nathaniel C. Hart, *Documents Relative to the House of Refuge Instituted by the Society for the Reformation of Juvenile Delinquents in the City of New-York, in 1824* (New York, 1832), pp. 132, 134 (editor's lib.)

[THEATRES OF NEW YORK AS CAUSES OF JUVENILE DELINQUENCY, 1828-1831]

The assembling together of so large a number of the vagrant, corrupt, and wicked youth of the city as are collected in the House of Refuge, the entire confidence which the Superintendent is able to gain in his conversations with them, and the full confessions, which, in due time, they make of their past lives and actions, furnish data from which it is easy to deduce conclusions relative to the principal causes of that degradation and abandonment to vice which lead the culprit to prison or to infamy. . . . Among these causes of vicious excitement in our city, none appear to be so powerful in their operation as theatrical amusements. The mention of the number of boys and young men who have become determined thieves in order to procure the means of introduction to the theatres and circuses, would appal the feelings of every virtuous mind, could the whole truth be laid open before them. A small sum is at first pilfered, to obtain a single sight of amusements respecting which they hear so much, and whose entertainments the street advertisements exhibit in such conspicuous and alluring characters. The first gratification prompts powerfully to the means of renewal,—new acquaintance is formed—the secrets of others still deeper in crime become known—other passions are elicited—dishonesty and falsehood, once rendered habitual, and the vicious propensities of the mind gaining a complete ascendency—the barriers of the law, and a regard for character, present no further impediments, than a desire to evade the one and to conceal the abandonment of the other.

In the case of the feebler sex, the result is still worse. A relish for the amusements of the theatre, without the means of honest indulgence, becomes too often a motive for listening to the first suggestions of the seducer, and thus prepares the unfortunate captive of sensuality for the haunts of infamy, and a total destitution of all that is valuable in the mind and character of woman.

. . . From the rivalship which prevails between these places [theatres], and the necessity of resorting to some means in order to sustain a reputation for numbers, the terms of admission are reduced to a modicum; and, if our information be correct, tickets of admission, even in some of the largest of these establishments, are freely granted to that class of females which it is expected will be able to bring companions with them, and thus add to the emoluments and appearance of the house.

[An eleven year old boy's infatuation for attending the theatre is described as follows:]

"His first theft was sixpence from his mother; the second was two shillings from her, with which he went to the Chatham Theatre, and told his mother that he had been playing with boys in the street; then six shillings from his mother, which he spent in going to the Bowery Theatre twice; next five dollars from his Aunt H. M., of which he spent three dollars, in going to the Park Theatre three times, and concealed the rest under his mother's back stoop; then four shillings from Miss J. M., which he spent in going to the Chatham Theatre, including ice cream, oranges, &c, &c.; then five dollars from Miss S., one of his mother's boarders—spent three dollars in going to the Bowery Theatre, and concealed the rest as before; next two dollars from Mrs. D., which he hid under the back stoop as before; then ten dollars from his mother, spent the greatest part in going twice to the Chatham Theatre, put the balance as before under the back stoop. The object of his hiding these little amounts, was, that he might have a sufficiency on the ensuing fourth of July"

. . . The number of boys that occupy the lower seats of the theatres and of those too whose appearance indicates the poverty in which they live, is said to be very great; and the examinations of the Refuge would lead to the conclusion, that these places are the resort almost universally of those, who, by the dishonesty of their lives become candidates for the Refuge and City Prison. But it is much easier to point out these evils than to prescribe the remedy.

[Taken from the *Third Annual Report*, etc., 1828.]

[D] Nathaniel C. Hart, *Documents Relative to the House of Refuge Instituted by the Society for the Reformation of Juvenile Delinquents in the City of New-York, in 1824* (New York, 1832), pp. 249-52 (editor's lib.)

In *indenturing* the children, committed to the Manager's care, the most patient consideration is bestowed upon the selection of suitable occupations and places of abode, and every means within the power of the Managers is diligently employed in the investigation of the character and circumstances of the person to whom an apprentice is indentured. The wishes of the child are carefully attended to, and an apprenticeship rarely takes place without the perfect accordance of his feelings. The execution of this important branch of the Directors' duties, involves in it perhaps the greatest degree of labor attending the management of the Institution. Three of the Managers, forming what is termed the *Indenturing Committee*, are specially charged with this employment. This Committee meets always once, and frequently twice or three times a week at the House of Refuge, often spending the greater part of a day in a meeting. Before this Committee are laid the applications for apprentices; and all such certificates and evidence as it is possible to obtain of the character and circumstances of the applicants, are required and minutely examined: and as far as a personal investigation into every circumstance connected with the proposed Indenture is within their power, it is industriously prosecuted by the Members of the Committee in the recess of their Meeting.

It is felt by the Managers, to be due to the gentlemen to whom this important department of the management of the Institution has been confided, to bestow a further remark upon the additional labors with which they charge themselves. The supervision of this Committee over the children of the Refuge, ceases not with the departure of the latter from our walls. As far as is practicable, a tutelary observation is still maintained over the situation of the youth who have been indentured, and particularly over the treatment which they receive from their employers. And in some instances, where an interference on behalf of the apprentice was demanded, as where it was discovered that he had been cruelly treated, or that his morals had been neglected, or that the character of his master was different from what it had been represented, and likely to affect injuriously the welfare of the indentured boy, a change was effected by the exertions of the Committee, and the child transferred to a more humane and advantageous situation.

The discipline and government of the children within the House of Refuge, are enforced and improved by the collateral labors of the

Indenturing Committee. In guiding their judgments in the selection of Apprentices, the Members of the Committee render themselves minutely acquainted with the individual character and circumstances of the different children, and are enabled to assist the Officers of the Institution by their counsel, in the details of their treatment of the inmates of the House. The children are separately called before them, and examined in private; their good or bad standing is inquired into, and its causes ascertained; those who are subject to censure are exhorted, advised and reproved, while the meritorious are commended and encouraged to persevere in the performance of their duties: and a regular classification of all the persons in the House is made, with a view to the relative standing of each individual, and the distribution of rewards or the application of punishments. . . .

[Out of 102 boys indentured during the year (1832), 35 were indentured to farmers, 24 to sea service, 9 to blacksmiths, and the remainder to a scattering of occupations. All 20 girls were indentured to housewifery. Most of the boys indentured to sea service were sent on long South Sea whaling voyages. Speaking of these the Superintendent said, "A large number have returned this season, and almost uniformly come to see us; dressed without exception like gentlemen; some with watches in their pockets, the fruits of their own industry. The greater part of them return to the same employ again. Many are shipped as boat-steerers, and one, I am informed, has been made second mate of one of the whaling ships." All the early reports of the House of Refuge contain copies of appreciative letters from the indentured children and from their generally well-pleased masters. It is reported that of the first 275 children who were indentured only 22 were returned because of given dissatisfaction to those to whom they were apprenticed. Taken from the *Seventh Annual Report* 1832.]

Discipline at the Boston House of Reformation for Juvenile Offenders, 1832-1833

[A] G. de Beaumont, and A. de Toqueville, *On the Penitentiary System in the United States, and its Application in France,* tr. Francis Lieber (Philadelphia, 1833), pp. 118-19 (editor's lib.)

In Boston, corporal chastisements are excluded from the house of refuge; the discipline of this establishment is entirely of a moral character, and rests on principles which belong to the highest philosophy.

Everything there tends to elevate the soul of the young prisoners, and to render them jealous of their own esteem and that of their comrades: to arrive at this end, they are treated as if they were men and members of a free society. . . .

A book of conduct exists, likewise, in Boston, where everyone has his account of good and bad works; but that which distinguishes this register from those of other houses of refuge is, that in Boston, each child gives his own mark. Every evening the young inmates are successively asked; everyone is called upon to judge his own conduct during the day; and it is upon his declaration that the mark, indicating his conduct, is inscribed. Experience has shown that the children always judge themselves more severely than they would have been judged by others; and not unfrequently it is found necessary, to correct the severity and even the injustice of their own sentence.

If any difficulty arises in the classification of morality, or whenever an offence against the discipline has been committed, a judgment takes place. Twelve little jurymen, taken from among the children of the establishment, pronounce the condemnation or the acquittal of the accused.

Each time that it becomes necessary to elect among them an officer or monitor, the little community meets, proceeds to the election, and the candidate having most votes is proclaimed president. Nothing is more grave than the manner in which these electors and jurymen of tender years discharge their functions. . . .

Children, whose conduct is correct, enjoy great privileges. They alone participate in the elections, and are alone eligible; the vote of those who belong to the first class, counts for two—a kind of double vote, of which the others cannot be jealous, because it depends upon themselves alone to obtain the same privilege. With the good are deposited the most important keys of the house; they go out freely, and have the right to leave their place, when the children are assembled, without needing a peculiar permission; they are believed on their word, on all occasions; and their birthday is celebrated. All the good do not enjoy these privileges, but whoever belongs to a good class, has a right to some of these prerogatives. The punishments, to which the bad children are subject, are the following:

Privation of the electoral right, and the right of being elected; they are not allowed to come into the room of the superintendent, nor to speak to him without permission, nor are they allowed to converse with the comrades; lastly, if it should be required, a physical punishment is applied. Sometimes "bracelets" are put on; sometimes, the offender is blindfolded; or he is shut up in a solitary cell. . . .

[B] City of Boston, *Report of the Standing Committee of the Common Council on the Subject of the House of Reformation for Juvenile Offenders* (Boston, 1832), pp. 78-84 (editor's lib.)[1]

ON INITIATION

1. When a boy is received into the Institution, his person shall be examined and washed, and new dressed, if there be occasion therefore; and if medical or surgical aid be required, it shall be administered as soon as may be.

2. The Chaplain shall also examine him, as to his habits of life, principles and passions—state to him the cause of his coming, the object of his remaining, and the improvement and time necessary for his leaving.

3. He shall then be introduced by name to the boys, while assembled, and receiving a copy of these laws (if he can read,) he shall be placed in the second or third mal grades, as his case may require; in both or the former of which, he shall remain one week on probation. If during this probation he has behaved well, he shall be so reported to the boys, and their vote taken whether he shall be received into their community.—If there be one of the first Bon Grade; two of the first two; four of the first three, or five in all, who vote against him, he shall not be admitted till another trial.

4. If a boy of peculiar circumstances, extra age, or committed by the Municipal Court, be received, he shall remain in a solitair one or more weeks, before being introduced to the boys.

DIVISION AND OCCUPATION OF TIME

1. There shall be in each day three meals—the time for eating, which shall not be less than one hour for the three: three seasons

1. See also *Rules for the House of Reformation, at South Boston. Reported by the Chaplain, E. M. P. Wells, to the Board of Directors, and by them approved.* In Francis Lieber's translation of de Beaumont and de Toqueville, *On the Penitentiary System in the United States,* Appendix pp. 216-23; and Part III, Ch. I, "On Houses of Refuge," pp. 108-24.

for play, three quarters of an hour each: two seasons for school, and two for work—except Sundays.

2. The exact time of beginning and ending each division of time, as also the hour for rising from and going to bed, shall be definitely fixed and regularly marked by the ringing of the bell as often as necessary. This division of time may be varied according to the season of the year, by consent of the Committee.

3. On Sundays, the Chaplain may regulate the exercises as he pleases, except that there shall be the two usual morning and evening services. There shall be prayers every morning and evening.

THE DISCIPLINE

Shall be chiefly moral, rather than physical.

1. No member of the community (see Initiation, art. 3d) shall be punished by whipping, or the cells; but solitary rooms, visors to obscure the sight, bracelets to restrain the hands, privation of conversation, of play, of work, of the regular food, or of one meal entirely, shall be substituted therefor.

2. A boy shall not be punished for a fault not expressly prohibited, either by the laws of God, of the country, or of the institution; and not unless he knew it was so prohibited, as far as can be judged from circumstances.

3. No boy shall be required to give information of the faults of another; nor shall he be allowed so to do, unless he be apparently conscientious in it.

4. No boy shall be punished for a fault, however great, which he frankly and honestly confesses, unless he is influenced by his being suspected, or partially known; nor shall any boy be punished for faults which come out in the confession of another, except by consent of the one confessing.

A Dr. and Cr. account shall be kept with each boy;—Dr. marks shall be given for small faults, and at the close of each day the names shall be called over, and every boy shall pass judgment on his own conduct, and answer to his name good, bad or indifferent. No opinion shall be given to the boy by which to regulate his answer; and if his answer be given better or worse than it should be, it shall be corrected by the instructors, or monitors. And if it be and ought to be good he shall receive a Cr. mark.

6. There shall be a court held in each day, before morning or evening prayers, for the examination and settlement of cases of conduct.

7. As man is not capable of punishing disrespect or irreverence to God: therefore, if a boy be irregular in his behaviour at religious services he shall not be allowed to attend them—leaving the punishment to a higher power and for a future day.

8. The accounts shall be settled every Saturday night. If a boy have a balance of two bad marks, they may be carried to a new account; but for a greater number of marks he shall be degraded one or more grades, according to the rules of those grades; except in the first mal a boy may lose his supper on Sunday night for his bad morals, if they do not exceed four.

If the balance of the marks be Cr. they shall be passed to new account for the purchase of passers to the city, books, paper, pencils, combs, handkerchiefs, and various other advantages.

9. In cases of extraordinary bad conduct, whether from its nature or long continuance, a boy may be expelled from the community; after which he shall have no intercourse with the boys; and if circumstances should again favor a readmission to it shall not be except by the regular course of probation.

10. As the government of the Institution is in part committed to monitors, the following regulations respecting them are adopted.

The monitors to whom the government and business of the House are at all committed, shall be appointed at the beginning of each month: A head monitor who shall preside in the absence of the officers: Two keepers of the keys, who shall take charge of the keys, ring the bells, open and shut the doors, morning, night and other set times, and tend the door bells: A sheriff and two deputies, who shall take charge of the second and third mal grade, one of them at all times, except sleeping hours and the first mal grade during play hours: A steward, who shall have a boy with him, and shall attend to the marketing; the boys meals, and provisions: A monitor of police, who shall have two or three boys under him, who shall daily sweep clean and arrange the boys' part of the house, except the chambers and dining-room: A monitor of the chambers, who shall attend to their daily and weekly clearing and arranging, who shall also keep order in the upper entry at night: A monitor of the wardrobe, who shall attend to the brushing, putting up, and giving out of the clothes; Three door-keepers, who shall attend to particular doors or gates, as may be required; other monitors may be occasionally appointed. The monitors of divisions and of the first grade shall be elected monthly by the boys of such divisions and grades, and shall march them, and see that their heads are combed, and their face and hands washed before breakfast.

The principal enforcement of discipline shall be by promotion or degradation, according to the following system of Grades of Character with their privileges and privations.

The members of the community shall be divided into the following grades of Character.

Bon Grades—First Grade

Those who make *positive,* REGULAR and CONTINUED effort to do right.

Their faults can be those only of mistake, or very rarely those of carelessness.

PRIVILEGES

1. The same as the inferior grades, and also
2. To walk without the stockade without a monitor; to sail and swim without a monitor.
3. To go to their rooms without permission, and into the dining room, when necessary.
4. To leave their seats in the assembling room, without permission.
5. Other things being equal, this grade have a choice before all others.
6. The use of the recreation room.
7. To be entrusted, when necessary, with the most important keys.
8. To have their word taken on all common occasions.
9. To have their birth-days celebrated.
10. To wear the undress uniform.

Second Grade

Those who make *positive* and REGULAR efforts to do right.

Their faults are those only of carelessness; faults not evil in themselves, or if so, not intentional; or a balance of bad marks. Also faults which are simply legal.

PRIVILEGES

1. The same as all inferior grades.
2. To go to the city for twenty-five good marks without a monitor, if it is the third time.
3. To be entrusted with the keys of secondary importance.

358

4. To be capable of holding the offices of appointment.

5. To take books from the reading-room.

6. To use the papers in the assembling room without permission.

7. Other things being equal, this grade have a choice before all inferior.

THIRD GRADE

Those who make *positive* effort to do right.

Their faults are those only of carelessness or of momentary erring; faults evil in themselves, perhaps, but immediately repented of, on reflection; or a balance of three bad marks.

PRIVILEGES

1. The same as the inferior grades, and also

2. To go to the city for twenty-five good marks under a monitor.

3. To walk about the grounds without a monitor.

4. To go to the gymnasium and reading room.

5. To use the books and papers in the assembling room by permission.

6. To hold offices by election.

MAL GRADES—FIRST GRADE

Those who are *positively* inclined to do wrong.—Their faults are only legal faults, (that is, things not wrong in themselves) or moral faults rarely committed, or a balance of five bad marks.

PRIVATIONS

1. To be deprived of play and of conversation except with those of this grade, or when necessary to those they are at work with.

2. Not to go to the superintendent's room.

3. Not to vote at elections.

4. For faults committed while in the grade, marks of degradation.

SECOND GRADE

Those who are positively and regularly inclined to do wrong. Their faults are moral or legal ones often committed, or a balance of ten bad marks.

1. The same as the first grade.

2. Not to converse with any boys except when necessary about their work.

3. Not to speak to the superintendent except when permitted.

4. To be deprived of their regular seats, and kept distinct under a sheriff and never be dismissed, except in their bed rooms.

5. To be deprived of cake, or any other extra food.

6. For faults committed while in this grade, to be degraded, unless for trifling ones, which *may* be settled by bad marks.

THIRD GRADE

Those who are positively, REGULARLY and CONTINUALLY inclined to do wrong.

PRIVATIONS

1. The same as all others.

2. To have their food bread and water, to wear bracelets or a visor, or to be put in a solitary room. The first of these deprives of the use of the hands; the second of the eyes; and the third of the usual liberty.

3. For faults committed while in the grade, or if a boy be degraded to this grade for any extra fault such as lying, dishonesty, profane language, or such faults, he may be deprived as above.

The time necessary to remain in the above grade before promotion is 4 weeks in the 2 Bon 2 weeks in the 3 Bon 1 week in the first mal and in the second or third mal grades one day each and the term for each must be correctly passed according to each grade.

The following things not before mentioned are also forbidden.

1. To use profane, vulgar or angry language.

2. To use tobacco.

3. To pass through any door or gate or up and down stairs without permission.

4. To cut, scratch, break, write upon or in any other way disfigure the buildings furniture or fences.

5. To engage in any game or play which is not specially allowed of.

6. To fire stones about the house, or any thing in the house.

7. To go out of the paths in the garden or pull up or eat any thing except by permission.

8. To carry food from the dining room to throw it about or pass it to others.

9. To bring any thing to the house without permission.

10. To have any buttons belonging to the clothes.

11. To converse with different grades except among the Bon Grades.

12. To have any thing of the knife or cutting kind except regular pocket knives.

13. To have yarn, thread, twine or balls except by permission.

14. To run in any part of the house except the two arches.

15. To climb any where except in the Gymnasium.

BED ROOMS

Every boy shall have a bed to himself and he shall not change his bed or sleep in the bed clothes of another or wear his clothes without permission.

There shall be no playing, laughing, singing or other noises except that of conversation in a low voice, in the chambers.

The boys shall make their beds and do the other chamber work immediately after the ringing of the first bell and the opening of the doors between which there shall be one quarter of an hour.

No boy shall keep any thing whatever in his room except books without permission.

No boy shall go into his own or any other boy's room (except he be of the first Bon Grade) without permission.

CLEANLINESS

The bed rooms, assembling room, reading room and wardrobe entries and stairs shall be washed and scoured alternately once a week when in use. The winter bed clothing shall be washed in the Spring before putting away. The sheets shall be changed at least once in two weeks—The shirts shall be changed once a week at all seasons and in the summer twice a week as circumstances require. The summer jackets and trowsers shall be changed every week, extraordinaries excepted. The chamber utensils shall be rinsed every day and washed every week.

2. During the warm weather the boys shall bathe in salt water three times a week unless the weather prevent.

3. Out of the bathing season the small boys shall be washed all over, and the large boys the upper and lower part of their bodies at

least once a week, and their heads shall be combed twice a week specially.

4. The hair shall be cut once a month.

Food

The breakfasts and suppers shall consist of one pint of tea or shells and as much bread as each boy wishes but he shall return all that he does not want.

1. The Dinners, as nearly as convenient shall be as follows:

Baked Beef with vegetables once per week
Boiled   ″   ″   ″   ″   ″   ″
Stewed Beef or soup ″   ″   ″   ″
Fish or Beef minced ″   ″   ″   ″
Baked Beans   ″   ″   ″
Puddings   ″   ″   ″

3. On Christmas, Thanksgiving, 4th of July and Election day, the boys shall have extra food and recreation.

4. A boy shall not be deprived of his food more than one meal for the same fault, nor in ordinary cases shall he be kept on bread and water for more than three or four days.

Dress

1. On Sundays and on special occasions, the boys shall be dressed in a uniform, to consist of a blue cap and jacket single breasted and white trowsers, in summer, and in winter some other light colour.

2. The ordinary dress shall be of a plain and durable kind, except the first Bon Grade who shall wear the first grade uniform.

The foregoing rules apply to females as well as males, varying only as circumstances dictate.

Childrens' Theatres, 1833

Fifth Annual Report of the House of Refuge of Philadelphia, with an Appendix (Philadelphia, 1833), p. 14.

In the investigations to which the duties of the Managers have necessarily invited their attention, they have learned that a new source of juvenile corruption has been opened in this city, which deserves to be noticed. They allude to what for want of a more appropriate phrase may be called childrens' theatres. As they have understood, the actors and the audience are minors of both sexes, though it is supposed that the whole is under the direction and for the benefit of adults. They are established in obscure places, the price of admission is low, and there is unlimited license in them for every sort of vicious indulgence. They are visited by stealth, and the money paid for admission must be known by those who receive it, to have been very often dishonestly acquired, as the visitors are of an age and a class not to have money of their own. There can be no doubt that such establishments are common nuisances, obnoxious to prosecution and punishment, and that it is in the power of the law, as it is manifestly for the interest of the public, to break them up. . . .

The Design and Advantages of the Philadelphia House of Refuge, 1835

Committee of the Board of Managers of the Philadelphia House of Refuge (Peter Hay, Chairman), *The Design and Advantages of the House of Refuge* (Philadelphia, 1835), pp. 3-4, 8-12, 14-17 (editor's lib.)

[An excellent discussion of the primary function of a house of refuge—reformation rather than punishment—contains much of the philosophy underlying the modern juvenile court.]

A very slight acquaintance with the state of society, especially in large cities, must satisfy any man that a vast number of the children and youth are entirely neglected.

A distinguished gentleman of this State,* long connected with the administration of the criminal law, in allusion to this subject, says:—

"Vicious propensities are imbided at a very early age by children, in the crowded population of a city. Parents, whose extreme poverty, casual calamity, or moral turpitude, induces a neglect of their offspring, expose them at once to be caught up by the profligate and knavish, to be made unsuspecting agents in the commission of offences, and to be trained into habits of idleness, cunning, and predatory vagrancy. A boy, nine, ten or twelve years old, cannot range uncontrolled through the streets for a week, without forming dangerous associations, or without being entrapped by some veteran rogue, who, conscious of his own notoriety, eagerly

*Hon. Geo. M. Dallas.

enlists, with affected kindness or exaggerated menace, an unknown instrument for his purposes. Children, too, accomplish petty thefts with ease, and with frequent impunity: they pass unnoticed by the busy, or, if detected, are treated with indulgence. Success gradually emboldens; they become proud of their skill, form combinations among themselves, and grow ambitious to surpass each other in their daily contributions to the hoard of a common guide and pretended protector."

It being obvious that a large class of persons of this character exists among us, humanity and public safety, are interested in the inquiry,

WHAT SHALL BE DONE WITH THEM, OR FOR THEM?

I. Shall they be permitted to pursue their present course until it ends in the commission of some flagrant crime—to be followed by a public prosecution, expensive to society and disastrous—fatally disastrous—to the future character of the subject of it? Surely such a principle can find few advocates. Immunity from criminal accountability up to a fixed period of life, and a consequent freedom from restraint and punishment until that period arrive, would be repugnant to every dictate of social prudence and justice. What means then shall be employed for their restraint and reformation?

II. Are the common prisons of the country suitable for this purpose? To seize upon the first dawn of the faculty of discerning between right and wrong, when childhood is manifest in the language, the deportment, and in the very person of the culprit, and subject the offending child to the same punishment, and condemn him to the same association, with the ripe and hardened offender, has in it something so revolting to humanity, that the spectacle never fails to enlist the feelings against the law; and judges and juries are often tempted to strain their consciences in order to produce an acquittal. Either alternative is dangerous to the future welfare of the unfortunate accused. If by the irresistible impulse of humanity, he is restored to liberty, he returns to his former haunts and habits, emboldened by impunity. If he be condemned, disgrace and infamy attend him. . . .

III. It is obvious, then, that the institution we want is neither a prison nor an alms-house—but an ASYLUM—a school of discipline and instruction, or (for there is no word more expressive of the thing to be signified)—a REFUGE.

IV. What then is the design of such an institution? The design of the House of Refuge is to furnish an asylum, in which boys under a certain age, who become subject to the notice of the Police, either as vagrants or houseless, or charged with petty crimes, may be received, put to work at such employments as will tend to encourage industry and ingenuity, taught reading, writing, and arithmetic, and most carefully instructed in the nature of their moral and religious obligations, while at the same time, they are subject to a course of treatment, that will afford a prompt and energetic corrective of their vicious propensities and hold out every possible inducement to reformation and good conduct.

The Refuge is not a place of punishment; it is not a provision simply, nor even principally, for the security of society against offence, by the confinement of culprits, nor for inflicting the vengeance of society upon offenders as a terror to those who may be inclined to do evil. It presents no vindictive or reproachful aspect; it threatens no humiliating recollections of the past; it holds out no degrading denunciations for the future—but, in the accents of kindness and compassion, invites the children of poverty and ignorance, whose wandering and unguided steps are leading them to swift destruction, to come to a home where they will be sheltered from temptation, and led into the ways of usefulness and virtue.

It is to be looked upon as a school for reformation, not a place of punishment. An Asylum for poverty and helplessness and ignorance, not a prison for malefactors. Its directors are the friends and instructors of its inmates. Instead of being outcasts from society, with scarcely a possibility of return, they are withdrawn only for a season, in the trust that by a course of right but not cruel or ignominious discipline, they may be prepared to partake of its enjoyments and even to hope for its rewards. In the mean time the restraint imposed, merely interdicts a fellowship with the vicious, which could not fail to be disastrous, and substitutes one of a beneficial character.

It imposes restraint, for restraint is necessary no less for the good of the subject, than for the security of society.

Idleness being the prolific parent of vice, the House of Refuge is designed to be a place of never ceasing occupation, to every inhabitant. It is not contemplated that every moment shall be devoted to arduous and painful labour; or even that recreation and amusement shall be denied. These are the natural and innocent, and often the laudable desire of the young. In the intervals between labour and rest, they are recurred to as subservient to the work of reformation and instruction. They are relied on, to afford relaxation from past, and zest to future employment. Recreation is regarded as part of the business of the institution; and in its introduction is as remote from idleness as from extreme labour. It is encouraged at stated periods—for a short time—under the eye of a superintendent—and is of such a character as to exercise and invigorate the body, while it diverts the mind.

Whether accomplished or not, this is the design. And truly the whole community is deeply interested in its accomplishment. It has for its object, and promises to realize in its results, employment of the idle;—instruction of the ignorant;—reformation of the depraved; —relief of the wretched;—a general diffusion of good morals;—enlargement of virtuous society;—and the universal protection of property and life.

"The establishment of an asylum for juvenile delinquents," says the late Recorder of the City of Philadelphia, in a charge to the Grand Jury, "is an event at which, as guardians of the laws, we may heartily rejoice. The pain attendant on the performance of our duty, will, in future, be alleviated by the reflection that the sentence of the law removes the unpractised convict from the influence of evil example, to an asylum, where lessons of industry, virtue, and religion, will be taught. It has been founded to rescue the unwary from temptation and evil example, and, from the too easy paths of iniquity and crime. For its support, as identified with the salutary administration of justice, I earnestly solicit your co-operation."

Some have supposed the restraints imposed in this establishment, were inconsistent with the liberty of the citizen, and especially with that clause of the Constitution, which secures to every one a trial by jury. To the candour of such, the following remarks, directed more particularly to this point, are respectfully submitted:—

The House of Refuge is intended to obviate not merely the sentence of infamy and pain, which follows a trial and conviction, but to prevent the trial and conviction itself. If a trial is to take place, the legitimate form is by jury. No substitute can be adopted, which our republican institutions would tolerate. By no other means can guilt be satisfactorily ascertained. But the inquiry which precedes admission here, is not necessarily into the guilt or innocence of the subject, with a view to punishment. Such inquiry may be made; and the law provides for the reception of children, who have been thus exposed to it, in the regular and accustomed form. Conviction is one of the circumstances which will justify admission here; and there is no other mode in which conviction can take place except by jury. One class of subjects, therefore, is formed by those who have been regularly tried and condemned.

A much larger class happily find a shelter here; where the inquiry has been directed mainly to the criminal tendency and manifestations of their condition, to their means of support, to the protection and guidance they receive from their natural friends. If adequate securities against guilt are wanting, and they must in all probability become criminal as well as wretched, they are entitled to a place within these walls, even though they may not have committed specific crimes. The imputation of a crime is not a necessary passport to admission. If it has been committed, it furnishes strong evidence of the absence and necessity of proper guardianship; since it would not have taken place, if neither necessity, nor bad example, had been the inducement. But it is only in this respect that the crime is adverted to. A child is not the less wretched because guilty. Its wretchedness alone gives it a just title to reception. The addition of criminality does not take away its claims. Almost every child that steals is a vagrant as well as a thief; for theft is the result of a want of honest occupation and support; and a want of honest means of subsistence is vagrancy. When a commitment, therefore, is made by a magistrate, it is not simply nor even necessarily because of a crime, but because of want and bereavement, of which crime is both the proof and the consequence. It would be equally cruel and unnecessary to subject to trial and conviction, and thus to lasting infamy, when the requisitions of the law are fulfilled without them, and the child is instructed, cherished, saved, without exposing it to the melancholy satisfaction of knowing, that there are two motives for its restraint when one is sufficient.

Let the law be read, and it will appear, that punishment is not named. The system is introduced for the purpose of preventing punishment. It humanely ascribes the errors of early youth, to the unconscious imitation of evil examples, to accident, to the disregard to parents, to any thing rather than moral guilt. It, therefore, treats them as deficiencies of education, and provides means by which those deficiencies may be supplied. If the parent or the natural friend will show that there are no such deficiencies, or that proofs are wanting to substantiate them, the discipline of the House is at once withheld for other objects.

Whoever will investigate the actual course of instruction and discipline at the House, must be convinced that wholesome restraint does not necessarily imply that there has been crime; that infamy is not the consequence of a residence here; that the leading object is to avoid disgrace, by cherishing a laudable pride in those who may become inmates; that punishment (except for offences committed in the institution, and with a view to preserve its discipline) is not mentioned in the law or contemplated by the plan. In a word, that the whole system is the reverse of that which prevails in prisons—the object being to prevent contamination and infamy, to prevent crime, to inform the ignorant, to support the friendless and forsaken, and to qualify all to maintain themselves by virtuous industry, and to enter the world with a knowledge of what is right, and a capacity to pursue the paths of rectitude.

It should be borne in mind that the managers themselves have no authority to send a subject to the House of Refuge. They merely receive those who are committed to them by the proper authorities; they are indeed a BOARD OF GUARDIANS, composed of thirty-one gentlemen, five of whom are appointed by the public authorities, and the residue by private contributors.—When a youth is brought to the House they consider him as committed to their guardianship and in every subsequent measure that is adopted for his discipline and instruction, this same principle of guardianship or parental oversight is a paramount feature. If by any modification of the institution a public prosecution with all the formalities of complaint, indictment and trial becomes necessary in order to place a subject under their care; a multitude of parents will see their children pursue a course of crime to the end rather than become prosecutors of their own offspring, and contributors to their early and indelible disgrace.

V. Does the House of Refuge accomplish the end proposed? The late De Witt Clinton expressed the opinion in one of his messages to the Legislature of New York, that the House of Refuge was the best institution of the kind that has ever been devised by the wit, or established by the beneficence of man. "It takes cognizance of vice in its embryo state, and redeems from ruin and sends forth for usefulness, those depraved and unfortunate youth, who are sometimes in a derelict state, sometimes without subsistence, and at all times without friends to guide them in the paths of virtue. The tendency of this noble charity is preventive as well as remedial; its salutary power has been felt and acknowledged in the haunts of vice and the diminution of our criminal proceedings."

Evil communication and example are the attendants of confinement in prison, and their effects are to corrupt the thoughtless, and harden the ill-disposed; to render all who are so unfortunate as to be subject to them, infamous and wretched. This establishment affords no means of indulgence in vicious habits or conversation, and can occasion no loss of virtuous feelings, and that honest pride

368

which is essential to good conduct. The term *punishment* is unknown, except in the necessary correction of idleness or disorder within the house. All former errors are forgotten. A new course of life is adopted, and as the *disgrace of trial and conviction* has not preceded admission, the pain of punishment does not follow it. Education, employment, and instruction in some useful trade; constant association with men of character and purity; frequent exercise in religious duty; rational amusement; the use of books calculated to gratify youthful taste, such as travels, voyages, history, fables, and other well written works; cleanliness in dress and person; the absence of falsehood and profanity: these are the chief objects and occupation to which the young inmates are destined. Let them be compared with the corresponding incidents of a jail, and it will be easy to perceive the difference in substance as well as name, between the one establishment and the other. . . .

VI. What is the discipline and instruction of the House of Refuge, and who are the proper subjects of it?

1. As to the subjects—they are generally those who are neglected and destitute, very frequently without parents or friends to advise or direct them; and there are not wanting numerous instances in which abandoned parents, for their own gratification, direct their children into the paths of vice, by sending them into the streets to beg or to steal. There is besides, a case of by no means rare occurrence, appealing if possible, still more powerfully to our sympathy—the case of a widowed mother, who sees her son rushing upon destruction, and is unable by any authority she can employ, or by any influence she can exert, to reclaim him from his evil ways, or arrest him in his progress to ruin. Where can she look for assistance or relief? If the power of the law be interposed, it sends him to jail, where he becomes still more degraded, and is perhaps condemned to deeper contamination. The true judgment of a mother's never-dying affection would readily assent to restraint, if accompanied with care and instruction, and freed from the stigma and the poison of a confinement in prison. But the jail she regards as an extremity so disastrous, that tears and prayers, and every exertion she can employ, are used to avert it, and when at last it comes, it is an overwhelming calamity. Thus is she doomed to witness the downward course, and perhaps the ruin, of her child, without the power to save or to help him.

This is no fancy sketch; nor is it drawn from other countries, or from other times. More than one unhappy and anxious mother has already applied to the managers, and found a new hope in the prospect of a Refuge for her child.

If such be the nature of the law and of our ordinary institutions, and such their inadequacy, or worse than inadequacy, in the case of juvenile delinquents—if the security of society requires, that without regard to their feebleness, their destitution, their inevitable ignorance, they should be treated as criminals, surely it is a noble charity which seeks to devise and to execute a plan for extending to them parental aid, affording them the means of instruction, and leading them into the ways of industry and innocence—which endeavours to rescue them from the effects of their unfortunate condition, ascribing, with equal justice and humanity, their errors, and even their vices and their crimes, to the want of that aid which childhood always requires.

The character of the subjects is also disclosed in the act of incorporation.—

Sect. 6. And be it further enacted by the authority aforesaid, That the said managers shall at their discretion receive into the said House of Refuge, such children who shall be taken up or committed as vagrants, or upon any criminal charge or duly convicted of criminal offences, as may in the judgment of the court of oyer and terminer, or of the court of quarter sessions of the peace of the county, or of the mayor's court of the city of Philadelphia, or of any alderman or justice of the peace, or of the managers of the Alms-House, and house of employment, be deemed proper objects; and the said managers of the House of Refuge shall have power to place the said children committed to their care during the minority of the said children at such employments, and cause them to be instructed in such branches of useful knowledge as may be suitable to their years and capacities, and they shall have power in their discretion to bind out the said children with their consent as apprentices, during their minority to such persons, and at such places to learn such proper trades and employments as in their judgments will be most conducive to the reformation and amendment, and will tend to the future benefit and advantage of such children. *Provided* That the charge and power of the said managers upon and over the said children, shall not extend in the case of females beyond the age of eighteen years.

2. And as to the discipline of the institution it is intended to be constant and firm, while it is kind and affectionate. It consists in the watchful guardianship of friends, not the severe and rigorous exaction of task masters. But it is a part of its theory that it shall

370

be only *temporary*. As it is designed to make its objects useful and respectable in life, it cherishes the hope of putting them in the way to usefulness and respectability at an early period. Experience has shown elsewhere, that habits of industry and good conduct necessarily persevered in for a few months, not in general exceeding *a year*, so withdraw the inclinations from the vices of earlier infancy, and the pursuits that might have been the consequence of them, that there is little danger of a relapse. As soon as this happy effect is clearly manifested, and the elements of school learning, and some knowledge of a trade, have also been communicated, the power to bind out the pupils, *with their consent*, to apprenticeships, is at once exercised. In this the Managers have, by law, an authority similar to that of parents over their offspring, and to that of the *Guardians of the Poor*. It differs in being exercised only upon those who have been the victims of crime, in being preceded by the judgment of a lawful magistrate, as well as their own, and in a course of preparation and discipline, which render the apprentice more fit for his station than he would be, if taken at once from a course of idleness and a state of entire ignorance.

An important feature in the character of the House of Refuge, distinguishing it from all systems of penitentiary discipline, is, that no pupil is sent thither for a definite period. No boy can be retained after he is 21, and no girl after she is 18. Within these limits the term of each child's residence is to be governed by his capacity, docility and diligence. As soon as he becomes fit for a place, and a suitable place offers, he is indentured. The section of the by-laws on this subject is as follows:—

SECTION IV. THE INDENTURING OR APPRENTICING COMMITTEE.

The Board of Managers shall elect by ballot an Indenturing Committee of five members, whose duty it shall be to decide upon all applications from persons who wish to have such children as have become sufficiently reformed, apprenticed to them. The inmates shall be bound only to persons of good moral character, who in the opinion of the Committee will feel a deep interest in the reformation of the children placed under their care.

No inmate shall be apprenticed to a tavern keeper or distiller of spirituous liquors; and girls shall not be apprenticed to unmarried men, or placed in boarding houses or public academies.

No child shall be put to service out of the House of Refuge, unless under regular indentures from the Board of Managers; and

371

none shall be apprenticed to any person or persons residing within the city of Philadelphia, or within twenty miles thereof, unless with the consent of the Executive Committee; and in all cases, preference shall be given to applications from persons who do not reside in towns, but in the most distant parts of the country.

A Bible, and printed paper of advice and instruction relative to his or her future conduct, shall be given to each inmate when apprenticed; a printed letter shall also be given with the Indenture to those under whose control the children are placed, recommending them particularly to their parental care and affection.

No child shall be apprenticed until he or she have resided at least one year in the House, given satisfactory evidence of reformation, and learned to read and write, except in special cases, and then only with the consent of the Executive Committee.

The Committee shall keep regular minutes of their proceedings, which shall be laid before the Board of Managers at each stated meeting.

The Boston Society for the Prevention of Pauperism Seeks to Prevent Juvenile Delinquency, 1837-1839

Frederick T. Gray, An Address Delivered at the Odeon Before The Society for the Prevention of Pauperism, January 14, 1839 (Boston, 1839), pp. 6-7, 18 (editor's lib.)

[In 1834 representatives from some twenty or more alms-giving agencies in Boston met and formed an Association of Delegates from the Benevolent Societies of Boston. The purposes of the Association were more efficient relief giving and the prevention of fraud and deception by applicants for relief. These objectives were to be secured through avoidance of indiscriminate alms-giving, careful case investigation of all applicants, the keeping of central case records, and frequent exchange of information between member agencies. In 1837 the volume of work of the ministers-at-large (voluntary case workers) became so great that the Association was forced to employ a full-time agent—the man who was serving as Superintendent of the House of Industry at South Boston—and the Association changed its name to that of the Society for the Prevention of Pauperism.]

But their [the managers of the Society] great object is to assist in the right way the morally exposed, and particularly children of the poor and unfortunate,—those who are not in school, without regular employment, or practicing beggary and petty theft, and preparing by these means, for a life of dependence and crime. They hope to place as they have already, a large number of these in good families in town and country, beyond the reach of strong temptations and influences that lead to ruin. Many juvenile delinquents may doubtless be saved from future infamy, by simply withdrawing them from unfavorable associations, and placing them in respectable families, where they will be trained to good habits. . . . It is sufficient to show . . . that in the past year, eighty girls and boys, from nine to fourteen years, have been supplied with places at this office. Of the one hundred and eleven young persons at South Boston [House of Reformation], many might have been saved from their ignominy, if in the earlier stages of their career, they had only been sent to such an office as the Society's for which we plead; where they could have found a friend and watchful guardian, such as the agent has been and is, in seeking out and saving these little ones. . . . The usefulness of this Society is great in the prevention of moral ruin to the young—in promoting industry—procuring for them happy homes, and in rescuing them from evil examples and the company of the depraved and vicious.

To my own mind, its importance in this respect is vastly increased, when I consider the fact that ninety-four young persons, under seventeen years of age, have been imprisoned in the Leverett Street Jail, within the last six months.

Children on Probation in Boston, 1843-1850

> John Augustus, *A Report of the Labors of John Augustus, for the last ten years, in aid of the unfortunate: containing a description of his method of operations; striking incidents, and observations upon the improvement of some of our city institutions, with a view to the benefit of the prisoner and of society* (Boston: Wright & Hasty, 1852), pp. 13, 34-35, 95 (Lib. Cong.)

During the year 1843, I bailed a number of persons who were charged with various offences, my efforts hitherto having been exclusively for the benefit of the drunkard. In the latter part of this year, I bailed two little girls, aged eight and ten years, and one little boy aged eleven. The girls were sisters. These children had been indicted at the October term, and of course their cases were entered on the docket of the Municipal Court. The girls were charged with stealing five or six dollars from a grocery store on Washington street.—These girls sold apples, and entered the store daily to offer their fruit for sale, and at such times those employed in the store would often teaze them by playfully seizing their apples. This familiarity of course, caused the children to be pert and to act in a similar manner with the property of the grocer, and on one occasion one of them took a small sum of money from a drawer; they shared it equally, and were soon after arrested for larceny from a shop and confined in jail. The next day they were brought before the Police Court for examination. The father of the little ones was present and was allowed to speak for them if he desired, but he was evidently intoxicated; he spoke in a very un-feeling manner of the older child, saying that "she was to blame, and might go to jail, it was good enough for her," but spoke in a different manner of the other. The Justice ordered them both to find surety each in the sum of $100, and for default to be committed to jail. I offered myself as surety for the little one and was ac-cepted. I took the child to my house, and placed her in charge of my wife; the other went to jail. The next day I went in quest of her mother, and after some difficulty found her, but in a state of intoxi-cation, and of course unable to converse about her children. It was not a fit place for these little ones, neither were those whom nature intended as their guardians, at all competent to take proper care of them. A few days after I had witnessed this melancholy sight, a humane gentleman, Mr. H., called on me, and expressed his desire to take the little girl who was then in jail, into his own family. I offered to bail her, and immediately proceeded to the Police Court, for that purpose, and was at once accepted as her surety. We pro-ceeded directly to the jail, where we found the little one crying bitterly. The iron door swung creaking on its hinges, to allow of the egress of the little prisoner, I took her tiny hand in mine, and led her from the place, while the child looked up into my face, and there beamed from her eyes an expression I can never forget. Who would know true joy, let him be a participant in a scene like this. I could fancy a language proceeding from that gaping cell which was now untenanted; it said in unmistakable language, "Take this infant under thy guardian care, for she has none to help her; be thou her father and her guide, then shall the blessings of those that are ready to perish come upon you. Say to her, remember this day in which you came from out the prison of bondage, for by strength of hand the Lord has brought thee out of this place."

My friend took the little one to the bosom of his own family, and the sequel is soon told;—they both became good girls, and were brought up aright; the elder one is now married happily, and resides in Worcester County of this State. . . .

In 1847, I bailed nineteen boys, from seven to fifteen year of age, and in bailing them it was understood, and agreed by the Court, that their cases should be continued from term to term for several months, as a season of probation; thus each month at the calling of the docket, I would appear in Court, make my report, and thus the cases would pass on for five or six months. At the expiration of this time, twelve of the boys were brought into Court at one time, and the scene formed a striking and highly pleasing contrast with their appearance when first arraigned. The judge expressed much pleasure as well as surprise, at their appearance, and remarked, that the object of the law had been accomplished, and expressed his cordial approval of my plan to save and reform. Seven of the number were too poor to pay a fine, although the court fixed the amount at *ten cents* each, and of course I paid it for them; the parents of the other boys were able to pay the cost, and thus the penalty of the law was answered. The sequel thus far shows, that not one of this number has proved false to the promises of reform they made while on probation. This incident proved conclusively, that this class of boys could be saved from crime and punishment, by the plan which I had worked out, and this was admitted by the judges in both courts.

Great care was observed of course, to ascertain whether the prisoners were promising subjects for probation, and to this end it was necessary to take into consideration the previous character of the person, his age and the influences by which he would in future be likely to be surrounded, and although these points were not rigidly adhered to, still they were the circumstances which usually determined my action. In such cases of probation it was agreed on my part, that I would note their general conduct, see that they were sent to school or supplied with some honest employment, and that I should make an impartial report to the court, whenever they should desire it.

This course adopted by the court I hailed as one extremely favorable to the success of my efforts, and I soon found, that it spared me an immense amount of labor which I should otherwise have been compelled to perform; I was pleased too, to observe that the opposition on the part of the District Attorney was gradually and rapidly giving way. But the toil thus saved was required in another manner, for I had frequent occasion to provide indigent girls with suitable places, and often young females were brought to my house, sometimes late at night, who required a shelter, and frequently these cases were extremely urgent; although by no means situated in a manner suited to open an asylum of this kind, I accommodated them as well as my humble means would allow. That year I took seven young girls from houses of ill-fame; these girls were from ten to thirteen years of age, the most of whom had been placed there by applications at *intelligence* offices. For these children I was obliged to incur considerable expense, in providing them with a temporary home. Sometimes young girls were brought to my house by express-men and cab-men, who felt a kind interest in their welfare. . . .

In August, 1850, as I was walking around in Leveret street jail, I found a small boy who was crying. I asked him why he was there, and he said he did not know. I inquired of the officers and they informed me that he was there on charge of committing a rape; at first, I paid no attention to the reply, thinking of course, that the statement was false, but I afterwards learned, that such was the fact. He was but *seven* years old. I proceeded directly to court, and informed his Honor, Judge Hoar, who was then presiding, of the fact. The judge immediately issued a *capias* and the child was brought into court. By advice, he pleaded not guilty. A jury was impanneled in the case, and though the presumption was that the judge's instruction to the jury would result in the boy's acquittal, just as the trial was about to proceed, I told the judge that I thought it a shame and a disgrace to all present to proceed with the case; his Honor asked what could be done; I replied, "let him be sent to his mother and placed in her lap;" I stated that I would bail him, and to this the court readily assented. I bailed him, then moved to have the indictment placed on file, which was done, and I carried the child to his home in Chelsea. . . . The Grand Jury were not aware that the charge which they investigated was against so young a child. The girl upon whom the assault was alleged to have been committed was but ten years old.

A Connecticut Survey of Juvenile Offenders, 1844

Connecticut House of Representatives, *Report of the Committee on the Punishment and Reformation of Juvenile Offenders*, May Session, 1844 (New Haven [Conn.], 1844) pp. 1-8 (Brit. Mus.)

The Committee appointed at the last session of the General Assembly to prepare and report a system for the punishment and reformation of Juvenile Offenders, either by the establishment of an Institution for that purpose or in some other manner, together with an estimate of the expenses thereof—respectfully ask leave to submit the following

REPORT

. . . The Committee . . . thought it necessary to make some inquiry into the extent of the evil proposed to be remedied, not with the view of ascertaining whether it was of sufficient magnitude to require the interposition of the Legislature; but for the purpose of adjusting the system they might suggest, to the nature and extent of the existing evil.

With this view the Committee, since the first of January last addressed a circular to the deputy Jailers of the several Counties in the State, requesting from them a statement of the number of offenders of fourteen years of age and under, committed to the respective Jails under their care, specifying the particular offence for which each was committed. They have received returns from most of the Jailers, and giving to those counties, from which they have not heard, a number equal to the other counties, in proportion to their population; the Committee are induced to believe that the whole number in the State committed to the several Jails within the time mentioned, was not less than eighty. Of this number a very great proportion was committed for the crime of theft—and so far as the Committee could learn from the respective Jailers, their parents were either deceased, had absconded, or under the influence of intemperance, had entirely neglected the care and the education of their children. If to this number are added those committed to work-houses, as well as those who are suffered to escape, from a reluctance, to cause the laws as they at present exist, to be executed upon offenders so young, together with those between the ages of fourteen and sixteen,—the Committee are fully convinced, from the information they have been able to obtain, that the whole number in the State, who come within the class of Juvenile Offenders, is not less than one hundred and fifty.

That youthful violators of the law, under our present system of punishment, should be suffered to escape prosecution, cannot be a matter of very great surprise. If convicted, they must necessarily be sentenced to the County Jail or the State Prison—in either case the effect would generally be, to destroy in the offender, all self-respect—to familarize him with scenes and associates of crime, and confirm him in his course of vice and infamy. On the other hand, if his offences are overlooked, there is a possibility of his being thrown under influences that may favor his reformation.

Considerations of this description have doubtless often operated to screen the young offender from prosecution and consequent punishment; but whether the house of reformation, from which these considerations have arisen, has often, or ever been realized, is a question of great uncertainty.

With then, a class of not less than one hundred and fifty juvenile offenders within our State, constituting as they doubtless do the source of supply of the great mass of convicts in our State Prison, the Committee feel assured that the wisdom and the humanity of the Legislature will permit them to remain no longer unheeded; but that the measures commenced in their behalf will be prosecuted to a speedy and successful result. . . .

[The Committee tell of their visits to the New York House of Refuge and the Boston House of Reformation, in both of which the boys were employed in some branch of mechanical labor. The Committee feel that in Connecticut the new institution should train for agricultural labor and that the farm should be not less than fifty acres in size, with a capacity for employing seventy-five boys. Power should be given the courts to sentence juveniles under sixteen, guilty of offences, etc., to the institution, where they could be kept until twenty-one years of age.]

> SAMUEL H. HUNTINGTON
> JOHN T. NORTON   } Committee
> THADDEUS WELLES
> Hartford, May 1st, 1844

Juvenile Delinquency and Vagrancy in New York City, 1849-1850

[A] George W. Matsell, *Report of the Chief of Police Concerning Destitution and Crime among Children in the City* ([New York], 1849). This Report is found as an Appendix to Thomas Lake Harris, *Juvenile Depravity and Crime in Our City. A Sermon* (New York: Norton, 1850) pp. 14-15.

To Hon. Caleb S. Woodhull, Mayor of the City of New York.

Sir: I herewith transmit to you the Semi-Annual Report of the

378

Police Department, commencing with the 1st of May, and ending with the 31st of October, 1849.

In connection with this report I deem it to be my duty to call the attention of your Honor to a deplorable and growing evil which exists amid this community, and which is spread over the principal business parts of the city. It is an evil and a reproach to our municipality, for which the laws and ordinances afford no adequate remedy.

I allude to the constantly increasing numbers of vagrant, idle and vicious children of both sexes, who infest our public thoroughfares, hotels, docks, &c. Children who are growing up in ignorance and profligacy, only destined to a life of misery, shame and crime, and ultimately to a felon's doom. Their numbers are almost incredible, and to those whose business and habits do not permit them a searching scrutiny, the degrading and disgusting practices of these almost infants in the schools of vice, prostitution and rowdyism, would certainly be beyond belief. The offspring of always careless, generally intemperate, and oftentimes immoral and dishonest parents, they never see the inside of a school-room, and so far as our excellent system of public education is concerned, (and which may be truly said to be the foundation stone of our free institutions,) it is to them an entire nullity. Left, in many instances, to roam day and night wherever their inclination leads them, a large proportion of these juvenile vagrants are in the daily practice of pilfering wherever opportunity offers, and begging where they cannot steal. In addition to which, the female portion of the youngest class, those who have only seen some eight or twelve summers, are addicted to immoralities of the most loathsome description. Each year makes fearful additions to the ranks of these prospective recruits of infamy and sin, and from this corrupt and festering fountain flows on a ceaseless stream to our lowest brothels—to the Penitentiary and the State Prison.

Reports have been made to me from the Captains of the 1st, 2d, 3d, 4th, 5th, 6th, 7th, 8th, 10th, 11th and 13th Patrol Districts—from which it appears that the enormous number of 2,955 children are engaged as above described in these Wards alone. And of these *two-thirds are females, between eight and sixteen years of age!* This estimate I believe to be far short of the number actually thus engaged. Astounding as it may seem, there are many hundreds of parents in this City who absolutely drive their offspring forth to practices of theft and semibestiality, that they themselves may live lazily on the means thus secured,—selling the very bodies and souls of those in whom their own blood circulates, for the means of dissipation and debauchery. These *embryo* courtezans and felons may be divided into several classes, as follows:

1st: Those who congregate around the piers, &c., where merchandise is chiefly landed. Cunning and adroit in their operations, they daily pilfer immense quantities of cotton, sugar, spirits, coffee, teas, &c., from the bales, hhds, casks, bags, chests, &c., with which the wharves are generally, more or less, loaded; and in the absence of other articles of plunder, they wrench the knobs from doors, steal building hardware from unfinished dwellings, lead and copper pipe, and even tin roofing! They will even, with the owner and consignee looking on, cut open a coffee bag in a manner so sly and artistical, that he is forced to believe the bag burst by accident, and in a few moments some 15 or 20 lbs. are transferred from the planking of the pier to their capacious baskets or aprons. It is no uncommon thing for a hogshead of sugar to be short from 50 to 100 lbs. through their undetected depredations, and the same system of petty abstraction prevails in regard to all exposed articles of moveable nature. In one instance an entire bale of cotton was stolen piecemeal, by this process, and the perpetrators were only caught when they returned for the purpose of filching the bag itself!

To guard all the property exposed along our docks, would require a policeman upon *each pier* in the lower Wards—a disposition of the force, which the present state of the Department will in no wise warrant, and which indeed would not, in my opinion, be advisable under any circumstance.

The number of children engaged in this nefarious occupation, is estimated at seven hundred and seventy in the districts enumerated.

Arrests are, indeed, frequently made, but it is my duty to inform your Honor, that, so far as I can learn from the Captains of the river districts, these juvenile rogues generally manage to escape. Parents appear in their behalf with tears and promises of a more careful supervision in future, and the petite pilferer is released from durance, with a simple reprimand from the sitting magistrates, to return in one hour to the docks a more confirmed, thieving vagabond than ever.

This course of procedure has become so universal that policemen are discouraged, and, as the owners of the property will seldom take the trouble to appear upon the witness stand, it seems to be proper that some further remedy should be sought.

In the investigation of this unpleasant subject I would beg to direct your Honor's attention to the numerous junk shops, and places where second-hand articles are bought and sold, now existing in this city. It is notorious to those who, as ministers of the law, are obliged to keep a record of these establishments, that more than a moiety of them might more properly be designated "receptacles for stolen goods." They offer a reward for theft, and an encouragement to crime, by the facilities they afford to thieves, both old and young, for the disposal of their stolen wares. There are about two hundred and fifty junk and second-hand dealers in New-York, and of this number, only 129 are licensed in accordance with the ordinances of the Corporation!—under the present law it is necessary to report those not licensed to the Corporation Attorney, who should sue for the recovery of the penalty for the violation of the ordinance. This process is found to be wholly inadequate to the suppression of the evil complained of, the operation being so slow that the offenders pay but little attention to it. It is therefore suggested to your Honor, that Legislative action upon this important, and, as it appears, dangerous branch of business is necessary, so that by placing junk and second-hand dealers in a position similar to hack and stage drivers, they may, for infractions of law, be dealt with in the same summary manner.

I have reason to believe that a statute properly framed in accordance with the above suggestions, would very materially tend to abate the amount of juvenile crime, which is now increasing so rapidly, and that by bringing these always suspicious concerns under the more immediate control and prompt action of the constituted authorities, a great incentive to these petty thefts would be destroyed.

The Second Class of youthful vagrants, are the "Crossing's Sweepers." They are entirely different from those first mentioned, and in regard to moral degradation, they still occupy a lower position. Clothed in rags—filthy in the extreme, both in person and language, it is humiliating to be compelled to recognize them as part and portion of the human family. Consisting mainly of small girls, one looks in vain for a single attribute of innocent childhood in their impertinent demands. Their persevering advances, and the lewd billingsgate of their voices, involuntarily gives rise to the question, "what fearful fruit will the seeds of sin, thus early sown, bring forth in womanhood?" Citizens generally suppose that in bestowing pennies upon these children, they are performing acts of charity and of mercy. This is a mistake. Whatever may be their gains during the day, the amount is almost always spent during the night in visiting the galleries of the minor theatres, or in the lowest dens of drunkenness and disease which abound in the Five Points and its vicinity. And they oftentimes waste large sums of money amid half-grown boys of similar stamp, in the most disgusting scenes of precocious dissipation and debauchery. The number thus engaged is estimated, in the lower districts, at about one hundred.

The Third Class are also sufficiently well marked to present distinctive features. They likewise are mostly girls of tender years, and frequently neatly dressed, modest-looking and in many instances even pretty. Their ostensible business is the sale of nuts, fruits, socks, tooth-picks, &c.; and, with this *ruse*, they gain ready access to counting-rooms, offices, and other places, where, in the secrecy and seclusion of a turned key, they submit for a miserable bribe of a few shillings to the most degrading familiarities. By these practices they frequently are enabled to carry home some two or three dollars daily. And this very money, to obtain which the miserable child endangers its present and future welfare, is easily grasped by the often inebriate parents, who, with a full knowledge of the sacrifice by which it is obtained, scruple not to use it, and on the morrow the girl is again sent forth upon the same disgusting errand.

The Captain of the 11th Patrol District, in speaking of this class of citizens, says it may be proper to state that most of these children are of German or Irish Parentage, the proportion of American born being not more than one in five. Scenes of almost nightly occurrence might, if necessary, be related, which for vileness and deep depravity would absolutely stagger belief.

These enormities have long been known to the Department, and they have come to me in such an unquestionable shape that I cannot doubt the truth of the statement.

I am aware that there are honorable exceptions to the above, and that some among the hundreds, included in this third class, are in reality honest children, endeavouring to gain a living by the legitimate sale of trifles, but the majority are vicious, and only so; their number is computed in the districts named at 380.

The Fourth Class are *boys*—they are termed "Baggage Smashers;" they congregate around steamboat landings, and railroad depots, apparently for the purpose of carrying parcels for individuals arriving in the city. A large proportion of them have no homes whatever; they will not hesitate to steal when opportunity offers, and live idle and dissolute lives, generally sleeping in the markets, under sheds, and occasionally in cheap lodgings; but the luxury of a bed is an article, however, which they seldom indulge in. Of an average larger growth, and more experience than those classes before mentioned; there is more method in their evil propensities, and not unfrequently are small burglaries traced home to them. There are about 120 thus engaged.

A Fifth Class consists of boys similar to those last mentioned, with this exception—they *have homes*, and many of them are the children of respectable parents, but through a mistaken leniency or a criminal carelessness, they are suffered to spend their evenings and Sabbath in small gatherings on the corners of the streets, annoying the neighborhood and passers by with their wrangling and fighting practices, and with the most reckless oaths and blasphemies. They will often steal, and many of them absent themselves from the roof of their parents or guardians for weeks together, sleeping in market wagons and other places of shelter; consorting with the vilest of both sexes, and forming habits of vice and dissipation which cling to them through all their after years. Frequent complaints are made by citizens in regard to the practices of these juvenile rowdies, but under existing regulations the efforts of the police are found inadequate to the suppression of the nuisance. The number of these is estimated at between 1,600 and 1,700. Besides these, there are reported to me from the above named districts, 2,383 children that do not attend school.

In presenting these disagreeable facts for the consideration of your Honor, I trust that I may be pardoned for the suggestion, in conclusion, that in my opinion some method by which these children could be compelled to attend our schools regularly, or be apprenticed to some suitable occupation, would tend in time more to improve the morals of the community, prevent crime, and relieve the City from its onerous burden of expenses for the Alms-House and Penitentiary, than any other conservative or philanthropic movement with which I am at present acquainted.

Respectfully submitted,
GEO. W. MATSELL, Chief of Police.

[B] "The Dens of Death." *New York Daily Tribune*, June 5, 13, 19, 1850 (Duke Univ. Lib.)

[INHABITED CELLARS IN NEW YORK CITY—THE BREEDING GROUND OF JUVENILE VAGRANCY AND CRIME]

No. I

At the request of Dr. James Stewart, the Chief of Police lately completed a Census of Inhabited Cellars in this city, the number of rooms in each, and the number of occupants. The document is one of great length, extending to a hundred pages of manuscript, and develops startling facts in regard to what we might characterize as a Subterranean City, from whose damp and filthy portals oozes up the foul and poisonous miasma which continually pollutes the air and sows the seeds of disease broadcast among the inhabitants of the Upper City. The document is too long to publish entire, but we will go over it by Wards, and point out some of its most important facts.

[Each of 18 Wards is described in detail with reference to the cellar population.]

No. II

Around the doors of many cellars you may see, at any time when the weather is not too cold, swarms of children whose appearance is the best argument that can be found in favor of public washhouses; covered in rags, encased in a coat of dirt, that from long hardening has become a sort of water and fire-proof paint, their hair matted into one mass with grease and dust, their limbs distorted by disease or bruised and disfigured by accident, constantly in contact with the more vicious of the street-roaming vagabonds of larger growth, utterly ignorant of such a place as a school, perfectly oblivious of the use of the alphabet they grow up in ignorance and wretchedness to a future of vice and misery. It is from these subterranean fountains of poverty and infamy, in a great measure, that the great army of Juvenile Vagrants is constantly recruited. . . .

The Boarding and Lodging Cellars are the last we shall mention. In several of these there are three classes of boarders taken; the first class pay 37½ cents per week for board and lodging; having straw (loose on the floor) to sleep upon, and being entitled to the first table; the second class pay 18¾ cents per week, sleep on the bare floor and eat at the second table; the third class pay 9 cents per week, are turned out when there is a lack of lodging room, and eat at the third and last table. These cellars are generally bare of furniture except one or two benches and a large table. The marketing is done by the children who are sent out to beg cold victuals, except in some instances where there are too many boarders to risk such a hazardous source of supply, and then the keeper of the celler makes a special contract with three or four professional beggar women, who sell the product of their appeals in behalf of starving children and sick husbands, for a mere trifle. All the baskets are got in at a certain hour, when the boarders assemble, and at the time of feeding, the whole mass is emptied upon the table. The "first class" or three-shillings-a-week boarders have the first picking, and in a trice the fingers of the first table gourmands are knuckle deep in the feast of fat things, and for a quarter of an hour they poke over the pile selecting the choice bits—the scraps of chicken, chop, ham, muffins, clean bread, &c. seasoning the variety with pickle, salad, and such condiments as fancy and a delicate appetite may select. Having satisfied their tastes, they depart, with contemptuous glances at the eighteen-penny table, or a look of pity upon the expectant nine-pence folks. The second class go over the table in a less dainty manner, and by the time their omnivorous appetites are appeased there is little left but stale pieces and bare bones for the last feeders. The nine-penny wretches fall like wolves upon their lean portion, and not unfrequently a general fight ensues, in which the bones that a few hours before graced aristocratic china above Bleeker, are whirled about the cellar in most admired disorder, to the great damage of the heads and limbs of the "boarders." It will be at once surmised that the beings who board in these places are of the lowest classes of Society—professed thieves of all kinds, young burglars, broken-down gamblers, homeless loafers and beggars. The simple innocence of the beggar girl, who, when questioned as to what she did with such quantities of cold victuals, replied, "Mother takes boarders," has been ridiculed as a mere fiction; yet, it is literally true.

The lodging system in these places is, to spread along one side of the room a layer of straw on which the first class boarders stretch themselves, lying generally very close together; the next tier, on the bare floor, are of the second class, and if the patronage be extensive the whole floor outside the straw will be packed with these persons as closely as it is possible to make human beings lie. Should this class fill the room, the nine-penny vagabonds are unceremoniously thrust into the street, regardless of rain or snow, to crawl into alleys and under door steps for the night. Thus packed, the room becomes in a few minutes filled with nitrogen and carbonic gas sufficient to poison a regiment. The door being barred and the windows closed, there is not the slightest chance for fresh air to get in, and the appearance of the wretches as they issue forth in the morning, shows plainly the effect of their dreadful confinement.

There are cellars devoted entirely to Lodging, where straw at two cents and bare floor for one cent a night can be had. The piling and packing here does not differ from that of the Boarding Cellars. In some of the dens males and females are promiscuously lodged together, and scenes of depravity the most horrible are of constant occurrence. Black and white, men, women, children, are mixed in one dirty mass. But we need not dwell upon this phase of subterranean infamy.

[Long discussion follows of evil effects of breathing impure air, etc.]

No. III

The average number of people living in *one room* among the very poor in our city is about six, the extreme number is twenty. The average number occupying one house among this class of people is about sixty. These are the permanent dwellers—the occasional lodgers swell the number to an incredible amount. . . .

Sleeping together in such numbers in one room always produces a feeling of exhaustion and physical misery, and where it can be done resort is had to low priced alcoholic drinks for its temporary relief. . . .

Children suffer the most from a crowded mode of living; the children of the poor die in frightful numbers, the greatest number is from this cause alone. In the year 1848 the whole number of deaths from diseases was 14,199 of which 6,847 were children under five years, and in 1849, deaths 22,006, children under 5 years, 9,057.

Juvenile Delinquents in Massachusetts, 1852

> *First Annual Report of the Trustees of the State Industrial School for Girls, at Lancaster* (Boston, 1857), pp. 44-46 (editor's lib.)

In 1852, the city marshal of Boston says, in his annual report: "Allow me to renew my appeal in regard to the young in this city, and to the large and increasing number of poor and destitute children of both sexes, who are growing up in vice and crime. In an investigation made to ascertain the number thus exposed, between the ages of six and sixteen, 1,064 were found; 880 males, and 182 females. My opinion is that of the whole number, from eight to nine hundred, (from neglect and bad habits,) are not fit to enter any of our present schools. From the best information which I can obtain, I am satisfied that the whole number in the city at the present time, (including the above number,) is not less than 1,500 of the same class as those described. I earnestly call your attention to them, and the necessity of providing some means to have these children properly brought up, either at public or private expense." "And," he adds, both forcibly and truly, "I am satisfied that it will *cost the State and the City more for police, courts, and prisons, if they are suffered to go at large, than it would to take them now, maintain and make them useful citizens.*" In 1855, the chief of the police of the same city, in making his annual report of the labors of his department, gives in his aggregate statement, as the number of arrests in the city, 14,464. Of this number 2,393 were minors, and 2,837 were females. The same officer, in response to the inquiry as to the number of girls exposed to vice and likely to become criminals in the city of Boston, returns to the mayor,—that under 16, the number is 393, while over 16, but still girls, he returns 884. These numbers were obtained by the captains of police, and of those under 16 at the present time, the chief remarks: "I fear that the actual number is larger than above stated." Here, then, in the city of Boston, are to be found of girls alone, exposed children sufficient to fill four times our accommodations at the Industrial School; and a few years since, the terrible band of 884 young female criminals were to be reckoned in the same class. It must occur at once to every intelligent mind, that there is no mystery in the growth of crime, or in reference to the material out of which criminals are made. In some wise these four hundred girls must be provided for at public expense; for if now neglected, how short will be the period before they will enter as fresh recruits the larger army, to fill up the ranks which are continually decimated by death and the jail.

Hon. James Ritchie, late mayor, now a city missionary of Roxbury, in a letter to the writer, says: "The number of children in Roxbury exposed to a life of sin and crime through lack of adequate parental care, is very great. Our streets are infested with those educated either in the street school or in homes of profanity and impurity. Notwithstanding our truant law for absentees, many children of suitable age never attend our schools. It is safe to say that there are 500 children in Roxbury, between the ages of eleven and fifteen, who do not attend school, and who have never done so with any degree of regularity. Many of these, from ten years of age and upwards, work in our factories, without suitable parental training, and with no prospect of future education in useful knowledge, independent of the routine of their particular employment. Besides these whose moral training is little regarded, a vast number of those who do attend our schools, from five to fifteen, have but little care from parents. In school, they must submit to rules and require-ments; out of school they resort to shops, engine-houses, or the streets, and become adepts in all the filthy conversation and unholy practices of sunken and degraded men. This of boys, and the girls in less numbers, thank God, yet in a sad proportion, assemble among the vile and low of their own sex, and very shortly lose all inherent modesty and maidenly reserve." In Fall River, in answer to the inquiry, how many children are there under sixteen, peculiar-ly exposed to a life of crime and sin, through a lack of proper parental training, the late clerk of the police court, Hon. J. E. Dawley, says: "After consulting various sources of information," he should estimate the number evidently very much within the prob-able limit, to be one hundred and eighty; and the majority of this number he believes "will become a burden to the community through vicious poverty or crime." Rev. Moses G. Thomas, a minis-ter at large in the city of New Bedford, writes in answer to the same question, that there are three hundred in that city of this class, and that in some form they must be provided for by the public.

Results bearing the same relation to population, would be found to follow inquiries throughout the cities and towns of the State; an astonishing number of children would be discovered, who, in one form or another, must be provided for by the community. It can hardly be considered as admitting of a query which will be the most economical for the State—to place herself at once *in loco parentis,* assume the burden; support and train them for useful stations when they shall reach their majority, or leave them in their present neglect and viciousness, to become inevitably the prodigals of her court house, and the population of her jails.

Prize Essays on Juvenile Delinquency, 1855

Board of Managers of the House of Refuge, Philadelphia, *Prize Essays on Juvenile Delinquency* (Philadelphia, 1855), pp. 6, 59, 62-68, 81, 109-13 (New York Pub. Lib.)

PUBLISHERS' NOTE

. . . It was with a view to draw the attention of legislators and philanthropists to this great subject, and to elicit such suggestions as the wisdom and observation of others might furnish as to the causes of Juvenile Delinquency, and the means of checking or counteracting it, that the Board of Managers of the *Philadelphia*

House of Refuge, in February, 1853, offered a premium of $100 for the best, and $50 for the second best Essay, pointing out the errors in modes of training the young, and other causes cooperating to the increase of Juvenile Delinquency, and so presenting them as to claim the serious consideration of parents and guardians throughout the land.

Forty-four essays were offered—several of them possessing great merit, and all of them evincing, in a very gratifying manner, the interest which is felt in the great subject to which they relate. In awarding the premiums reference was had, not exclusively to the intrinsic merit of the essays, but rather to their appropriateness to the *precise object* which they were intended to accomplish. . . .

The Publishers.

Philadelphia, March 25, 1855.

I. Edward E. Hale, "The State's Care of its Children: Considered as a Check on Juvenile Delinquency," pp. 9-44.

[Abstract: In America the State assumes responsibility for the intellectual education of all its children, leaving to parents their moral, religious, and vocational training. When parents fail to meet their responsibilities in this respect and their children become delinquent, then the state should take full charge of the education of these children. The state plan would consist essentially of a "restoration of the pure system of apprenticeship." A Receiving School would take the state children, both boys and girls, from their old, unsuccessful homes, would wash them, establish regular habits for them, and retain them long enough to judge their abilities and, in some measure, their character. Then the Receiving Home would indenture them to proper private masters, according to the children's abilities and tastes, to learn in the master's own home—a dozen or so children to each master—such trades as printing, gardening, teaching, scholarship, and on through the "whole calendar of the higher range of employments." Such training would be superior to that given in congregate institutions for delinquents.]

II. Rev. Thomas Verner Moore,[1] D.D., "God's University; or, The Family Considered as a Government, a School, and a Church . . . A Prize Essay," pp. 45-89.

[A well-written and at times an eloquent essay with a strongly religious tone.]

1. Pastor of the First Presbyterian Church, Richmond, Va.

1. [SOME COMMON MISTAKES OF PARENTS IN DISCIPLINING CHILDREN.]

. . . The growing amount of juvenile depravity in our towns and cities is owing, in great measure, to the want of family discipline and control. . . .

. . . Let us then consider, in brief terms, some common mistakes in family government. . . .

1. *The want of self-government* . . .

(a) *Punishing in anger* . . .

(b) *Choosing the easiest mode of punishment, rather than that most adapted to the nature of the offense, or the nature of the child* . . .

(c) *Grading the punishment rather to the inconvenience that the offence has caused, than its moral turpitude* . . .

2. *Another error is a want of wise adaptation of government to the differences of character in the SAME FAMILY* . . .

3. *Allowing discipline to be incomplete* . . .

4. *Postponing all discipline until character is formed* . . .

5. *Undue severity* . . .

6. *Constant fault-finding and scolding* . . .

7. *Vacillation and caprice* . . .

8. *Differences of opinion in the united head of the fâmily* . . .

9. *Deception* . . .

10. *Undue indulgence, and allowing children to do as they please* . . .

2. [THE FAMILY AS A SCHOOL]

. . . It [the family] must be a place of education, and its agencies are as pervading and ceaseless as those of the atmosphere on the earth that it envelopes. The teachers in this seminary are countless. The words of direct instruction are the smallest part of these educational agencies. The smile of love that looks down on the nestling babe; the lullaby of hymns that soothes its infant slumbers; the placid face of content, or the anxious front of uneasy and complaining fretfulness; the gentle tones of kindness, or the grating accents of anger; the loving light of meek-eyed charity, or the scowling brows of fierce revenge; the words that drop at the fireside or the table unheeded, or the gossip of the day; the visitors and friends; the servants and companions; the books and newspapers; the habits of acting and speaking in regard to holy things; all these, and ten thousand yet more invisible and impalpable things, are ceaselessly acting to educate and train the forming characters of the children of a family. . . .

III. [A. H. GRIMSHAW], "AN ESSAY ON JUVENILE DELINQUENCY," PP. 91-159.

[Abstract: It is impossible to name any *one* permanent cause of juvenile delinquency. Crime is the result of a combination of circumstances and a variety of causes, among the chief of which are: (a) ignorance on the part of parents and children; (b) the construction of the houses of the poor; (c) poverty (increased by poor laws and charities); lack of training or domestic discipline; the system of apprenticing now in vogue; lack of religious instruction; early orphanage; and drunkenness on the part of parents.]

[INADEQUATE HOUSING AS A CAUSE OF DELINQUENCY]

. . . It is almost impossible for the poor . . . to train up children in habits of order, obedience, sobriety and economy. Ignorance, poverty and vice are the unholy inmates of the same house. . . .

Why is it that the corners of the streets are crowded with boys? Why has "the street schoolmaster—the Devil"—so many pupils? Ask some boys in that noisy congregation at their nightly rendezvous to lead you to their homes. The houses are situated in courts or closed alleys—or in the streets, "most of the narrowest (in New York) are mere alleys, and many of these closed at the end." The internal ventilation is as bad as it can be. "The dwellings of the people inhabiting these parts are of the worst possible description; old, dilapidated, filthy and crowded with people to an extent scarcely to be believed. As many as twelve to fifteen have been known to occupy one room; sixty may be the entire number in one house." In Philadelphia: "In such a court, the houses are, of course, built against a dead wall, and unprovided with any means for the access of air or light in the air; they are without privies or hydrants, and from the height of the surrounding walls, and the confined situation of the street on which the court has an outlet, it is often deprived of currents of air through it, and from the access of sunlight, except during a small portion of the day."

"At the upper end of such courts, a pump or a hydrant, to be used in common by the occupants, is placed, and nearby a range of privies; which in warm weather affect the atmosphere with a sickening effluvium; while, in some instances, the privy is even placed in the cellar of each house, which is still worse." . . .

Go to Lowell, the boast of America. See how the working man is accommodated there. See what *cupidity* has done towards fostering juvenile delinquency. "One week ago," says a writer in the *Lowell Courier,* of September, 1847, "I entered a house, in a central location, and found it occupied by one store, and twenty-five different families, embracing one hundred and twenty persons, more than half of whom were adults! In one of the rooms, which was inhabited by two families, I found one of the families to consist of a man, his wife, and eight children, (four of whom were over fifteen years of age,) and four adult boarders!"

"In Cincinnati," Dr. Harrison says, "as in all cities of any magnitude, too many persons among the poor occupy the same building. Among the Germans, especially, eight or ten families are seen to occupy the same house—a family in each room." . . . I say, that in these foul abodes, teeming with vermin and foul air,—reeking with noisome diseases—oppressive with sickening effluvia—moral maladies are developed. . . . Is it not plain,—the reason why boys congregate at the "corners?" They are driven there by sickening effluvia!

. . . If the child stays in the house his health is ruined, and he witnesses scenes of brutality, and listens to horrid imprecations and fierce denunciations of family and neighbors, children and employers.

Progressive Administration of the Chicago Reform School, 1855-1862

> [A] Rev. D. B. Nichols [Supt.], *Second Annual Report of the Officers of the Chicago Reform School . . . for the Year Ending November 30, 1857* (Chicago, 1857), pp. 18-20, 22.

[In October, 1856, the poor-house buildings that had been renovated to serve as a Reform School were destroyed by fire, and for about two months, "during the coldest weather of the last terrible winter," the boys were housed in an old packing house. The School was rebuilt and the boys occupied their new quarters in December, 1856.]

CELLS, BARS AND FENCE

When our school was first opened on the 30th of November, 1855, we thought it necessary to adhere to the plan generally adopted by institutions of a kindred character for the safe keeping of our inmates. We received, at the opening of our school, 7 boys from the county jail; some of them had been inmates of the jail a number of times previous to their present confinement. It was suggested that irons had better be put on these hardened juvenile subjects, in order safely to remove them from the jail to the school. No one thought that such *sorry* looking subjects could be appealed to by the principles of honor. It was supposed that these subjects were beyond the influence of all such appeals.

In our old buildings we had cells wherein each boy was locked up for the night. I confess that with all my endeavours to make myself believe that these boys were not prisoners, that the building was not a prison, that I was not a jailer, were utterly unavailing. In vain did I tell the boys that after I locked them in, I should go and lock myself in. But, oh, says one of the discerning ones, "Mr. Nichols, *you hold the keys.*" The boys also, when they took their meals, had a man put to watch them, while the professed father of the family eat [ate] in another room. This did not appear to be the family system. There seemed to be some defect, some friction in the wheels of the machinery.

Then I was ordered to put bars on the windows, to keep the inmates inside.

This looked still more jail-like. And I confess that when I placed these bars on the windows I *began myself* to lose confidence in my boys. Night and day I feared that they would *break jail.* I tried to reason myself into the belief that it was necessary, that we could not keep the boys by any other method. This was the *universal* feeling. At first I thought I would put all the bars on at night, for I feared the results when the boys came to see, after all, they were in a *jail or lock-up.*

In vain did I endeavor to tell them that we feared that bad boys *might* come to the school who would require safeguards like these. Yet I saw by their countenances that I had lost *power* over their minds; that when I threw away my confidence in their honor I had severed the strongest bond by which I was to bring them back to the path of duty, and to God.

The house was all barred, at length, and the cells had strong and massive bars and locks upon the doors. But the day came when the bars, bolts and locks lay scattered in the wildest confusion about the yard. The fire did this work, and so far the fire did a *good work.* We gathered them together in heaps, and there they remain.

In the occupancy of the old packing house we learned a very instructive lesson. We had there no bars, cells nor fence, yet we lost comparatively few of our inmates. Some boys did escape from that *comfortless* abode, and no less than four came back of their own accord, while we yet occupied the packing house. In this building we learned enough of the confidential system to give it a fair trial in the new building. . . .

. . . When we removed into our new buildings we had no fence, bars or lock-ups. We were without a fence until last May, when we were so exceedingly annoyed by the parents and friends of the inmates, on the *Sabbath especially,* that we were obliged to have a fence as a matter of self-protection, to keep outside influences from our boys. Some of the boys were told by their parents to escape the first opportunity that offered itself. Some did escape from the known repeated solicitations of their parents or friends. Thus a fence was deemed necessary to the wholesome discipline of the school. As to this fence we can say that the keys of the gates were placed in the hands of a boy, and I can say that not a key to one of the four gates have I ever turned, and I do not know that any of the employes about the Institution have ever turned a key, though it is very possible that they have turned some of the keys of the gates, though with them it is a thing very seldom, if it has ever been done. We have had ten different gate-keepers since the middle of last May. Not one day passes but these gate-keepers could permit all of our boys to leave if they were so inclined. Yet we are glad to record that not a *single* case has occurred where the gate-keeper has violated the confidence imposed in him; neither have these boys who have been appointed to this responsible office been taken from that class who have never been detected of dishonesty before they came to this school. Some of our gate-keepers have earned for themselves a reputation for wickedness before their commitment here. . . .

We have no bars on our buildings, neither have we any lock-ups. Our beds are arranged either in berths or hammocks; the latter we think preferable to the former. . . .

POLICE ARRANGEMENT

. . . We found that it worked well to put boys in to superintend the several departments . . . we have police boys and various superintendents. We have found that boys in this department are far more efficient than any employes we can obtain. If a boy escapes we permit the captain of the police department to take his own way to bring back the fugitive. The chief of police with us is a boy who came to us a little over one year since. He came in irons, and as he left the cars, by his hands being confined, he stumbled. I met him at the cars, and saw him stumble; this vexed him, and he gave way to his feelings by the use of profane language. I mildly remarked to him that "you will not use such language here, my son." He looked me in the eye, and I saw that his heart was touched. Those irons, I also remarked, will not be allowed to be on you either. After we went to the old packing house this boy ran away. He escaped on Saturday afternoon, and came back of his own accord, alone, on Sabbath evening. . . . I have sent him to the city from seven to twelve times in a week; have sent money by him, and have always found him prompt to his word, and honest in all of his business transactions. . . .

We have had, I should think, a dozen boys run away, and come back of their own free will, and some of them have turned out to be among our best class of boys. . . .

[B] Rev. D. B. Nichols [Supt.], *Fourth Annual Report of the Officers of the Chicago Reform School . . . for the year ending September 30, 1859*, p. 13.

[This report contains twenty-two tables emphasizing the social conditions of the inmates and their families. In addition to the usual data on admissions and discharges, offences for which committed, ages, etc., there are tables giving nativity and occupation of parents, moral conditions of the home, sanitary conditions of the home, marital status of parents, probably causes of delinquency, moral condition of inmates before admission, industrial condition, educational attainments before admission, results of reformatory education, amount of labor performed in the school, etc. The Appendix shows the author's wide acquaintance with the literature on crime and delinquency, including English writers such as Samuel P. Day, Fredrick Hill, John Clay, etc.]

[CAUSES OF JUVENILE DELINQUENCY]

Showing the probable cause, of delinquency as ascertained from the facts of the inmates previous history

Intemperance of parents	91	Half orphans	25
Bad company	33	Cruelty of parents	14
Want of parental control	24	Bad occupation	31
Orphanage	48	Bad home	21

Parental neglect	33	Truancy from school	13
Step parents	9	Familiarity with vice	13
Hereditary criminality	10	Squalid poverty	6
Naturally ugly	198	Love of a wandering life	9
Love of strong drink			
Idleness	12	Total number included	
Improper recreations	6	in this table	428

[C] George W. Perkins [Supt.], *Sixth Report of the Officers of the Chicago Reform School . . . for Eighteen Months, Ending March 31, 1862* (Chicago, 1862), pp. 25-26, 18, 11-12, 29.

GOVERNMENT

We have no need of cells for ugly boys, or any place that might be called a secure place of confinement. Several boys during the year, to whom our attention has been especially called by the police when bringing them to the School, have always, on understanding our good wishes for their welfare, conformed cheerfully to the rules of the School. . . .

We believe our boys have realized more fully than ever before the fact that the Reform School is a *home* and place for good training, rather than a place of punishment for wrongs they may have committed, or ills they may have suffered.

The appointment of a Commissioner about a year ago, in accordance with an act of our Legislature, has been of great service to the School. Before a boy, often on account of the hasty examination necessarily given him before the Police Court, frequently came to the School with the impression that he was unjustly sent, or that some other boy connected with him needed reformation the most. The thorough examination of our Commissioner take away these excuses in a great measure. Frequently the boy is dismissed by the Commissioner the first time, on the promise to do better, and coming before him the second time, is sent to the School. . . .

Our hours of labor are the same as reported last year—five hours per day—three in the morning and two in the afternoon. We do not believe in over-tasking a boy for the few cents he may earn in a day, to the detriment of his study and recreation. . . .

[TICKETS OF LEAVE]

We have not discharged from the School as rapidly lately on account of a preference being given to the tickets of leave. We frequently grant a ticket of leave to a boy who is doing well, when we could not grant his discharge. We find that these tickets, in many instances, shield a boy from temptation, and keep him from doing wrong. . . . These tickets are renewed each month if the boy is doing well, and the fact of having to return the ticket every month and obtain a new one does much towards regulating the conduct of the boys who receive them. In cases where the boy returns to his own home the parents frequently give more careful attention to the boy's conduct than they otherwise would do, fearing that if the boy does not do well he will be returned to the School.

We have lately heard from or seen nearly all of the seventy-two boys now absent on tickets, and with but one exception they are doing well. Generally these tickets are continued for a year, and then if the holder is doing well a discharge is granted. . . .

TRUSTS

We have given the boys in connection with the School the same trust and confidence during the past eighteen months that has been granted to them heretofore. The visits of the whole school to the lake and to adjoining fields for recreation have been even more frequent than in previous years. December 24th, 1860, we gave permission to all the boys in the three highest grades in school, who desired so to do, to go to the city [Chicago] and spend Christmas with their friends, with the understanding that they were to return before six o'clock Wednesday evening, the 26th. Forty-six boys accepted the privilege, and all returned as agreed before the time specified. Our boys in honor have attended the State Fair and other similar places since our last report. We have also granted permission to the usual number of boys to visit their friends in the city on Saturdays, remaining over the Sabbath and returning Monday morning.

Two National Conventions of Managers and Superintendents of Institutions for Delinquents Held in New York City, May, 1857, and May, 1859

[A] *Proceedings of the First Convention of Managers and Superintendents of Houses of Refuge and Schools of Reform in the United States of America; held in the City of New York, on the Twelfth, Thirteenth and Fourteenth Days of May, 1857* (New York, 1857) (editor's lib.)

[Abstract: As a result of a suggestion made by Dr. John J. Graves of the Baltimore House of Refuge in May, 1856, that "a Convention of representatives, from each House of Refuge in the Union" be held in New York, with a view to exchange of information on problems of administration of reform schools, the New York Society for the Reformation of Juvenile Delinquents, after circularizing these institutions and receiving an enthusiastic response, called the meeting for the House of Refuge in New York in May, 1857. The First Convention was attended by delegates from seventeen institutions. Among the resolutions discussed were those relating to the separation of the sexes in reform schools; the classification of the delinquents according to character; the "Family System" of government as contrasted with the "Congregated System;" the parental nature of the institutional government; an improved system of education; more emphasis on religious training, and appeals to the honor of the inmates, etc. While no formal action was taken on most of the resolutions for fear of tying the hands of future conventions, one resolution was unanimously adopted, as follows: "That committals to Houses of Reformation should always be until the children are of age—to be released only at the option of the managers of such reformatories; that the object of such committals is not punishment, but reformation, and that no delinquent should be discharged until satisfactory evidence of reformation be given." (p. 60.)

Another resolution (p. 45) of particular interest requested that there be established "in the city of New York, if practicable, a Depository of Documents relating to all Provident and Benevolent Institutions, as well as to Preventive, Correctional, and Reformatory Institutions, and Agencies for Juvenile Destitution, Delinquency and Crime in different States and Countries, and to organize a system of International correspondence and Documentary Exchange, especially with the Central Agency of the 'Congrès de Bienfaisance,' at Brussels, Belgium."

The Appendix contains extracts from historical documents by John Griscom and James W. Gerard relating to the establishment of the New York House of Refuge; reports of various committees appointed by the Convention; letters from such foreign correspondents as Mary Carpenter and John Cropper, of England, M. Ed. Ducpetiaux, of Belgium, etc.; and formal papers presented to the Convention.]

398

[B] *Proceedings of the Second Convention of Managers and Superintendents of Houses of Refuge, Schools of Reform, and Institutions for the Prevention and Correction of Juvenile Destitution, Delinquency and Crime in the United States of America, held in the City of New York, on the Tenth, Eleventh and Twelfth Days of May, 1859* (New York, 1860), pp. 4-5, 83-86, 28-29, 136-37 (editor's lib.)

[The Second Convention was attended by about one hundred delegates and friends representing not only houses of refuge and reform schools but such other institutions and agencies as the Home for the Friendless (New York), the Society for the Prevention of Pauperism (Boston), New York Association for the Improvement of the Poor, New York Prison Association, New York Children's Aid Society, Five Points Mission School, etc.]

SUBJECTS FOR DISCUSSION

I. The Distinction which Should be Observed between Vagrancy and Destitution, on the One Hand, and Crime on the Other. . . .

II. The Comparative Value of the Family and Congregated Systems in Reformatory Institutions. . . .

III. The True Principles of Legislation in Respect to Vagrant and Criminal Children. . . .

IV. The Training of Instructors, Both Male and Female, for Reformatory Institutions, Asylums, &c. . . .

V. The Best System of Education in Reformatories. . . .

VI. The Best System of Discipline. . . .

A. SPECIAL POLICE FOR VAGRANT CHILDREN.

A Delegate:

I would ask the gentleman from Philadelphia, whether they have any police there, who look after juvenile delinquents?

Mr. McKeever [House of Refuge, Phila.]:

Mayor Henry did appoint officers who were especially detailed to arrest vagrant children; and through their instrumentality a number have been sent to our institution. . . .

Mr. Browne, of the Philadelphia House:

. . . I will merely state, that the records of our institution, which contain the histories of the little girls sent to us, show . . . that, in nine cases out of ten, these children are tampered with in point of personal purity: their persons are prostituted for some small gain, at an age almost incredible, and they are abused to an extent that will scarcely bear allusion. It was found that in almost every case

399

the pretense of peddling small wares was only the means of disguising their real object. Acting upon the information received, our Mayor detailed a special police to follow up these children and to arrest them, making, of course, the proper inquiries to distinguish between those who are out in the streets upon legitimate errands, and those who are engaged in vicious ways. This course, on the part of our city authorities, has been attended with beneficial results, and now there are comparatively few children to be met with in our city who yield to these vicious habits. . . .

Mr. Fay, of Lancaster, Mass.:

I wish to make a single remark about this matter of a special police. I think favorably of such a regulation, but I am satisfied that the most extraordinary exercise of discretion should be made in selecting the men for this duty. The gentleman from Philadelphia speaks of these young girls being tampered with. I have good reason to believe that a good many of the girls are quite as much tampered with by police officers as by any other class of the community. . . .

Mr. Hewitt, of New York:

Probably after we have received the information from our friend from Brooklyn (Mr. Van Epps) . . . where they have a special police to arrest vagrant children, we may think it proper to adopt a resolution recommending such a course to be adopted by all our other large cities. I am aware of the difficulty connected with this subject, growing out of the crowded state of our population; but still the evils that exist in respect to this class of street vagrants might be remedied, to a very great extent, by a police of judicious men, of higher order than the average police, who would have some sympathy for the condition of these children, study their habits and the temptations to which they are exposed. . . .

B. CAUSES OF JUVENILE VAGRANCY AND CRIME.

Mr. R. N. Havens, of the New York Juvenile Asylum:

. . . In our own institution, the Juvenile Asylum, we have no right to receive those who are technically guilty of crime as defined by our statutes; but we may receive beggars—those found in a state of abandonment, destitution, and desertion. . . . I suppose we have occasionally sent to us children who are guilty of what may be defined to be petty larceny. . . .

With regard to the proximate causes of juvenile vagrancy and crime . . . eighty-one percent of the committals to us, and following a remarkable uniformity of rule for a period of years, are either the children of emigrants born abroad or after their arrival here. . . .

With regard to the question of orphanage . . . our experience . . . runs likewise with remarkable uniformity. Taking a period of four or five years, the percentage of half-orphans and those cast-off foundlings is from forty-one to forty-four percent.

. . . in our own investigations and inquiry into the character of the parents . . . it was found that a very considerable portion of juvenile delinquents are the children of criminals, and a somewhat larger proportion are the children of intemperate persons. There is another cause of juvenile vice and crime . . . and that is the prevalence of licentiousness. . . .

C. CHILDREN SHOULD NOT BE REGARDED AS CRIMINALS.

[Appendix, "The True Principles of Legislation in Respect to Vagrant and Criminal Children," by Francis B. Fay, Mass.[1]

. . . Now, it is asked whether the usual proceedings in our criminal courts, so far as they relate to the reputed criminal, are calculated to have a favorable effect upon him, and to produce a happy and serene state of mind. It is believed that juveniles should never be brought into our criminal courts, nor before any court where spectators are admitted. They should be examined as privately as possible, consistent with the protection of their rights and to obtain the necessary evidence. The magistrates to consist of humane and discreet men, selected expressly for this particular duty, and who shall act rather in the character of physicians than of judges, and to determine whether the juveniles require to be sent to the school or moral hospital provided for them, to be healed and restored to moral health, and, if so, to direct that they be transferred accordingly; but they should not be branded or recorded as convicts, to depress their spirits or to be taunted with in after life. . . .

The City of Hartford, Connecticut, Proposes to Establish an Institution for Delinquent and Neglected Children, 1862-1863

> Report of the Joint Special Committee, to the Hon. Court of Common Council, upon the Subject of Juvenile Vices, Exposures and Wants in the City of Hartford (Hartford, 1863), pp. 2-7.

1. State Industrial School for Girls, Lancaster, Mass.

CITY OF HARTFORD, NOVEMBER 24, 1862

By concurrent action in Court of Common Council, it was

Resolved, that a Joint Special Committee, consisting of one from the Board of Aldermen and three from the Council, be appointed, to act in connection with two citizens, to be appointed by the Mayor, to take into consideration that part of the Chief of Police's late report, that refers to the deplorable condition of some of the children in our city, and the necessity of providing some public institution for them, in order to their reformation: said Committee to report to this Council, as soon as practicable, the most feasible plan for the City Government to adopt, to make proper provision for this neglected and degraded portion of our community.

A true copy as approved,

Attest, LEVI WOODHOUSE, *City Clerk.*

Committee:
Alderman,

FREDERICK S. JEWETT,
Councilmen

S. A. ENSIGN, THOS. K. BRACE, W. S. BRONSON.
Citizens
NATHANIEL H. MORGAN, NATHANIEL SHIPMAN.

To the Honorable Court of Common Council of the City of Hartford:

The Committee raised under the resolution hereto appended, have given their attention to the subjects therein referred to them, and respectfully

REPORT

The first subject of their inquiry, in order to determine whether any further action might, in their judgement, become necessary on their part—was to ascertain, as far as practicable, the character and extent of the evil complained of; and to this end they have made inquiries and investigations, in detail, by themselves in person, assisted by the chief and members of the police force of the city, among that class of our population, and in those localities, which seemed to offer the most fruitful sources of information, upon which to base their judgment as to its character and extent.

These investigations have disclosed to the notice of the Committee, sources of vice and depravity, scenes of abject misery, and spectacles of squalid wretchedness, which they little expected to find existing in our opulent and highly cultivated city. They know but little of the condition, in this regard, of other similar cities, and cannot therefore speak comparatively of our own. It may be, and probably is true, that we have but our fair share of these wretched elements among us. But one thing is quite certain: we have enough, and more than enough, to call forth our deepest sympathies, and our most earnest efforts to discover and apply some remedial agency.

The Committee do not propose to give a detailed description of the scenes and conditions of life which came under their observation. Many of the habitations they visited presented phases of human existence too revolting for public description. They propose to give the general result of their inquiries, and that only so far as relates to the numbers and conditions of the particular class to which their attention was directed by the resolution referred to.

They have assumed that the scope of their inquiries was not intended to embrace any provisions for children of a more tender age than six years; and have, therefore, made no note of the number found below that age.

Of those above it, they find vegetating amid the pestiferous atmosphere of these abodes of vice and wretchedness, some 160 children of various ages and both sexes, many of whom are under no moral or salutary restraint whatever, and many others over whom such parental or moral restraint as is exercised, is positively and exceedingly pernicious in its character and influence. A considerable proportion of these, however, could, in the opinion of the Committee, have their condition essentially ameliorated through the instrumentalities of our Public Schools and Sabbath Schools, and the many other philanthropic appliances already in operation in our city, if some more effectual measures could be devised to bring them within the sphere of their influence. But there are others, some 50 or more at present, whom these influences can never be made to reach. They are the children of profligate, abandoned parents—the sons of fathers brutalized by dissipation, vice, and crime—the daughters of mothers beastly licentious, who train and even compel their own offspring to follow in their own infamous footsteps, as a source of abhorrent revenue. . . .

What remedial measures can be devised and recommended as the most feasible and efficient in the reclamation and moral training of this class of juvenile outcasts?

The State Reform School is open only to boys; and to such of that sex only as find an entrance through the medium of judicial interposition. Its agency, as an auxiliary, is excellent, as far as it goes; but it is only auxiliary, and can never reach or properly remedy the wants of this case.

The Orphan Schools in the city . . . are merely special and limited private corporations and associations, and have neither the means, the powers, or the capacities adequate to grapple with this formidable evil.

The common Jail might, indeed, be made to open its ponderous jaws wide enough to receive them all; but, unless it emtombed them forever from human society, it would only disgorge them again, with the additional stigma of public disgrace stamped upon them, and thus more surely launch them upon a career of crime.

There is, then, but one conclusion to which . . . the Committee can come; and that conclusion is—that some public institution, other than any or all now provided, is imperatively demanded by the exigencies of the case, for the reception, restraint, education, and moral culture of these neglected and abandoned children; and that our city, in its municipal capacity, should take the initiative and the responsibility of providing such an institution—at the same time invoking the aid and cooperation, in its support and management, of such individual or other auxiliary assistance as may be enlisted in the enterprise.

In the first place, then, we are not, in point of fact, assuming any new burden. This whole mass of pestilent and pestiferous juvenility is already supported at your expense, and in a manner which imposes burdens upon you greater than you can well bear. They all have mouths to feed, and bodies to be clothed; and they are fed and clothed, not only at the expense of your purses, but at the far more extravagant and alarming expense of your public and private morals. . . .

Some proper building near the city already erected, or which may be erected and fitted at small expense, for the reception and safekeeping of these neglected ones, is all that is needed. Add to this the holy and softening influences of a quiet moral and Christian home and family, and we are complete. Nor do the Committee believe it wise or necessary ever to retain long, or to aggregate large numbers, even in such a home. Whenever, and just as fast as better homes in private families can be found, there, to the bosom of these most natural and best of all institutions, these children should be at once transferred. . . .

404

[The Committee calls attention to a bequest amounting to some seventy-five thousand dollars, lately left by David Watkinson, of Hartford, for the purpose of founding and supporting just such an institution as the Committee had in mind and suggests the desirability of consulting the Board of Trustees with a view to joining forces in setting up the institution. The city authorities, however, would have to receive additional powers from the General Assembly to exercise jurisdiction and supervision. The report is signed by N. H. Morgan, Chairman, March 26, 1863.]

Aid of Private Families Should be Enlisted in Reclaiming Juvenile Delinquents, 1866

[Massachusetts] *Second Annual Report of the Board of State Charities* . . . *January, 1866* (Boston), pp. lxxvii, lxxix, lxxxi (editor's lib.)

INTERCOURSE WITH GOOD ASSOCIATES AS NECESSARY AS SEPARATION FROM EVIL COMPANIONS

Whatever may be the causes of evil conduct, the first want of a boy or girl who is growing up in habits of vice and of crime, is immediate and entire separation from vicious associates, and temptations to vice; but, since the cravings of the social nature are irresistible, and will find food in some direction there arises a second and not less imperative want—that of virtuous companions.

The first can be of little use without the second.

We cannot supply either of these wants by shutting him in a house with other boys of like thoughts, feelings and habits. . . .

A CHANGE OF OUR REFORMATORY SYSTEM PROPOSED

Now in view of all the difficulties, and expenses, and complications of various kinds which our great reformatories are producing . . . and in view of the importance of enlisting wider public sympathy, and a larger number of citizens in the work of reform, it is proposed to modify the present system with a view of getting rid of the central establishments altogether; or, at least, of so reducing the number of inmates that they will be merely temporary receiving stations. Some of the Board are ready to recommend the adoption of the change; and all consider that it is worthy of attention and discussion.

The principal feature of the change would be to renounce the attempt to instruct and train the children for any length of time in the reformatory, and to commit the charge to private families; or, if they could not be found in sufficient numbers, then to societies of benevolent persons. . . .

It is suggested that every respectable family who will adopt a pupil from the Reform School, and train him in virtuous and industrious habits, keep him comfortably clad, give him a trade or calling, and send him to school, at least in winter, shall not only have the advantage of his services during his minority, but shall be paid therefore a sum not exceeding the actual cost to the State of keeping the boy two years at the reformatory. The average time, now, is three years: there would be, therefore, a reduction of expense on this item. A small portion of the payment might be made at fixed periods for clothing; or the clothing might be provided by the State; but the bulk be reserved until the end of the apprenticeship, and then paid only upon condition that all the obligations of the party had been faithfully discharged. The proof of this would be easy, for there would be the young man, or woman, to speak for themselves. . . .

EFFECTS OF THE PROPOSED CHANGE

If this system should succeed, and the demand for apprentices be greater than the supply, the first effect would be to stop the increase of numbers at the State Reform Schools, and soon to reduce those establishments to mere places of reception and detention of boys and girls, until something could be learned of their disposition and wants, and a suitable home selected for them. Instead of a great household of three or four hundred boys, we should have, perhaps, twenty-five or thirty awaiting places, and several apprenticed out and to be watched over; and no more officers would be needed than would suffice for that duty.

The cost of supporting two or three hundred boys being cut off, the expenses of the establishment would be reduced, we may suppose, to $10,000; leaving the balance to be expended, in whole or in part, for the supervision of the apprentices, the allowance for their clothing, and for the reserve fund to be paid to the family at the end of the apprenticeship. It is probable that a large saving of money could be made; but this is of less importance; and the main question is whether with the expenditure of any given sum, we can reform a greater proportion of boys, by keeping them altogether during two or three years in one great household, or keeping them scattered over the country, singly, or by twos and threes, in private families.

The Condition of the Destitute and Outcast Children of the City of New York, 1868

Oliver Dyer, "The Condition of the Destitute and Outcast Children of the City of New York," *Fourteenth Annual Report of the Superintendent of Public Instruction of the State of New York . . . 1868* (Albany, 1868), pp. 126-28, 138-40, 144, 150 (editor's lib.)

[This paper was presented at "a public meeting of the friends of missions and charitable works among the poor of New York, held at the Howard Mission on the first Monday evening of January, 1868." As a factual basis for his discussion, the author cites the number of people living in tenant-houses, cellars, etc., as found in a survey made by the sanitary inspectors of the Council of Hygiene of the Citizens' Association of New York. The author also presents police figures on the number of saloons and rum shops in New York, the number of people patronizing them, annual amount spent for drink, etc. The social and health conditions of the dwellers in these squalid abodes as given here are almost unbelievably sordid. Extracts can hardly do justice to this report. It should be read as a whole.]

The tenant-house and cellar populations of this ward (the fourth) is the most dense of any in the city, being packed together at the rate of 290,000 to the square mile. And a great portion of the ward covering what was originally a swamp, and other portions of it consisting of "made land," and being cursed with a most unequal proportion of the vilest rum-holes, dance-houses, and other dens of infamy, in the city, and its population abounding with the most abandoned of both sexes, it presents a concentration of poverty, ignorance, degradation, vice, crime and wretchedness, such as can be found on no other spot of equal size in America. And yet the number of children resident in this vice-infested, sin-polluted, rum-steeped ward, under the age of fourteen, is 3,967 (2,610 of whom are under ten years of age); whereby it appears that this one wretched little patch of our city would give ample employment to, and in fact tax the resources of five such institutions as this (the Howard Mission). . . .

... They [the apartments] usually consist of two rooms, a living room and a sleeping room, the first being about eight feet by ten, and the second seven feet by ten, and averaging seven feet in height. The bed room has no ventilation except what it gets by the door opening from the living room; and the living room, when in the center of the floor—that is to say, when it is not a front or rear room—has no ventilation or light except what it gets through the door and a window opening into the narrow hall. The so-called living room is used to cook and wash in, and is also frequently used as a shoe shop, tailor's shop, or for other manufacturing purposes.

Not unfrequently two families—yea, *four* families, live in one of these small sets of dens; and in this manner as many as 126 families numbering over 800 souls, have been packed into one such building, and some of the families taking boarders and lodgers at that. And worse yet, all around such tenements, or in close proximity to them, stand slaughter-houses, stables, tanneries, soap factories and bone-boiling establishments, emitting life-destroying exhalations. Nor have we yet reached the climax of these horrors. *One* such nest of pest pits would be bad enough, even if planted on a wide-spreading prairie; but here in New York, we have scores of them towering in such close proximity as to shut out the air and sunlight from their inmates—with noisome, stench-reeking alleys leading to the rear houses, with yawning cesspools and privies in the areas, and steaming garbage-boxes on the sidewalks, and gutters running with festering filth, altogether forming a conglomerate mass of indescribable nastiness, from which ceaselessly go up such rank-smelling odors as might well cause the Man in the Moon to hold his nose as he passes over them. . . .

CHILDREN TRAINED TO DRUNKENNESS AND THEFT.

. . . Hundreds of them [children] have already become confirmed drunkards, and thousands of them are accustomed to strong drink. Children from the age of fourteen years down to infants of four, are daily met in a state of intoxication. They come drunk to the mission schools. The little creatures have many a time lain stretched upon the benches of this institution (Howard Mission) sleeping off their debauch.

Hundreds of these children have also become veteran thieves, and thousands more are in training for the same end. Nine hundred and sixty girls, and 3,658 boys, between the ages of ten and fifteen years—making a total of 4,618—were arrested during the year ending October 31, 1867, for drunkenness and petty crimes. . . .

Girls Trained to Worse than Drunkenness and Theft.

The girls often become not only drunkards and thieves, but something far worse—something too hideous to be put into plain English. But the children who travel this road are seldom responsible for their degradation. They do not have a fair chance in any respect. They are so hemmed in by wickedness, and so constantly exposed to the cunning manipulations of those who traffic in their ruin, that, humanly speaking, it is impossible for them to escape. They are enticed into the cellar dancing-schools, yea, they are often sent thither by their own parents, and there they are taught to dance and to practice all the arts of the wanton, so as to be fitted to play the part of decoys, or to take their places as experts in the pretty-waiter-girl saloons, or in the Water street dance-houses.

The officers of the House of Refuge . . . not long since developed the following facts concerning a den kept by a dehumanized hag, in James Street. . . . The keeper of this den was in the habit of enticing girls, from eight to fourteen years of age, into her rooms, between half-past seven and nine o'clock in the morning, where, with hellish cunning, and all manner of seductive appliances, they were trained to lewd debauchery; and when their principles could not be undermined, nor their moral resistance defeated, they were overcome by violence, and then bribed or intimidated to silence. . . .

. . . According to the testimony of the children, many of the men whom they met in that James-street den were *gentlemen,* and some of them old men—old enough to be their grandfathers. . . .

Stopping the Leak.

It is obvious . . . that the fundamental fact which physically and socially underlies all this wretchedness, and is the chief cause of its existence, is the *Tenant-house and cellar packing,* and that next to it, in demoralizing power, comes drunkenness. It necessarily follows, therefore, that the first comprehensive and fundamental step towards remedying the evils hereinbefore set forth, toward getting at and stopping the leak, must be *to unpack these people,* and that the second step must be *to protect them against strong drink.*

These things can only be accomplished by legislative aid. . . .

TWO GREAT FACTS

The truth is . . . that no community, whether town, city, or State, can, with impunity, ignore the sufferings or the vices of any portion of itself, any more than the healthy portions of a human body can with impunity neglect a part diseased; and also that—

So long as Anybody's child is neglected, Nobody's child is safe.

Delinquent Children in North Carolina, 1869-1899

[A] *First Annual Report of the Board of Public Charities of North Carolina. February, 1870* (Raleigh, 1870), pp. 101, 104, 106 (UNC Lib.)

GENERAL STATEMENT SHOWING AGES OF PRISONERS [IN THE COUNTY PRISONS]

Age	No.
10 years	1
12 "	1
13 "	2
14 "	1
15 "	4
16 "	4
. . . .	. . . .
. . . .	. . . .
	372

. . . As a general thing our jails are miserably constructed, and there is little or no attention paid to the division and classification of prisoners. Every offender, or even one accused of crime—the boy of twelve, put in for a street fight, or some slight misdemeanor, and the hardened criminal, deep dyed in infamy, are all thrown together in filth and idleness, thereby making the jail a seminary of crime and corruption. . . .

[The Board recommended the establishment of a house of industry or correction where vagrant boys and girls might be sent—as an experiment, at least.]

[B] *Second Annual Report of the Board of Public Charities of North Carolina* (Raleigh, 1871), pp. 14, 18 (UNC Lib.)

[This report in made up almost entirely of a discussion of "the causes of Crime and Pauperism" as required by law to be made to the General Assembly of 1871. It is not based on data secured from visitation of prisons and poor houses, or on reports from prosecuting attorneys, as the Board realized should be done, but is based on reports from other states and countries, etc. The chief causes of crime and pauperism are set forth as follows: the grog-shop or intoxicating drinks; want of home training; ignorance; idleness; brothels; gambling hells; poverty; our prisons; pernicious books and pictures; pauperism; want of economy; extravagance in dress; and wild speculations. The state is described as the public guardian of all the children of the commonwealth.]

WANT OF HOME TRAINING

. . . There is but little doubt, and we believe the annals of crime will prove it, that nine out of ten cases of crime can be traced for their ultimate source to bad training or the utter neglect of training in early youth. . . . It needs only a visit to our penal and reformatory institutions to learn what a very large proportion of this criminal and vicious class are yet only youths, and inquiry will in almost every case give assurance that they came there from bad homes—or never had homes or ran away from home very early or either received bad training in such as they had, or were left without restraint to indulge their wayward propensities. Doubtless it is true that large cities furnish more of such youthful criminals than do the rural portions of our country. Yet the children of vice and crime will be met from every place where there are neglected orphans— homeless children and ungodly homes that train for crime. Every village depot—every cross-road grog shop will pour out to the traveller's view and annoyance that unrestrained and untutored crew of bad children who make night hideous with their yells and wild songs—who are experts in mischief and who are in training for the prison or the gallows. . . .

. . . In our country the results of the war have cast thousands of children on society that have been bereft of one or both parents—the manumission of the slaves has thrown upon the state many with none to care for them. Is there not due these care, guardianship, education and proper training?

[C] *Biennial Report of the Board of Public Charities of North Carolina, 1893-'94* (Raleigh, 1895), pp. 117-18 (UNC Lib.)

A city paper has well commented upon the cost to the State of the imprisonment in Wake County jail, for months before trial, of a boy accused of the theft of two cantaloupes, at a period when such were selling at about ten cents a dozen. The costs of trial, and subsequent cost of workhouse life, while such a boy is being trained in evil by his older companions in iniquity, is another part of this criminal administration, which would be absurd if it were not so injurious to the tax payer, and to the remaining hopes of a virtuous life for the juvenile offender. . . .

The Need of a Reform School

The number of children in the State Penitentiary under 16 years of age when admitted was 97. . . .

Many sad cases have come under notice during the past year. . . . A notable case is that of a boy confined in jail at a county seat in Western North Carolina for the crime of arson. He was the child of a woman of bad reputation, who abandoned him, and he was kindly taken in by a family, where, for some childish fault, he was punished. His age was only 9 or 10. In revenge he set fire to the home of his benefactors. The judge who held court in April last declined to try a child so young for this offence, capital by the laws of the State. The community was unwilling for his release upon *nolle prosequi* by the Solicitor, because the boy's brother was accused of setting fire to the jail of an adjoining county, and it was feared that the influence of heredity might induce a repetition of the offense. But his health was suffering from the confinement of many months in jail, and application was made by the clergy, and certain officials, to the Governor, for the disposal of his case, by asking for his reception, through executive courtesy, into the reformatory of some State fortunate enough to possess such an institution. [He was accepted by the Thomasville (N.C.) Baptist Orphanage before arrangements could be made to send him to another state.]

Another case is of recent occurrence. A young white girl, not yet seventeen years old, of gentle retiring manners and reserved disposition, was brought in chains to the State Penitentiary under sentence of imprisonment for fifteen years for murder in the second degree, her crime being a blow inflicted with a penknife upon a man who was accusing her of unchastity in the presence of her mother. Her surroundings had been bad, with a dissolute mother, and father of weak intellect, and her own character had not been unassailed. After confinement from that period to the present time His Excellency issued a conditional pardon, granted upon her entrance into a reformatory . . . in a sister State. . . .

The reception, some weeks ago, of two boys at the State Penitentiary, one of whom was but nine years old, sentenced for four years for larceny, is another sad illustration of our want of a Reform School.[1]

[D] *Some Cases of Children Included in the Governor's Lists of Pardons, Commutations and Respites, 1869-1899.*[2] (UNC Lib.)

George Hill, New Hanover County, was convicted of larceny at the Spring term of the Superior Court, 1869, and was sentenced to the work house for six months at hard labor. He was pardoned Nov. 2, 1869. The prisoner was only 14 years of age. It was thought the punishment was too severe, and that the ends of justice had been secured.

David Wortham, New Hanover County, was convicted of assault and battery at the special court, Fall term, 1869, and was sentenced to six months in the workhouse. He was pardoned Nov. 26, 1869. The prisoner is a youth thirteen years of age. Petition signed by prominent citizens.

John L. Davis, City of Wilmington, was convicted of assault at the special Court, 1869, and sentenced to twelve months in the Penitentiary. He was pardoned Dec. 6, 1869. Prisoner only ten years of age, and was led into the crime by bad company. Petition signed by prominent citizens.

John Ledbetter, Henderson County, was convicted of burglary at the Fall term of Superior Court, 1869, and was sentenced to serve 25 years in the State Prison. He was pardoned Dec. 18, 1869. Prisoner only 15 years of age at time of conviction, and considered an idiot. It was thought that the punishment was too severe.

Baldy Stewart, New Hanover County, was convicted of larceny at the July term, 1870, and was sentenced to twelve months in the

1. In the annual report of the State's Prison for 1894 it is stated (p. 44) that of 1265 convicts in the prison, 99 were under 16 years of age when received.

2. In the public documents of each session of the General Assembly the Governor's list of pardons, etc., is usually found appended to the Governor's message. The cases presented here may be taken as representative samples. In many cases not included the age of the child is not given. For the sake of uniformity slight adaptations have been made in the arrangement of the facts in a few cases without altering the facts themselves.

workhouse. He was pardoned Oct. 24, 1870. Application by prisoner's father, stating his extreme youth, between 10 and 13 years. Endorsed by Superintendent of Workhouse on account of good conduct.

Ben Sneed (colored), Mecklenburg County, was convicted of larceny at the Fall term, 1868, and was sentenced to twenty years imprisonment, He was pardoned March 14, 1872. The prisoner, was a boy aged about 14 years and this was the first offence charged against him. Having served three and a half years, he was pardoned on the recommendation of the Solicitor and a number of citizens.

Stephen Lewis (white), Wilkes County, was convicted of arson at the Fall term, 1869, and was sentenced to five years imprisonment. The petition sets forth that the accused is a weak-minded, almost idiotic boy of fourteen years, who was convicted on circumstantial evidence, of setting fire to a barn. He was pardoned May 12, 1873, on recommendation of [the judge, county officials, and others].

David Martin (col.), New Hanover County. Convicted at Fall term, 1873, for the murder of Willie Carter, and sentenced to be hanged. Sentence commuted to imprisonment for life at hard labor in the Penitentiary, Dec. 16, 1874. Martin was only 12 years of age, and the petitioners say, "His extreme youth and his demeanor upon trial preclude the certainty that he was perfectly conscious of the magnitude of his guilt. He knew not what he had done or the awful penalty of the crime. His extreme youth suggests a doubt whether our civilization and the more humane feelings of the age would permit his execution." The application is signed by ten of the jurors who tried the case [by county officials and others].

Lee Haywood, Wake County, was convicted of larceny at the May term, Criminal Court, 1877, and was sentenced to fifteen months in the workhouse. He was pardoned Jan. 10, 1878, on condition that his mother would *bind* him out; the reason for pardon being that boy was only 11 years of age; his application was signed by Solicitor and many prominent citizens.

Charles Gilmer, Guilford County, was convicted of rape at the Fall term, 1871, and sentenced to death. Sentence commuted to 20 years imprisonment in the Penitentiary, October 21, 1871. Pardoned Jan. 6, 1881. Upon the recommendation of Judge Gilmer. The boy was but 12 years old when he is said to have committed the offence. He has served over nine years, and his deportment has been reported to me as uniformly obedient and good—his health having much of the time been bad.

414

James G. White, Guilford County, was convicted of larceny at the Spring term, 1889, and was sentenced to serve three years in the Penitentiary at hard labor. Pardoned Dec. 5, 1891. It appearing upon recommendation of the Judge who tried the case that criminal is only fourteen (14) years of age, he very reluctantly sentenced him to eighteen (18) months imprisonment. When sentence was pronounced, criminal said in open Court, "I don't give a damn for that," whereupon the Judge, before the sentence was recorded, changed it to three years in the Penitentiary. After final sentence was pronounced and recorded, the Judge says that he is satisfied that the boy was prompted to make the remark by three bad men, who were in jail with him. . . . In consideration of these facts, and the extreme youth of the prisoner, and the statement of the Judge endorsed by the Solicitor, and of the further fact that prisoner has served two and one half years of his sentence; with the hope that the boy will lead a different life, this pardon is granted.

Handy Timberlake, Franklin County, was convicted of assault with intent to commit rape at the Fall term, 1891, and was sentenced to five years in the Penitentiary. He was pardoned, Sept. 27, 1894. This is the case of a feebleminded boy convicted of assault with intended rape upon a notorious bad character. After due consideration and investigation I am satisfied that the ends of justice have been met by sufficient punishment. In this I am more confirmed by the character of the petitioners, they being numerous and of both races. Clemency is also asked by the judge and Solicitor, and a large proportion of the jurors.

Ben Brittain, Forsyth County, was convicted of larceny and receiving in Feb. 1894, and was sentenced to serve one year on the public roads. He was pardoned Dec. 3, 1894. Upon the recommendation of the Chairman of the Board of County Commissioners and the County Physician, who state that Brittain is about sixteen years of age, he has been sick since August last, is in a bad condition and cannot get well—with consumption. The doctor states he will die in prison unless pardoned; therefore in the interest of humanity, and with the hope that a full, free pardon will enable him to live a few years longer, this is granted.

Ester McGuire, Watauga County, was convicted of murder in the second degree at the Fall term, 1896, of Watauga Superior Court and sentenced to two years in the State Prison. The prisoner is a boy, convicted . . . for the killing of another boy. It is reasonably certain that the homicide was accidental. Every man on the jury states in writing that he does not believe the boy to be guilty, and urges his pardon. The pardon is also recommended by the trial judge, by the chairman and other members of the Board of County Commissioners and all the county officers and by several hundred citizens. It is evident that the jury would not have convicted but for an unfortunate misconception of their duty for which they were not to blame. Pardon granted, May 6, 1897.

The Massachusetts State Visiting Agency and Juvenile Offenders, 1869-1873

[A] *Sixth Annual Report of the Board of State Charities of Massachusetts . . . for the Year Ending September 30, 1869* (Boston 1870), pp. 25-26, 28-30, 163, 165-66, 175 (editor's lib.)

THE MASSACHUSETTS VISITING AGENCY.

I. ITS IMPORTANCE AND NECESSITY

Since the establishment of her State Almshouses and Reformatories, Massachusetts has assumed the guardianship of many thousands of indigent and unfortunate children, large numbers of whom have disappeared in the ever-varying currents of human destiny, no accurate record of their locality, condition or life, having been preserved. Of their hopes and their struggles, their successes and their fate, no history exists. How many of them went forth to honor or to dishonor, to virtue or to vice, cannot now be known.

The records of the three Reformatories and the three Almshouse Establishments, show the names of more than three thousand four hundred children, including past and present inmates, who are *now nominally* the wards of the Commonwealth; but a careful investigation indicates that nearly four hundred of those who have gone out from these Institutions, have been removed from the care and custody of the State, chiefly by death, marriage and other causes. Massachusetts therefore has at the present time, not less than three thousand of these youthful and dependent beneficiaries, all needing her kindly sympathy and vigilant protection.

Of these, more than one thousand have been "placed out" or indentured from the State Primary School and Almshouse at Monson. . . . About nine hundred more "placed out" or indentured from the State Almshouses at Tewksbury and Bridgewater, from the Reform Schools for Boys, and from the Industrial School for Girls, have been mainly under the supervision of the officers of those Institutions. Of the remainder, about seven hundred are now inmates of the three Reformatories [State Reform School for Boys, Massachusetts Nautical School, State Industrial School for Girls], nearly three hundred are pupils in the State Primary School, and one hundred and sixty-eight are in the Almshouses. . . .

II. ESTABLISHMENT AND ORGANIZATION OF THE AGENCY.

In view of the increasing number of juvenile wards claiming public charity and protection, and of the manifest advantages to be gained from a systematic and efficient supervision, it was felt, during the past year, that the time had come for the establishment of a State Visiting Agency. Foreseeing the importance and necessity of its humane and benevolent mission . . . the present Executive of the Commonwealth, Governor Claflin, earnestly advised and aided its adoption. Receiving the endorsement of the Legislature of 1869, the proposed measure was sanctioned by one of its enactments, Chapter 453, approved June 23d, viz.:—

AN ACT IN ADDITION TO AN ACT TO ESTABLISH THE BOARD OF
STATE CHARITIES.

Be it enacted, &c., as follows:

Sect. 1. The governor, with the advice and consent of the council, shall appoint an agent to visit all children maintained wholly or in part by the Commonwealth, or who have been indentured, given in adoption or placed in the charge of any family or person by the authorities of any state institution, or under any provision of this act.

He shall hold his office for one year, subject to removal by the governor and council, and shall receive an annual salary of twenty-five hundred dollars; and, with the approval of the board of state charities, he may employ such assistants and incur such expenses as may be necessary for the discharge of his official duties.

Sect. 2. It shall be his duty to visit the children aforesaid, or cause them to be visited, at least once in three months to inquire into their treatment, their health and their associations, and especially to ascertain whether their legal rights have been invaded, and whether all contracts or stipulations made in their behalf have been duly observed, and to collect such other information respecting them as the board of state charities may direct; and, for this purpose, he shall have the right to hold private interviews with the children, whenever he may deem it advisable.

Sect. 3. All applications to take any of the children above specified, by indenture, adoption or any other method fixed by law, shall be referred to the aforesaid agent, who shall investigate the character of each applicant, and the expediency of so disposing of the child applied for, and report the result to the board or magistrate having jurisdiction over the child, and no such child shall be indentured or otherwise disposed of until such report is received; and in case any child shall be placed in a home which the said agent may deem unsuitable, he shall forthwith report the facts to the board of state charities for their action thereon, and the governor and council may at any time annul any indenture by which such child may be held.

Sect. 4. Whenever application is made for the commitment of any child to any reformatory maintained by the Commonwealth, the magistrate before whom the hearing is to be held shall duly notify the visiting agent of the time and place of the hearing, by written notice mailed one week at least before the time of hearing, and directed to said agent at the state house, and the agent shall attend at said hearing in person or by deputy, in behalf of the child; and if it shall appear to the said magistrate that the interests of the child will be promoted by placing him in a suitable family, he may, instead of committing him to a reformatory, authorize the board of state charities to indenture the child during the whole or a portion of his minority, or to place him in such family. And the board of state charities is hereby authorized to provide for the maintenance of any child placed in a family as aforesaid at an expense not exceeding the average cost of the support of such child in any of the state reformatories. And it shall be the duty of said agent to seek out families willing and suitable to receive such children, and furnish the names and places of residence of the same to the boards or magistrates who are to provide for the commitment or indenture of a child under this act: *provided,* that the provisions of this section so far as they require notice to the visiting agent shall not apply to the superior court.

Sect. 5. The visiting agent shall make a monthly report to the board of state charities of all his proceedings, especially concerning children placed in families under the fourth section of this act and any person aggrieved by his action shall have the right of appeal to the board or magistrate having original jurisdiction of the child.

Sect. 6. The duties required in sections three and four of this act shall, in case of the industrial school for girls, be performed by the officers of that institution under the supervision of the board of state charities.

The Visiting Agency established by this Act was duly inaugurated on the first of July of the present year [1869], by the appointment, as its Chief, of Lieut. Col. Gardiner Tufts, so well and so favorably known during and since the late war for his efficient services as the Massachusetts Agent at Washington to look after the interests and comfort of her sick and disabled soldiers. Colonel Tufts entered at once upon the new service assigned to him, organizing his Bureau and apportioning its labors to suitable assistants. . . .

As nearly as could be ascertained from the records of the institutions, twenty-two hundred and seventeen (2,217) children had been released therefrom, by indenture, adoption, probation, &c., who were under the age of twenty-one years, and were therefore wards of the Commonwealth to be accounted for. To ascertain the location of these wards was the initial movement towards a systematic plan of

Visiting.

A transcript of the records of the Reform School at Westborough, the Nautical Branch and the Almshouses at Tewksbury, Bridgewater and Monson, was made upon convenient blank forms, which were then assorted and grouped in divisions of towns and cities, in order that all in each place, from every institution, should be included in one and the same visitation, rather than to repeat a canvass by visits arranged in institutional order. . . .

After the work of transcribing and arranging had been accomplished, visiting was commenced. Central points in districts were reached by railroads, from which journeys in all directions were taken on foot or by horse, as expediency or necessity demanded. The task of finding the children was difficult. The records gave the location of them and names of the parties to whom they had been sent, somewhat imperfectly; there had been no tidings from many of them for several years; they had been subject to change without official knowledge; they were in remote and diverse quarters of farming towns, or obscured in the multitude of large places.

Thoroughness of search and inquiry was the requirement, and a good degree of success is the result. . . .

Visits have been made in New Hampshire, Connecticut, and all the counties of this State, except Suffolk, Dukes and Nantucket. . . .

Visits have been made to the places where fourteen hundred and nine (1,409) of the children were reported to have been sent.

The distance travelled in making these visits is nearly ten thousand miles. . . .

[The results of the follow-up visits on 1409 dependent and delinquent children from six state institutions (not counting the industrial school for girls) are presented in a table, p. 167. A check up on 694 boys from the Reform School and the Nautical School showed that 76 were in place, 40 had joined the army or navy, 36 were dead, and 186 could not be found. Of the remaining 356 cases, 52 were in prison or reformatories, 13 in almshouses or insane asylums, 221 were in the community "doing well," and 70 were in the community "not doing well." This study of outcome represents roughly 62 per cent success and 38 per cent failure.]

ATTENDANCE AT HEARINGS

We have attended hearings in all the counties of the State, except Hampden, Dukes and Nantucket. The Agency has received no notices from those counties. I have appeared in person or by deputy at every hearing that has been had except in cases of girls; from such I am exempted by law, that duty being conferred upon the officers of the Industrial School for Girls. . . .

Usually during the week that has intervened between the notice and the hearing, a thorough examination of the cases has been made, by personal interviews with the child, the parents, or persons who made complaint, police officers and such other persons as were supposed to have knowledge of pertinent facts. The result of these investigations are written out at length for the files of this office, and shown to the magistrates, and sometimes copies are furnished them at their request. The facts brought out by these investigations, and the conclusion drawn therefrom, are usually accepted as the basis of action on the part of the magistrates.

[B] *Seventh Annual Report of the Board of State Charities of Massachusetts . . . January, 1871* (Boston, 1871), pp. 80-81, 262, 266-67, 269, 280, 282, 298 (UNC Lib.)

This Act is a new draft of chapter 453 of the Acts of 1869, which established the Visiting Agency, together with the addition of important provisions relative to proceedings in court in the cases of juvenile offenders. . . .

The Act in question has two divisions, one comprising sections 2-6, inclusive, which makes more complete the system of visitation of the wards of the State established by the Act of June 23, 1869, Chapter 453 . . . and the other, comprising sections 7 to 13, inclusive, which relates to the proceedings in the courts in the cases of children accused of crime. . . .

[Act of June 15, 1870, chapter 359] Sect. 7. When a boy or girl, except in the county of Suffolk, is brought before a trial justice, police or municipal court, on complaint for any offence not punishable by imprisonment for life, except for an offence against a town or city by-law or ordinance, and, in said county of Suffolk, is so brought for any offence first described, but not now within the final jurisdiction of any police or municipal court therein, and it appears at or before the trial that such boy or girl is under the age of sixteen years, the justice or court shall make an endorsement of the fact upon the original warrant, and the officer who served said warrant or any other officer qualified to serve the same, shall take said boy or girl, with said warrant, and the complaint, before the judge of the probate court, who shall have jurisdiction thereof in like manner as if originally brought before him. And in the county of Suffolk, all boys and girls under sixteen years of age, complained of for any offence before any police or municipal court, shall have the complaints against them heard and determined, by themselves, separate from the general and ordinary criminal business of said courts: in all such cases, the notice provided in section eight shall be given to the visiting agent, and they may be disposed by the judge of said court in the manner provided in section ten, if deemed expedient.

Sect. 8. When a complaint against any boy or girl for any offence is made or pending before a judge of the probate court or a commissioner, notice in writing thereof shall be given to said agent, who, by himself or an assistant, shall have an opportunity to investigate the case, attend the trial, and protect the interest of, or otherwise provide for such child. Said notice may be sent by mail to said agent, or he may waive the same or the service thereof.

Sect. 9. [Child may be committed to jail until time for trial or admitted to bail.]

Sect. 10. [Child may be committed to the board of state charities for indenture or for care in state primary school until he is twenty-one years of age at cost of the state, etc.]

Sections 11-12. [Children convicted of offences may be committed to appropriate state institutions.]

Sect. 13. Judges of the probate courts may receive complaints, issue warrants, and hear cases against juvenile offenders referred to in this act, at such times or places in or out of their respective counties as convenience may require. And any judge of a probate court may act in any case for the judge of any other county, whether absent or not when so requested.

ATTENDANCE AT TRIALS

As already stated, all cases of juvenile offenders under sixteen years of age, except in the county of Suffolk, are brought before judges of the probate court. To better accommodate the local officers, these magistrates hold court in various places in their counties, at convenient times, and to such sittings are the accused brought. . . .

Trial is usually had the day following complaint, sometimes on the same day; rarely, if ever, later than four days subsequent to complaint. So good are the facilities of the Agency that its representatives are ready to attend trials in any part of the State as soon as the court and officers deem it necessary to proceed. Certainly the children are entitled to enough delay to secure investigation and preparation for defence in all cases, especially so when decisions unfavorable to them may result in their incarceration for a long term of years. Undue haste in matters so important to the State and vital to the child should be discountenanced everywhere. The convenience of an officer or community should always be subordinate to the interests of a child. . . . Investigation is made before the trial by such legitimate inquisition as will bring out the pertinent facts concerning the circumstances of the case, the character of the accused, and his or her situation and surroundings at home. At the trial the Agent or his assistant appears, listens to the testimony, and sifts the evidence by examination of the witnesses, if it is deemed expedient. After the testimony in the case has been offered, he gives the judge the information gained elsewhere by the investigation, and urges such considerations in favor of the accused as appear worthy. The policy of the Agent is not to secure, if possible, in all cases, an acquittal of the child, but to bring about, so far as is in his power, the thing which is best for the child. The investigations shape largely our action and purpose and we urge discharge, probation or committal to a reformatory as circumstances and facts will warrant. It is often a greater mercy to commit a child to a State reformatory during his minority than to give him or her a discharge. . . . .

The Agent has not, as has been intimated in some quarters, the power of decision in the cases of juvenile offenders. He is but the friend of the child—a legally commissioned friend—who appears by authority of the law. The judge hears only with judicial fairness the Agent's statements. . . . With him is the verdict. When that has been reached, the question arises, What shall be done for and with the child? At this stage of proceedings the law gives the Visiting Agent the opportunity of suggestion and request. The judge may punish by the ordinary methods of fine and imprisonment in jail, house of correction or State prison; he may commit to a State reformatory, he may put on probation, or "upon *request* of said Agent, may authorize the Board of State Charities to take and indenture or place in charge of any person, or in the State Primary School, such child until he or she attains the age of twenty-one years, or for a less time." . . .

As already stated, and as appears by the law, Suffolk county is made by some sections an exception to the other counties of the State. The jurisdiction of the municipal court therein was not disturbed by the legislation of 1870. . . .

The duties of the Agent in reference to cases arising in Suffolk are the same as in cases occurring in other counties, but are necessarily differently exercised. So numerous are the cases in Boston, and such are the necessary modes of procedure in the courts, that similar opportunity for the issue of "notices" to the Agent, and for his investigation, permitted in other counties, could not be insisted on without complications and delay that would involve unfavorable incidents.

To facilitate the business of the court, as well as to conform to the requirement of the law, an assistant of the Visiting Agent is in daily attendance at the sessions of the municipal court. Each morning he visits the "Tombs" to ascertain if minors are there among other prisoners waiting the opening of the court, and, if found, an examination of their cases is made, and he appears for them at the session, proceeding in their behalf in same general way as has been indicated in reference to other courts.

The law requires that minors under sixteen years of age, before municipal courts, "shall have complaints against them heard and determined by themselves, separate from the general and ordinary criminal business of said courts." The practice is to hear such cases after the docket has been cleared of others. As the adult cases are numerous, varying from thirty to one hundred and fifty daily, and as they may require a long or a short time for disposal, and as juveniles are sometimes brought to the court after its sessions have commenced who were not among those arrested before its opening, the attendance of the assistant upon the court during its entire session is usually compelled. . . .

The grand purpose of the Visiting Agency is the salvation of children. Its effectiveness in that particular alone should challenge consideration. . . .

Upon the points of reformatory effectiveness and economical methods, the following statements are offered.

Of the five hundred ninety-six (596) children convicted since the establishment of the Visiting Agency, the Agent has taken from the courts one hundred fifteen (115), or nearly one-fifth of the whole. He took twenty-two from the hands of magistrates and officers without formal trial, making a total of one hundred thirty-seven taken by the Visiting Agent. It secured the probation of one hundred eighty-nine (189) of the remaining number; of those taken by the Agency twenty-four were put in the Primary School and one hundred thirteen (113) were placed in families. Most of these have done well; but eight of them have been subsequently committed to any institution, while there are some luminous examples of well-doing. Of the whole number placed on *probation* twenty-five have again come under arrest. . . .

It is a part of the policy of the Agency, to secure the probation of as many juvenile offenders as circumstances and the best good will permit, and assure their subsequent good conduct by frequent visits and careful oversight of them in connection with their relatives, friends and the good citizens of the community. The Agency receives much encouragement and assistance from the interest worthy people in the community take in the wayward and unfortunate children it attempts to reclaim without commitment to public institutions. . . .

Most of the children [placed on probation] . . . have done well.

They are frequently visited and earnestly advised of the necessity of well-doing, while a knowledge of the consequences of wrong-doing is not hid from them. As many of this class of children as are in Boston or vicinity are required to report at this office every week or fortnight, and they are expected to give an account of themselves. On Saturday afternoons they come in groups to the State House to tell the stories of their behavior, usually putting in a bright and tidy appearance, with a fair history. We do not trust altogether, however, to the reports they give, but by other means learn of their well or evil doing. It is believed that many even unpromising subjects, may be carried safely over the period when temptations can be least resisted, in a state of continued probation, to years of discretion.

[C] *Eighth Annual Report of the Board of State Charities of Massachusetts . . . January, 1872* (Boston, 1872), 278-80 (editor's lib.)

VISITATION OF PROBATIONERS

. . . When the child is put on probation by the court, he or she is supplied with the card of this Agency, whereon is inscribed the name of the child, the residence, charge, court, time of hearing, when to report, employment and remarks, and is requested to appear at this office every Saturday or fortnightly, if in Boston or its vicinity, as most are, during the probationary period, and to report their conduct. The attendance of such probationers at the office during the early hours of Saturday afternoon is often quite numerous, and their tidy appearance and cheerful looks generally betoken well-doing. They often bring certificates from teachers, employers and other persons showing how they have conducted themselves during the intervals of their visits to us. Meanwhile, by visits to their homes and inquiries of truant and police officers and other persons, we know for ourselves how they have behaved. . . .

When the probationary period is ended, the child goes again before the court, and the Visiting Agent or his assistant reports their conduct during the time to the judge. If it has been unexceptional he orders the complaint dismissed; if for reasons it appears best to extend the term of probation, that is done, and the oversight described is continued. The police officers are charged by the judge to bring immediately before him for sentence, without a new hearing, all probationers doing badly during their term.

425

Juvenile Offences in Massachusetts: Causes, Dispositions, and Remedies, 1871-1872

[A] *Eighth Annual Report of the Board of State Charities of Massachusetts . . . January, 1872* (Boston, 1872), pp. 222-31. (editor's lib.)

[The tables presented below have been adapted from statistical and descriptive data found on pages 222-31.]

Delinquency Cases[1] handled by the Courts of Massachusetts for the Year Ending September 30, 1871, by Sex and Charge

Offence	Total	Boys	Girls
Larceny	591	548	43
Assault and Battery	194	191	3
Stubborn	155	110	45
Malicious Mischief	154	152	2
Breaking and Entering	106	106	
Trespass	59	59	
Violation of Lord's Day	47	47	
Vagrancy	40	36	4
Drunkenness	20	19	1
Idle and Disorderly	12	5	7
Disturbing School	11	11	
Disturbing Peace	11	11	
Stealing Ride	9	9	
Burglary	7	7	
Assault, intent to ravish	6	6	
Larceny from person	6	6	
Setting Bonfire	5	5	
Running Away	5	5	
Receiving Stolen Goods	4	3	1
Lewd and lascivious	3	3	
Assault and Battery with Knife	3	3	
Common Drunkard	3	3	
Night walking	2	1	1
Embezzlement	2	2	
Forgery	2	2	
Selling without license	1	1	
Goods on False Pretences	1		1
Profanity	1	1	
Fornication	1		1
Neglected Child	1	1	
Rescuing beasts from officer	1	1	
TOTAL	1463	1354	109

1. All offenders under seventeen years of age—except for offences against city ordinances and town by-laws, and those punishable by imprisonment for life (p. 222).

Disposition of Delinquency Cases Handled by the Courts of Massachusetts for the Year Ending September 30, 1871, by Sex

Disposition	Total	Boys	Girls
Probation	456	436	20
Fined	289	282	7
Discharged	241	228	13
Taken by Visiting Agent	128	93	35
Reform School	96	96	
Nautical School	90	90	
House of Reformation for Juvenile Off. Boston	30	29	1
Failed to Appear	28	26	2
Industrial School	27		27
Taken by Private Institutions	20	19	1
Adjusted before Trial	15	15	
Sent home out of State	10	10	
House of Industry, Boston	9	6	3
House of Reformation for Juvenile Off., Lowell	9	9	
House of Correction	4	4	
Taken by Truant officer	4	4	
Common Jail	2	2	
Bail to Superior Court	2	2	
To go to sea	2	2	
Transferred to Probate Court	1	1	
TOTAL	1463	1354	109

[B] *Ninth Annual Report of the Board of State Charities of Massachusetts . . . January, 1873* (Boston, 1873), pp. 502 pp. 303, 307-14 (editor's lib.)

It is evident from the statistics of these pages, and from a consideration of the places from whence offenders come, of the influences which surround them and from the character of the offences committed, that poverty, overcrowded and incommodious dwelling-places, neglect, intemperance and ignorance are leading causes in the production of juvenile offenders in Massachusetts as well as elsewhere.

To our own view [Gardiner Tufts, Visiting Agent] poverty seems the leading cause of vice in children; it compels crowded and incommodious dwelling, and from it results neglect, intemperance and ignorance. . . . Stealing heads the list of offences in our calendar of juvenile crime. To the children of poverty is often presented for their choice the alternative, "either to steal or starve," and "it is not human nature quietly to submit to the latter, while the former means of deliverance is within reach." . . .

The personal necessities of children are not their only compulsions to crime; the necessities of parents also compel and sometimes they are forced by their parents or those with whom they live to the commission of crime, in order that their appetites and lusts may be gratified. It may not be often that children are taught to steal by their parents or guardians, but they frequently learn to do so from the demands of the family necessity. Its wants send the children to the wharves and to the buildings being erected or torn down, to pick up chips and wood; to the houses of the better provided, to beg food; to the streets to gather rags and junk; and they not having the moral intelligence which distinguishes in such pursuits between lawful and unlawful possession, readily and without knowledge pass the bound that divides honest getting from stealing, and thus they contract the habit of taking whatever their wants demand, if exposed to sight or seizure. . . .

In order to show the facts and conclusions of this agency in reference to juvenile offence and offenders in the light of the opinions, judgment and data of those whose knowledge and experience convey confidence and respect relative to the causes of juvenile offence, and the best methods of dealing with juvenile offenders, I introduce several answers received in reply to a series of questions addressed to the chiefs of police and city marshals in our State. Those here quoted were from Fall River, Charlestown, Lowell, Lawrence and New Bedford. . . . The answers given, in the main express the opinions of many other like officers in the State. There is great unanimity of opinion in regard to the desirableness and value of local truant schools as preventive means, the belief being quite general that habitual truancy leads almost always to juvenile criminality. . . .

[Five quoted answers are given by chiefs of police and city marshals from the above-named cities to eleven questions, as follows:—

    1. From what classes do juvenile offenders mostly come?

    2. From what causes do juvenile offences arise?

    3. What are the first public manifestations of a wayward course among children?

    4. What, in your opinion, are the best means for preventing juvenile offence?

    5. What are the best methods of restraining juvenile offenders, and in what way can they best be dealt with?

6. What is your opinion of the value of Reform Schools and the reformatory processes which present laws contemplate?

7. What percent of the juvenile offenders sent to the Reform Schools of this State are reformed, according to the data you have; or in your judgment?

8. What is the value of punishment in correcting and preventing juvenile offence?

9. Would a Truant School in your city diminish the cases of juvenile offence?

10. Would County Reformatories be likely to bring better results than a State one, equally well officered and managed?

11. What, in your judgment, is the comparative value of terminate and indeterminate sentences, in cases of juvenile offenders?]

Juvenile Vagrants and Delinquents in New York City, 1872

Edward Crapsey, *The Nether Side of New York; or, the Vice, Crime and Poverty of the Great Metropolis* (New York, 1872), pp. 119-23, 125 (Brit. Mus.)

[A New York journalist presents "without extenuation or exaggeration" the facts acquired in a four year study "in the hope that I might furnish a basis of fact for the operations of the social reformers of the future."]

Outcast Children

. . . At the beginning of the undertaking I discovered that notwithstanding the many earnest agencies at work among these outcasts to ameliorate their condition, very few precise facts concerning them were known. The intelligent and sympathetic agents of the Children's Aid Society, the Howard Mission, the Catholic Protectory, and other organized charities, were constantly among them; yet no one of them could give any exact data as to the number, haunts, or habits of the outcast children of New York, nor did the reports of any of these institutions contain such information in manageable shape. The moral and physical destitution of these child-vagrants, and the causes which produced them, are the topics chiefly discussed by these societies; but the statements of facts are almost entirely confined to the means of reclamation which they so constantly and unselfishly exert. . . . The only positive statement I have seen is that "the vagrant and neglected children of the city; if placed in double file three feet apart, would make a procession eight miles long." In this estimate are included the neglected children as well as the true nomads of the streets, and it is under rather than above the truth. . . .

The first and most natural recourse of the outcast who has just passed from a neglected babyhood into a vagrant childhood, is beggary. It is these forlorn creatures whose naked feet smear the gutter ice with blood, whose hands eagerly search the garbage barrels for morsels of refuse food which the homeless dogs will not touch, but which they devour; it is they whose eyes have the frightful glare only privation can give, and whose voices are often so weakened by want that they cannot audibly articulate their needs at area doors; it is they who are found at night under stoops, in wagons, in lumber yards, or timidly asking for lodging at the police stations. I am fully aware that all this means that there are homeless children who are actually starving in the streets of New York, and I am also conscious that I have not exaggerated nor set down aught in malice. There are such children, and hundreds of them. Despite the constant and systematic efforts made by organized charities, there are constantly in the streets fifteen hundred fragile boys and girls under the age of ten years, who have no conception of the meaning of the word home, and who are dying by inches for the want of sufficient nutriment. . . .

Juvenile delinquents are infantile mendicants ripened by time and circumstances. Foremost among them are the boy burglars and thieves who have become at least a grave annoyance of metropolitan life. There is nothing too trivial to escape the attention of these young marauders, and their physical insignificance is to their advantage in their work of depredation. They go with nonchalant ease where bolder spirits would fear to tread and larger bodies fail to penetrate. . . . Their particular depredation is to enter unoccupied houses and strip them of whatever they can conveniently carry away. The summer months, when large numbers of families go into the country for weeks, leaving their homes entirely unprotected, offer an opportunity to burglars which is never neglected, and very few of these houses escape pillage. Sometimes a clean sweep of everything portable is made, which is satisfactory evidence that adults have been at work; and sometimes only a few trifling articles are missing, but much wanton damage is done to what is left, which is sure proof that boys have been about. But the especial field of juvenile burglars is found in houses which are to let, and are therefore left to care for themselves by the police. The boys easily gain entrance, and once in are secure in the intrusion, however protracted it may be. There is nothing to operate upon apparently but the bare floors and walls, but the boys find portable plunder in the gas and water fixtures. Not only do they wrench off faucets and burners, but they pull the pipes out of the walls, and frequently do a damage of hundreds of dollars in obtaining plunder for which they get only a few cents from the junkmen. . . . There are others who are engaged in breaking show-cases incautiously left on the sidewalks at night and robbing them of their contents. There are some who loiter about the doors of the smaller shops watching an opportunity to slip behind the counter and rob the till. This also is an every day occurrence and the small size of the thieves pecularily adapts them to the crime and renders them remarkably successful in it; where a man or half-grown boy would be sure to be seen or heard, the urchin of eight or ten years glides noiseless and invisible. These same advantages are apparent in his depredations upon the property exposed at the doors of shops where he lingers unsuspected to snatch up a pair of shoes, a jacket, or something of like nature which he can easily carry off.

. . . Every case of crime develops some distinctive features which tend to remove it from the class to which it seems to belong, and the means of robbery are therefore almost as varied as the peculiarities of cases. This is especially true of the depredations of vagrant girls. . . . They never commit burglary and rarely street robberies or from stores, and they principally confine themselves to what is called "the domestic lay." Gaining access to dwelling by pretence of begging or selling matches carried in a large basket, they snatch up and secrete whatever is presented by opportunity, if it is nothing better than a handkerchief or a pewter spoon. But almost the only method of robbery which is peculiar to vicious street girls is that practiced by the flower girls, who are about twelve years of age, rather handsome in features and modest in demeanor. Sufficiently attractive to make the story probable, and having enough adroitness to give it the further probability of an opporunity having been had, they boldly demand hush money of gentlemen for alleged improper liberties taken with them. There are scores of these girl blackmailers, and they are the most dangerous and profligate of all juvenile offenders. . . .

It is impossible to give the exact numbers of the juvenile thieves of all classes to be found at all times in New York. All outcast children are so liable at any moment to pass the line between vagrancy and crime, that the two classes are practically only one. . . .

The army of juvenile vagabondage has been briefly reviewed in its leading divisions, and the sources of its recruitment can be briefly and distinctly stated. Liquor is at the bottom of all of it. If not the immediate cause, the traffic in alcoholic liquors is remotely responsible for the casting adrift from the anchorage of home of every juvenile outcast found in the streets. Years ago I read in an English periodical the short, sad story of Elsie, a St. Giles child. The father died, and

> Twas hard upon his death, I think,
> That Elsie's mother took to drink,
> And harder still on Elsie

That told the whole story. The St. Giles unfortunate became an outcast and worse. In New York and in London the same causes produce the same effects. Only the rum traffic could make the tenements of Greenwich and Cherry streets possible, and only the profligate debauchery produced by it could cast ten thousand children out of a million people, in such a country as this, homeless upon the world. . . . Ordinary prudence and industry will enable any adult in the United States to earn sufficient to keep those dependent upon him from want, and I dare affirm the same of a place so exceptional to the country at large as New York. But there is not ordinary industry and prudence in the mass of the population of a city which has 7,500 grog-shops, or one to every one hundred and twenty-six of its people. At least $15,000,000 are swallowed up every year by these grog shops, and three dollars in every ten come out of the pockets of the tenement classes. The $5,000,000 thus wasted, if legitimately used, would more than provide a comfortable home for every vagabond child in New York.

Children in Jails in Ohio, 1875

Report of the Prison Reform and Children's Aid Association of Ohio. Columbus, Ohio, December 31, 1875 (Cincinnati: Western Methodist Book Concern Press, 1876), pp. 47-48 (Lib. Cong.)

[A detailed account of conditions in county jails and infirmaries in Ohio as revealed by personal visits of Rev. A. G. Byers, Corresponding Secretary of the Association.]

JUVENILE DELINQUENTS

Another outrage upon humanity, and corresponding injury to society, is the fact that children are thrown into our county jails. During the past year as in other years, while visiting our jails, the Secretary has found little boys imprisoned, of course, in the common jail, where men, old and hardened men, were not only their associates, but, of necessity for the time, the tutors of these children. It is no relief to say that these boys are bad boys, precocious in the development of vicious habits, or of actually criminal character, often equally bad, if not worse, than the men. This may be so. Then so much the more should the State provide against, rather than for, the confirmation of these injurious habits and hurtful character. It is not an unusual thing to find boys of eight and ten years of age in the county jails. It is far more common, however, that these boys, most of whom need restraint and discipline, are set at large to learn defiance of law, just because there is no alternative but the county jail. Of the number of these juvenile delinquents we have no means of knowing beyond the fact that, for several years, the State Reform School has not been able to receive one in ten of the number committed to its care.

Juvenile Delinquency Statistics from New York Police Reports, 1875-1890

C. Loring Brace, "How Boys Come to be Bad," *The Independent* (March 3, 1892), p. 296.

Some brief statistics will serve to illustrate the progress of juvenile reformation during the past fifteen years. The following table from the police reports shows the number of juvenile delinquents arraigned and committed:

Year	Total	Males	Females	Committed
1875	1139	932	207	917
1876	1186	888	298	976

1877	1035	748	287	794
1878	905	654	251	605
1879	552	436	116	266
1880	628	499	129	357
1881	610	467	143	330
1882	642	510	132	316
1883	610	496	114	393
1884	548	443	105	323
1885	515	420	95	320
1886	580	465	115	400
1887	531	416	115	363
1888	575	431	144	380
1889	646	485	161	461
1890	536	440	96	390

This remarkable decrease in juvenile vagrancy and crime during the past twelve years as well as the decrease from previous years, is one of the most striking evidences ever offered of the effects of such labors as those of this society [New York Children's Aid Society] and of many similar charities.

Newspapers, Nickel Novels, and Obscene Prints as Defilers of Youth, 1883

Anthony Comstock, *Traps for the Young* (New York, 1883), pp. ix-x, 24-26, 134, 141 (editor's lib.)

PREFACE

... This book is designed to awaken thought upon the subject of *Evil Reading,* and to expose to the minds of parents, teachers, guardians, and pastors, some of the mighty forces for evil that are to-day exerting a controlling influence over the young. There is a shameful recklessness in many homes as to what the children read.

The community is cursed by pernicious literature. Ignorance as to its debasing character in numerous instances, and an indifference that is disgraceful in others, tolerate and sanction this evil.

The author, during an experience of nearly eleven years, has seen the effects of the evils herein discussed. If strong language is used, it is because no other can do the subject justice.

This work represents facts as they are found to exist. ...

434

Recently I purchased a book offered for sale on the railroads and recommended by the newsboy on a train . . . as the "boss book," the "fastest selling book of the day." The web of the story consisted of four murders, three highway robberies, two burglaries, one blackmailing scheme, three attempts to murder women, one attempt to poison a young woman, two conspiracies to ruin a pure girl, one den of counterfeiters in full blast, two gambling hells, one confidence game, one brothel, procurers abducting a young girl for a rich man, three cases of assault and battery, one street fight, two dens of thieves, one forced marriage, two suicides, and oaths, lies, wine drinking, smoking cigars, *et cetera*. The character that figured throughout all this was a beautiful young wife, who was the murderess and principal actor in all these horrible and disgusting scenes.

Again, these stories give utterly false and debasing ideas of life. All high moral purposes are made to give way to self-gratification. The great safeguard of human society—reverence to law—is broken down. Disobedience to parents is encouraged. The healthful restraint of parental authority is treated as a species of tyranny which the hero first chafes under, then resists, and lastly ignores. . . .

Again, these stories breed vulgarity, profanity, loose ideas of life, impurity of thought and deed. They render the imagination unclean, destroy domestic peace, desolate homes, cheapen woman's virtue, and make foul-mouthed bullies, cheats, vagabonds, thieves, desperadoes, and libertines. They disparage honest toil, and make real life a drudge and burden. What young man will serve an apprenticeship, working early and late, if his mind is filled with the idea that sudden wealth may be acquired by following the hero of the story? In real life, to begin at the foot of the ladder and work up, step by step, is the rule; but in these stories, inexperienced youth, with no moral character, take the foremost positions, and by trick and device, knife and revolver, bribery and corruption, carry everything before them, lifting themselves in a few short weeks to positions of ease and affluence. . . .

I proceed to give a truthful synopsis of one of the "ten-cent" pamphlets recently issued by a publisher of boy literature in New York City.

This book opens with an account of an assault on a woman. It contains a number of shooting scenes. It tells of several seductions and murders. It describes with minuteness of detail a burglary, and a den of thieves from which a band of burglars and assassins is hired. It gives an account of a gambling saloon, where a young man wins $30,000, which in turn is won from him by a beautiful woman, whereupon he drinks to the health of King Death and shoots himself dead. There is an account of a negro and a beautiful but abandoned woman making their home in a cave, where in four days they dig gold to the amount of $1,750,000, to which they add $200,000 by speculation in Wall Street. There is a story of a man illegally imprisoned and bound to an iron bedstead. Several prisoners are walled into a room and left to die, and the monstrous story ends with the man on the iron bedstead calling a fellow prisoner to him, when he discovers that he is his father. Thereupon the son fastens his teeth into the throat of his father and they die together. . . .

Death Traps by Mail

. . . Many a parent, before sending the child away from home to school, canvasses the country over for a proper and desirable institution where the child shall have all the comforts and advantages of home and culture. All the details are inquired into with greatest care. At last the child reaches the school, and his or her name appears upon the roll and is printed in the catalogue. These catalogues are sought for by those who send circulars through the mails advertising obscene and unlawful wares. . . .

To say that twenty-five tons weight of contraband matter has been seized by the Society for the Suppression of Vice, while it sums up the facts, does not present to the ordinary mind the fearful magnitude of this evil.

In 1872, when the work of extermination against this evil commenced, there were 165 different books published in New York and Brooklyn. Numerous establishments were in full blast, turning out obscene pictures and articles for indecent purposes, and of the vilest character. In all the so-called sporting papers, in many otherwise respectable weekly journals, in the daily, and sometimes covertly in the religious papers, these foul articles and things were advertised. According to the account books of the publishers and manufactures seized by the above society, there were about 4000 dealers scattered throughout the country. These supplied themselves from the headquarters for the production of these nefarious goods in New York and Brooklyn. All the known manufactories and publishing houses of these obscene articles have been closed. . . . A vigilant watch is kept to discover any new enterprises. . . .

Some Causes of Delinquency in New York City, 1892

[A] Elbridge T. Gerry,[1] "Cause of Juvenile Delinquency," *The Independent* (March 3, 1892), p. 294.

Crime is undoubtedly a moral disease. It is both contagious and infectious. Contagious when acquired by intercourse or contact with others already afflicted with it; infectious when the atmosphere in which the victim lives is saturated with it; and any youth of either sex is more susceptible to criminal influences than the adult, just as children are more susceptible to ordinary physical disease than grown persons.

The children of the poor are driven to the streets in three different ways: first, in consequence of the inadequacy of the dwellings in which they live to furnish them with the proper comforts of life. Thus, for instance, in an ordinary family where the children are sent to school during the day and return home at night, all the members of the domestic circle are huddled into small and miserable apartments where the air, during the winter season, is permeated with the odors of cooking from a hot stove, and where, in summer, the external heat renders life in such quarters almost absolutely unendurable.

A second cause is a desire to find comfort and leisure. The boy who goes out on a cold winter's night finds the air, to a certain degree, refreshing. Passing along the street he sees the barroom. It suggests warmth and comfort. He enters the place and there soon meets associates, none of the best. Before long he is induced to drink, and then he soon falls into crime. . . .

Lastly, children are driven into the streets by the conduct of their parents: particularly, the intoxication of either, surliness of temper and want of appreciation. The trials and troubles of children, and of their parents, all combine to make the lives of the children of the poor unhappy. These causes, often coupled with personal violence, administered under the pretense of punishment (usually the outbreak of bad temper), render the home so distasteful that but little domestic feeling is left in the mind of the child.

1. President of the New York Society for the Prevention of Cruelty to Children.

The cheap variety shows of this city, together with the sensational publications which are weekly read by the young, also tend
to create a distaste for home life.

In addition to this, the greed of the parents of poor children,
especially of married foreigners, is remarkable. Well-to-do families
will not hesitate to send their children out on the streets to peddle,
entirely regardless of the exposure to them. The result is that boys,
at an early age, are beginning to peddle and to steal, and the girls,
in selling newspapers and flowers, fall from virtue.

Worse than all is the effort which is continually being made to
obtain for these wretched children employment in low theatres
where, for forty cents a night, they are compelled to labor night
after night in spectacular pieces, losing their sleep, without the opportunity for rest, and being very scantily fed, long after midnight
going back to their wretched homes in all sorts of weather, only to
repeat their work the next night.

The atmosphere of the theater is never very congenial to the
development of morality in children. . . .

There is a necessity of trying the cases of children in courts
specially provided for them; they should not come in contact with
older offenders. There is now a bill before the legislature making
provision in this direction; and it certainly ought to pass.[2]

[B] Samuel Colgate,[3] "Ways of Debauching the Young," *The
Independent* (March 3, 1892), p. 298.

. . . After its organization the work of this society was directed
against obscene literature, then lotteries, and finally gambling.
Those were the three vices that we aimed to combat. . . .

Lotteries and policy are great sources of demoralization in the
young. . . . There are all kinds of small gambling enterprises to
attract the young.

Some time since the city was flooded with candy lotteries. Con-
fectionery stores were turned into gambling saloons for the
children. Manufacturing firms which had thereto forborne a good
reputation, blinded by the spirit of gain, and under the force of

2. A new subdivision was added to the Penal Code, as follows: "All cases
involving the commitment or trial of children for any violation of the Penal
Code, in any police court or court of special sessions, may be heard and determined by such court, at suitable times to be designated therefor by it,
separate and apart from the trial of other criminal cases, of which session a
separate docket and record shall be kept." *Laws of the State of New York,*
1892, Chapter 217.

3. President of the Society for the Suppression of Vice, organized in 1873.

competition, were making the goods to supply the demand. We instituted proceedings against five manufacturers, arresting the principals and seizing 1,483 candy lotteries. These lotteries disposed of a series of prizes according to the numbers upon slips of paper wrapped about small sticks of chewing gum, which were sold for a penny each.

Should Delinquent Children Be Placed in Free Foster Homes after a Period of Institutional Care or in Foster Boarding Homes Directly? Contrasting Experiences of the New York Juvenile Asylum and the Pennsylvania Children's Aid Society, 1893

Elisha M. Carpenter,[1] "The Placing Out of Juvenile Offenders," in *Proceedings of a Conference on the Care of Dependent and Delinquent Children in the State of New York, held under the Auspices of the State Charities Aid Association of New York . . . November, 14, 15 and 16, 1893* (New York: State Charities Aid Association, 1894), pp. 118-23 (editor's lib.)

In 1855, thirty-nine years ago, the New York Juvenile Asylum established an agency in Illinois for apprenticing juvenile offenders and homeless children to the farmers of that State. During that year 100 children were placed out by the Asylum, and during the past thirty-nine years, 5,456 children have been placed out among the best farmers of Illinois, an average of 139 each year.

The writer of this paper has been in charge of the New York Juvenile Asylum as its General Superintendent for the past twenty-three years, during which period 3,053 children have been placed in homes. In this paper is presented very briefly the knowledge and experience thus acquired, including eleven years' previous experience in a similar institution.

We now ask, first, what shall be done with these children? Shall they be removed at once from their homes, if they have any, or from their vagrant street life, to homes in the country? Certainly not, for any one acquainted with such children and their habits knows full well that a change of place is not followed by a change of habits. And no family will tolerate children with such habits. It is just here that people not acquainted with such children labor under a grave mistake. They think the half-starved children that roam the streets by day, committing all sorts of depredations and sleep in boxes, wagons or under stairways at night, mourn over

1. Superintendent, New York Juvenile Asylum.

their wretched condition and long for the comforts of a home. Nothing is farther from the truth. They enjoy that kind of a wild life, and, if removed from it, seek to return to it, just as wild animals when captured strive to regain the freedom of their native wilds.

Before such children can be placed out in families, with any reasonable prospect that they will remain there and do well, they must first be prepared for such homes by a course of training and discipline under proper restraint. They must undergo to some extent a change in their ideas, tastes and habits. To effect such a change is the object of a reformatory institution. Time is required, for it is a matter of growth and development under right instructions and influences. A brief period of a few months will not suffice. Observation and experience have convinced me that a period of about two years is requisite to effect a change and growth in the right direction. The asylum apprenticing agent states that the children who have spent two years in the asylum do much better than those who have remained in the institution but a year or so.

... I will state the method [of procuring homes] usually pursued by our apprenticing agent. Having selected the most central point in any given county, usually the county seat, he advertises for three weeks in the principal papers of the county, and by means of hand bills distributed through the country, that a company of children from the New York Juvenile Asylum will arrive at the place named. on the day named, and will stop at the hotel named. The notice states that "homes are wanted for these children with farmers where they will receive kind treatment and enjoy fair advantages. They have been in the Asylum from one to two years and have received instruction preparatory to a term of apprenticship. They may be taken at first upon trial for four weeks, and afterward, if all parties are satisfied, under indentures, girls until eighteen, boys until twenty-one, years of age. The indenture provides for four months' schooling each year, until the child has advanced through compound interest, and at the expiration of the term of apprenticeship, two new suits of clothes and the payment to the girls of $50, and to the boys of $150. All expenses of transportation will be assumed by the Asylum and the children will be placed on trial and indentured free of charge. Those who desire to take children on trial are requested to meet them at the hotel at the time above specified."

The result usually is, that at the time and place specified a large number of people will be assembled to see the children; some from curiosity and others for the purpose of obtaining children. Among the latter will be found well-to-do farmers and their wives, whose children have grown up and left home, and feeling lonesome, they desire a child for companionship, and for such services as parents require of their own children, at the same time taking an interest in the child's welfare, very often ready to do for the child in education and otherwise far more than required by the indenture. For like reasons, young farmers and families that have never been blessed with children, desire them. Oftentimes a family having boys only will desire a girl, or, having girls only, will desire a boy. Again, there will be poor people seeking cheap help. Against the latter our agent carefully discriminates.

The agent is prepared with printed blanks on which is entered the name of the child applied for, the name of the applicant, his residence, post-office address, railway station, financial condition (size of farm and whether owned or rented, etc. etc.), number of children and ages, distance from church and day school, church membership, etc.

In permitting an applicant to take a child on trial, the agent first satisfies himself from the appearance of the applicant and from conversation with him, that he would be a desirable person to take a child. He then seeks information about him from written recommendations, or through the hotel proprietor, postmaster, minister or other persons who are usually present to render such assistance.

At the close of the trial period of four weeks, and in some cases a longer period according to circumstances, he meets the applicant and child by appointment, and if they are mutually satisfied and no unfavorable information has been obtained during the trial period, indentures are executed according to the terms in the notice published at first.

If at the close of the trial period, the applicant or the child is not satisfied, the child is replaced on trial with another family. Sometimes a child is replaced several times. In one instance a girl was replaced eleven times before a family was found who understood her case and was able to manage her successfully. It is not strange that two or three trials should often be made before the applicant or child should become suited. The child may think the family at fault, until two or three trials lead him to discover that he is the one at fault, and to make an effort to mend his ways. . . .

It would be very difficult, if not impossible, to state the exact percentage of juvenile offenders who have been restored to a right life by placing them in country homes in Illinois after a course of training in the Juvenile Asylum. . . . Nevertheless we feel assured that a very large percentage of such children are finally reclaimed, judging from the great mass of information obtained by our agent and his assistants, by the numerous letters constantly received at the Asylum from the children, from the children themselves who are constantly returning to New York for a visit, usually after the term of indenture expires, and through whom we receive much information respecting those who have lived in the neighborhood with them or with whom they have met from time to time. . . .

DISCUSSION: MISS C. H. PEMBERTON[2]

When the Children's Aid Society of Pennsylvania started a few years ago to take charge of the so-called criminal and delinquent children of police stations and courts, it was said that to place such children directly in families was an exceedingly hazardous experiment. These children had hitherto been held up to the public as something little short of monsters. They were the victims of hereditary influences, the offspring of degraded criminals, the outcasts of society, and only stone walls could hold in check the unnatural depravity of their instincts, so we were told.

The Children's Aid Society examined carefully the antecedents and home surroundings of every child brought to it as incorrigible and criminal, and was much surprised and deeply impressed by the fact that nearly every case was traceable to neglect or lack of parental oversight.

It seemed to us that we were announcing a great discovery when we published our statistics on this subject, and demonstrated that such children were not necessarily depraved by instinct, and different from other children. They were only more unfortunate, in the respect that they were the victims of circumstances and had been neglected. It seemed to us as if that part of the charitable public which loves to take care of little children gave a great sigh of relief when it was made known that they need no longer look upon a great multitude of little children as incipient monsters. They could regard them still as children, making allowance only for the fact that they had been neglected. There was no such thing, we boldly declared, as an "incorrigible child." . . . Thus did we justify our bold experiment of putting little pickpockets and thieves directly into country families to board, to be educated, and to be taken care

2. Assistant Superintendent, Children's Aid Society of Pennsylvania.

of. It needed very little argument on our part to prove that if the child was merely suffering from want of care, the sooner you turned around and began to take care of him, the better for all concerned.

You may judge, therefore, of my surprise on listening to the paper just read and hearing the same arguments that we had so courageously advanced as good reasons for not putting young children into a reformatory, now brought forward as the very reasons why they should be put into a reformatory. Mr. Carpenter states very clearly that *lack of care* is the chief cause of juvenile delinquency, and argues that, having acquired the habits engendered by neglect, the *only alternative* is the reformatory.

The question of placing any kind of child directly in a family is a question of practicability. Mr. Carpenter asserts that no family can be found willing to receive a juvenile offender until he is supposed to be reformed. The Children's Aid Society of Pennsylvania asserts that the juvenile offender is not so much in need of *reform* as he is of *care*, and that no child is a proper subject for reform if it is possible to meet his needs by taking care of him. We have found it entirely possible to *take care* of the juvenile offender, and it is an easy task to find a very large number of good persons in rural communities ready to assist in taking care of him, provided we are willing to share with them the burden of his support and the responsibility of his future. This is just what we are doing constantly, and we speak from much experience. . . .

The care and education of a child, and especially a neglected child, are worth paying for in dollars and cents, and as well worth it *out* of an institution as *in* an institution, and if paid for *out* of an institution you have the advantage of killing two birds with one stone. While you are purchasing month by month the care and education of the child you are also giving opportunity for the growth of bonds which are stronger than indenture papers—the bonds of affection and mutual interest, and when the business of dollars and cents comes to an end you may find *something left* which is more powerful *to restrain* than the highest stone wall that was ever built around a group of unfortunate children.

The First Juvenile Court in Chicago (Cook County), Illinois, 1899-1900

[A] *Proceedings of the [Fifth Annual] Illinois Conference of Charities at Champaign, November 14-15, 1900* (Springfield, Illinois, 1900), pp. 10, 12-14 (Lib. Cong.)

THE JUVENILE COURT LAW IN COOK COUNTY, BY HON. R. S. TUTHILL, JUDGE CIRCUIT COURT

. . . Illinois has claimed and in many respects has justly claimed the right to be classed with the advanced States of the Union. . . . Yet a deplorable condition with respect to the treatment of children has existed in the State from its organization up almost to the present time. This condition in Cook county is stated in moderate language in the official reports of grand juries, month after month, in substantially these words:

"There is at present in this county no proper place for the detention or final committment of youthful offenders. We have no institution where friendless children of tender age, who have been arrested for offences against the law, can be sent, educated, and possibly saved from a criminal career. A committment to the Glenwood School under sentence for crimes committed, is not allowed, as that institution is simply for incorrigible children. We call attention to the fact that there are at present confined in our county jail, children of eleven, twelve, thirteen and fourteen years of age, where they are exposed to the evil association of older criminals.

"Indeed, in the county jail, we found children of nine years of age, who had been bound over to the grand jury by incompetent or corrupt justices of the peace, in disregard of the fact that the laws of Illinois recognize no capacity for criminality in a child of that age."

This condition, especially in Cook county, grew worse from year to year, until at length the people of the State awakened to the fact that the State by the inadequacy of its laws and failure to care for these children who were without proper parental care was creating, —breeding as it were, an army of criminals who in a short time would be its open and avowed enemies. . . . An appeal was made to the General Assembly at its last session for relief. A law was prepared as a result of extended consideration of the subject by men and women of all creeds and political affiliations and was submitted for enactment. It was, in the form originally agreed upon, probably as well considered, as wise and humane a measure as was ever presented to the law making body of the State. The Bar Association of Chicago composed of the ablest and best members of our metropolitan bar was active in the preparation of the bill and gave its powerful influence towards its enactment. The good women of the State, always quick and earnest in everything which tends to the proper care of children, were leaders in the movement, laboring in season and out of season to induce the representatives of the people by the passage of this bill to place Illinois *primus inter pares* in respect to provisions made for the exercise of this highest duty of a State,—a civilized State,—to stand in *loco parentis,* to be a parent to all the neglected and delinquent children of the State. It is to be regretted that various antagonistic interests made themselves manifest and opposed the bill with such mistaken pertinacity as that some of the most essential features in it were per force dropped.

Yet what is known as the Juvenile Court Law became the law of Illinois, going into effect July 1, 1899. . . .

The law made it the duty of the judges of the circuit court in Cook county to designate one of their number to preside in this new branch which for convenience was designated as the Juvenile Court. This designation was promptly made. The duty of inaugurating the work was placed upon me.

There are three classes of children mentioned in the law as coming within its purview.

First—The "dependent child" and

Second—"The neglected child;" which classes are defined to "mean any child who for any reason is destitute or homeless or abandoned; or dependent upon the public for support; or has not proper parental care or guardianship; or who habitually begs or receives alms; or who is found living in any house of ill-fame or with any vicious or disreputable persons; or whose home by reason of neglect or depravity on the part of its parents, guardian or other person in whose care it may be, is an unfit place for such child; and any child under the age of eight years who is found peddling or selling any article or singing or playing any musical instrument upon the street or giving any public entertainment."

Third—The "delinquent child," which it is declared, "shall include any child under the age of sixteen years who violates any law of this State, or city or village ordinance," and "who is not now or hereafter an inmate of a State institution or any training school for boys or industrial school for girls." Section 5 of the law has this provision: "Pending the final disposition of any case, a child may be retained in the possession of the person having the charge of the same or may be kept in *some suitable place* provided by the city or county authorities."

Section 11 provides: "That no court or magistrate shall commit a child under the age of twelve years to a jail or police station."

Here was an immediate difficulty inasmuch as neither city or county had a place of detention such as the law contemplated for the children brought under this operation.

The county had prior to the enactment of the law cared for the dependent and neglected children in a building at the county hospital used for the temporary detention of insane persons. This, while not a proper place to house babies and children of tender age within hearing of the outcries, the cursings, and screamings of the unfortunates who were always found within its walls, even for a day or night, has from necessity been continued as the place where the dependent and neglected children have been cared for pending the hearing of their cases in the Court and placing them in care of various charitable associations and persons with the ultimate purpose of having them placed in suitable family homes at the earliest possible moment.

A more serious difficulty was to secure a place other than the jail or police station of the city for the detention, pending the hearing of the *delinquent*. . . . The generous action of the Board of Directors of the Illinois Industrial Association . . . gave the use of their cottage . . . for this purpose. This has since served as a detention home. . . .

The law makes provision for the appointment by the Court of probation officers. It declares that "it shall be the duty of the said probation officer to make such investigation as may be required by the court; to be present in Court in order to represent the interest of the child when the case is heard; to furnish to the Court such information and assistance as the Judge may require; and to take such charge of any child before and after trial as may be directed by the Court.

Printed instructions are given to each probation officer when appointed. These give a good conception of the work a probation officer is expected to do. They are as follows:

INSTRUCTION TO PROBATION OFFICERS

In appointing probation officers the Court places a special reliance upon the faithfulness and wisdom of the persons so designated. There is no more important work than that of saving children, and much will depend upon your faithfulness.

This appointment is made under the provision of the law, enacted by the Legislature of 1899. Your attention is particularly called to the last section of that act. (Section 21) which declares the purpose of the law as follows:

"This act shall be liberally construed to the purpose that its end may be carried out, to wit: That the care, custody and discipline of a child shall approximate as nearly as may be that which should be given by its parents, and in all cases where it can be properly done, the child be placed in an approved family home and become a member of the family by legal adoption or otherwise."

It will be the endeavor of the Court to carry out both the letter and the spirit of this act, and to this end the Court will have in mind the following considerations in order named:

First.—The welfare and interests of the child—It is the desire of the Court to save the child from neglect and cruelty, also to save it from the danger of becoming a criminal or a dependent.

Second.—The welfare of the community—The most practical way of lessening the burdens of taxations and the loss of property through the ravages of the crime class is by the prevention of pauperism and crime. Experience proves that the easiest and most effective way of doing this is by taking hold of the children while they are young—the younger the better.

Third.—The interests and feelings of parents and relatives—It is right and necessary that parental affection should be respected, as far as this can be done without sacrificing the best interests of the child and without exposing the community to unnecessary damage.

Dependents and Delinquents—The law divides the children into two classes, Dependents and Delinquents. Cases of both classes will be referred to you; (a) For investigation pending action of the Court; (b) for temporary supervision pending action of the Court; (c) for supervision after action by the Court.

(a) Investigation—When cases are referred for investigation, you will be expected to make personal inquiry into the facts of the case, with the view to assist the Court in deciding what ought to be done. To this end, it will be necessary to record the history and the circumstances of the child as fully as possible, and blanks will be provided for this purpose. The Court will desire to ascertain the character, disposition and tendencies and school record of the child; also, the character of the parents and their capability for governing and supporting the child, together with the character of the home as to comforts, surroundings, inmates, etc.

This information will be obtained in your own way, from the child, from the parents, neighbors, teachers, clergymen, police of-

447

ficers, and from the records of the poor department, the police department and the various charitable agencies.

The court will wish to determine, from these inquiries, whether the child should be separated from the parents, guardian, or custodian; if so whether it should be committed to the care and guardianship of some individual or to some suitable institution. The Court will not ordinarily separate children from their parents unless: (a) the parents are criminals; (b) the parents are vicious or grossly cruel; (c) the parents are entirely unable to support the children; (d) the home is in such condition as to make it extremely probable that the child will grow up to be vicious or dependent.

This Court can not be used as a convenience for the purpose of relieving parents or relatives from their natural obligation. Even in the case of illegitimate children the question will be carefully considered whether the mother and child ought to be kept together, at least for the time being.

(b) Temporary care. The law forbids the keeping of any child in any jail or police station. A place of detention for children, under the care of the Court will be provided, but it is the desire of the Court to avoid congregating children even in this temporary home. Whenever practicable, therefore, the child will be left in the care of the parents or of some suitable family, under the supervision of the probation officer, pending the final action of the Court. In your investigations you will have in mind the question whether the child can be suitably cared for in his own home, and, if not, whether a suitable temporary home can be secured without expense.

(c) Supervision after action of the Court—The law makes it the duty of the Court, as far as possible, to locate its young wards, both dependents and delinquents, in family homes. When practicable, the child will be remanded to its parents, or will be placed directly in the family of some suitable citizen. In such cases the probation officer will be expected to maintain a special oversight of the child, either by personal visits at frequent intervals or by written report from parents or custodian. All visits to wards of the Court will be reported on blanks provided for that purpose.

You will please familiarize yourself thoroughly with the new law, and will apply to the Court for such instructions or information as you may need from time to time.

The probation officer feature is in my judgment the keystone which supports the arch of this law, an arch which shall be as a rainbow of hope to all who love children and who desire that *all*

448

children shall be properly cared for. . . . While the law gives to the Court power to appoint probation officers, no provision is made in it for the payment of compensation to any of them for their services. Whether it was supposed that valuable services of this kind could be obtained from charitably disposed men and women who would without compensation and at their own expense do the work in a satisfactory manner, I do not know. I, from the first, was convinced that the services of a probation officer to be valuable must be *persistent,* and that such persistent service could not be had except upon the payment of a moderate salary and a re-imbursement of expenses necessarily incurred in the work. The experience of sixteen months during which the work has been in progress has proved this to be true. . . .

An appeal was made to the mayor of the city, Honorable Carter H. Harrison, to detail a number of fatherly and humane men from the police force in the city (in citizen's clothes without batons or arms and with no badge to indicate their character save a star worn under the coat) to be appointed as probation officers of the Juvenile Court. The detail was at once made. These police officers have been of great service in the work. In fact, it is hard to see how without their assistance the work could have been carried on.

The Woman's Club of Chicago, represented by Mrs. Lucy L. Flower and her associates upon the committee appointed to look after the workings of the Law saw clearly that if the law was to be a success, capable probation officers, paid for their services, must be provided. They at the opening of the Court tendered the services of one who might be taken as a model for this class of work, Mrs. Alzina P. Stevens of Hull House. . . .

Other Woman's Clubs of the city churches and charitable persons have employed and paid for the services of five other probation officers who have thus been able to give all of their time to the work.

[B] Mrs. Joseph T. Bowen, "The Early Days of the Juvenile Court," in *The Child the Clinic and the Court*[1] (New York: New Republic, Inc., 1925), pp. 298-300, 303 (UNC Lib.)

I first heard of the Juvenile Court through Mrs. Lucy L. Flower. . . .

1. This is a collection of papers "given at a joint commemoration of the twenty-fifth anniversary of the first Juvenile Court and of the fifteenth anniversary of the first Psychopathic Institute, which was held in Chicago in early January 1925." The selection presented here is by permission of the New Republic, Inc.

449

Mrs. Flower soon demonstrated to me the great need of a court where children should not be treated as criminals but as delinquent children needing wise direction, care and correction; and also the need of a place where they could be confined awaiting their hearing in the court. She told me of many pitiful cases of little children confined in the police stations or the jails and of one boy, in the former place, who had been bitten by rats. . . .

Mrs. Flower at this time founded a committee of citizens called the Juvenile Court Committee, with Miss Julia Lathrop as its first president. . . .

I have said that we had no place to confine children pending their hearing. They could not be kept in the jails or the police stations so we took an old house on West Adams Street which had been fitted up as a Detention Home and run by the Illinois Industrial Association. They could not support it, so it was taken over by the Juvenile Court Committee. The girls and the dependent children were kept in the house, which was a very simple homelike place. Behind it was a large, two-story building which had been used as a stable. We fitted this up, using the first floor as a kitchen and sitting room and the second floor as a sleeping quarters. It contained fifty beds for the boys who were confined there. We maintained this house for seven years in cooperation with the city and county, from twenty-six to twenty-eight hundred children passing through it yearly. The city allowed us eleven cents a day for food for each child and the county gave us certain things, among others the services of the county physician, transportation to and from the Court, etc. During these seven years the insitution was never quarantined on account of contagious diseases. When a child was ill the county Physician was immediately called and if the child had a contagious disease he was at once removed to what, I think was the contagious ward in the County Hospital.

This Detention Home was under the charge of one of the members of our committee, now Mrs. Harry Hart. She was at the Home every day and looked after every detail, using the greatest economy in purchasing. . . .

We had at that time, a fine body of men and women who were most anxious for the success of the Court and for the good of the children, and we finally secured the passage of a law which provided that probation officers be placed on the payroll of the county. I well remember how that law was passed, because it gave me a feeling of great uneasiness that it was so easy to accomplish.

I happened to know at that time a noted Illinois politician. I asked him to my house and told him I wanted to get this law passed at once. The legislature was in session; he went to the telephone in my library, called up one of the bosses in the Senate and one in the House and said to each one, "There is a bill, number so and so, which I want passed; see that it is done at once." One of the men whom he called evidently said, "What is there in it?" and the reply was, "There is nothing in it, but a woman I know wants it passed"— and it was passed. I thought with horror at the time, Supposing it had been a bad bill, it would have been passed in exactly the same way.

The Juvenile Court Committee was at that time made up of women delegates from the various clubs. These clubs took a great interest in the Home: they visited it frequently; they pulled down the covers of the beds to see if they were clean; they tasted the food to see if it was good. Seldom a day passed without a visitor from one of these organizations and it certainly tended to keep us alert and active on the job. I remember at one time we were summoned into Court charged with having served worms to the children in their soup. When we responded to the summons and listened to the evidence, it was found that one of the parents of the children had seen vermicelli in the soup and thought it was worms. Another time we were berated by a club because we only had one sheet on the beds. It was difficult for us to get the boys to use sheets at all or even to undress or take off their shoes. They would strip the clean sheets off the beds, saying they could not bear to get them dirty, and one of their favorite tricks (smoking was not allowed) was to take the shoe strings out of their shoes to bed with them and smoke them in comfort until the guard for those fifty boys smelt the burning strings and hastened to confiscate them. . . .

On one occasion one of our best boys escaped from the Home. We were rather unhappy about it because we had given him certain privileges and he seemed a reliable boy. He returned at the end of the day, very triumphant, carrying in each hand several chickens tied by the legs, and he said, "I felt so sorry for you ladies. You seemed to have such a hard time raising money to feed up kids that I just went out to Mrs. Story's chicken yard and got these chickens for you." He was very much upset, and we felt almost apologetic, to take the chickens away from him and return them to the rightful owner.

It was very difficult to get the city or the county authorities to give us any money or necessary equipment for the Home. The county had given us an old omnibus, drawn by a very small horse, which struggled painfully to drag the omnibus between the Court and the Home. The old vehicle grew older and older and became very rickety, and one day the driver came to say that some of the boards had fallen out of the bottom and he had nearly dropped the children on the street. The omnibus could not be repaired, so I went to the county for relief and was told that this was a city matter and I must go to the chief of police. I went to his office and stood up against the wall all day; the office was full of expectorating gentlemen who occupied chairs and were rather amused at a woman wanting to see the chief of police. When I went to luncheon Miss Lathrop took my place in holding up the wall and we spun the day out that way, until the chief left by a back door when it was dark. Next day I was in my place again and this time saw him. He said he had nothing to do with the matter and referred me to the repair department; they said the omnibus could not be repaired and referred me to the construction department. The construction department could do nothing about it unless it was O.K.'d by the mayor, who referred me to the county commissioners, who referred me to another department.

After six weeks of seeing one man and then another, in desperation the Juvenile Court Committee bought a new omnibus. It was too heavy for the little horse to pull, so I went all over the ground again, to get another horse. Finally, after having been referred to the fire department, I was informed that there was a horse out on a farm that had been laid off because he was lame, but perhaps he could draw the omnibus. He was brought to the city and proved to be a large husky animal. He was harnessed to the omnibus with the little horse, but evidently thought he was going to a fire and rushed down the street so rapidly that the driver had to stop him, as the pony was nearly strangled from having been lifted off its feet.

We then bought a pair of horses and the city gave us a barn four miles from the Home. We were told several days later by the driver that the stalls in the barn were so small that the horses had not been able to lie down for four days and nights. Finding we could not do anything about the matter, we rented a stable ourselves and tried to get the city to provide us with food for the horses. We even let them go three days without food, hoping in this way to force the city to provide for them. The whole thing ended in the committee buying its own omnibus, its own horses, renting its own stable and furnishing its own horse-feed.

Some of the children who were brought into the Detention Home in these early days were pitiful objects. I remember two children, a boy and a girl, who had been found in a pigpen; their mother and father must have been out of their minds because they had kept the children in with the animals, wearing no clothes and eating only the food furnished the pigs. They did not know how to talk and jabbered like little animals.

The early days of the Juvenile Court were without the services of a psychiatrist and we were not able to detect any dangerous tendencies on the part of the children. One day a sweet-looking little boy, aged seven, with long curls down his back and a face like a cherub, took the kerosene can and when he was alone in the dormitory, poured kerosene over all the beds and set fire to them. Be it said to the credit of all the other boys in the institution that they assisted in putting out the fire which, fortunately, did very little damage.